THE SCIENTIST AND THE HUMANIST

THE SCIENTIST AND THE HUMANIST

A Festschrift in Honor of Elliot Aronson

Edited by
Marti Hope Gonzales
Carol Tavris
Joshua Aronson

Psychology Press
Taylor & Francis Group
New York London

Psychology Press
Taylor & Francis Group
270 Madison Avenue
New York, NY 10016

Psychology Press
Taylor & Francis Group
27 Church Road
Hove, East Sussex BN3 2FA

© 2010 by Taylor and Francis Group, LLC
Psychology Press is an imprint of Taylor & Francis Group, an Informa business

Printed in the United States of America on acid-free paper
10 9 8 7 6 5 4 3 2 1

International Standard Book Number: 978-1-84872-867-7 (Hardback)

For permission to photocopy or use material electronically from this work, please access www.copyright.com (http://www.copyright.com/) or contact the Copyright Clearance Center, Inc. (CCC), 222 Rosewood Drive, Danvers, MA 01923, 978-750-8400. CCC is a not-for-profit organization that provides licenses and registration for a variety of users. For organizations that have been granted a photocopy license by the CCC, a separate system of payment has been arranged.

Trademark Notice: Product or corporate names may be trademarks or registered trademarks, and are used only for identification and explanation without intent to infringe.

Library of Congress Cataloging-in-Publication Data

The scientist and the humanist : a festschrift in honor of Elliot Aronson / editors, Marti Hope Gonzales, Carol Tavris, Joshua Aronson.
  p. cm. -- (Modern pioneers in psychological science: an APS-Psychology Press series)
Includes bibliographical references and index.
ISBN 978-1-84872-867-7 (hbk. : alk. paper)
1. Aronson, Elliot. 2. Social psychology. I. Gonzales, Marti Hope. II. Tavris, Carol. III. Aronson, Joshua.

HM1031.A76S35 2010
302.092--dc22   2010011730

Visit the Taylor & Francis Web site at
http://www.taylorandfrancis.com

and the Psychology Press Web site at
http://www.psypress.com

CONTENTS

List of Contributors   ix

Introductions

The Wizard of Santa Cruz   1
    MARK R. LEPPER

Editors' Introduction   7
    MARTI HOPE GONZALES, CAROL TAVRIS, AND
    JOSHUA ARONSON

A Tribute to Elliot Aronson   11
    WALTER MISCHEL

Honoring Elliot Aronson   15
    PHILIP G. ZIMBARDO

PART I   Issues in Social Psychology

Chapter 1   The Ultimate Lewinian   21
    THOMAS F. PETTIGREW

Chapter 2   Forbidden Toys and Transgressive Thoughts   31
    MARK R. LEPPER

Chapter 3	Dealing With Conflict: Experiences and Experiments LEE ROSS	39
Chapter 4	Rejection, Consistency, and Interpersonal Processes ROY F. BAUMEISTER	67
Chapter 5	The Rise and Fall of the High-Impact Experiment PHOEBE C. ELLSWORTH	79

PART II Cognitive Dissonance and Its Descendants

Chapter 6	Decisions, Action, and Neuroscience: A Contemporary Perspective on Cognitive Dissonance EDDIE HARMON-JONES	109
Chapter 7	The Power of the Self-Consistency Motive in Social Life JEFF STONE	133
Chapter 8	Riding the D Train With Elliot: The Aronsonian Legacy of Cognitive Dissonance JOEL COOPER	159
Chapter 9	Self-Persuasion When It Matters to Self: Attitude Importance and Dissonance Reduction After Counterattitudinal Advocacy MICHAEL R. LEIPPE AND DONNA EISENSTADT	175

PART III Research and Applications

Chapter 10	A Tiller in the Greening of Relationship Science JEFFRY A. SIMPSON	203
Chapter 11	Lies, *Damned* Lies, and the Path From Police Interrogation to Wrongful Conviction DEBORAH DAVIS	211
Chapter 12	Giving Psychology Away to Energy Policy PAUL C. STERN	249
Chapter 13	Under What Conditions Does Intergroup Contact Improve Intergroup Harmony? ANTHONY G. GREENWALD	269

| Chapter 14 | Jigsaw and the Nurture of Human Intelligence
JOSHUA ARONSON | 285 |

PART IV Writing and Teaching

Chapter 15	Writing About Psychological Science CAROL TAVRIS	313
Chapter 16	Chance Encounters TIMOTHY D. WILSON	321
Chapter 17	The Art of Teaching: Lessons From a Teacher Who Was Never Taught How to Teach MARTI HOPE GONZALES	325

PART V Codas

| Chapter 18 | Elliot Aronson and the Spirit of Yom Kippur: The Adjustment to Atrocity
RABBI HILLEL COHN | 337 |
| Chapter 19 | The Last Word
ELLIOT ARONSON | 343 |

| Elliot Aronson's Awards, Books, and Publications | 347 |
| Index | 359 |

LIST OF CONTRIBUTORS

Joshua Aronson, Elliot Aronson's youngest child, is associate professor of psychology at New York University. He received his PhD in 1992 from Princeton University. Before coming to New York University, he was on the faculty at the University of Texas and was a postdoctoral scholar and lecturer at Stanford University. His research focuses on social and psychological influences on academic achievement. Aronson is internationally known for his research on "stereotype threat" and minority student achievement. He is the editor of *Improving Academic Achievement: Impact of Psychological Factors on Education* and coeditor with his father of *Readings about the Social Animal*. His current work focuses on interventions to improve learning and test performance of underachieving youth. Aronson has received Early Career awards from the Society for the Psychological Study of Social Issues and the National Science Foundation, and the G. Stanley Hall Lecturer Award from the American Psychological Association. The founding director of the Center for Research on Culture, Development, and Education at NYU, he is currently writing a book titled *The Nurture of Intelligence*.

Roy F. Baumeister is the Eppes Eminent Professor of Psychology and head of the social psychology program at Florida State University. He received his PhD from Princeton in 1978, spent over two decades at Case Western Reserve University, and has worked at the University of Texas, the University of Virginia, the Max Planck Institute, and the Center for Advanced Study in the Behavioral Sciences. Baumeister's research spans multiple topics, including self and identity, self-regulation, aggression, self-esteem, and self-presentation. He has received research grants from the National Institutes of Health and from the Templeton Foundation. He has over 400 publications, and his books include *Evil: Inside Human Violence and Cruelty*, *The Cultural Animal*, and *Meanings of Life*.

Joel Cooper is professor of psychology at Princeton University. He received his BA degree from the City College of New York in 1965 and his PhD from Duke University in 1969. He has been teaching at Princeton since 1969, serving as chair of the department from 1985 to 1992. He has had visiting appointments at the University of Queensland, University College London, University of Auckland, and Hebrew University. Cooper is a past chair of the Society for Experimental Social Psychology and currently serves as editor of the *Journal of Experimental Social Psychology*.

Deborah Davis began her academic career at the University of Texas, where she took one of her all-time-favorite courses from Elliot Aronson. She received her PhD from Ohio State University in 1973, and is now professor of psychology at the University of Nevada, Reno; president of Sierra Trial and Opinion Consultants; and principal clarinetist of the Reno Chamber Orchestra. She publishes and serves as an expert witness in the areas of witness memory, coerced confessions, and issues of sexual consent. She also publishes in the area of interpersonal relationships, with particular interests in the role of adult "attachment style" in romantic relationships, and in changes in relationship preferences and behavior across the life span.

Donna Eisenstadt is a social psychologist who has held tenured positions at Saint Louis University and Illinois State University, and taught at St. Mary's College of Maryland and John Jay College (where she is currently affiliated with the Psychology Department). She earned her BA at Brooklyn College and her PhD at The Graduate Center of the City University of New York. Her research and numerous scholarly publications focus on self and social identity, prejudice and prejudice reduction, and psychology and law. Eisenstadt has won teaching awards at two universities. She has completed postdoctoral clinical training to assist her in integrating social and clinical insights about the self, self-threat, and self-concept change.

Phoebe C. Ellsworth is the Frank Murphy Distinguished University Professor of Psychology and Law at the University of Michigan. She received her AB from Harvard and her PhD in Psychology from

Stanford, where she worked with Elliot Aronson and Merrill Carlsmith on *Methods of Research in Social Psychology*. This exciting collaboration sparked a lifelong interest in the art and science of research, and she continues to teach and write about research methods. She is known for her basic research on human emotion, and for her research on psychology and law. She is a Fellow of the American Academy of Arts and Sciences.

Marti Hope Gonzales earned her PhD in 1987 at the University of California at Santa Cruz, where Elliot Aronson was her mentor. A Fellow of the Association for Psychological Science and an associate professor of psychology at the University of Minnesota, she is a Horace T. Morse–Minnesota Alumni Distinguished Teaching Professor, and has won teaching awards from the University of Minnesota, the Minnesota Psychological Association, and the State of Minnesota. Gonzales is coauthor, with Elliot Aronson and Phoebe Ellsworth, of *Methods of Research in Social Psychology* (2nd ed.). Her research interests include interpersonal conflicts, and the personal and social benefits of mediation, political psychology, and self-presentation. Minnesota weather permitting—and it seldom does—she gardens and takes walks around one of the nearby 10,000 lakes with her spouse, Michael, and Akita, Kashi.

Anthony G. Greenwald received his PhD from Harvard University in 1963 and is professor of psychology at the University of Washington. He has published over 170 scholarly articles, served on editorial boards of 13 psychological journals, and received the Donald T. Campbell Award for research career contributions from the Society of Personality and Social Psychology, and the Distinguished Scientist Award from the Society of Experimental Social Psychology. In 1995 Greenwald invented the Implicit Association Test (IAT), a measure of individual differences in implicit social cognition, which has numerous applications in clinical psychology, education, marketing, and diversity training. Greenwald was elected a member of the American Academy of Arts and Sciences in 2007.

Eddie Harmon-Jones is professor of psychology and faculty of neuroscience at Texas A&M University. He received his PhD from the University of Arizona in 1995. His research focuses on emotions and motivations, their implications for social processes and behaviors, and their underlying neural circuits. He has coedited three scholarly books: *Cognitive Dissonance: Progress on a Pivotal Theory in Social Psychology* (1999); *Social Neuroscience: Integrating Biological and Psychological*

Explanations of Social Behavior (2007); and *Methods in Social Neuroscience* (2009). In 2002, he received the Distinguished Award for an Early Career Contribution to Psychophysiology from the Society for Psychophysiological Research. He has served as associate editor of the *Journal of Personality and Social Psychology: Personality Processes and Individual Differences,* and is currently on the editorial board of eight other journals.

Michael R. Leippe is professor of psychology at John Jay College of Criminal Justice, City University of New York. He received his BA degree from the University of Rochester in 1974 and his PhD in 1979 from Ohio State University. After teaching at St. Norbert College, he held tenured positions at Adelphi University, Saint Louis University, and Illinois State University, serving as department chair at the latter two institutions. His research interests are in the areas of social influence and legal psychology. In the social influence realm, he has focused on both persuasion and dissonance, and studied change in social attitudes, self-concepts, and prejudice. In legal psychology, he is an authority on eyewitness testimony, especially social influences on and memory of eyewitness reports. Leippe coauthored *The Psychology of Attitude Change and Social Influence* with Phil Zimbardo, and is a Fellow of the Association for Psychological Science.

Mark R. Lepper is the Albert Ray Lang Professor of Psychology at Stanford University, where he has taught since 1971. He did his undergraduate work at Stanford and his graduate work at Yale in social and developmental psychology. His primary research interest has long been the study of motivation and, in particular, the effects of intrinsic or internalized versus extrinsic motivation, as observed in the laboratory, in children's school classrooms, in educational computer games and activities, and in the strategies of effective human tutors. His second main research interest, pursued largely with colleague Lee Ross, has concerned motivational and cognitive biases in information processing that lead people to persist in erroneous beliefs and dysfunctional theories.

Walter Mischel earned his PhD in clinical psychology at the Ohio State University in 1956, spent 21 years on the faculty at Stanford University, and is now the Robert Johnston Niven Professor of Humane Letters in Psychology at Columbia University. His research focuses on the structure and organization of individual differences, and the psychological mechanisms underlying self-control. He is a member of the National Academy of Sciences and the American Academy of Arts and Sciences.

His honors include the Distinguished Scientific Contribution Award from the American Psychological Association, the Distinguished Scientist Award of the Society of Experimental Social Psychology, the Distinguished Contributions to Personality Award of the Society of Social and Personality Psychology, and the Distinguished Scientist Award of the American Psychological Association Division of Clinical Psychology. He is past editor of *Psychological Review*. He has served as president of APA Division 8, the Association for Research in Personality, and the Association for Psychological Science.

Thomas F. Pettigrew is research professor of social psychology at the University of California, Santa Cruz. A Harvard PhD, he also taught at Harvard (1957–1980) and Amsterdam (1986–1991). He was a Fellow at the Center for Advanced Study in the Behavioral Sciences and the Netherlands Institute for Advanced Study and has conducted intergroup research throughout the world. He was president of the Society for the Psychological Study of Social Issues and has received the Society's Lewin Award, twice its Allport Intergroup Research Award, the American Sociological Association's Spivack Award, the Society for Experimental Social Psychology's Distinguished Scientist Award, the International Academy for Intercultural Research's Lifetime Achievement Award, and the University of California's Panunzio Award.

Lee Ross is professor of psychology at Stanford University and cofounder of the Stanford Center on Conflict and Negotiation. The author of four books (including *Human Inference* and *The Person and the Situation*, with Richard Nisbett) and many papers, his research on attributional biases and shortcomings in humans influenced both social psychology and the field of judgment and decision making. More recently, he has explored barriers to dispute resolution and participated in conflict resolution efforts in the Middle East and Northern Ireland. Ross was elected in 1994 to the American Academy of Arts and Sciences, and has received distinguished career awards from the Association for Psychological Science and the Society of Experimental Social Psychology.

Jeffry A. Simpson is professor of psychology and director of the doctoral minor in interpersonal relationships at the University of Minnesota. His research interests center on adult attachment processes, human mating, idealization in relationships, empathic accuracy, and dyadic social influence. He has served as editor of the journal *Personal Relationships*. He was associate editor for the *Journal of Personality and Social Psychology: Interpersonal Relations and Group Processes* and is currently editor. He has served on panels at the National Science Foundation and the National Institute of Mental Health, and has served as chair of the Social, Personality, and Interpersonal Relations grant panel at NIMH.

Paul C. Stern is a principal staff officer at the National Research Council/ National Academy of Sciences and director of its Standing Committee on the Human Dimensions of Global Change. He is coauthor of the textbook *Environmental Problems and Human Behavior*, and coeditor of numerous National Research Council publications, including *Public Participation in Environmental Assessment and Decision Making*; *Decision Making for the Environment*; *Environmentally Significant Consumption*; *Global Environmental Change*; and *Energy Use: The Human Dimension*. His research interests include the determinants of environmentally significant behavior, particularly at the individual level; participatory processes for informing environmental decision making; processes for informing environmental decisions; and the governance of environmental resources and risk.

Jeff Stone is associate professor of psychology in the School of Mind, Brain and Behavior, appointed faculty in the Marketing Department of the Eller College of Management, and a research associate in the Arizona Cancer Center, all at the University of Arizona. He received his PhD from the University of California at Santa Cruz in 1993 and completed postdoctoral training at Princeton University before joining the Arizona faculty in 1997. Stone conducts research on attitudes, persuasion, and social influence processes in health, intergroup relations, and sports.

Carol Tavris earned her PhD in social psychology at the University of Michigan. In her writing, lectures, and teaching, she has sought to educate the public about the importance of scientific thinking in psychology and to educate psychologists about the importance of clear writing in psychology. Her books include *Anger: The Misunderstood Emotion*, *The Mismeasure of Woman*, and, with Carole Wade, *Psychology* and *Invitation to Psychology*. But the project that most qualifies her to be a contributor to this volume is the trade book she wrote with Elliot Aronson, *Mistakes Were Made (But Not by Me)*, an experience that showed her all of his Festschrift-worthy qualities: knowledge, wisdom, and the ability to turn work into play.

Timothy D. Wilson received his BA from Hampshire College and his PhD from the University of Michigan. He has taught at the University of Virginia since 1979, where he is currently the Sherrell J. Aston Professor of Psychology. He served as chair of the department from 2001 to 2004. He is the author of *Strangers to Ourselves: Discovering the Adaptive Unconscious* and numerous articles on self-knowledge—its limits, how people attain it, and its value. He is also coauthor, with Elliot Aronson and Robin Akert, of *Social Psychology*, a text now in its seventh edition. He has served as associate editor of the *Journal of Personality and Social Psychology*. In 2001 he received an All University Outstanding Teaching Award and in 2009 was elected to the American Academy of Arts and Sciences.

Philip G. Zimbardo is an internationally recognized scholar, educator, researcher, and media personality, winning numerous awards and honors in each of these domains. He earned his PhD in psychology at Yale University, and is now professor emeritus at Stanford University, where he has been on the faculty since 1968, having taught previously at Yale, NYU, and Columbia. Zimbardo's career is noted for giving psychology away to the public through his popular PBS TV series, *Discovering Psychology*, along with many text and trade books, including *Psychology and Life*, now in its eighteenth edition, *Shyness* (1977), *The Lucifer Effect* (2007), and *The Time Paradox* (2008), among his 400 publications. He is past president of both the Western Psychological Association and the American Psychological Association.

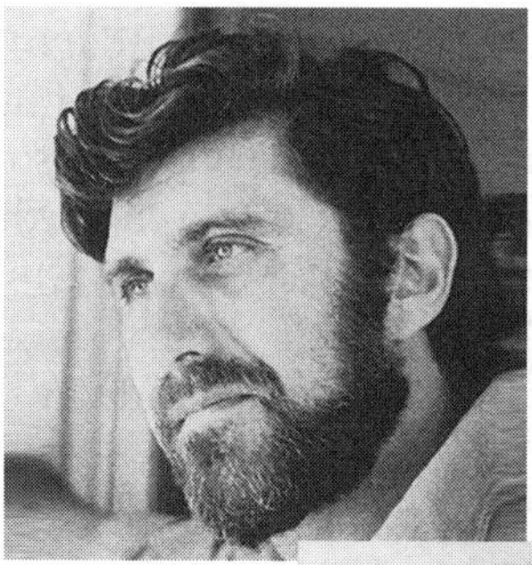
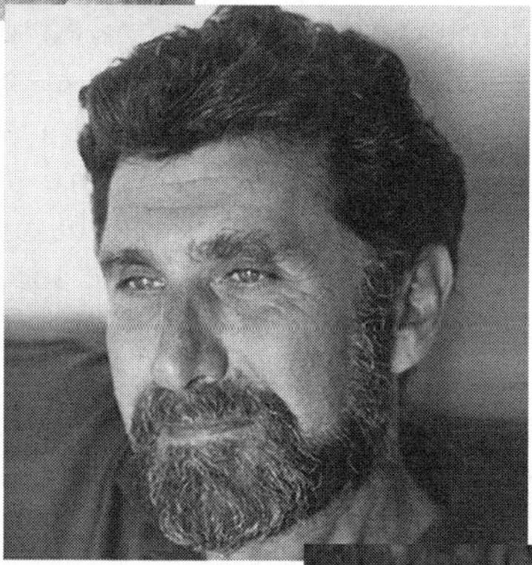
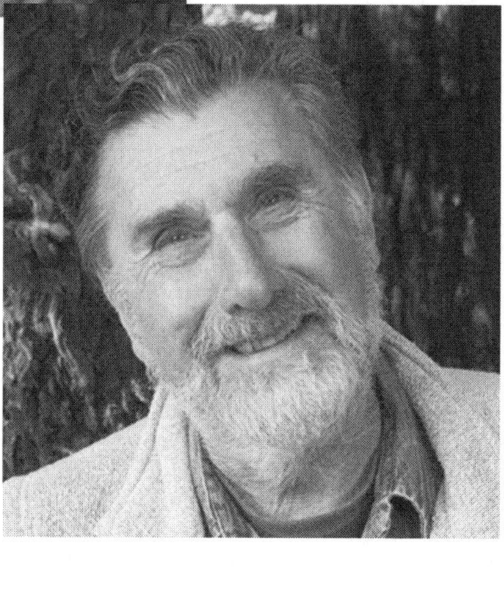

Introductions

Introduction

THE WIZARD OF SANTA CRUZ

Mark R. Lepper
Stanford University

Not all that long ago, in a country not so very far away, a small band of travelers set out in search of the legendary Wizard of Santa Cruz in the fabled state of Oz (more commonly known, these days, as California). They were four: the Scarecrow, the Tin Man, the Cowardly Lion, and some young girl named Dorothy. Typical citizens of the Western world at the start of the second millennium, they all shared but a single overriding goal: What can the Wizard do for *me*?

The Scarecrow, in particular, wished that the Wizard might give him a brain, to replace the damp and malodorous bundle of straw that currently filled his head. In the tradition of so-called rational economic theorists everywhere, the Scarecrow presumed that an actual brain would help him make better decisions, to understand the world economy, and to appreciate the vast social wisdom of the unfettered marketplace. Certainly, he had heard a lot about the wonderful effects of hedge funds, derivatives, and deregulation. Moreover, he was sure that possession of an actual brain would be pretty much a prerequisite for his later participation in any exciting fMRI studies of social cognition that might come his way.

The Tin Man hoped that the Wizard might find him a heart to fill the huge metal cylinder that comprised his torso. Only with such an organ, he felt, would he be able to identify and experience the undifferentiated arousal that, coupled with various appropriate cognitions, his friend Stanley had told him constituted the emotions. He knew that the as-if feelings that he experienced from directly injecting epinephrine via his trusty oil can clearly did not qualify as real emotions; indeed, they felt even less authentic than the filmed efforts of Chuck Norris trying to display emotional states other than anger or disgust.

The Cowardly Lion, as discerning readers may already have guessed from his unusual name, was concerned about the abject fear and terror he so often experienced—whenever he was exposed to, for example, hockey-masked strangers bearing large chain saws, to TV shows hosted by Donnie and Marie Osmond, or to social policies hatched by George Bush and Dick Cheney. The Wizard, he was hopeful, would be able to give him some courage that he could then screw to its sticking point (wherever that might turn out to be).

Then there was Dorothy. No one knew quite what her story was, but it appeared that she had inadvertently left her home in search of something called a career. None of the others had quite heard of such a thing, but at least she had a melodious singing voice and was better company than that greedy freeloader Goldilocks. Besides, all of them were certain that the Wizard would know how to deal with such a request, not to mention the question of where one ought to stick a career.

After many trials and tribulations—including encounters with vicious tree-huggers, Fighting Banana Slugs, overgrown elephant seals, the state's own Governator himself, and various Puritanical social psychologists enraged by the very thought that social psychology "is and ought to be fun"—the four travelers approached the famed Emerald City of Santa Cruz, where they sought an audience with the Wizard who was said to live there. After several false starts, kind neighbors eventually showed them to his office, right across from the town's fabled and funky boardwalk.

As they entered the Wizard's inner sanctum, there were flashes of lightning and the rumbling of thunder, and they heard a disembodied synthesized voice emerging from the ether. A peculiar haze also filled the room; it was not a smell the travelers recognized, like tobacco and pipe smoke, but it filled them with a sense of calm and contentment. "I have an enormous yearning for a good brownie," Dorothy murmured, channeling the sentiments, such as they were, of the group.

Once their awe of being in the virtual presence of the storied Wizard himself had subsided, the travelers remembered their reasons for seeking this audience. All four sought to speak at once, before they collectively recalled the ancient Gricean rule that communication works better if we all take turns and only one person speaks at a time.

The Scarecrow spoke first: "O great Wizard, I am a fool, for I have no brain. Could you give me a brain, so that I can more efficiently calculate my rational self-interest in any situation and make fun of those who propose that people might sometimes prove altruistic or abide by their own moral values even when no one is watching?"

Sadly, the Wizard replied, "Actually, I can't help you in that way. I don't have a supply room full of fresh, or even of factory-reconditioned preowned, brains. Perhaps you have me confused with that electronics geek, Dr. Frankenstein. But," he added, "I can tell you how to become a very smart person. There is a famous psychologist, Elliot Aronson, who lives right in this city and is one of the wisest and cleverest men in the country. He has conducted innovative and important research in many areas. He has won all the most prestigious awards that his colleagues in that field can offer. His writings have enlightened and inspired hundreds of thousands of readers. He has taught at the best institutions of higher learning in this country from the north to the south and the east to the west. Find this smart man, study carefully his thoughts and actions, and perhaps you too can become wise like him. He might even enlighten you about the distinction between human rationality and human rationalizing."

"But what about me?" the Tin Man cried. "I have no heart, and I have traveled all this way hoping that you can give me one."

"Alas," the Wizard responded, "I cannot do that, either. Do you have any idea what a new heart costs these days? And you don't even have health insurance. Fortunately, however, I can tell you how to develop a magnificent one. There is a famous psychologist, Elliot Aronson, who is widely known for his enormous heart. Throughout his career, he has dedicated himself to making this world a better place for everyone. He has fought for peace and for social equality and justice, even when these causes were not so popular. He has developed techniques that help to level the playing field for disadvantaged students, and methods for encouraging citizens to help save our planet from global warming and other manmade disasters. He is a prototype of the sort of loving, caring, open person for whom the term *mensch* was originally invented. Seek him out, absorb and imitate his values and his interactions with others, and, with luck, you too may develop a heart as large and caring as his."

"That's all well and good," interjected the Cowardly Lion, "but I came here to get some courage."

"Ah, so," replied the Wizard. "Do you think that gaining courage is as simple as my pinning a Good Player Award or a Legion of Valor Medal on your chest? Well, think again! Acquiring real bravery is a difficult and effortful process. Fortunately, there is a famous psychologist, Elliot Aronson, who is known far and wide for his courage. He has faced (if not courted) a lifetime of controversy with courage and aplomb. Some might say that he stands ever ready to fight for a good cause, or an elegant theory, at the drop of a hat. Others might go further and note his occasional penchant for dropping that proverbial hat himself. Most recently, he has faced the loss of his eyesight with hardly a complaint, much less a significant lessening of his activities. If you were to apprentice yourself to him, perhaps you could acquire some of his courage in the process."

Finally, it was Dorothy's turn to speak: "O magnificent Wizard, my internal organs are largely in working order. All that I am looking for is a good career—one that would be fun, one that would provide intellectual excitement and challenge, and one that would allow me to address important social problems using sound theories and actual evidence. Though I guess I wouldn't object if that career also came with lifetime tenure and academic freedom."

"Young lady," the Wizard intoned, "have I got a career for you! There is a famous psychologist, Elliot Aronson, whom you may have heard me mention, who has carved out exactly that sort of career for himself. Perhaps if you were to go and study with him, you could do the same—although you may need to ditch those shiny ruby slippers in favor of some greener Birkenstocks. This is Santa Cruz, after all. If you are lucky, you might learn some of the knowledge and skills that have contributed so critically to his great success: the ability to script, for instance, the most inane and boring discussion of sex (among beetles) ever written, the cleverness to turn satirical writings (say, by C. Northcote Parkinson) into elegant empirical investigations, the panache to remain a respected intellectual leader even when clad in lumberjack shirts or buckskin jackets, the skill to make even Mother Teresa feel like a bit of a hypocrite, the nerve to introduce the technical term *pratfall* into the scientific literature, or the chutzpah to remain happily married for over half a century yet still have a 'Law of Infidelity' named after himself. At the very least, you would certainly learn the basic arts of elegant experimentation, eloquent writing, and exciting theorizing."

Suddenly, a big gust of wind blew aside the curtain obscuring the far corner of the room, revealing a short, pot-bellied, bespectacled man speaking into a microphone in front of a massive computer console. "Why, you're a fraud!" said Dorothy, never one to pass up a chance to state the obvious.

"You are right," the ersatz Wizard replied. "To be sure, I do not have the same tall, dark, handsome, and bearded persona as my favorite psychologist. But then again, who does? Aren't we all just players strutting and fretting our hour upon the stage? Or, perhaps, avatars in some elaborate cyberworld? Characters in a Borges labyrinth or a Courtney Davenport romance novel?"

With that, the ersatz Wizard turned and exited, but the four travelers had learned a crucial lesson: that in academia, one can meet many people who are very smart, a smaller number who have a strong social conscience and a deep concern about social justice, and fewer still who prove courageous. What is exceptionally rare and praiseworthy is someone who displays all these qualities simultaneously. And so our four travelers journeyed down the road, this time to meet the real wizard, Elliot Aronson.

The moral of the story is this: We must always make sure to recognize the real wizards who walk among us and savor our opportunities to be inspired, educated, and entertained by them. For they, collectively, are what make the world, or at least a field like social psychology, interesting and fun. And perhaps, once in a while, we should be asking, in paraphrase of John F. Kennedy, not just what these wizards can do for us, but what we can do for them—for they, like Elliot Aronson, have certainly earned our admiration, our love, and our respect.

EDITORS' INTRODUCTION

Marti Hope Gonzales, Carol Tavris, and Joshua Aronson

Elliot Aronson probably needs no introduction. Still, he deserves one and is going to get one. The three of us are well placed to edit this Festschrift volume in honor of his life and work; we love social psychology, we love writing and teaching, and we love him. It's true that one of us has an edge in his personal familiarity with Elliot, given he first met the honoree upon being born. But we other two have cultivated friendships and professional partnerships with the man going back some 30 years, so we know a little something about him.

Elliot is the only psychologist in the entire history of the American Psychological Association (APA) to win the trifecta—its three highest awards—for scientific contributions, for teaching, and for writing. As impressive a feat as this is, it nonetheless falls short of conveying the impact he has had on the field as one of the most influential founders of social psychology. With scant precedent to draw upon, his work showed younger scientists what the field was about. He taught them, directly and indirectly, that experiments did not have to treat internal mental events as hopelessly encased in a black box, and that with artistry and hard work they could answer questions about complex cognitive and motivational processes by carefully crafting experiments that were as rich in dramatic detail as they were in scientific rigor. Likewise, his example demonstrated that to conduct first-rate research, the social psychologist need not—indeed should not—stay stuck in the laboratory, but should venture into the field to test theories by applying them to the problems of the day.

Contributors to this volume—former students and colleagues, coauthors, a family member, and even one social psychologist who never met Elliot—write warmly of how Elliot influenced them in one or more of these ways. *Warmly*, you will see, is key; as chapters came in, we were struck (though unsurprised) by the recurring expressions of affection, admiration, and respect for Elliot that infuse them. The result was that this collection of essays, reflections, research, and songs of praise does just what we had hoped it would do: It honors Elliot for the rare combination of passion and intelligence he has always brought to the field, for his intellectual courage, for his inspiration and creativity, for his humor and heart, and for his storytelling and straight talk. In short, it honors both the man and his work.

You will find here a fascinating assortment of chapters by some of the greatest social psychologists in the business. Walter Mischel and Phil Zimbardo start things off with their personal reflections, most of which were suitable for print.

In Part I, Tom Pettigrew, Mark Lepper, Lee Ross, Roy Baumeister, and Phoebe Ellsworth write about diverse issues in the discipline itself, from its "golden years" of high-impact experimentation in the late 1950s and 1960s to the present.

In Part II, Eddie Harmon-Jones, Jeff Stone, Joel Cooper, and Mike Leippe and Donna Eisenstadt write about their own excursions into one of Elliot's greatest scientific contributions: his pioneering research on cognitive dissonance theory.

In Part III, the authors describe Elliot's influence as they followed his example of applying social–psychological insights to diverse areas of research and application. Jeff Simpson writes on relationship science, Debbie Davis on the legal system, Paul Stern on energy efficiency, Tony Greenwald on prejudice, and Joshua Aronson on education.

In Part IV, three chapters are devoted to two of Elliot's passions: writing and teaching. Tim Wilson describes the pleasure of learning to deacademicize textbook writing as Elliot's coauthor; Carol Tavris reflects on writing for the general public and writing a trade book with Elliot; and Marti Gonzales shares lessons learned about the art of teaching, when Elliot was her graduate advisor at the University of California, Santa Cruz.

We regret that one central domain of Elliot's life is not represented in this collection: his work with T-groups in the 1960s and 1970s, when most of his academic colleagues thought he had gone a bit loony, lost in the touchy-feely world of gurus and goofiness. Elliot loved this phase of his life and has always claimed that his work as a scientist made him a better encounter-group leader, and his work with groups made him a better social psychologist. But perhaps it is just as well that we have no chapter reflecting that era. The substantive lessons he learned from his humanist work as an encounter-group leader, especially about straight talking, risk taking, and the importance of identifying the feelings behind accusations and insults, can be found in *The Social Animal,* particularly if one seeks out earlier editions of the book. But the feelings of enlightenment and exhilaration that so many encounter-group participants experienced probably could not have been captured well anyway. "Trying to describe what happens in an encounter group," Elliot often says, "is like trying to describe what happens during sex. If you're doing it, you know how much fun it is. If you're observing it, the activity looks preposterous."

Everyone who knows Elliot knows that you cannot honor him without honoring his remarkable partnership with Vera, who has been his best friend ever since they were undergraduate research assistants for Abraham Maslow (who pegged Vera as the star). Leon Festinger, in a letter of recommendation he wrote for Elliot in the 1970s, expressed awe that Elliot was able to do so many things—research, write textbooks, do applied work, lead T-groups, and teach—and do them all so well. "I really don't know how he manages to do it," he wrote. (For Leon, only the research part mattered.) But there's no mystery here. He managed to do it all because he had Vera.

Elliot and Vera's four children are an integral part of their shared story. Each went into a different career, yet all chose work for the same reason that Elliot has always valued social psychology—for its inherent excitement and its benefit to others: Hal as an expert on alternative sources of energy, Neal as a firefighter, Julie as an educational consultant, and Joshua as a professor of psychology. Elliot and Vera encouraged their children to do whatever made them happy and never pushed them toward academia or public service. Yet despite this laissez-faire attitude, it would have been utterly inconceivable for any of the Aronson children to have become a stockbroker or corporate lawyer. The value they place on serving the common good is a testament to both parents' definition of what it means to live the good life. They are a living Festschrift for their father.

This volume has two codas. One is an excerpt from a Yom Kippur sermon, which we included because we love it and because it is, well, so Jewish. And you can't celebrate Elliot's life without tipping your hat to the Jewish sense of humor and love of argument that pervade his soul, as does *tikkun olam,* the secular obligation to do one's part to heal the world. The second coda is Elliot's. If he doesn't get to have the last word, who does?

At the end of Mark Lepper's opening fable, he advises us to ask not just what our wizards can do for us, but what we can do for them. And that is exactly what the contributors to this Festschrift volume had in mind: to honor the real wizard among us, Elliot Aronson.

A TRIBUTE TO ELLIOT ARONSON

Walter Mischel

Columbia University

For more than half a century, beginning in the late 1950s, Elliot Aronson and I shared many of the experiences, big joys and heart-rending pains, small jokes and goofs, and shit-fits that make life meaningful. We began together as eager assistant professors in the Social Relations Department at Harvard. We bonded quickly because we were among the few in that department then who knew how to do an experiment and actually did a few.

We also bonded by sharing Tony Greenwald as a graduate student. We competed to see how we could separately and collectively torture Tony into being less obstinate about insisting on having his own ideas. Ultimately he won by torturing us even more than we tortured him and showing some of his ideas were actually well worth listening to. In time of course, he's managed to convince not only us but the rest of our field, and to make both of us proud of him, and delighted at any opportunity to claim him as our student.

In retrospect, life themes, which could not be seen when we were so busy living them, become clearer with the passage of time. Looking back, Elliot knows that much of his life reflects two influences on him that for most of us in psychology seemed irreconcilable: Abraham Maslow and Leon Festinger. Maslow electrified Elliot's college experience, his value system, and his personal vision. Festinger transformed Elliot, the smart but raw graduate student, and inspired him to become a great researcher and rigorous scientist. If psychology had a *Saturday Night Live* spoof show, an act that tries to reconcile these two people might become its most hilarious moment. Maslow and Festinger would not have wanted to find themselves together on the same side of the street. Elliot loved them both, and still does.

At points in his life, unsystematically sampled by me over a lifetime, Elliot seemed to become a sharpened, sped-up version of his two utterly contrasting mentors, sequentially. In an early phase, as an academic with the "hot hand" of a basketball star, he represented the best of what Leon offered as a laser-sharp experimentalist and dazzling thinker. Elliot began his career by doing some of the most elegant and significant experiments in social psychology, giving dissonance theory its sharpest teeth, and showing how far incisive, original ideas and rigorous, intuitively sensible experiments can take social psychology. Elliot's experiments made genuine discoveries that would have surprised grandma ("Bubbe" in Yiddish)—the golden criterion for Leon. In a later period, in which the great teacher and missionary in him emerged, he personified the best of what Abe Maslow was all about and made his life a case study of "self-actualization." And he didn't give a damn what Bubbe might have thought about it.

In time, Elliot even managed to reconcile the best from both of his mentors in much of his work and in how he lived his life. It took me a long time to believe it could be done. For a while at the height of the counterculture in the early 1970s, I was a bit worried about Elliot—his popularity and charisma became so great as a teacher and model to the young I feared he was on the way to becoming a guru. I began to anticipate his hair growing down to his shoulders, a beard moving toward the navel, and flowing white robes—sort of a Gandhi type who would captivate enthralled college audiences. He got the captivated audiences, but instead of becoming a guru, Elliot became a model for "translational research" decades before translational was even a word within psychology. And what Elliot found in translation showed powerfully how much of a difference psychology can make in the real world. Soon the model for enviable social psychology experiments became the model for how to fuse the scientifically important with the humanly meaningful and consequential.

One of the gratifications of watching Elliot's evolution over a long lifetime is to see how his two mentors ultimately merged seamlessly in his identity, in his character, in his work, and in his relationships to other people. His commitment and caring concern with other people reached out not just to his own beloved Vera and family, but also—yes, Leon would have winced, and Maslow would have glowed—to the community and, indeed, humanity.

This phase began when the Vietnam War and the civil rights movement galvanized him to venture beyond the classroom and the lab into the crazy real world swept up in turbulent changes all around him. His involvement took many forms, supported many vital social causes, and is perhaps best illustrated in his creation of the Jigsaw Classroom. Elliot saw that, contrary to expectations, following desegregation, prejudice increased, while the self-esteem and performance of minority kids did not. So he made the elementary school classroom his lab, observing that the competitive school situation confirmed and magnified the kids' existing stereotypes about each other. The Anglo children generally saw the minority kids as stupid and lazy; the minority children thought the Anglos kids were snooty show-offs. So he restructured the dynamics of the classroom, changing the structure from competitive to cooperative. He created small interdependent groups, in which students of different ethnic backgrounds were placed in a situation in which they had to cooperate with each other to make sense of the material. It was dubbed the Jigsaw Classroom because it resembled how a jigsaw puzzle gets assembled. And it worked. Like most of what Elliot did, it also had huge impact.

No tribute to Elliot could begin to get at who he is and who he became without including a tribute, as he himself often says, "for Vera, of course." Vera's role in Elliot's life and career deserves its own biography: I suspect that their relationship, and Vera's love, guts, brains, and wisdom, account for much of those "underlying processes" that we psychologists care so much about in our efforts at explanation. While I don't have a clue about the specific processes that caused the kid from Revere Beach to become the Elliot Aronson we honor in this volume, I am sure that Vera was vital to how it all happened. And I know that there was and is much beauty in the details of how they built a life together, even though the medals went to him, while Vera quietly glowed.

Talking about the life of Leon Festinger, Stanley Schachter once memorably said that Leon had a mind curse: He listened, he really listened. I think that Elliot also has that curse: He listens, he really listens; he also responds honestly to what he hears. But, in addition to a mind curse, Elliot also has a blessing: He cares, he really cares, and even better, he goes on to make a difference in the lives of people. I expect he always will. Looking at Elliot's life, not even Maslow could have hoped for more. And Leon would be smiling his warmest grin.

HONORING ELLIOT ARONSON

Philip G. Zimbardo
Stanford University

In 1970, Elliot invited me to spend a week at the University of Texas, Austin. I would be staying at his home, giving some talks and working with his graduate-student research team. I had met him a year before in Lincoln, at the Nebraska Symposium on Motivation, where we bonded in a flash, dazzling the joint with our ideas and storytelling style. So I accepted his offer at once. As I deplaned, the Armadillo Marching Band was blasting away and dozens of students and colleagues were shouting welcomes, holding high all kinds of signs. The entire event was, of course, orchestrated by the impresario in his top hat, long cape, and cane—Master of Ceremonies Elliot Aronson. I happened to be wearing my British Bobby cape and identity pin ("Z—He Lives"), so I was not out of local fashion as our motorcade roared through Austin. That visit was a great gift from Elliot—one of the most memorable gifts I have ever received—and the start of a lifelong friendship and funship. Our professional and personal lives intersected often over the next four decades, at home and abroad, together, and with our families.

Elliot survived his early life trials and tribulations in Revere, Massachusetts, while I did the same, making it through my South Bronx ghetto experience. We also shared being picked on, and even abused, by the bad-assed bullies—for being Jewish. In Elliot's case, he really was; in my own case, it was because I looked Jewish enough to the Irish toughs. Like many early social psychologists who were from minority backgrounds, immigrants to the United States, or both, we felt the stigma of being outsiders. Still, on the positive side, we became observers of the human condition when we were not participating in it fully, as do cultural anthropologists.

I know in my case, and in that of my James Monroe High School classmate little Stanley Milgram, and in Elliot's case as well, we became situationists rather than dispositionists in response to seeing more failures than successes around us. If you are privileged, you come to believe that success is in your genes, legacy, and personality. But who wants to claim poverty and the economic failure of your family and friends? My own mantra was: Things would be different if a few things in the situation were changed for the better.

Elliot and I nearly crossed paths many times en route to our Austin event. We almost shared Abe Maslow, who was a guru at Brooklyn College when I arrived in 1950, but he soon left for Brandeis to become one of Elliot's early influences. And we almost shared Leon Festinger. Elliot was working with Leon at Stanford, joining the Lewinian lineage, as had Leon with his own mentor, Kurt Lewin. I was at Yale, where my major influences were Carl Hovland and Neal Miller, both from the Clark Hull tradition. Jack Brehm had just come to Yale from Minnesota, having completed one of the first experiments testing cognitive dissonance predictions. Jack arranged for a small group of us students to read Leon's dissonance theory in manuscript form before it was published. Leon was invited to give a colloquium at Yale, and his brilliance was captivating. I knew I wanted to study with him and asked if I could do a postdoc with him at Stanford; he said, sure, if I could get funding, which I could not. So I drifted off to NYU, while Elliot headed up the social lab at the University of Minnesota, with much success both as a mentor and creative researcher.

I envied Elliot's close connection with Leon, but always appreciated how he took the best his mentor had to offer and enriched it with his own originality and flair. First, there was the emphasis on starting with simple theories about specific phenomena, then creating compelling laboratory analogues of real-world events or experiences. Second, there was his eventual passion for T-groups, which went far beyond Leon's origins in group dynamics. Elliot became one of the most effective and sought-after T-group leaders at Bethel, Maine, and later, in Austin, where he ran encounter groups with his wife, Vera. Elliot told me this was one area in which he and Leon parted company because Leon disdained that whole movement and suggested that Elliot abandon it, but Elliot hung tough and embraced it fully.

Elliot cared more than Leon did about addressing social problems, such as understanding and changing prejudice and academic performance, and about popularizing scientific social psychology. Visit Scott Plous's Social Psychology Network, SPN, to view a module on the Jigsaw classroom; the site has been visited by over 3 million people since its inception in 2002. And, of course, Elliot's deep concern for applying social-psychological thinking to solutions to social and political problems has always been evident to generations of readers, including students introduced to our field via the joys of reading *The Social Animal*, perhaps social psychology's premier textbook. In *Nobody Left to Hate*, in the aftermath of the 1999 tragedy at Columbine High School, he explains how and why otherwise typical kids become "shooters." And in his most recent trade book, *Mistakes Were Made (But Not by Me)* (with Carol Tavris), he compellingly explains why we are so much better at rationalizing our mistakes after the fact than we are at making rational decisions in the first place. And the hits just keep on coming.

Elliot and I forged our friendship on trips to conferences in Hungary, where we overdosed on pastries, and Spain, where we spent days lecturing and nights drinking sangria and barhopping. We shared an amazing experience during a visit to the Arabic gem, Al Hambra, in Granada, Spain. Al Hambra—the "Red Fortress"—is one of the most spectacular temples in the Western world, and was a refuge for Muslim artists and intellectuals during Christian victories in the 14th century. We were there on a weekday, when a light rainy mist made it both more magical and solitary, as few visitors were evident. We had a chance to dig deep into our souls about our careers and ambitions, amazed at how far we had come from where we started, yet eager to do more and better research, teaching, and work to improve the human condition. It was the quiet, gentle yang of our rowdy, collective yin experience in Austin those many years earlier.

Although I got the job at Stanford replacing Leon, a position that should have gone to Elliot, he never (seemed!) to begrudge it to me, and our families continued to share milestone events—weddings, birthdays, honorific events, even illnesses and other challenges. Not for many years was I able to reciprocate his unflagging generosity. Upon his retirement from University of California, Santa Cruz (UCSC) in 1994, despite Elliot's having won every award for outstanding research, teaching, and writing from the American Psychological Association (APA) and other groups, the university did not permit him to continue teaching his introductory social psychology course, the most popular course in the university. I seized the opportunity and arranged for him to teach a special course at Stanford, which he did until his failing eyesight made the travel up from Santa Cruz more arduous than pleasurable. But what a joy it was to sit in his class, reveling in his mastery of the art of teaching through his original narratives about a host of timeless themes, all centered on understanding and appreciating the nature of human nature.

Here's a toast to the kind of person who comes around all too rarely, but when they do, they cut a permanent place in the firmament of enduring ideas that change how we think about ourselves and our natures as social animals. That's Elliot—impresario, scholar, friend.

I
Issues in Social Psychology

1
THE ULTIMATE LEWINIAN

Thomas F. Pettigrew
University of California, Santa Cruz

Kurt Lewin reshaped the discipline of social psychology. His field theory and his innovative approach to high-impact experiments on basic issues injected excitement and distinctiveness into the discipline's work. But in recognizing the field's enormous debt to Lewin, we have obscured two key points in social psychology's history.

First, there was a vigorous, if small, social psychology in the United States prior to and right after Lewin's flight from Hitler Germany and his arrival in America in 1933 via the Trans-Siberian railway. In this sense, the claim that Lewin was the "founder of social psychology" (Kurt Lewin, 2008) is an exaggeration. By 1935, a series of classic studies had already established social psychology in the United States. Consider Floyd Allport's (1920, 1934) study comparing the performance of individuals acting alone versus in groups and his J-curve for conforming behavior, John Dashiell's (1930) study of group effects on a series of cognitive tasks, Gordon Allport and Hadley Cantril's (1935) study of radio effects, and Otto Klineberg's (1935) ground-breaking research revealing that African Americans' intelligence test scores increases after moving from the South to the urban North. To be sure, the field remained tiny and suffered low status within psychology departments. What was missing were the dynamic theories and vivid experimentation that the German immigrant was soon to introduce.

Second, only one side of Lewin's genius and contributions has been sufficiently emphasized. In addition to his influence on the discipline's approach to experimentation, Lewin also stressed the application of social psychology's insights to "real-world" problems. In social psychology, Lewin's applied side is largely confined to knowledge of a few famous experiments, such as his work on group decisions and food habits (Lewin, 1947).

But Lewin actually involved himself in many other, directly applied endeavors. In response to a Connecticut state government request for methods to diminish racial and religious prejudices, he set up a workshop to try out what is now known as "T-groups" and "sensitivity training." This led in 1947 to the establishment of the National Training Laboratories (NTL) in Bethel, Maine. Also following World War II, the former World War I soldier worked on the psychological rehabilitation of former occupants of displaced persons camps. "Action research" was his concept although it has had its greatest impact in organizational psychology (Lewin, 1946).

Moreover, Lewin worked hard at linking his two emphases. In the 1940s, he carefully established two centers—one at the Massachusetts Institute of Technology for his basic research, another in New York City for applied work. He then shuttled back and forth by train between Cambridge and New York to connect his dual efforts of expanding both theory and meaningful social action.

Just how much current social psychology has obscured this duality of Lewin's contributions is illustrated by the abbreviated motto of the Society for the Psychological Study of Social Issues. Throughout its long history, this group—of which Lewin was a cofounder, together with three dozen other eminent scholars in 1936—has effectively advanced applied work with direct social policy implications. Yet its motto is only a partial citation from Lewin: "There is nothing so practical as a good theory ..." This motto omits the remainder of his pointed sentence that admonishes theorists not to "look toward applied problems with highbrow aversion or with a fear of social problems" (Lewin, 1951, p. 169). Obviously, he fully understood that applied work had lower status than more fundamental research and theory, and that this situation should not be allowed to deter applied work by social psychologists.

LEWIN'S STUDENTS: THE FIRST-GENERATION LEWINIANS

After his untimely death in 1948, Lewin's tradition was institutionalized in social psychology by the efforts of the remarkable cohort of talented students whom he had trained. Their names today read like a who's who of leading social psychologists: Kurt Back, Roger Barker, Alex Bavelas, Morton Deutsch, Leon Festinger, Harold Kelley, Ronald Lippitt, Al Pepitone, John Thibaut, Ralph White, Alvin Zander, and many others. Their contributions were wide ranging. In theory, Festinger's cognitive dissonance and social comparison theories and Deutsch's conflict resolution theory enriched a theory-starved discipline. In research, they perfected the high impact laboratory experiments on central issues that reoriented the field's empirical work. And, in all their work, the influence of their teacher is clearly apparent.

These first-generation Lewinians encountered and overcame the low status that social psychology occupied during the 1950s in psychology departments dominated by experimental psychologists. Thus, it is not surprising that they typically followed the basic theory and research side of the Lewinian tradition. White laboratory coats were the order of the day, not applied work in the field. Consequently, the applied tradition received far less attention as social psychologists of the period struggled to acquire full acceptance within academic psychology (see also Jones, 1985).

There were, of course, exceptions to this trend. For example, Ronald Lippitt and Alex Bavelas continued Lewin's interest in organizational psychology, sensitivity training, and the NTL in Bethel. Even rarer were first-generation Lewinians who evinced both sides of their mentor's legacy—basic and applied social psychology tightly intertwined. Here the influential work of Morton Deutsch is the conspicuous exception. He stands as the ultimate Lewinian of his generation. Not only has Deutsch long studied and practiced conflict resolution (Deutsch, 1949), but he also pioneered policy-relevant field research on interracial contact (Deutsch & Collins, 1951). At Columbia University's Teachers College, he founded the International Center for Cooperation and Conflict Resolution, an organization highly reminiscent in its approach and aims to the applied center established by Lewin in the late 1940s in New York City. And, fittingly, Deutsch established an honor that sums up the tradition's two sides: the Morton Deutsch Award for Distinguished Scholarly and Practical Contributions to Social Psychology.

THE SECOND-GENERATION LEWINIANS

Following their teacher's example, all of Lewin's star-studded cast of students proceeded to train another generation of leading social psychologists. Not surprisingly, these second-generation Lewinians typically followed the laboratory-bound experimental side of the tradition practiced by their mentors. Leon Festinger, in particular, provided the discipline with an array of outstanding students; the most renowned of whom is Elliot Aronson. And, like Deutsch, Elliot has proven to be the ultimate Lewinian of his generation, for he, too, combines the two sides of the tradition. Elliot's dual contributions are described in detail throughout this volume. A brief summary here underlines the point and its significance for social psychology as a developing discipline.

Elliot's strikingly powerful and important experiments conducted early in his career are perhaps the best known of his many works. His classic severity of initiation experiment with Jud Mills (Aronson & Mills, 1959) was conducted while Elliot was still a graduate student at Stanford. Together with such other classics as Muzafer Sherif's Robbers Cave study (Sherif, Harvey, White, Hood, & Sherif, 1961) and Stanley Milgram's (1974) obedience research, this early work brilliantly demonstrated what social-psychological research could distinctively contribute to social science knowledge. A quick search of five recent social psychology texts on my shelf all cite it, half a century later.

Equally cited today is Elliot's dissonance research with Merrill Carlsmith, research that showed the extremes people will go to preserve a consistent, even if negative, self-concept (Aronson & Carlsmith, 1962). Indeed, the results of this provocative study and others like it led Elliot to restructure dissonance theory with a new emphasis on the self-concept. He specified the theory by showing that dissonance predictions proved most valid when subjects failed to behave consistently with important aspects of their sense of self. Later, he and Ruth Thibodeau demonstrated that hypocrisy that challenged one's self-concept could induce dissonance without there being aversive consequences (Thibodeau & Aronson, 1992).

Elliot credits his grasp of rigorous experimentation to the stern instruction of Leon Festinger (Aronson, 2007). But, in fact, it was Elliot who was the first to convey in forceful prose just how to conduct laboratory experiments in the unique Lewinian style. He did so in two books, *Research Methods in Social Psychology* (Aronson, Carlsmith & Ellsworth, 1976) and *Methods of Research in Social Psychology* (Aronson, Ellsworth, Carlsmith & Gonzales, 1990), and in a series of influential chapters in the various editions of the *Handbook of Social Psychology* (Aronson, Brewer, & Carlsmith, 1985; Aronson & Carlsmith, 1968; Aronson, Wilson, & Brewer, 1998). These works completed the full diffusion of the Lewinian approach to experimentation throughout social psychology.

Diffusion also resulted from Elliot's popular graduate seminars on experimental methods in the four universities in which he has taught. His influence can be seen, I believe, in the later research of his Harvard University students (e.g., Merrill Carlsmith, John Darley, and Anthony

Greenwald), his University of Minnesota students (e.g., Ellen Berscheid and Darwyn Linder), his University of Texas students (e.g., Kay Deaux, Bill Ickes, Dave Mettee, and Harold Sigall), and his University of California, Santa Cruz (UCSC) students (e.g., Mark Costanzo, Marti Hope Gonzales, and Jeff Stone). Elliot has also won repeated awards for his colorful undergraduate teaching. Here I have the testimony of my own son, Mark, to support this acclaim. Mark enjoyed every lecture of Elliot's introductory social psychology course. One evening at the family dinner table he exclaimed that now he finally understood what I had been talking about all these years.

Later in his career, Elliot turned his talents to a great variety of important applications of social-psychological principles, and became the complete Lewinian. Best known, of course, is his Jigsaw Classroom technique (Aronson, 1978; Aronson & Patnoe, 1997). Drawing on a wide range of social-psychological principles from G. W. Allport's (1954) intergroup contact theory to Deutsch's (1949) theory of cooperation and competition to Sherif's (Sherif et al., 1961) theory of common goals and cooperation, the ingenious Jigsaw application is one of the most widely adopted and effective social-psychological interventions ever advanced. With ethnically diverse classrooms, the technique substitutes intragroup cooperation for individual competition and achieves not only academic gains, but also improved intergroup relations. Moreover, it has proved itself in a wide variety of cultures around the world, supporting the contention that many social-psychological phenomena possess near-universal applicability. Hence, positive Jigsaw Classroom results for children have been reported in Australia (Walker & Crogan, 1998), Germany (Eppler & Huber, 1990), Israel (Hertz-Lazarowitz, Sharan, & Steinberg, 1980), Japan (Araragi, 1983), and in the United States for Mexican Americans (Aronson & Gonzalez, 1988).

But Elliot has also contributed to our understanding of many other practical problems. He has offered strategies for encouraging condom use to combat the spread of AIDS (Stone, Aronson, Crain, Winslow, & Fried, 1994), for conserving water (Dickerson, Thibodeau, Aronson, & Miller, 1992) and energy (Gonzales, Aronson, & Costanzo, 1988; Stern & Aronson, 1984), and for the relief of career burnout (Pines & Aronson, 1988). These applications of social psychology are all ingenious, but they are also often surprisingly simple and straightforward. The use of hypocrisy to induce greater use of condoms is one example. Another involves ways to encourage people to turn off the hot shower while applying soap—a habit I still continue two decades later.

One might ask how much the Lewinian tradition inspired Elliot's many applications. I maintain that they are all mainstream Lewinian approaches that would have delighted Lewin. In addition to his training with Festinger at Stanford, Elliot attended NTL in Bethel for nine weeks, and learned how to conduct T-groups and sensitivity training—an opportunity that had a major influence on him (Aronson, 2007). And he and his wife, Vera, have both successfully directed T-groups. These experiences in the Lewinian tradition relate directly to how Elliot thinks about social problems and devises possible remedies.

A FINAL PERSONAL NOTE

Elliot and I are only nine months apart in age, and our careers have intersected at both Harvard and UCSC. We met for the first time in 1959 on the third floor of Emerson Hall in Harvard Yard just as Elliot arrived fresh from his graduate work at Stanford.

Because we came from sharply different backgrounds, traditions, and training, one might have thought we would have very little in common. But, actually, we shared three strong bonds. We both were highly identified and enthusiastic social psychologists who believed strongly in the potential of our chosen discipline. We both cared deeply about prejudice and discrimination and wanted to find practical ways to combat these intergroup afflictions, each of us having experienced their consequences early in life. And finally, we were both apprehensive assistant professors in the old Department of Social Relations, which boasted such luminaries as Gordon Allport, Clyde Kluckhohn, Henry Murray, Talcott Parsons, Samuel Stouffer, and Robert White. We were justifiably apprehensive, for Harvard was then a scary place for assistant professors (hopefully, less so now).

I recall our first meeting vividly, because I still have a Zeigarnik going for the article we carefully planned but never managed to write. We were going to explain, in part, white American resistance to racial change using—what else?—dissonance theory.

I also fondly recall the warm welcome that Elliot provided me when I joined him at UCSC in 1980. His presence at UCSC was one of many reasons why I left Harvard to come to UCSC. And I recall our engaging deliberations of the discipline between sets of our early morning tennis—great discussions but appalling tennis!

Of our three decades together at UCSC, I remember in particular the fun and excitement we had with Dane Archer in conducting energy conservation research for the California State Energy Commission—and our largely vain attempts later to put what we learned into social policy (Archer, Pettigrew, & Aronson, 1992; Costanzo, Archer, Aronson, & Pettigrew, 1986). And now, years later, the wonderful graduate students with whom we worked on that project are prominently placed in social psychology throughout the nation and are represented in this volume.

Thus, for both professional and personal reasons, I am delighted to join in this richly deserved Festschrift for the ultimate Lewinian of his generation.

REFERENCES

Allport, F. H. (1920). The influence of the group upon association and thought. *Journal of Experimental Psychology, 3*(3), 159–182.

Allport, F. H. (1934). The J-Curve hypothesis of conforming behavior. *Journal of Social Psychology, 5,* 141–183.

Allport, G. W. (1954). *The nature of prejudice.* Reading, MA: Addison-Wesley.

Allport, G. W., & Cantril, H. (1935). *The psychology of radio.* New York: Harper.

Araragi, C. (1983). The effect of the jigsaw learning method on children's academic performance and learning attitude. *Japanese Journal of Educational Psychology, 31,* 102–112.

Archer, D., Pettigrew, T. F., & Aronson, E. (1992). Making research apply: High stakes public policy in a regulatory environment. *American Psychologist, 47*(10), 1233–1236.

Aronson, E. (1978). *The Jigsaw Classroom.* Beverly Hills, CA: Sage.

Aronson, E. (2007). An autobiography. In G. Lindzey & M. Runyan (Eds.), *The history of psychology in autobiography* (Vol. 9, pp. 3–41). Washington, DC: American Psychological Association Books.

Aronson, E., Brewer, M., & Carlsmith, J. M. (1985). Experimentation in social psychology. In G. Lindzey & E. Aronson (Eds.), *Handbook of social psychology* (3rd ed., Vol. II, pp. 441–486). New York: Random House.

Aronson, E., & Carlsmith, J. M. (1962). Performance expectancy as a determinant of actual performance. *Journal of Abnormal and Social Psychology, 65,* 178–182.

Aronson, E., & Carlsmith, J. M. (1968). Experimentation in social psychology. In G. Lindzey & E. Aronson (Eds.), *Handbook of social psychology* (2nd ed., Vol. II, pp. 1–79). Reading, MA: Addison-Wesley.

Aronson, E., Carlsmith, J. M., & Ellsworth, E. (1976). *Research methods in social psychology.* Reading, MA: Addison-Wesley.

Aronson, E., Ellsworth, E., Carlsmith, J. M., & Gonzales, M. H. (1990). *Methods of research in social psychology* (2nd ed.). New York: McGraw-Hill.

Aronson, E., & Gonzalez. A. (1988). Desegregation, jigsaw, and the Mexican-American experience. In P. A. Katz & D. A. Taylor (Eds.), *Eliminating racism: Profiles in controversy* (pp. 301–314). New York: Plenum Press.

Aronson, E., & Mills, J. (1959). The effect of severity of initiation in liking for a group. *Journal of Abnormal and Social Psychology, 59,* 177–181.

Aronson, E., & Patnoe, S. (1997). *Cooperation in the classroom: The jigsaw method.* New York: Longman.

Aronson, E., Wilson, T., & Brewer, M. (1998). The experimental method in social psychology. In G. Lindzey, D. Gilbert, & S. Fiske (Eds.), *Handbook of social psychology* (4th ed., pp. 99–142). New York: Random House.

Costanzo, M. A., Archer, D., Aronson, E., & Pettigrew, T. F. (1986). Energy conservation behavior: The difficult path from information to action. *American Psychologist, 41*(5), 521–528.

Dashiell, J. F. (1930). An experimental analysis of some group effects. *Journal of Abnormal and Social Psychology, 25,* 190–199.

Deutsch, M. (1949). A theory of cooperation and competition. *Human Relations, 2,* 129–152.

Deutsch, M., & Collins, M. E. (1951). *Interracial housing: A psychological evaluation of a social experiment.* Minneapolis: University of Minnesota Press.

Dickerson, C. A., Thibodeau, R., Aronson, E., & Miller, D. (1992). Using cognitive dissonance to encourage water conservation. *Journal of Applied Social Psychology, 22,* 841–854.

Eppler, R., & Huber, G. L. (1990). Wissenserwerb im Team: Empirische Untersuchung von Effekten des Gruppen-Puzzles [Acquiring knowledge in teams: Empirical examination of the effects of puzzle groups.] *Psychologie in Erziehung und Unterricht* [*Psychology in Education and Instruction*], *37,* 172–178.

Gonzales, M. H., Aronson, E., & Costanzo, M. (1988). Increasing the effectiveness of energy auditors: A field experiment. *Journal of Applied Social Psychology, 18,* 1049–1066.

Hertz-Lazarowitz, R., Sharan, S., & Steinberg, R. (1980). Classroom learning style and cooperative behavior of elementary school children. *Journal of Educational Psychology, 72,* 99–106.

Jones, E. E. (1985). Major developments in social psychology during the past five decades. In G. Lindzey & E. Aronson (Eds.), *The handbook of social psychology* (2nd ed., pp. 47–107). Reading, MA: Addison-Wesley.

Klineberg, O. (1935). *Negro intelligence and selective migration.* New York: Columbia University Press.

Kurt Lewin. (2008). In Wikipedia. Retrieved August 22, 2009 from http://en.wikipedia.org/wiki/Kurt_Lewin

Lewin, K. (1946). Action research and minority problems. *Journal of Social Issues, 2*(4), 34–46.

Lewin, K. (1947). Group decision and social change. In T. M. Newcomb & E. L. Hartley (Eds.), *Readings in social psychology* (pp. 330–344). New York: Holt.

Lewin, K. (1951). *Field theory in social science.* New York: Harper.

Milgram, S. (1974). *Obedience to authority: An experimental view.* New York: Harper & Row.

Pines, A., & Aronson, E. (1988). *Career burnout.* New York: Free Press.

Sherif, M., Harvey, O. J., White, D. J., Hood, W. R., & Sherif, C. F. (1961). *Intergroup conflict and cooperation: The Robbers Cave experiment.* Norman, OK: University of Oklahoma Book Exchange.

Stern, P. C., & Aronson, E. (Eds.). (1984). *Energy use: The human dimension.* New York: Freeman.

Stone, J., Aronson, E., Crain, A. L., Winslow, M. P., & Fried, C. B. (1994). Inducing hypocrisy as a means of encouraging young adults to use condoms. *Personality and Social Psychology Bulletin, 20,* 116–128.

Thibodeau, R., & Aronson, E. (1992). Taking a closer look: Reasserting the role of the self-concept in dissonance theory. *Personality and Social Psychology Bulletin, 18,* 591–502.

Walker, I., & Crogan, M. (1998). Academic performance, prejudice, and the jigsaw classroom. *Journal of Community and Applied Social Psychology, 8,* 381–393.

2

FORBIDDEN TOYS AND TRANSGRESSIVE THOUGHTS

Mark R. Lepper
Stanford University

I cannot actually recall the first time I met Elliot Aronson in person, but I do know that it was many years after he had already acquired legendary status in my mind as a master of experimental social psychology. I suspect that many in my cohort, entering this field in the 1960s, may have had similar feelings, but I also suspect that I may have been particularly susceptible to the lures of Aronson mania.

To begin with, my introduction to psychology of any sort was a Stanford course in social psychology taught by J. Merrill Carlsmith, one of Elliot's earliest and most successful students and collaborators. The year was 1964, and right at the top of the list of hot, new studies in social psychology were the three paradigmatic "insufficient justification" demonstrations of Aronson and Mills (1959), Festinger and Carlsmith (1959), and Aronson and Carlsmith (1963), along with the first, brief report of Milgram's (1963) new work on obedience to malevolent authorities, and Schachter and Singer's (1962) novel two-process or "jukebox" theory of emotions.

Wow! Not only were these studies exemplary of what would later be called high-impact experimentation, in which experimenters sought to create "slice of life" dramas that placed participants in situations of real conflict and immediate personal relevance, they were also studies that routinely fascinated readers and convinced them that they had learned something new and important because the results that were reported were so strikingly counterintuitive. Even more impressive, to a naïve undergraduate, was the fact that these master experimenters made it all look so easy.

Indeed, Merrill Carlsmith persuaded me to become a psychology major following that first class and eventually inveigled me into doing a senior honors project under his supervision, in part by mentioning casually to me that *his* Stanford honors thesis had been the famed Festinger and Carlsmith (1959) study. Somehow, though, he neglected to mention that to this day that article remains perhaps the most famous senior honors thesis in all of psychology. More typically, although my senior honors project was subsequently published, no more than half a dozen people (and that includes both my parents and my two coauthors) have ever actually read that article.

Yet, at the time the mere possibility of winning fame and fortune (the latter aspiration demonstrating how truly naïve I was then), all while still a mere undergraduate, seemed unaccountably attractive. Indeed, these prospects probably loomed especially large when contrasted with my then-current chemistry major, since only two weeks earlier I had inadvertently "blown up" a portion of the organic chemistry laboratories. Blown up, I should admit, is slightly too strong a phrase, but it does convey the general idea. My laboratory notebook, not to mention a considerable amount of glassware, sadly paid the ultimate price for my mishap.

Having made the decision to become a social psychologist, then, the question was what should I study, and the answer seemed clear, at least by elimination. I quickly ruled out the Aronson and Mills paradigm, reasoning that I myself would probably be unable to pass the severe initiation procedure of reading lurid passages to a person of the opposite sex. I also quickly gave up on the Festinger and Carlsmith procedure, once I heard from Merrill that he had to use his own $20 to pay subjects and then beg for it back from each participant at the end of the study. Schachter and Singer's study seemed similarly out of my price range, since it required a licensed M.D. to administer the epinephrine shots and to remain on the premises in case of any adverse reactions.

Finally, by the time I had gotten to graduate school, Milgram had already published a second paper that revealed he had already run over 1,000 more subjects, and his critics had so strongly excoriated his studies on ethical grounds that it would have been virtually impossible to follow up on his obedience studies. To be accurate, I did try some studies on children's obedience to everyday requests from adults, but although we found a few results of interest—for example, that the vast majority of children were more likely to comply with requests from other children's mothers than from their own mothers—these studies remain, perhaps mercifully, unknown (Landauer, Carlsmith, & Lepper, 1970).

Thus, it was the Aronson and Carlsmith (1963) experiment on the effects of variations in the severity of a threat on children's later devaluation of the forbidden activity that captured my attention. In fact, my very first publication featured two replications of their basic paradigm, in which we examined the hypothesis that making salient the dissonant cognitions would increase dissonance reduction. My major contribution to these first studies (aside from the usual running of subjects, analyzing data, and the like) involved creating a means for us to make an old-fashioned goose-necked lamp flicker on and off (with accompanying sounds of electrical crackling and popping) on demand—thus drawing, in the high salience conditions, the child's attention to the attractive but forbidden toy. This attentional manipulation, in turn, produced increased dissonance reduction, in the form of greater subsequent derogation of the previously forbidden activity under both mild and severe threat conditions (Carlsmith et al., 1969).

In later work, Mark Zanna and I continued to work with this paradigm, showing the differential effects of manipulations that drew attention to the nature of the experimenter's threat at the same time as to the attractive but forbidden toy (Zanna, Lepper, & Abelson, 1973). We did this by having the experimenter place a large sticker with an X (the skull and crossbones seemed just a bit too harsh) on the forbidden toy "to remind" the child not to play with it. Here, we manipulated the children's attention by having a "janitor" walk through the room as they were resisting temptation and suddenly ask, in a puzzled voice, "How come you're not playing with that [forbidden toy]?" This procedure produced increases in derogation of the forbidden toy in the mild threat, but not the severe threat, conditions.

Still later, in my own dissertation research (Lepper, 1973), I showed that resisting an initial temptation to play with a forbidden toy (under mild, but not severe, threat) not only increased children's derogation of the specific forbidden toy, but also increased their resistance to a quite different form of temptation (i.e., avoiding the temptation to only slightly inflate one's score on a "bowling" game in order to win an attractive prize) two weeks later in the first experimenter's absence. This last result made this study one of relatively few studies in the dissonance tradition that examined subsequent overt behavior as well as the more common attitude change measures. Had there been more such studies, I have always suspected, Daryl Bem's (1965, 1972) self-perception challenge to dissonance theory might have proved considerably less persuasive to the field.

Although, sadly, these early studies did not attract even the minimal attention that they might have warranted—had not dissonance theory at that same time been headed into a state strongly resembling hibernation—I have always had a soft spot for these studies because I think of them as carrying on not only the theoretical traditions of Elliot and Merrill, but also a bit of their methodological style as well. Besides, they were, dare I say it, kind of fun. And we all know Elliot and Merrill's view of fun in research: Go for it (Aronson & Carlsmith, 1968).

Likewise, I still have a certain fondness for my early studies that attempted to extend some of the logic of the dissonance theorists from the problem of psychologically "insufficient" justification to the problem of psychologically "oversufficient" justification (e.g., Lepper, 1981; Lepper & Greene, 1975, 1978; Lepper, Greene, & Nisbett, 1973), which I initially considered a fairly small extrapolation beyond previous findings. Procedurally, these studies seemed to me quite close to our prior work. They used similar high-impact, slice-of-life settings and manipulations, once again with my particular insistence on obtaining behavioral measures in real-world settings, whenever possible.

Strikingly, our overjustification research (Lepper, 1981; Lepper et al., 1973) and related work by others (see Deci, 1971, 1975; Deci & Ryan, 1985; Lepper & Greene, 1978), produced far more than their fair share of controversy, debate, and downright hostility (e.g., Deci, Koestner, & Ryan, 1999; Lepper, Henderlong, & Gingras, 1999). For reasons I still do not fully understand, something about these studies—perhaps partially their use of behavioral measures—even more than the much larger body of evidence on dissonance theory, evidently hit a particular nerve among certain Skinnerians. Some claimed that the studies simply were not true, and that even if they were accurate, they should never have been done, and even if they had been done, they never should have been published. Indeed, some critics formally accused these experiments of "preventing the alleviation of human suffering" and their findings were characterized as a "myth." And those were only some of the nicer comments that actually made their way into print.

As empathic readers may already suspect, I had certainly not intended to come out quite so strongly in favor of human suffering. Rather, I had thought that our two lines of work on psychologically insufficient and psychologically oversufficient justification, taken together, had some potentially important implications for how parents (Lepper, 1983) and teachers (Lepper & Hodell, 1989) could use promised rewards and threatened punishments in more effective and supportive ways. To the extent that a central goal of socialization, at least in the United States, is not only to produce immediate compliance with adult requests or prohibitions, but also to produce internalization of the adult standards underlying them as well, attention to these issues seemed important.

Nonetheless, as I gave the usual colloquia and conference talks focused on this early research, I could not help but notice that even my closest friends had developed a tendency to introduce me as one of the world's experts on undermining children's intrinsic motivation, quashing their creativity, and generally stifling their spirits. I must admit that I found this a bit unnerving, and in the end, although I have remained interested in the ways that adults may sometimes unwittingly turn "play" into "work" (e.g., Lepper, Henderlong, & Iyengar, 2005; Lepper & Henderlong, 2000), I also felt it prudent to branch out from the study of how to turn play into work to the study of how one might do the reverse as well and turn work into play (e.g., Lepper, 1985). Thus, in recent years, my students and I have investigated various techniques for *enhancing* students' intrinsic motivation and, empirically, their concurrent learning as well. In some studies, we have sought to design and assess the effects of highly motivating educational computer activities (e.g., Cordova & Lepper, 1996); in others, we have examined and evaluated the motivational strategies and techniques of highly effective human tutors (e.g., Lepper & Woolverton, 2002).

Most recently, we have presented a general taxonomy of different sources of intrinsic motivations for learning that we have described as the "Seven C's" (plus or minus two) of intrinsic motivation (Lepper, Master, & Yow, 2008). Systematic attention to these factors—namely, competence, challenge, control, curiosity, contextualization, community, cooperation, and competition—we argue, can help in the design of more highly motivating and more instructionally effective learning environments in virtually any setting or domain of study.

Obviously, all these years later, I have no right to complain. Indeed, it has been a great privilege to be able to spend my career in the company of students and colleagues as bright and interesting and creative as those I have encountered at Stanford and elsewhere. So I know that I should have nothing but profuse thanks for Elliot Aronson and Merrill Carlsmith, for Leon Festinger and Stanley Schachter, and for Stanley Milgram and all the others of their generation whose research and theorizing so inspired the students in mine.

Still, I cannot help it: I do have a small bone to pick with them. How come nobody warned me, and the others in my generation, that *après lui, le deluge*? I mean, who knew that within a year of the publication of the massive consistency-theory opus, *Theories of Cognitive Consistency*

(Abelson et al., 1968), all of the grown-ups (or the generals, depending on your age and preferred metaphor) would have left that field for the next decade or more? Suddenly, Festinger was studying the resolution of "dissonance" between efferent and afferent perceptual feedback, and his students seemed to have dropped dissonance research like a hot potato. In tandem, Schachter had turned to studying the differences between "fats" and "skinnies," and Milgram had begun dropping "lost letters" to assess the political attitudes of different groups and started asking people to make cognitive maps of their neighborhoods.

More generally, who knew not long thereafter the field of social psychology would begin to eschew high-impact experiments of any sort (Ellsworth, this volume; Ross, Lepper, & Ward, 2010), or that the field would turn to the study of verbal reports and finger movements in lieu of behavioral measures of social phenomena like altruism, aggression, achievement, or obedience (Baumeister, Vohs, & Funder, 2007). Likewise, who would have guessed back then that the strategy of directly manipulating hypothesized mediating variables would be replaced by correlational statistical analyses relying heavily on potentially suspect verbal reports of hypothesized mediators (Spencer, Zanna, & Fong, 2005), or that traditional literature reviews would be supplanted by meta-analyses that permitted, if not sanctified, the use of overtly deceptive reports of experimental findings (Lepper, Keavney, & Drake, 1996)? Nor would most of us have expected that the top journals would effectively stop giving investigators credit, as it were, for the added difficulty and evident relevance of doing applied research in real-world settings (Cialdini, 2009).

Now, not to put too fine a point on it, if only our mentors had ... "spoink" (the official sound made by "cognitive dissonance taking over," according to *Dilbert*, September, 8, 1999). So, as I was about to say, obviously no one is perfect, and if mistakes were made, it certainly would not have been by them. Besides, if I and others in my generation had known what was in store, perhaps we would all have gone into some other field of study and missed out on the excitement and the challenges and the fun of the first golden age of experimental social psychology.

REFERENCES

Abelson, R P., Aronson, E., McGuire, W. J., Newcomb, T. M., Rosenberg, M. J., & Tannenbaum, P. H. (Eds.). (1968). *Theories of cognitive consistency: A sourcebook*. Chicago: Rand-McNally.

Aronson, E., & Carlsmith, J. M. (1963). Effect of the severity of threat on the devaluation of forbidden behavior. *Journal of Abnormal and Social Psychology, 66*, 584–588.

Aronson, E., & Carlsmith, J. M. (1968). Experimentation in social psychology. In G. Lindzey & E. Aronson (Eds.), *Handbook of social psychology* (2nd ed., Vol. II, pp. 1–79). Reading, MA: Addison-Wesley.

Aronson, E., & Mills, J. (1959). The effect of severity of initiation in liking for a group. *Journal of Abnormal and Social Psychology, 59*, 177–181.

Baumeister, R. F., Vohs, K. D., & Funder, D. C. (2007). Psychology as the science of self-reports and finger movements: Whatever happened to actual behavior? *Perspectives on Psychological Science, 2*, 396–403.

Carlsmith, J. M., Ebbesen, E. B., Lepper, M. R., Zanna, M. P., Joncas, A. J., & Abelson, R. P. (1969). *Dissonance reduction following forced attention to the dissonance.* Proceedings, 77th Annual Convention, American Psychological Association.

Cialdini, R. B. (2009). We have to break up. *Perspectives on Psychological Science, 4*, 5–6.

Cordova, D. I., & Lepper, M. R. (1996). Intrinsic motivation and the process of learning: Beneficial effects of contextualization, personalization, and choice. *Journal of Educational Psychology, 88,* 715–730.

Deci, E. L. (1971). Effects of externally mediated rewards on intrinsic motivation. *Journal of Personality and Social Psychology, 18*, 105–115.

Deci, E. L. (1975). *Intrinsic motivation.* New York: Plenum.

Deci, E. L., Koestner, R., & Ryan, R. M. (1999). A meta-analytic review of experiments examining the effects of extrinsic rewards on intrinsic motivation. *Psychological Bulletin, 125,* 627–668.

Deci, E. L., & Ryan, R. M. (1985). *Intrinsic motivation and self-determination in human behavior.* New York: Plenum.

Festinger, L., & Carlsmith, J. M. (1959). Cognitive consequences of forced compliance. *Journal of Abnormal and Social Psychology, 58*, 203–210.

Landauer, T. K., Carlsmith, J. M., & Lepper, M. R. (1970). Experimental analysis of the factors determining obedience of four-year-old children to adult females. *Child Development, 41*, 601–611.

Lepper, M. R. (1973). Dissonance, self perception and honesty in children. *Journal of Personality and Social Psychology, 25*, 65–74.

Lepper, M. R. (1981). Intrinsic and extrinsic motivation in children: Detrimental effects of superfluous social controls. In W. A. Collins (Ed.), *Aspects of the development of competence: Minnesota symposium on child psychology* (Vol. 14, pp. 155–213). Hillsdale, NJ: Erlbaum.

Lepper, M. R. (1983). Social control processes and the internalization of social values: An attributional perspective. In E. T. Higgins, D. N. Ruble, & W. W. Hartup (Eds.), *Social cognition and social development* (pp. 294–330). New York: Cambridge University Press.

Lepper, M. R. (1985). Microcomputers in education: Motivational and social issues. *American Psychologist, 40*, 1–18.

Lepper, M. R., & Greene, D. (1975). Turning play into work: Effects of adult surveillance and extrinsic rewards on children's intrinsic motivation. *Journal of Personality and Social Psychology, 31*, 479–486.

Lepper, M. R., & Greene, D. (Eds.). (1978). *The hidden costs of reward*. Hillsdale, NJ: Erlbaum.

Lepper, M. R., Greene, D., & Nisbett, R. E. (1973). Undermining children's intrinsic interest with extrinsic reward: A test of the "overjustification" hypothesis. *Journal of Personality and Social Psychology, 28*, 12–137.

Lepper, M. R., & Henderlong, J. (2000). Turning "play" into "work" and "work" into "play": 25 years of research on intrinsic versus extrinsic motivation. In C. Sansone & J. Harackiewicz (Eds.), *Intrinsic and extrinsic motivation: The search for optimal motivation and performance* (pp. 257–307). San Diego: Academic Press.

Lepper, M. R., Henderlong, J., & Gingras, I. (1999). Understanding the effects of extrinsic rewards on intrinsic motivation: Uses and abuses of meta-analysis. *Psychological Bulletin, 125*, 669–676.

Lepper, M. R., Henderlong, J., & Iyengar, S. S. (2005). Intrinsic and extrinsic motivational orientations in the classroom: Age differences and academic correlates. *Journal of Educational Psychology, 97*, 184–196.

Lepper, M. R., & Hodell, M. (1989). Intrinsic motivation in the classroom. In C. Ames & R. E. Ames (Eds.), *Research on motivation in education* (Vol. 3, pp. 73–105). New York: Academic Press.

Lepper, M. R., Keavney, M., & Drake, M. (1996). Intrinsic motivation and extrinsic rewards: A commentary on Cameron and Pierce's meta-analysis. *Review of Educational Research, 66*, 5–32.

Lepper, M. R., Master, A., & Yow, W. Q. (2008). Intrinsic motivation in education. In M. Maehr, S. Karabenick, & T. Urdan (Eds.), *Advances in motivation and achievement: Social psychological perspectives* (Vol. 15, pp. 521–555). London: Emerald.

Lepper, M. R., & Woolverton, M. (2002). The wisdom of practice: Lessons learned from the study of highly effective tutors. In J. Aronson (Ed.), *Improving academic achievement: Impact of psychological factors on education* (pp. 135–158). Orlando, FL: Academic Press.

Milgram, S. (1963). Behavioral study of obedience. *Journal of Abnormal and Social Psychology, 67*, 371–378.

Ross, L., Lepper, M. R., & Ward, A. H. (2010). A history of social psychology: Insights, challenges, and contributions to theory and application. In D. Gilbert, S. Fiske, & G. Lindzey (Eds.), *Handbook of social psychology* (5th ed., pp. 3–50). Hoboken, NJ: Wiley.

Schachter, S., & Singer, J. E. (1962). Cognitive, social and physiological determinants of emotional state. *Psychological Review, 69*, 379–399.

Spencer, S. J., Zanna, M. P., & Fong, G. T. (2005). Establishing a causal chain: Why experiments are often more effective than mediational analyses in examining psychological processes. *Journal of Personality and Social Psychology, 89*, 845–851.

Zanna, M. P., Lepper, M. R., & Abelson, R. P. (1973). Attentional mechanisms in children's devaluation of a forbidden activity in a forced-compliance situation. *Journal of Personality and Social Psychology, 28*, 355–359.

3

DEALING WITH CONFLICT
Experiences and Experiments

Lee Ross

Stanford University

When writing a Festschrift piece one normally begins with a heartfelt tribute to the honoree that highlights major contributions to the field and the debts one owes, both personal and intellectual, to the honoree. Then, after some throat clearing, one gently and only implicitly suggests, "but enough about *him* and *his* work, let me tell you about *me* and *mine*." There usually also is a promise to say a bit about how and why there are more connections between one and the honoree than the reader might imagine—a promise one struggles, often with only modest success, to keep—and a concluding paragraph or two with more laudatory remarks in which one tries not to embarrass the honoree with excess. This chapter will be no exception, except that I will not work too hard to avoid excess because Elliot does not embarrass easily.

I will leave it to others to summarize the content of Elliot's contributions. Suffice to say that in my eyes he has been the Willie Mays of social psychology. Mays was remarkable, in fact incomparable, because he had all the tools in extravagant measure: excellence in hitting both for average and with power, legendary skill and dash in fielding his position, a golden throwing arm, and tremendous speed and savvy as a base runner. Moreover, he did it all with verve, grace, and seeming ease, and was loved by the fans. The incomparable Elliot Aronson has a similarly multifaceted claim to fame, for he has contributed mightily in all possible ways a psychologist can. He has been a major theory builder and theory tester. He harnessed the same skills and insights that produce good results in the laboratory in service of successful application and intervention. He also has been a distinguished mentor and perhaps the best undergraduate lecturer in the business. (I say *perhaps* because I expect to be called upon someday to write a Festschrift piece honoring our mutual friend, Phil Zimbardo, and I may need the same accolade again.)

What is more, Elliot writes beautifully and has legions of fans who never saw him perform in person or read his scholarly work but read *The Social Animal,* or his candid and iconoclastic methodology chapter and textbook, or the *Jigsaw Classroom,* or his later, more popularly oriented books, *Nobody Left to Hate* and *Mistakes Were Made (But Not by Me).* Moreover, although both Mays and Aronson are giants, Elliot produced something that the "Say Hey Kid" never did—a son Josh, who has launched a promising career in the family business. Also, to the best of my knowledge, Mays never edited the *Handbook of Baseball* (although, in fairness, he probably never had a collaborator with the organizational talents of Gardner Lindzey).

The only thing wrong with this tribute and comparison is that, given his sports loyalties, Elliot probably would prefer to be compared to Ted Williams, the greatest batsman ever. But although Williams had other prodigious skills (as a fighter pilot and fisherman), he was famously cool, aloof, and indifferent to fans and media alike, attributes that no one would ever apply to our honoree!

Anyway, enough about Elliot and sports icons of yore; let me say a bit about me, or at least about the bonds, beyond a long friendship that I cherish, that attach us. First, and foremost, we are both direct descendants in the ancestral line that started with Kurt Lewin, the "practical theorist" and the father of modern social psychology. Second, we both benefited enormously from distinguished mentors—Leon Festinger in his case and Stanley Schachter in mine—who, together, transformed social psychology and first showed the full possibilities of the laboratory experiment by bringing a dedication and genius to that task that inspired their students to look, listen, learn, and emulate. Third, and less obvious, we both disregarded our mentors' shared reservations about the wisdom of concerning ourselves with questions of direct application, or God forbid, getting personally involved in real-world intervention.

After a period of theory building and doing laboratory experiments that helped shape, and then nicely conformed to, the tastes and priorities of our leading journals, Elliot looked back to his intellectual grandparent, Kurt Lewin—both to his humanistic inclinations and to his interest in addressing the problem of intergroup conflict or, more specifically, how to make intergroup contact fruitful rather than a source of hostility and occasion to express it. As will be apparent in this chapter, the latter part of my own career arc has led me to address the same issue. After many years of experimental work on strategies and shortcomings of the layperson or "intuitive scientist"(Ross, 1977), I turned my attention, both as a researcher and concerned citizen, to the problem of intergroup disagreement and enmity, and to the barriers that make fruitful dialogue between members of conflicting societies in pursuit of dispute resolution such daunting tasks.

In my applied work, as in Elliot's, the goal of successful intervention has demanded attention to some hard-won lessons from the laboratory. Our mentors both helped us to appreciate that designing experiments, at least in broad brush terms, is relatively easy. What requires a bit of skill, some insight about people, a lot of informal and formal pretesting (and schmoozing with very bright students and colleagues), and of course a good theory, is figuring out the specific procedures that will make them come alive and *work*—that is, produce significant results. Elliot's two methodology texts (Aronson & Carlsmith, 1968; Aronson, Ellsworth, Carlsmith, & Gonzales, 1990) offer lots of sage advice about how to do this; and Phoebe Ellsworth's chapter in this volume provides some compelling examples of this art in a discussion of the dissonance classics that should be required reading for contemporary graduate students.

The same is true, in many respects when one tries to design an intervention, although the concern with alternative explanations for successful results is largely replaced with a concern about whether the effect shown is robust, that is, whether the success of the intervention can readily be duplicated in other settings and, in fact, be "scaled up" to meet the relevant challenge in a way that can make a real difference in addressing the problem at hand (see Ross, Lepper, & Ward, 2009). The Jigsaw Classroom procedure was a case in point. The broad theory had been spelled out long ago. Interracial or interethnic conflict, and presumably other forms of intergroup hostility, it was hypothesized, could be eased if one could arrange intergroup contact (i.e., integration) wherein members of the estranged communities interact as individuals, and differing viewpoints and experiences are shared in a way that promotes greater understanding, dispels stereotypes, permits friendly contact, leads to friendships, and so forth.

But school integration per se generally failed to produce this happy outcome. The legally mandated experiment did not work, and when Elliot was asked to consult with education and local government officials who had clumsily conducted that experiment with Anglo and

Hispanic kids in Austin during the late 1960s, the reason was clear. The intervention manipulation did not create the social and psychological context envisioned in the theory. Contact between the groups was minimal, and the only thing shared was mutual resentment. The remedy he devised—periods in which members of the two communities had to work together cooperatively to achieve a common goal—was both clever and in good accord with theorizing by Gordon Allport (1954), Morton Deutsch (1977), Muzafer Sherif (1966), and other social psychologists who had written about intergroup hostility. But, as is so often the case, for the experiment to work various nagging problems and potential barriers to success had to be addressed.

Students simply instructed to work together cooperatively and given the material they needed to complete their project would not really be inclined to cooperate, and certainly not with members of other groups, whom they did not really know, like, or trust, and with whom they did not share language or styles of engagement. Left to their own devices, the Anglo kids would have dominated any interaction and been disinclined to seek or accept input from the Hispanic kids. The Hispanic kids, in turn, would likely have withdrawn from the task or at best gone it alone. The further remedy, as all students of Aronsonia know, was to give each student his or her own unique piece of the puzzle (i.e., unique knowledge about the topic at hand) such that the students needed, and were sure to benefit from, one another's input. Moreover, patience and encouragement were required to secure that input from some students who would otherwise have remained on the sidelines, or who would have been ridiculed or disregarded if their initial efforts had been less than satisfactory. So creating a shared goal and guaranteeing cooperative efforts to that goal was necessary. But it was not quite sufficient. At least one other barrier remained.

Even with the jigsaw intervention, efforts and contributions were bound to be of unequal quality. Some students would inevitably work harder and more effectively than others or hold themselves to higher standards. Free-riders would be resented if all got the same rewards (i.e., the same high grades on the project), and students who cared most about grades would be disinclined to have others taint their product and diminish their chances both at getting that high grade and at standing out as individuals. Hence, there was a nonobvious feature to the otherwise shared undertaking. Although students needed and made use of one anothers' contributions, final products were submitted and graded individually.

I am sure that a dozen other nagging problems and challenges had to be addressed, and that many small features of the specific intervention were introduced to create the types of motivations, perceptions, and sentiments required for the experiment to succeed. But succeed it did! The students did cooperate, informal contact between Hispanic and Anglo kids did increase, and relationships did improve, as Aronson and his colleagues documented (see Aronson, Blaney, Stephan, Sikes, & Snapp, 1978; Aronson & Patnoe, 1997). The challenge that remained, and still remains, was that of getting educators to implement this and other successful interventions when the sense of crisis has passed, and when the attention of school and government officials has returned to normal matters of budgets, building maintenance, and bureaucratic maneuvering.

My own applied work has similarly required attention both to underlying theory and to details of implementation. Before I begin my account of that work, however, let me acknowledge a debt that is particularly relevant to this chapter. Elliot recently urged me, and in a sense thereby gave me permission, to write about conflict and dispute resolution in a looser, more reader-friendly way—even at the risk of being labeled a popularizer or, worse, a do-gooder rather than a sober scientist who refuses to go beyond his data (and, of course, resists all temptation to discuss mere anecdotal evidence and personal experience).

This Festschrift piece represents a first attempt at exercising such authorial freedom. The reader can rest assured that I will include some theory and even some experimental evidence that I hope will meet Elliot's approval, for he has never lost his appreciation of a nicely designed and executed lab or field experiment that brings alive, and tests, a contention born in theory. (Indeed, the colleagues with whom I have tried my hand at intergroup dialogue and conflict resolution have teased me by claiming that I waste time trying to prove that what is true in practice is also possible in theory, and that one can generalize from the real-world to the laboratory.) However, the bulk of what follows will be a combination of armchair theorizing, storytelling, and pontificating. This chapter will have three sections, each dealing with work that brings theory, research, and real-world experience into productive contact, and a few concluding, wistful words about hopes for the future and our honoree.

WHEN RESEARCH, THEORY, AND EXPERIENCE CONVERGE

The False Consensus Effect

My gradual journey toward the study of disagreement began with a relatively dull alternative explanation for an interesting phenomenon:

the "divergent perceptions (i.e., attributions) of actors and observers" that Ned Jones and Dick Nisbett (1972) had provocatively described in an important paper. In several illustrative examples they had pointed out that when people think about their personal choices of things like academic majors and girlfriends (and presumably things like careers and political affiliations as well), they attribute their own choices to properties of the alternatives but the choices of their peers to properties or dispositions of the person doing the choosing.

My coinvestigators and I suggested that this might occur simply because people assumed that their own choices were more common and reasonable than those of peers who made alternative choices. Initially missing the point that this conjecture was interesting in its own right, we set out to see whether people would be less likely to view their own choices as attributable to dispositions than they would view other people's choices when such perceived consensus was held constant or corrected for statistically. The answer, which ended up a mere aside in the paper that ultimately resulted (Ross, Greene, & House, 1977), was "yes." But fortunately, we had come to recognize that the "false consensus" bias was interesting and worthy of explanation in its own right, and most of that paper reported research simply documenting that people who personally like, do, or expect something believe those likes, actions, and expectations to be more common, and less diagnostic of the traits of the actor, than do people who personally have opposite likes, make opposite behavioral choices, or offer opposite predictions.

Even more fortunately, Tom Gilovich (1990) cleverly documented one of the explanations that had been offered for that finding. That is, different people construe the same objects of judgment differently, and they do not make sufficient allowance for the fact that differences in construal will produce differences in response. Gilovich first showed that the size of the false consensus effect proves to be a function of the ambiguity or latitude for differences in construal. ("Do you think most politicians are honest? What percentage of your classmates would agree?" would be a high latitude item. "Do you think there will be a female president within the next 20 years? What percentage of your classmates would agree?" would be a low latitude item.) He then showed that if one removes the ambiguity in an item ("Do you prefer the bands of the '60s to the bands of the '80s?" vs. "Do you prefer '60s bands A, B, and C or '80s bands X, Y, and Z? What percentage of your classmates would agree?"), one greatly reduces the effect.

The Hostile Media Effect

The second step in the journey began with a simple extension of existing research. Philosophers (like Hume) and psychologists (like Hastorf and Cantril) alike had long recognized that people assimilate experience and information in a biased or partisan manner, which serves to reinforce their prejudices and expectations. My colleagues Mark Lepper and Bob Vallone and I (Vallone, Ross, & Lepper, 1985) simply reasoned that this type of assimilation bias would lead people to be dissatisfied by the efforts of any third party who offered a relatively unbiased account of the evidence on opposite sides of an issue or argument. If I see an object or set of facts as virtually all black, and you see the object or facts as virtually all white, we both are going to be chagrined by a third party who says there is both a lot of black and a lot of white here. In this case, we hardly needed to do the study to prove that this abstract conjecture was correct. Every day we see the left and right complain about media bias, each claiming that the other side gets a free ride while their side is subjected to unfair criticism. Partisan viewers of presidential debates feel certain that their party's candidate clearly outperformed the other party's candidate and are aggrieved when the pundits claim that neither candidate won a decisive victory.

Our job was just to bottle the phenomenon in the lab, which we did by showing pro-Israeli and pro-Palestinian viewers taped media coverage of a particular event (the massacre of refugee camp civilians by Falangist Christian gunmen with alleged ties to the Israeli side) in the long and tragic Mideast conflict. The results were decisive (Lord, Ross, & Lepper, 1979). Both sets of opposing partisans saw the same two hours of coverage by the major news networks and viewed the producers of that coverage as biased in favor of the other side. Moreover, pro-Israelis and pro-Palestinians alike thought that partisan viewers would be turned against their own side by the coverage in question. In other words, they felt that they knew what an objective account should look like, and to the extent that the coverage they viewed deviated from that account, it was biased, and therefore evidence of hostility on the part of those responsible for the coverage.

Naïve Realism

The two phenomena described above can be seen as manifestations of one of the deepest truisms in social science, and one of the foundations for an understanding of human behavior: the assumption that one sees and experiences the world as it is in some objective reality. Albert Einstein once stated what every physicist knows, that "reality" as we experience it is an illusion, a product of the particular interaction between what is "out there" (a bewildering assortment of unimaginably tiny particles, binding forces, and the like) and the particular properties of our sensory system, which is, of course, itself made up of the same stuff. Indeed, modern physicists are wont to suggest that time itself is, in an important sense, similarly epiphenomenal or illusory. But neither physics lessons nor electron microscopes, functional magnetic resonance imaging (fMRI) magnets, or other scientific instruments, change our *subjective* experience of reality. Most important, they do not prevent us from continuing to assume that the perceptions (and judgments following from those perceptions) that guide our everyday actions are faithful, essentially unmediated and objective, reflections of the way things "really" are.

From this basic tenet of naïve realism (Ross & Ward, 1996) the first corollary that follows is that we expect other reasonable, objective folks to share our perceptions and judgments (essentially the false consensus bias) if not immediately, then certainly after we enlighten them about the "real" facts and considerations that should be taken into account. At the height of the crisis in Iraq, the media reported that President George W. Bush had called more than a dozen foreign policy leaders from previous administrations (including Colin Powell, Madeleine Albright, George Shultz, Robert McNamara, William Perry, Lawrence Eagleburger, William Cohen, and Harold Brown) to the White House for a detailed briefing on the situation. Did he assemble this august group so that they could share their views and advice in the face of an obviously deteriorating situation, and perhaps learn something and change his policy? Not a chance! As the media reported, "The White House's hope was that the prominent figures, many of whom have publicly opposed Bush on Iraq, would be persuaded by the president's argument that he has what he called a 'dual-track strategy for victory,' and they would then spread the word."

This news report may prompt some readers merely to reaffirm their low regard for the ex-president; if so, they would be missing the larger phenomenon. I have helped to organize and facilitate "dialogue groups" involving citizens and politicians from rival communities in various parts of the world, including the Middle East, Northern Ireland, Armenia-Azerbaijan, and the United States. The participants generally have been people of good will, acting in good faith, who are genuinely interested in promoting an end to violence and hatred, and more productive future relations and joint enterprises. They are eager for dialogue and to exchange views. They are optimistic that when they explain the way things "really" are—including their real goals and pressing needs, and the historical bases for their legitimate grievances and misgivings, those on the other side, provided that those individuals are also open-minded, fair, and objective, will see the light, become more accommodating, and urge their compatriots to do likewise.

What I have never experienced are opposing parties who are eager for dialogue in the hope that it might change their own hearts and minds, or that the exchange of information and viewpoints will lead them to see matters more objectively and to go forth and act accordingly. In any case, the dialogue participants are typically disappointed to find that their input does not produce any great and immediate change in the views of the counterparts across the table. That is not to say that such dialogue is fruitless, far from it. In many cases, relationships get built, the parties come to recognize that those on the other side are sincere in their views and aspirations and not merely engaging in strategic posturing, they get a better sense of each other's priorities and bottom-line demands, and mutual respect is created. But the dialogue rarely leads to any sudden enlightenment on the part of either side, and there is a real danger that the moderate participants will be disheartened, especially when greeted by many of their less moderate friends with the familiar words "I told you so."

The second corollary to the basic tenet of naïve realism is that we treat disagreement as evidence that those who disagree with us are not seeing and understanding things as they really are, that they are seeing and judging, or perhaps even worse, reporting and offering conclusions, in a biased fashion (hence the hostile media phenomenon). This corollary leads to a testable empirical prediction about a linear relationship. Benjamin Franklin anticipated this prediction more than two centuries ago with the following observation (1787, as quoted in Copeland, Lamm, & McKenna, 1999): "Most men, indeed, as well as most sections in religion, think themselves in possession of all truth, and that [to the extent that] others differ from them, it is so far error."

Emily Pronin, Tom Gilovich, and I (Pronin, Gilovich, & Ross, 2004) tested this prediction of a linear relationship in a simple experiment. Students first were simply asked to complete an attitude questionnaire requiring them to state their positions about various issues and to rate various political figures on suitable scales. These questionnaires were then collected and redistributed at random, after which the students were asked to rate how similar the views of the other person are to their own. Finally, they were asked to assess the extent to which that respondent's views versus their own views reflected valid considerations (i.e., reading and serious discussion, careful weighing of long-terms costs and benefits, attention to facts, concern with fairness and justice, and firsthand knowledge) and to what extent they reflected biases (desire for peer approval, the influence of new media, wishful thinking, individual or group self-interest, and political correctness). The results of the study (Pronin et al., 2004) could not have been clearer. The tendency for the students to see their peer's views as more susceptible to bias and less reflective of valid considerations than their own views proved to be a linear function of the perceived discrepancy between those views. In other words, the more you disagree with me, the more I know the source is cognitive or motivational bias—in *you*, of course, not in me.

This invidious comparison, it should be noted, does not apply only to perceptions and attitudes, it pertains to actions and values as well. The comedian George Carlin once joked to his audience, "Did you ever notice that anyone going faster than you (on the freeway) is a maniac and anyone going slower is an idiot?" Carlin could have said, "Did you ever notice that anyone more liberal than you is an unrealistic bleeding heart and anyone more conservative is a cold-hearted reactionary?" or "Anyone who wants to move faster in the peace process is naïve and putting our side in danger, whereas anyone who wants to move more slowly does not understand the true costs of maintaining the struggle or has a personal axe to grind?"

Again, the challenge facing us when we bring opposing factions together to discuss their views and aspirations is made more difficult by this product of naïve realism. Frank discussion can heighten rather than lessen the feeling that the other side, or those at opposite ends of the political spectrum from our side, are unreasonable and unrealistic, that they do not really understand the problem or see the obvious outlines of the deal to be made. Accordingly, the skilled planner and facilitator of such dialogue processes is well advised not to just let that process or "experiment in intergroup contact" go forward without direction and let the chips fall where they may. Steps must be taken to minimize the type of exchanges that encourage the parties to restate long-held positions and demands, and to voice again long-held grievances and narratives about the past. Mediators should plan activities that allow the parties to experience each other's humanity: their commitment to their families, the criticisms they have faced and sometimes the greater price they have paid for their willingness to meet with the enemy, and in many cases the road they have traveled in moving from militant to moderate. I will return to the question of how to make intergroup dialogue, and negotiation itself, more fruitful later in this chapter. But first, let me describe a different type of interplay between theory and experience.

WHEN THEORY COLLIDES WITH EXPERIENCE: PSYCHOLOGICAL BARRIERS TO DISPUTE RESOLUTION

The basic principle for successful negotiation or "interest-based bargaining" is simple, and it involves efficient exchanges or trades of concessions. That is, the negotiators or third parties try to arrange a deal whereby each party agrees to give up things that are more valuable to the other party than to itself in order to get things that are more valuable to itself than to the party that will be giving them up. This principle, which was stated long ago by the sociologist George Homans (1961), is enunciated in wonderfully clear terms in the slim *Getting to Yes* volume by Roger Fisher and William Ury (1982), which also offers a lot of sage advice about how to deal with people who use unfair tactics or make unreasonable demands.

Yet, as the history of the Middle East, Ireland, and many other parts of the world, as well as protracted disagreements between labor and management, corporate struggles, custody suits, and marital disputes attest, conflicts often persist at great costs to all concerned, even when it is possible to readily identify resolutions that would leave both parties better off. These and many other cases of protracted, often tragic, conflict raise a central question for those of us concerned with dispute resolution: Why do negotiations so often fail when agreement would better serve the interests of the parties? For psychologists in the Lewinian tradition, this question calls upon us to identify the constraints or barriers that must be overcome for negotiations to succeed when, logically, they ought to succeed. In some past articles and chapters (Mnookin & Ross, 1995; Ross & Ward, 1995; see also Arrow, Mnookin, Ross, Tversky, & Wilson, 1995), my colleagues at the Stanford Center on Conflict and Negotiation and I identified several types of such barriers—structural, strategic, relational, and psychological—but here I will only discuss the latter, and describe some research relevant to only one such barrier, that of "reactive devaluation" (Ross, 1995).

The Pursuit of Fairness, Justice, and Equity

In many conflicts of the sort I noted earlier, the problems of reaching an agreement go beyond that of devising a mutually beneficial exchange of compromises. The disputants demand and feel entitled to an agreement that is fair or just, an agreement that takes into account the comparative strength and legitimacy of their claims. Such demands raise the bar for the negotiators, especially when familiar motivational and cognitive biases lead them to have very different notions about what would constitute an equitable agreement and they see those differing notions through the prism of naïve realism. Disputants inevitably see the history of their conflict (i.e., who did what to whom in the past, and with what justification, provocation, and intent) in very different terms. Those on both sides are apt to feel that they are the ones who have acted more honorably in the past and that they are the ones who have been more sinned against than sinning, and they now are seeking no more than that to which they are entitled.

Members of both sides, moreover, are apt to feel that it is *their* interests that most require protection in any negotiated agreement—for example, by avoiding ambiguities in language that could provide loopholes that the other side could exploit (while, at the same time, avoiding unrealistically rigid requirements for their own side that could compromise their ability to deal with unforeseen future developments). They are also bound to have divergent views about the future (i.e., who will grow stronger with the passage of time and whose assurances can be taken at face value and trusted). These differences, in turn, lead to disagreements about the balance of any proposal. Even when the two parties recognize what compromises each side will have to make if agreement is to be reached at all, they both feel that they will be the party who is settling for less, and giving up more, than would be equitable.

Furthermore, disputants on either side think that any objective observer of the conflict should agree with them (if not, that observer would be less than objective) and that the other party is being disingenuous when it defends its unreasonable demands. Finally, when a third party puts the inevitable deal on the table, a deal that calls on both sides to make wrenching concessions and to accept a high degree of uncertainty about where the future will lead, each side is lukewarm in its response and angry that the other side did not quickly embrace the plan in view of the fact that disputants on the other side, unlike those on their own side, would not be giving up anything to which they were ever entitled. If this unhappy narrative seems to capture the history of the Israeli–Palestinian stalemate in the Middle East, it is no coincidence, for it has been the source and test case for much of the thinking that my dispute resolution colleagues and I have done about barriers to dispute resolution.

Cognitive Dissonance and Rationalization

The second barrier to be noted, the impact of dissonance and rationalization, is one that has both an obvious and nonobvious connection to the career of our honoree. The obvious connection, of course, is that Elliot was both part of that small cadre of researchers who first were inspired by Leon Festinger (1957) to demonstrate the power and subtlety of dissonance theory and a major contributor to the later elaboration and sharpening of that theory (Aronson, 1969). The nonobvious connection involves the way in which he ultimately rejected the Festingerian warnings about the folly of wasting one's time and effort on application if one had any real talent for experimental research.

This chapter is not the place for a discussion of the failure of the dissonance researchers to get involved in the most important "forced compliance" experiment in American history, that is, the implementation of court-ordered racial desegregation. But a moment's reflection makes it clear that the question of how to produce changes in racial attitudes and beliefs along with behavior was one that the Festingerians were ideally situated to tackle. But they stayed on the sidelines, and when years later, Elliot did his Jigsaw Classroom work, the conceptual framework applied was not really that of dissonance theory (although, of course, kids who are cooperating with one another in the absence of external force or potent extrinsic rewards were likely to have revised some of the sentiments toward the other group to the extent that such contact was dissonant).

Beyond the lack of support for such an applied mission from the commanding general, I think there was another subtler reason. As dissonance theory had developed, the emphasis had mainly been on the effects of behavior on attitudes. Whereas the manipulations and staging of the research had been carried out with great flair, the dependent variable measures almost without exception were rather pallid paper-and-pencil self-report measures. One of the many notable features of the Jigsaw Classroom saga was the emphasis on behavioral measures—on evidence that the students' experience made them treat each other differently.

For a social psychologist who observes protracted conflicts and failures to make the compromises that are the price for an end to those conflicts, the role of dissonance is palpably apparent. Its impact is most apparent not on the parties' actions, but on their failures to act, or, more specifically, on the role that previous actions and inactions play in heightening the psychic costs of such compromises. That is, the rationalizations and means of dissonance reduction that allowed the parties to justify their past sacrifices and suffering and their past rejection of potential agreements to put an end to such costs themselves create a barrier to now accepting a deal that is no better, and perhaps worse, than one that might have been available in the past.

The rallying calls of the rejectionists are all too familiar: The other side is the devil incarnate; we can't deal with them because we can't trust them; God (or history) is on our side; we are more resolute than the other side because right makes might; the rest of the world is bound to wake up one day and recognize the justice of our aspirations; we can't break faith with the martyrs who fell in service of the cause. These calls, and the threats issued by those in a position to punish those who do not heed them, help to perpetuate deadlocks even when circumstances favoring agreement have changed for the better or when the folly of continuing the struggle has become more apparent to all concerned.

Although the implications of dissonance reduction may be bleak in the context of protracted and costly stalemates, there is one optimistic note worth sounding before continuing this discouraging account of conflict resolution barriers. Once a settlement has been reached, the human penchant for reducing dissonance can play a rather constructive role—especially if the decision to settle has been freely reached, if effort has been expended or sacrifices made in doing so, and if public defense of the settlement has been demanded (Aronson, 1969; Brehm & Cohen, 1962). Thus, the process of dissonance reduction may compel leaders and followers alike to find and exaggerate positive features of the settlement, and to minimize or disregard negative ones. We saw such processes occur in dramatic fashion early in 1972 when Richard Nixon suddenly and unexpectedly reached detente with China and later when Nelson Mandela and the African National Congress (ANC) reached an accord with the former practitioners of apartheid. And we can have some optimism about what will ensue if and when Palestinians and Israelis have to deal with the aftermath of their long-awaited, inevitably dissonance-producing, agreements.

Reactive Devaluation, Loss Aversion, and Reluctance to Trade Concessions

Beyond the barriers discussed thus far, there is a further problem, one resulting from the dynamics of the negotiation process itself, that is akin to psychological reactance (Brehm, 1966; Wicklund, 1974). The evaluation of specific package deals and compromises may change when they are put on the table, especially if they have been offered or proposed by one's adversary. My colleagues and I have sought to demonstrate the operation of this *reactive devaluation* barrier in a number of laboratory and field settings in which participants evaluated a variety of actual or hypothetical dispute resolution contexts and proposals (see Ross & Ward, 1995). In doing so, we struck a compromise ourselves in terms of research strategy. That is, although the participants could not enact agreements that had real effects in terms of ongoing conflicts and negotiations, participants were, in all cases, partisans who cared about the issue and proposals in question, rather than individuals playing an assigned role.

We did make use of deception, sometimes in what participants were led to believe about proposed terms or their authorship, and sometimes through the use of an experimental confederate who made the relevant proposals (e.g., a Palestinian confederate making a proposal to Israeli business school students about how to divide funds between rival communities, or a graduate student pretending to be a university employee negotiating the content of a drug legalization proposal to be made to the state). But in all cases the issues were real and timely, and the proposals were ones that were very much current in debates and negotiation about the issues in question. In short, the research strategy was designed to exploit existing motivations and biases of the sort that play a role in ongoing intergroup conflicts. (I can't resist digressing here to note parenthetically that reviewers typically do not give much weight to such authenticity of roles and motives—indeed, one actually expressed a concern that in our study using Israeli and Palestinians participants there was a "confounding" of attitudes held and the identity of those holding them.) With that design feature in mind, let me summarize our main findings.

Perhaps unsurprisingly, people rate the terms of a given proposal calling for bilateral concessions less positively when it has been put forward by the other side than when the very same proposal has been put forward by a representative of one's own side. What *has* been surprising is the magnitude of this effect. Indeed in one study (Maoz, Ward, Katz, & Ross, 2002), the effect of putative authorship proved to be so strong that the Israeli participants in the study rated an authentic proposal made by their own side (in the post-Oslo negotiations in 1983) less positively than one made by the other side, when the former was attributed to their adversaries and the latter to their own leaders.

A particularly compelling real-world demonstration of reactive devaluation was provided in a study we did at Stanford. Students evaluated their university's responses to student and faculty demands for financial divestment from South Africa at a point when the anti-apartheid struggle was reaching its climax (see Ross & Ward, 1995). In the study, we measured students' evaluation of the plan ultimately adopted by the university—one that called for selective or partial divestment and fell short of the students' demand for full divestment—on two occasions, once before the adoption of the plan was announced (i.e., when it was merely one possibility among many) and then shortly after it was announced. For comparison purposes, we also measured students' responses to an alternative plan, a seemingly modest proposal that called for an increase in the university's investment in companies that had left South Africa, but otherwise no change in its current investments.

The results were clear: When students were led to believe that the university was preparing to adopt a particular plan, their assessments of its merits relative to the alternative plan became more negative.

Moreover, when the university did announce its selective divestment plan, students' evaluations of that plan became more negative after that announcement, and their evaluations of the initially unattractive hypothetical alternative (i.e., increasing investments in companies that had left South Africa) became more positive.

Reactive devaluation can be traced to several psychological mechanisms beyond pure Brehmian reactance. In particular, whenever a negotiation proposal calls for a change in the status quo that makes things worse on some dimension to achieve a gain on some other dimension, the phenomenon of loss aversion (Kahneman & Tversky, 1984) comes into play. Let me digress for a moment to offer a simple thought experiment to make clear the nature of this phenomenon, whereby prospective losses loom larger and receive more weight than prospective gains. Consider the answers to the following three questions. First, how much would you be willing to pay someone (perhaps a manufacturer or researcher on auto safety) to make the brakes in your car 10% *safer*? Second, how large a payment would you demand to let someone (perhaps the same manufacturer or researcher) make your brakes 10% *less safe*? Finally, exactly how safe are your brakes right now compared to those in other cars, or compared to how safe they could be made by a skilled mechanic or through installation of some new features?

If you are a typical motorist, the answer to the first question would be "a reasonable but not a huge amount—somewhere between $100 and $1,000," whereas the answer to the second question would be "a huge amount—at least many thousand dollars," and some in fact would say, "no amount would be enough." As for the third question, most people say, "I guess they are pretty safe, but I don't really know how they compare to other folks' brakes or how much safer they could be made if I were willing to spend some money." Israelis considering the prospect of decreased security as the price for ending the occupation and Palestinians considering the prospect of giving up cherished dreams by ending the conflict and granting full recognition to Israel in return for the immediate economic gains that might be afforded by a two-state solution are similarly loss averse.

Other mechanisms may also contribute to reactive devaluation. Concession offers may lead us to conclude that the other side is eager for an agreement and that our previous negotiation stance has been too moderate. Social processes can be involved as well. Critics who oppose agreement because they prefer conflict or have something to lose from agreement will inevitably dismiss preliminary proposals or even unilateral concessions as trivial, token, and insincere. But regardless of why reactive devaluation occurs, its potential contribution to the maintenance of negotiation deadlocks and to ensuing cycles of heightening enmity and mistrust should be clear. Not only are proposals likely to be received less positively than they ought to be in terms of the objective interests of the parties, but each side is apt to interpret the other side's negotiation behavior and rhetoric as at best strategic manipulation, and at worst as dishonest, cynical, and dictated by animus rather than a sincere effort to end the conflict.

In my own experience, seasoned negotiators are well aware of the reactive devaluation phenomenon, although they may not know about all of the psychological mechanisms that underlie it and, most important, may fail to recognize their own susceptibility to it. Indeed, one important role played by the mediator in any conflict is to short-circuit this process, to obscure the parentage of specific proposals and concessions, and to encourage more positive (and accurate) attributions on the part of the disputants as they struggle to reach terms of agreement that are personally and politically bearable. To this end, skilled mediators may oblige the disputants to clarify their priorities and interests, in particular to have each side indicate concessions it may value more highly than its adversaries and vice versa. The mediator then is free to propose possible exchanges of concessions that are not only based on but also readily attributable by the parties to their own particular expressions of priority.

OVERCOMING REACTIVE DEVALUATION AND OTHER BARRIERS

The study of barriers and biases, and of psychological processes that exacerbate them, can do more than help us understand why negotiations sometimes fail when they should succeed, and why the process of negotiation can escalate rather than attenuate feelings of enmity and mistrust. It can help us develop techniques for overcoming these barriers and reducing these sources of misunderstanding. Rather than provide a shopping list of techniques, a list that would highlight relationship and trust building, and framing the negotiation tasks in terms that are forward looking and pragmatic, and perhaps even a bit of social psychology education, let me again just describe a couple of examples of what I hope will serve as useful demonstration experiments. Again, the work represents a kind of compromise between, on the one hand, evaluating full-scale interventions, and on the other hand, theory building and theory testing intended mainly for colleagues in social psychology. The term I like is *applicable* (as opposed to applied or pure) research.

Kurt Lewin is famous for the claim that nothing is as practical as a good theory; I would add that sometimes a good theory requires a good demonstration experiment if it is to have any impact on practitioner thinking. And few if any social psychologists have been as skillful at providing such demonstrations, whether the target behavior was condom use (Dickerson, Thibodeau, Aronson, & Miller, 1992) or energy conservation (Aronson, 1990; Gonzales, Aronson, & Costanzo, 1988), as Elliot Aronson.

Managing Attributions

If, as our research suggests, reactive devaluation of proposals from the other side is a ubiquitous real-world phenomenon, the implication for mediators and other third parties should be clear. A proposal originating from one side can be made attractive to the other side if authorship is concealed, obscured, or even misrepresented. Experienced diplomats and other seasoned mediators have told us that one of the benefits of shuttle diplomacy and other "caucusing procedures" is the opportunity to discover what each side might be willing to give up in trade, and then to formulate a plan calling for the exchange of such concessions that is attributed to neither side. Instead it is represented as the product of the third-party mediator's dialogues with the parties—not as a reflection of what the mediator personally deems fair or proportionate (that would produce a "hostile mediator effect"!), but rather as a reflection of what the mediator understands to be consistent with the parties' differing interests and priorities.

Both parties are then invited to treat the proposal as a working document that they are free to improve upon, with neither party called upon to defend the relevant document. At that point, both sides inevitably find fault with the document and insist on changes, thereby helping the parties and the mediator alike to fine-tune the agreement in accord with the respective priorities, and thus to maximize joint gains.

There is also a subtler role for negotiators and other third parties to play, one that arises from an understanding of the role that attributions play in reactive devaluation. Parties engaged in hard bargaining try to come up with explanations for each other's behavior in general, and for the content and timing of each other's concession offers in particular. The recipient of a unilateral concession or proposed trade of concessions is apt to ask, "Why are they offering this *particular* concession or proposing this *particular* trade, and why *now*?" In the absence of other satisfactory answers, the recipient is apt to conclude that the concession is probably less substantial than it might have seemed at first.

The third-party mediator sometimes can help solve these attribution problems and also help to reduce some of the dissonance felt by the negotiating parties, merely by explaining to each party, in caucus, the political realities and constraints compelling the other side to make or reject particular proposals. The knowledge that the other side is being forced to offer concessions, and their explicit acknowledgment of this state of affairs, may make one tempted to reject the relevant proposal on strategic grounds (one may conclude that since the other side is in a weak position it can be induced to offer even better terms) and make one less likely to attribute the others' offer to friendly intent or a change of heart. But the existence of such force, and the adversary's acknowledgment of it, does encourage one to take the concession at face value rather than construing it in whatever manner minimizes its significance.

Although we have suggested the role that mediators, facilitators, and other third parties can play in dealing with attributional problems in negotiation contexts, the principal parties themselves can address such problems. In particular, they can link the content of their proposals to the expressed needs and desires of the other side. A recent demonstration experiment (Ward, Disston, Brenner, & Ross, 2008) illustrated this possibility in a negotiation between an experimental confederate and undergraduates who were seeking to soften their university's position on drug legalization. In both experimental conditions in the study, the confederate ultimately put forward the same "final offer" as time ran out in the negotiation (an offer to eliminate penalties for marijuana use for a test period, but to increase penalties for hard drug use).

In one condition, however, the confederate characterized that offer as the one he had come to the negotiation intending to propose. In the other condition, by contrast, the confederate conspicuously put aside a piece of paper containing the offer he allegedly had intended to propose and made a "new offer"—one that he claimed he was now making in light of the student's input earlier in the negotiation. The result, as predicted, was a more favorable reception of the proposal in the latter "acknowledgment" condition than in the former "no acknowledgment" (control) condition. Not only was the rate of acceptance higher (63% vs. 40%) but the magnitude of the concession was assessed as greater, and the confederate who offered it was rated in more positive terms.

I want to add one aside here about attribution theory before describing a final applicable demonstration experiment. When Ned Jones, Hal Kelley, and company were making their initial contributions to this theory, the dissonance theorists were unimpressed and somewhat bored by the tedious questionnaire methodology. As I noted earlier, dissonance theory seemed to offer the more interesting applied possibilities, even though the primary investigators chose to direct their attention elsewhere. But a particular change in research focus, from strategies and errors in the attribution process to the *behavioral consequences* of attribution, made that boring (at least to many of us) theory suddenly become anything but boring. In fact, its application to the problem of motivating and empowering disadvantaged students—a task close to the heart of our honoree in this volume—has been one of the most exciting developments in modern social psychology (see Ross, Lepper, & Ward, 2009).

Negotiation Expectations

The final attempt at applicable research I am going to describe (Liberman, Anderson, & Ross, 2009) has its roots less in theory than in observation of the real world, although in a different venue I could trace its origins to the long history of research on self-fulfilling prophecies and confirmation bias. Negotiations, it seems, are most likely to succeed when the parties undertake their task with the conviction that agreement can, must, and will be achieved. By contrast, when the parties undertake the task with grave doubts about the possibility of achieving any major breakthroughs, and negotiation stalemate is seen as an acceptable, even likely, outcome—merely another chapter in a history of failure—those misgivings almost always seem to be confirmed.

Such real-world sagas, of course, confound cause and effect in a way that raises an obvious experimental question. Does the expectation of success or failure influence negotiation processes and outcomes, or do the factors that give rise to those expectations simply prove to be as potent as the negotiators expect them to be? The interesting hypothesis, of course, is that expectations can exert an independent influence on the behavior of the negotiating parties. More specifically, and again postulating a role for attributional processes, we proposed that when parties expect to succeed, they not only have a shared motive to avoid failure, but they also have both a satisfactory explanation for any concessions that they are obliged to make, and a satisfactory attribution for apparent concessions by the other side (that is, "We *had* to reach an agreement, and so did *they*").

The origins of this optimistic, even idealistic, hypothesis lie in our observation of difficult real-world negotiations that succeed despite the seemingly intractable nature of the underlying conflicts in question. We had in mind both exceptional events (such as the election of a pope), and more ordinary but perhaps more vital ones (such as the passing of a federal budget or, more recently, the passage of various pieces of bailout legislation). In both cases, the conflicts and divisions are complex and deep, and there is a real sense in which no solution can command an authentic majority (much less the two-thirds majority required to elect a pope or a 60% majority to avoid filibuster) whose interests are better served by agreeing to compromise than by continuing to hold out for better terms. But the certainty of relatively timely resolution, buttressed by history and tradition, seems to guarantee that a resolution will be found within the expected time period. The resolution may involve major compromises and minimal satisfaction on the part of many who comprise the necessary majority, but one that is justified by the negotiators by a simple dictum: "We *had* to have a pope" or "We *had* to have a budget (or a bailout)."

We tested our hypothesis in two studies. One was conducted in the United States with American college students who engaged in a relatively mundane negotiation exercise involving the proposed allocation of resources to undergraduate versus graduate student activities. The other was conducted with Israeli business school students (all of whom had served in the military) who negotiated a structurally similar, but much more politically sensitive resource allocation problem that involved funds associated with the building of the fence or wall separating the West Bank Jews from Palestinians. In both cases, the experimental procedure involved the use of a confederate who followed a predetermined script. In the American study, the confederate was an older student ostensibly representing the interests of graduate students; in the Israeli study, she was an Israeli Arab ostensibly representing the interests of the Palestinians. In both studies, the negotiation proceeded in stages, with the confederate making an initial offer, the experimental participant making a counteroffer, and the confederate making a final offer as time was expiring. The participant assessed the offer and agreed or refused to accept it, knowing, in the latter case, that the result would be a forfeiture of the funds in question until some later date.

The experimental manipulation was simple. Half of the participants were informed at the outset of their negotiation that all (or in the case of the Israeli negotiation, "virtually all") previous negotiation pairs had succeeded in reaching agreement. Half were given no such induction; they were merely told to do their best to reach an agreement. Although the participants recognized the hypothetical nature of their role-play assignment, they did represent the interests of their own group and negotiated seriously, and, in some cases, especially in the Israeli study, quite passionately.

As predicted, the expectation manipulation had a dramatic effect not only on the proportion of acceptances of the proposal (85% vs. 35% in the Israeli study), but also on the generosity of the participants' counteroffer to the initial proposal and on their ultimate ratings of the negotiation process and their counterpart in that negotiation. Of course, there is no magic ingredient to make Israelis and Palestinians seeking an agreement in the Middle East, or North Korean and American negotiators trying to hammer out a deal whereby the North Koreans give up their nuclear weapon aspirations in return for economic and political concessions from the United States and the rest of the world, believe that their past experience in such negotiations augurs extremely well for the prospects of success next time. But it is possible to imagine strategies to make the negotiator less pessimistic and more inclined to believe that this time their counterparts seriously, indeed urgently, are seeking to succeed.

What does all this have to do with our honoree? First, he appreciates a nicely wrought study with a dependent variable that poses serious stakes for the participants. Second, he has always been a source of optimism about the future, both mine and his, in difficult times.

WHEN EXPERIENCE INFORMS THEORY AND APPLICATIONS: FOUR LESSONS FROM THE REAL WORLD

Although I have done my share of "giving psychology away," as Donald Campbell (1969) exhorted us to do four decades ago in his famous article on "reforms as experiments," I must start my concluding remarks with a confession. Practitioner experience did far more for my research and theorizing than my theorizing and research ever did for my practice. At times, the experience served mainly to reinforce fundamental, hard-won insights that social psychology has long offered to any who would listen. These lessons include the power of the situation in general and that of group norms and group pressures in particular; the importance of subjective construal or the need to attend to the actors' understanding of the situation and the meaning they attach to their own actions and outcomes in light of their values, goals, and beliefs; the meaning that people attach to the behavior directed toward them by others; the lengths people go to in order to see themselves as rational and good; and the importance of Lewinian insights about the dynamics of tensions systems.

But, at times, experience has alerted me to the importance of other, more specific influences. Let me share some of these in the domain of dispute resolution, each of which can be regarded as an idea or insight in search of a good demonstration experiment, and of practitioners skilled and wise enough to put each to good use. In each case I will state the lesson and where I think it might be helpful to the reader, then say a bit about its origin and relevance.

The Importance of a Shared View of (and Shared Commitment to) a Mutually Bearable Future

Repeatedly, we have found that parties come to dialogue groups and even negotiations with the other side, with a detailed proposal outlining what they need and want, why they are entitled to it, and even what they are prepared to offer in return. But they fail to offer a view of the future that specifies the place of the other in that future, a place that seems better than the status quo. We have learned to challenge participants in advance of a meeting with the other side to explain why the life they envision for those on the other side is better than the other side imagines that they, their adversaries, hope them to have. If they can't offer such a view of a shared future, we suggest there is no point in meeting with the other side because the meeting will merely confirm the other sides' misgivings and strengthen its resolve. Indeed, in our experience, unless there is explicit acknowledgment of the importance of a shared view of and commitment to a mutually bearable future, negotiation between leaders and their agents, and even second-track diplomacy, is doomed to produce failure and to heighten rather than ease distrust.

The Importance of Relationships and Trust, Especially in Dealing With Spoilers and the Demands of Internal Politics

Deals that affect the larger populations on both sides of a conflict will almost always leave some individuals or interest groups worse off. In the most virulent conflicts, some of these individuals and interest groups will go beyond the normal realm of political discourse to make their objections felt and to do their utmost, including resorting to violence and intimidation, to ensure that no agreement will be reached. The parties that want a lasting agreement must agree on how the efforts of such "spoilers" will be handled. Moreover, the two parties cannot treat the efforts of spoilers on the other side, and the lack of quick and effective action against them, as evidence of bad faith, but instead should insist that the other side should not be deterred by spoilers on their side, and that the other side should understand that the demands of internal politics prevent them from cracking down on such spoilers.

The Futility of Trying to Convince People of Something They Can't Afford to Understand

One of the underexplored implications of dissonance theory (and other theories involving dynamic psychic processes) involves the limits to the value of appeals to reason or even to ethical principles. When the threat of loss or cost of an agreement to the self is too great, people will find a reason or at least a rationalization for continued intransigence. The cost in question may involve the need to recognize that one has spent one's life in a fruitless endeavor or that sacrifices of blood and treasury have been in vain (i.e., the barrier to conflict resolution I discussed earlier). But it may simply involve the unacceptability of the life and status that awaits one postagreement. I vividly remember a Protestant militia leader who had come out of prison ready to renounce violence and willing to negotiate earnestly with the other side. But somehow no deal put on the table was ever good enough, no promise by the other side reliable enough, to get him to say, "Let's stop talking and close the deal!" Observing this charismatic but uneducated man, I could not escape the thought that right now he was a respected leader with a place at the negotiating table, but that in the aftermath of a real agreement, and with the emergence of a normal peaceful society, he would be lucky to get a job driving a brewery truck. The issue of a mutually bearable future pertains not only to societies but to interest groups and individuals within those societies that can exercise veto power.

Conversion From Militant to Peacemaker Need Not Involve Any Blinding Light Conversion: Sometimes It Is "51% versus 49%"

A common refrain we hear from self-labeled moderates looking for moderates on the other side is that you can't make a deal with some particular leader or that "what we are waiting for is a Mandela on the other side." Such comments tempt us to begin a windy lecture on the sins of dispositionism and the fundamental attribution error, which we dutifully resist. Instead, we point out that Mandela was able to make peace not because he made the compromises that no one else would make, but instead because he made himself the leader to whom white South Africans were willing to make compromises that they said they would never make (largely because he offered them a future in which they would have an acceptable place).

We also tell them about a provocative set of remarks that David Ervine, a Northern Ireland Loyalist and ex-bomber, made in an address at Stanford University in response to an inevitable question: What insight or personal transformation had changed him from a militant bomber to a mainstream politician dedicated to a peaceful solution to the conflict that had waged so long? He explained that, in his case, it was a matter of "51% versus 49%," that his change involved not a transformation of character but a kind of tipping point, whereby the futility and costs of violence became marginally more obvious and the prospects for securing an acceptable agreement through normal politics became marginally brighter. He then added the striking comment that when he was only 51% certain about the decision to embrace bombing as a tactic, he was still 100% a bomber, and now that he is only 51% certain about the prospects for change through peaceful means, he is 100% a politician and peace activist.

The moral of this story is clear: Not only does the situation matter, but small changes for the better in that situation are worth working for. A meeting with the other side that goes well, a small concession that makes life for the other side more bearable, and a single humanizing remark can provide the tipping point that makes the difference between peace and conflict.

A FINAL EXHORTATION AND FOND HOPE

In a recent chapter on the history of social psychology (Ross, Lepper, & Ward, 2009), we ended a discussion of the applied tradition in our field with a quote from Robert Kennedy: "Few will have the greatness to bend history itself," he said, "but each of us can work to change a small portion of events, and in the total of all those acts will be written the history of this generation." Elliot Aronson did more than his part to change events both in psychology and in society, and through his teaching and writing to inspire more than one generation of young social psychologists. But, despite his flair for the dramatic as a lecturer, I do not remember him engaging in much pompous rhetoric. Rather, what I remember is urging his students and younger colleagues to have "fun," to be excited about their work, to realize what a privilege it is to be involved in what he considered the most interesting thing a person could do, that is, to think and talk about the "social animal" and to design just the right experiment and come up with just the right procedure to change individual and collective behavior for the better.

Kurt Lewin's biographer Arthur Morrow used the German verb *quasselstrippe,* which roughly translates as "chatter," to describe the kind of free exchange with students and colleagues that Lewin employed to generate ideas and formulate his theories—a mixture of gossip, observation of real-world behavior, and speculation about principles of behavior. Well, there is no one with whom I enjoy quasselstripping more than Elliot Aronson. I can count on him to help me sharpen ideas, design nice manipulations and interventions, grumble about politics, gossip about friends, tell stories, share nostalgic recollections, give me permission to bypass the *Journal of Personality and Social Psychology* (*JPSP*) thicket, and figure out how to bring lessons from the real world to the laboratory, and vice versa. Sometimes we just relax and debate the merits of Williams versus Mays (or Asch versus Festinger). In either case, I can count on him to reaffirm a message I learned from Stan Schachter: Not only is it great fun to do serious work, but sometimes, when we are having great fun, we are, in fact, doing our most serious work.

REFERENCES

Allport, G. W. (1954). *The nature of prejudice*. Reading, MA: Addison-Wesley.

Aronson, E. (1969). A theory of cognitive dissonance. In L. Berkowitz (Ed.), *Advances in experimental social psychology* (Vol. 4, pp. 1–34). New York: Academic Press.

Aronson, E. (1990). Applying social psychology to desegregation and energy conservation. *Personality and Social Psychology Bulletin, 16*, 118–132.

Aronson, E., Blaney, N., Stephan, C., Sikes, J., & Snapp, M. (1978). *The jigsaw classroom*. Beverly Hills, CA: Sage.

Aronson, E., & Carlsmith, J. M. (1968). Experimentation in social psychology. In G. Lindzey & E. Aronson (Eds.), *Handbook of social psychology* (2nd ed., Vol. 2, pp. 1–79). Reading, MA: Addison-Wesley.

Aronson, E., Ellsworth, P. C., Carlsmith, J. M., & Gonzales, M. H. (1990). *Methods of research in social psychology*. New York: McGraw-Hill.

Aronson, E., & Patnoe, S. (1997). *The jigsaw classroom: Building cooperation in the classroom* (2nd ed.). New York: Addison-Wesley/Longman.

Arrow, K., Mnookin, R. H., Ross, L., Tversky, A., & Wilson, R. (Eds.). (1995). *Barriers to conflict resolution*. New York: W. W. Norton.

Brehm, J. W. (1966). *A theory of psychological reactance*. Oxford, UK: Academic Press.

Brehm, J. W., & Cohen, A. R. (1962). *Explorations in cognitive dissonance*. New York: John Wiley & Sons.

Campbell, D. (1969) Reforms as experiments. *American Psychologist, 24*, 409–429.

Copeland, L., Lamm, L. W., & McKenna, S. J. (Eds.). (1999). *The world's great speeches: Fourth enlarged (1999) edition*. Mineola, NY: Dover.

Deutsch, M. (1977). *The resolution of conflict: Constructive and destructive processes*. New Haven, CT: Yale University Press.

Dickerson, C. A., Thibodeau, R., Aronson, E., & Miller, D. (1992). Using cognitive dissonance to encourage water conservation. *Journal of Applied Social Psychology, 22*, 841–854.

Festinger, L. (1957). *A theory of cognitive dissonance*. Stanford, CA: Stanford University Press.

Fisher, R., & Ury, W. (1982). *Getting to yes*. New York: Penguin Books.

Gilovich, T. (1990). Differential construal and the false consensus effect. *Journal of Personality and Social Psychology, 59*(4), 623–634.

Gonzales, M. H., Aronson, E., & Costanzo, M. (1988). Using social cognition and persuasion to promote energy conservation: A quasi-experiment. *Journal of Applied Social Psychology, 18*(12), 1049–1066.

Homans, G. C. (1961). *Social behavior: In elementary forms.* New York: Harcourt Brace & World.

Jones, E. E., & Nisbett, R. E. (1972). The actor and the observer: Divergent perceptions of the causes of behavior. In E. E. Jones, D. E. Kanouse, H. H. Kelley, R. E. Nisbett, S. Valins, & B. Weiner (Eds.), *Attribution: Perceiving the causes of behavior* (pp. 79–94). Morristown, NJ: General Learning Press.

Kahneman, D., & Tversky, A. (1984). Choices, values, and frames. *American Psychologist, 39,* 341–350.

Liberman, V., Anderson, N., & Ross, L. (2009). *Achieving difficult agreements: Effects of positive versus neutral expectations on negotiation processes and outcomes.* Manuscript submitted for publication.

Lord, C. G., Ross, L. & Lepper, M. (1979). Biased assimilation and attitude polarization: The effects of prior theories on subsequently considered evidence. *Journal of Personality and Social Psychology, 37,* 2098–2109.

Maoz, I., Ward. A., Katz, M., & Ross, L. (2002). Reactive devaluation of an "Israeli" vs. a "Palestinian" peace proposal. *Journal of Conflict Resolution, 46,* 515–546.

Mnookin, L., & Ross, L. (1995). Introduction. In K. Arrow, R. Mnookin, L. Ross, A. Tversky, & R. Wilson (Eds.), *Barriers to conflict resolution* (pp. 2–25). New York: Norton.

Pronin, E., Gilovich, T., & Ross, L. (2004). Objectivity in the eye of the beholder: Divergent perceptions of bias in self versus others. *Psychological Review, 111,* 781–799.

Ross, L. (1977). The intuitive psychologist and his shortcomings: Distortions in the attribution process. In L. Berkowitz (Ed.), *Advances in experimental social psychology* (Vol. 10, pp. 173–240). New York: Academic Press.

Ross, L., Greene D., & House, P. (1977). The false consensus effect: An egocentric bias in social perception and attribution processes. *Journal of Experimental Social Psychology, 13,* 279–301.

Ross, L., Lepper M. R., & Ward, A. (2009). A history of social psychology: Insights, contributions, and challenges. In S. Fiske & D. Gilbert (Eds.), *Handbook of social psychology* (4th ed., Vol. 1). New York: Random House.

Ross, L., & Nisbett, R. E. (1991). *The person and the situation: Perspectives of social psychology.* New York: McGraw-Hill.

Ross, L., & Ward, A. (1995). Psychological barriers to dispute resolution. In M. Zanna (Ed.), *Advances in experimental social psychology* (Vol. 27, pp. 255–304). San Diego: Academic Press.

Ross, L., & Ward, A. (1996). Naive realism in everyday life: Implications for social conflict and misunderstanding. In E. S. Reed, E. Turiel, & T. Brown (Eds.), *Values and knowledge* (pp. 103–135). Hillsdale, NJ: Erlbaum.

Sherif, M. (1966). *In common predicament: Social psychology of intergroup conflict and cooperation.* Boston: Houghton-Mifflin.

Vallone, R. P., Ross, L., & Lepper, M. R. (1985). The hostile media phenomenon: Biased perception and perceptions of media bias in coverage of the Beirut massacre. *Journal of Personality and Social Psychology, 49,* 577–585.

Ward, A., Disston, L. G., Brenner, L., & Ross, L. (2008). Acknowledging the other side in negotiation. *Negotiation Journal,* 24(3), 269–285.

Wicklund, R. A. (1974). *Freedom and reactance.* Potomac, MD: Lawrence Erlbaum.

4

REJECTION, CONSISTENCY, AND INTERPERSONAL PROCESSES

Roy F. Baumeister

Florida State University

In the early 1970s, when I first entered the field of social psychology as a student, Elliot Aronson's name was heard constantly. His bold ideas, innovative methods, and well-written papers inspired admiration and a healthy dollop of controversy. It seemed no course reading list could be complete without some of his works.

One of his influential papers made a deep impression on me and challenged my thinking. By way of context, I had just signed on to do my undergraduate thesis with Joel Cooper. As he was among the most popular instructors at Princeton, this was a great stroke of good fortune to me. Cooper listed the topics of interest to him, and when he mentioned "self-esteem" my interest perked up. At the time, self-esteem was not the household word it has become today, but it sounded like it might have something novel and interesting to offer. Cooper gave me some readings to do, and these included one by Aronson and David Mettee (1968).

The core insight of that paper was articulated in the following example. I quote it for several reasons. One, it gets the point across. Two, it shows the fine writing and superb intuitive insight that characterized much of Aronson's work. Three, the fact that I spontaneously remembered the gist of this sentence as I sit here on a Caribbean island four decades after its publication is a remarkable testimony to Aronson's influence. Here is the sentence: "If a person is jilted by his girlfriend (and thus feels unloved), is he more apt to go out and rob a bank, kick a dog, or wear mismatched pajamas?" (Aronson & Mettee, 1968, pp. 121–122).

The article and even that line had a lasting influence on my thinking, and they echoed through my research for years afterward. Let me tell this story.

Theory development was at that time still in a fairly primitive state in social psychology. (Some would say it is still primitive today!) There were few major theories or even perspectives that had broad influence. Cognitive consistency was among these few. A great deal of research and thought was driven by the idea that people strive for consistency.

The paper by Aronson and Mettee (1968) built on consistency theory and previous supportive findings, most notably the influential paper by Aronson and Merrill Carlsmith (1962), which had concluded that people will reject success when they have expected failure. They would rather be consistent with their expectations (of failure) than succeed.

The experiment reported by Aronson and Mettee—and it is a telling fact about how far the field has come, that back then the modal article in the *Journal of Personality and Social Psychology* reported on a single experiment—sought to show consistency of manipulated self-concept carrying over into dishonest behavior. Participants (back then they were called subjects) took a personality test and received bogus feedback that was either rather favorable or rather unfavorable. This was presumed to produce (temporarily) high or low self-esteem, respectively. Then participants played a card game that was ostensibly a test of their ability for extrasensory perception, but that also involved the opportunity to win money. During the game, participants were occasionally dealt an extra card that enabled them to win the hand and get more money. They had been told that if an extra card were dealt, they should return it to the experimenter. The measure was how often they kept the extra card and thus enjoyed some ill-gotten gains.

The only analysis that worked focused on whether the subject never cheated or cheated at least once. (That is, analyses of total cheating were not significant.) Almost all the participants who had received the bad feedback cheated at least once. Fewer than half of the participants who received positive feedback cheated. The interpretation was that low self-esteem led subjects to engage in dishonest behavior as a way of confirming their negative views of self.

The self-esteem manipulation thus had a dramatic impact on behavior, in line with consistency theory. As an impressionable undergraduate just starting to learn how social psychologists worked, I was deeply impressed by the manipulation of self-esteem and the clever measures of dishonesty.

Yet I wondered whether self-esteem could be changed so easily. As it happened, around this time, I had recently been a participant in a study that sought to manipulate self-esteem in a similar manner. Looking back on this experience afterward, I recalled that the bad feedback had not really changed my view of myself, as far as I could remember. However, I recalled that my worry over the bad evaluation had been focused on whether the experimenter had read this information about me and formed a negative opinion of me. I also wondered who else would have seen this information.

This insight was crucial. As a research participant receiving the bad evaluation, I had not revised my self-esteem, but instead had focused on what others thought of me. Public self, not private self, was in play.

Hence, as I struggled to generate an idea for my undergraduate thesis, I thought that the first step would be to establish that self-esteem manipulations really alter self-esteem. (I thought I had not been thus affected, but I have seldom if ever relied on my own intuitions and experiences to generate hypotheses about what will work in the laboratory. The manipulations might well work on other people. I knew I was weird.)

My undergraduate thesis used the manipulation taken directly from Aronson and Mettee's work and then measured self-esteem using a standard self-esteem measure (Janis & Field, 1959). I spent hours analyzing the data by hand, adding up sums of squares and so forth. There was not the slightest hint of any effect. The subjects' self-esteem scores had not budged an iota on the basis of the feedback I had given them.

To be sure, null results are ambiguous. I certainly knew I was not the most gifted of experimenters. But I believed my results. Surely even a novice experimenter would have gotten at least a trend and moved some people's self-esteem, if the manipulation were effective.

That's what then moved me to reflect on my own experience as a participant. Maybe the impact of these false feedback manipulations was on the public self, not the private self (not that I had learned to think in those terms yet). At the time, such theorizing was in its infancy. The term *self-presentation* was being bandied about occasionally, but it was considered a marginal idea. Its association with Erving Goffman's (1959) book *The Presentation of Self in Everyday Life*, which was regarded as a highly creative but methodologically unsophisticated work, did not attract respect.

Still, I was able to convince my mentor in graduate school, the great Edward E. Jones, to let me try a study (Baumeister & Jones, 1978). Participants took a personality test and got false feedback on it, just as in Aronson and Mettee's experiment. Half of them, however, received the feedback in an anonymous, confidential manner. It was printed on a computer sheet (the old kind of computer paper with green stripes across it and holes down the sides), and it had only a subject number on it, thus no identifying information. The experimenter delivered it in a sealed envelope, emphasized confidentiality, and insisted that he leave the room before the participant opened the envelope.

In the public condition, there was no sealed envelope and no confidentiality. I entered the room holding the evaluation in my hand and looking at it. The participant's name and other identifying information were printed at the top of the paper, and, as I recall, his or her name was used in the text of the message as well. (In the private condition, the profile referred to the participant only as "subject," as in "Subject's personality profile has several notable patterns …")

To strengthen the manipulation further, we set up the experiment so that there were two (real) participants at each session. They were introduced briefly at the beginning and then separated, though they believed they were going to interact more later. In the private condition, the personality feedback was treated as simply a formality that had nothing to do with the interaction to come. In the public condition, however, each subject was told that his or her profile was being shown to the other person "so that he (or she) can get an idea of what you're like." Thus, they prepared to interact with someone who had seen the feedback. When they read their personality profile, they believed that multiple others had read or were reading it.

We then asked people to rate themselves for their partner. Afterward, they played prisoner's dilemma, though that part did not yield useful results.

The findings from this study confirmed the importance of the public self. If the false feedback mainly affected self-esteem, as was the prevailing thinking at the time, then it should have done so in the private condition. But the private evaluations had no discernible effects on how people described themselves. Whether they had received good or bad feedback produced no change in their self-ratings that we could find.

The public evaluations were another matter, however. On items that overlapped with the content of the personality profile, people rated themselves consistently with their feedback. Those who had received favorable evaluations rated themselves better than those who had received unfavorable ones. (Remember, they were describing themselves to someone who supposedly had seen the personality profile.)

Thus, consistency theory was upheld (I hope Aronson was pleased by this aspect of the work), but only with the aid of implicit social pressure.

That is, people did rate themselves consistently with the feedback they received, but only when others knew the feedback. The private consistency processes that so dominated the thinking of the time (cognitive dissonance theory and so on) were not in evidence.

There were other effects, too. On items that were unrelated to the content of the fake feedback, in the public condition, people exhibited dramatic shifts. Those who had received positive feedback tended to be modest on these other items. In contrast, those who had received bad feedback rated themselves quite positively on the unrelated items. This appeared to be a strategy to compensate for the bad feedback. In effect, they were saying, "I may have the bad traits listed in the personality feedback, but I have other, very positive traits that make up for them."

The compensation effects also can be seen as a form of consistency, for they help to sustain an overall favorable image despite the strong manipulation. They also offered an intriguing way of reconsidering the findings from Aronson and Mettee (1968). In that original study, people who had received false feedback had cheated more than others on the test for extrasensory perception. It is possible that they cheated to confirm a negative image of self, but it is also possible that they cheated to win, especially because winning not only brought them money—it would show the experimenter that they had a talent for extrasensory perception. That way, they could prove themselves to be capable and special, despite the bad feedback.

I was quite struck by the fact that the consistency effect was only obtained in the public condition. My other mentor, Joel Cooper, a staunch advocate of dissonance theory, and I had embraced it as well. I did not realize that at the time he was involved in ongoing battles with Barry Schlenker, James Tedeschi, and other researchers over whether dissonance effects involved self-presentation. The fight was at times bitter, I believe, because some took self-presentation as equivalent to lying, and so the implication was that if dissonance effects are based on self-presentation, then there was no real attitude change: Participants merely *said* that they changed their attitudes to make a good impression on the experimenter.

As a loyal student of Cooper, I believed that dissonance brought real attitude change, but I also thought that perhaps change was driven by self-presentation. For example, I did not believe that the participants in my experiment were thinking, "Well, the profile says I am impulsive. I don't think I am impulsive, but I better say I am, because that's what they expect." Rather, I thought that the fact that they were interacting with partners and experimenters who all regarded them as impulsive made them think of themselves as impulsive. Getting the same feedback confidentially made it easier to dismiss.

Emboldened by the findings of that paper and a couple other early experiments that manipulated public versus private feedback, I decided to tackle cognitive dissonance itself. There had been several studies suggesting that public behavior had more impact on dissonance than did private behavior. Some of those writings, as I said, sought to trivialize dissonance phenomena by suggesting that participants merely superficially claimed to change their attitudes, but did not really do so (see Tedeschi, Schlenker, & Bonoma, 1971, for an early statement of this view). To me, these seemed inconsistent with the findings that dissonance depended on choice (e.g., Linder, Cooper, & Jones, 1967). After all, wasn't choice an inner process?

Around this time I had the great luck to start working with Dianne Tice, who was a much more talented experimenter than I was. Together we put together a series of experiments (Baumeister & Tice, 1984) that would manipulate both choice and publicness. We had participants write counterattitudinal essays (saying that the dormitory food was terrific and that the company that provided it—which was the target of campuswide loathing—should be rehired). Half got the standard high-choice manipulation ("It's entirely up to you, though I'd appreciate it"). The rest got a strong no-choice manipulation, in which the experimenter said, "I am sorry but I cannot give you any choice about what position to take in your essay."

Cross-cutting these conditions we had a strong public–private manipulation. Half the essays were to be strictly anonymous. Instructions urged the participant not to say anything that could enable anyone to trace his or her identity. The rest were told to write a plethora of identifying information at the top of the essay sheet, including name, student number, major department, campus address, home address, and more.

Of particular interest to me was the idea that cognitive dissonance could be motivated by self-presentational concerns but would still produce genuine, lasting attitude change. To show this, we added an "audience transfer" procedure, in which participants wrote their essays publicly under the eye of one experimenter, but then rated their attitudes on a postmeasure for a different experimenter, in a different location, and ostensibly as part of a separate experiment.

The results of that experiment were, I think, surprising to all sides interested in dissonance. The argument had been over whether dissonance was all inner process (so that choice was necessary) or was all impression management (so that public circumstances were necessary). We found that neither was necessary. In effect, there were two routes to dissonance and attitude change. Compared to the baseline and control conditions, there was significant attitude change in the private, high choice condition. No doubt this pleased the traditional dissonance crowd. But we also found significant change in the public, no choice condition, which probably pleased the self-presentation researchers. Apparently either choice or publicness was sufficient, but not necessary, to produce attitude change. Moreover, the combination of both factors seemed to produce twice as much attitude change as either factor alone: the public high-choice condition produced significantly more change than either the private high-choice or the public no-choice, and the pattern of means suggested that the effects were simply additive.

As for the audience transfer, we had some problems with suspicion there. Some participants understandably were skeptical that the two experiments were completely unrelated, especially when both measured attitudes toward the campus food service. The suspicious participants showed no attitude change. But the ones who were not suspicious showed strong attitude change, indeed just as much as in the regular public high-choice condition.

To me, this confirmed the reality of dissonance-produced attitude change even when it is driven by self-presentation. Self-presentation is not just saying what will make a good impression even if you don't mean it. Rather, it is an important part of constructing the self. The inner self derives in substantial measure from interpersonal concerns and processes.

At the time, I naïvely believed that dissonance processes were still among the most important and valued phenomena in social psychology, and I had high hopes that our paper (Baumeister & Tice, 1984)—bolstered by being published as lead article in the volume of the *Journal of Personality and Social Psychology*—would have a big impact and help get my career going. However, it seemed to attract relatively little attention and has never been among my better cited articles. It seems that by 1984 the field had moved on to other topics and interests. I spent several years in unsuccessful attempts to get a National Science Foundation (NSF) grant to follow up that work and do more audience transfer studies, and, when that pursuit ended in failure, I rather gave up on that line of work.

Although Aronson's question about the mismatched pajamas receded to the back of my memory, the question later came to preoccupy me in a different way. What, indeed, were the effects on someone of being jilted by a girlfriend or otherwise rejected?

I was led to this question from the earlier work on self-presentation. The core thrust of that earlier work was to push me to look at interpersonal roots of behavior. That was the message that I took away from the self-presentation versus self-esteem debate in my dissertation and other early work. Not that I had given up so easily on self-esteem, which in a sense was the first love of my research career. But rather than seeing self-esteem as the fundamental driving force from which interpersonal behavior flowed, I wanted instead to understand self-esteem in interpersonal terms. This had led me to several major efforts. The first was to blend self-esteem and self-presentation in a different way (Baumeister, Tice, & Hutton, 1989), looking at responses to self-esteem scales as indicative of habitual self-presentational styles and reconsidering the published literature on self-esteem in self-presentational terms.

The second was sociometer theory, which Mark Leary had been developing, and he was kind enough to allow me to coauthor a theory paper with him in which we fleshed out the idea that the function of self-esteem is to promote interpersonal connection. By then I had (like many across the nation) become disillusioned with self-esteem and was abandoning the earlier hope that it would prove to be a powerful panacea for mental health and societal functioning (see Baumeister, Smart, & Boden, 1996; also, especially, Baumeister, Campbell, Krueger, & Vohs, 2003). That had left open the question of why people care so much about self-esteem. After all, if it provides few direct benefits, why should nature have it so strongly linked to such powerful emotions and motivations? Aronson and others were certainly correct in contending that a great many social behaviors seem driven by the desire to maintain a favorable image of self. Why bother?

Our answer (see Leary & Baumeister, 2000) was that self-esteem is an internal measure of something that does matter a great deal, namely, *belongingness*. Self-esteem is one's inner assessment, not of actual or current relationships, but of one's eligibility for relationships. It asks the question, "Am I the sort of person with whom others will want to be connected?" As one sign, we noted that the contents of self-esteem scale items correspond closely to the main reasons why individuals are included or excluded from groups and relationships. Nearly all self-esteem scales measure likability, and obviously people who are liked have more social bonds than those who are not. Likewise, nearly all self-esteem scales measure general competence, and many groups and organizations include or exclude persons on the basis of competence. The two other types of items that are included in many though not all self-esteem scales are physical attractiveness and moral virtue. Again, these correspond to criteria for social connection. People like to affiliate with others who are physically attractive, and most groups eventually cannot tolerate members who violate the basic moral rules of how people should treat each other.

This reconceptualization of self-esteem exemplified a principle that has been one of the unifying ideas of my career, going back to my reaction to the original experiment by Aronson and Mettee (1968), though I have only begun to articulate it clearly in more recent years: *Inner processes serve interpersonal functions.* To me, this should be what social psychology is all about. By looking at the requirements and consequences of social interaction, we can understand the *raison d'etre* of thoughts, feelings, and other inner phenomena.

A major turning point in my thinking was my work with Mark Leary on a different paper called "The Need to Belong" (Baumeister & Leary, 1995). It had its roots in reacting to the terror management theory of anxiety (see Greenberg, Pyszczynski, & Solomon, 1986). Attending the small conferences that Bibb Latané held annually on the Carolina coast, we heard that theory over and over. The core idea was that fear of death was the fundamental and supreme human motivation and the main cause of anxiety. Obviously to focus on one person contemplating death is not a very social or interpersonal context, and so, as usual, I began to wonder about whether it overlooked some important interpersonal dimensions. I knew very little about anxiety other than Freud's theories about castration, so at one point Dianne Tice and I set out to do a literature review. Our finding was that, yes, fear of death is a significant cause of anxiety—but fear of social exclusion is a larger and more common source of anxiety (Baumeister & Tice, 1990).

After that was finished, Leary remarked to me that he thought we were right about anxiety but were missing the bigger picture. Through a series of meetings and conversations, we began to pull together other phenomena that seemed tied to social inclusion and exclusion. At some point this took shape as a literature review manuscript that managed to find its way into *Psychological Bulletin* (Baumeister & Leary, 1995). To this day, it remains the most heavily cited article that either Leary or I have ever published.

Writing that article made me appreciate how strong and deep is the human drive to connect with others. It follows, therefore, that any sort of social rejection would thwart that need, and therefore ought to produce some sort of shock to the system. This returned me to Aronson and Mettee's (1968) question: If a person is rejected (and thus feels unloved), how will he or she react?

It took me a couple years to persuade any of my associates to want to collect data on this issue, but when Jean Twenge began to run studies with randomly assigned social exclusion and rejection manipulations, we immediately began to have giant effects. These studies on rejection have been a staple of my laboratory for the past decade.

To be sure, we never measured whether rejected people wear mismatched pajamas. But as for robbing a bank or kicking a dog, our findings would suggest that the answer to Aronson's 1968 question is a definite yes. Excluded and rejected persons show sharp increases in aggression and antisocial behavior (Twenge, Baumeister, Tice, & Stucke, 2001). Self-defeating behavior (would mismatched pajamas qualify as such?) also increases in the wake of rejection (Twenge, Catanese, & Baumeister, 2002). Prosocial behavior drops, partly due to a loss of capacity to empathize with others (Twenge, Baumeister, DeWall, Ciarocco, & Bartels, 2007).

In conclusion, it is fair to say that Aronson's pioneering work and provocative ideas had a lasting influence on me, as they influenced countless other social psychologists. Inevitably, the hard discipline of the data has forced some revisions and changes. But the core question about the effects of being rejected that I read in his 1968 paper has remained highly relevant, fresh, and productive of new research directions.

REFERENCES

Aronson, E., & Carlsmith, J. M. (1962). Performance expectancy as a determinant of actual performance. *Journal of Abnormal and Social Psychology, 65*, 178–182.

Aronson, E., & Mettee, D. R. (1968). Dishonest behavior as a function of differential levels of induced self-esteem. *Journal of Personality and Social Psychology, 9*, 121–127.

Baumeister, R. F., Campbell, J. D., Krueger, J. I., & Vohs, K. D. (2003). Does high self-esteem cause better performance interpersonal success, happiness, or healthier lifestyles? *Psychological Science in the Public Interest, 4*, 1–44.

Baumeister, R. F., & Jones, E. E. (1978). When self-presentation is constrained by the target's knowledge: Consistency and compensation. *Journal of Personality and Social Psychology, 36*, 608–618.

Baumeister, R. F., & Leary, M. R. (1995). The need to belong: Desire for interpersonal attachments as a fundamental human motivation. *Psychological Bulletin, 117*, 497–529.

Baumeister, R. F., Smart, L., & Boden, J. M. (1996). Relation of threatened egotism to violence and aggression: The dark side of high self-esteem. *Psychological Review, 103*, 5–33.

Baumeister, R. F., & Tice, D. M. (1984). Role of self-presentation and choice in cognitive dissonance under forced compliance: Necessary or sufficient causes? *Journal of Personality and Social Psychology, 46*, 5–13.

Baumeister, R. F., & Tice, D. M. (1990). Anxiety and social exclusion. *Journal of Social and Clinical Psychology, 9*, 165–195.

Baumeister, R. F., Tice, D. M., & Hutton, D. G. (1989). Self-presentational motivations and personality differences in self-esteeem. *Journal of Personality, 57*, 547–579.

Goffman, E. (1959). *The presentation of self in everyday life.* New York: Anchor Books.

Greenberg, J., Pyszczynski, T., & Solomon, S. (1986). The causes and consequences of self-esteem: A terror management theory. In R. Baumeister (Ed.), *Public self and private self* (pp. 189–212). New York: Springer-Verlag.

Janis, I. L., & Field, P. (1959). Sex differences and personality factors related to persuasibility. In C. Hovland & I. Janis (Eds.), Personality and persuasibility (pp. 55–68, 300–302). New Haven, CT: Yale University Press.

Leary, M. R., & Baumeister, R. F. (2000). The nature and function of self-esteem: Sociometer theory. In M. Zanna (Ed.), *Advances in experimental social psychology* (Vol. 32, pp. 1–62). San Diego, CA: Academic Press.

Linder, D. E., Cooper, J., & Jones, E. E. (1967). Decision freedom as a determinant of the role of incentive magnitude in attitude change. *Journal of Personality and Social Psychology, 6*, 245–254.

Tedeschi, J. T., Schlenker, B. R., & Bonoma, T. V. (1971). Cognitive dissonance: Private ratiocination or public spectacle? *American Psychologist, 26*, 685–695.

Twenge, J. M., Baumeister, R. F., DeWall, C. N., Ciarocco, N. J., & Bartels, J. M. (2007). Social exclusion decreases prosocial behavior. *Journal of Personality and Social Psychology, 92*, 56–66.

Twenge, J. M., Baumeister, R. F., Tice, D. M., & Stucke, T. S. (2001). If you can't join them, beat them: Effects of social exclusion on aggressive behavior. *Journal of Personality and Social Psychology, 81*, 1058–1069.

Twenge, J. M., Catanese, K. R., & Baumeister, R. F. (2002). Social exclusion causes self-defeating behavior. *Journal of Personality and Social Psychology, 83*, 606–615.

5

THE RISE AND FALL OF THE HIGH-IMPACT EXPERIMENT

Phoebe C. Ellsworth
University of Michigan

Few children dream of becoming a social psychologist. They imagine careers filled with excitement and applause: firefighters, ballerinas, basketball stars, artists, astronauts, kings and queens. Elliot Aronson was going to be a baseball player; I was going to be an artist. In high school the sensible ones begin to sort the world into medicine, law, and business, and the rebels into art, literature, and philosophy, with science somewhere in between. Most people scarcely know that the field of social psychology exists until they get to college. For a few, their first encounter with social psychology is an epiphany, especially if their textbook is *The Social Animal* (Aronson, 1972/2008). The foibles and biases and self-deceptions of people in everyday life can be scientifically studied, and so can their extraordinary acts of generosity, savagery, and love. In writing their personal statements for admission to graduate school, many applicants tell us that when they took their first course in social psychology they changed their major and were born again into a lifelong passion for the field.

What was it that so excited them? Not, I think, the latest issue of the *Journal of Personality and Social Psychology* (*JPSP*). It was Solomon Asch's conformity research, Leon Festinger and Elliot Aronson's dissonance research, Stanley Milgram's obedience research, Elaine Hatfield's research on romantic attraction, John Darley and Bibb Latané's bystander intervention research, Stanley Schachter and Jerome Singer's research on emotion, Phil Zimbardo's research on deindividuation and dehumanization, and other vivid, memorable experiments in which people found themselves in unexpected situations that demanded a response. These situations were engrossing and memorable for the people who experienced them and for the people who read about them decades later. In Aronson and Carlsmith's terms, they were high in *impact* (Aronson & Carlsmith, 1968). They are also *old*.

For some of these researchers the choice of a high-impact situation that required a behavioral response seemed natural, because behavior was what interested them. The research by Asch, Milgram, and Darley was designed to study particular types of behavior: conformity, obedience to authority, or altruism. We called this kind of work "phenomenon-oriented research." Asch wanted to find out what kinds of people would deny the evidence of their own eyes and conform to the majority. Milgram wanted to find out whether Americans, unlike the Nazis, would refuse to obey an authority who ordered them to harm another person. What was stunning about this research were the results: Most people conformed to the majority when they knew its judgment was wrong; most people overcame their concern for the welfare of the other person and administered severe electric shocks to him. Neither Asch nor Milgram set out to test a specific hypothesis, and neither one of them even had a control group. They asked, "What would happen if …?" and they are famous because what happened was so unexpected and so disturbing. The results of the Asch and Milgram studies did not answer questions but raised them.

The choice of involving, realistic research methods probably seemed obvious to the phenomenon-oriented researchers because they needed situations that would elicit actual behavior. Very often these behaviors were socially undesirable (like conformity or aggression or blind obedience to authority) or desirable (like helping others in need), and people's reports about what they *would* do were likely to be untrustworthy. Very few people would describe themselves as likely to conform to the majority when they knew it was wrong or to turn a blind eye to a person in need of help, so the researchers assumed that the only way to get a valid measure of what people would do was to set up a situation that called for the behavior and see what people *did* do.

The studies designed by researchers who were students (or grand-students) of Kurt Lewin, such as Festinger, Schachter, and Aronson, were different in that they were empirical tests of hypotheses derived from general theories. Rather than beginning with a specific kind of behavior (conformity, obedience, helping), they began with a theoretically derived motivational process—the need for social comparison or cognitive dissonance reduction, for example. The theories were not tied to any particular type of behavior, but could be applied to a wide range of responses. Social comparison theory could make predictions about friendship choices, competition, emotion, or conformity. Dissonance theory could make predictions about preferences, group solidarity, reaction to failure, and a host of other behavioral and mental responses.

In the late 1960s, Gardner Lindzey asked Elliot to write a chapter on experimental methodology for the second edition of the *Handbook of Social Psychology* (Lindzey & Aronson, 1969). Elliot begged off on the grounds that the topic was insufferably boring and that he had never even bothered to take a methodology course. But Lindzey, never one to be easily dissuaded, said in effect, "You've been doing experiments for the past decade. All you need to do is think about what you've been doing and write it down" (Aronson, 2010). Elliot enlisted his former graduate student, Merrill Carlsmith, to help him out, and the result was a discussion of methodology unlike anything that had ever been written on the topic, a chapter about what great experimenters actually do rather than about principles and rules, a chapter that was more exciting than most of the other chapters in the handbook.

Everyone was talking about the chapter, and publishers were begging Elliot and Merrill to expand it and publish it as a book. Of course, a book would have to cover some of the less exciting essentials of methodology, like rating scales and experimental design, and that's where I came in. Merrill Carlsmith was my advisor, and he persuaded Elliot that I would be a good person to help transform their brilliant chapter into a book. I was flattered to be asked, dazzled by Elliot, and working with him and Merrill on the book was a heady, challenging experience. We didn't want the book to look like other methods books, which were highly abstract and technical, soporific, or both. We wanted to capture the actual process of planning and doing research, and translating theoretically derived hypotheses into high-impact experiments.

High-impact experiments were not a necessary implication of social comparison or dissonance theory. If those theories were invented today, it is likely that researchers would use hypothetical scenarios and self-report measures to study them. The Lewinians advanced the field of social psychology by testing rigorous, theoretically derived hypotheses in settings that were real to the participants, that confronted them with dilemmas that had to be resolved, that left them no time to step back and analyze the situation, and that usually demanded that they actually do something.

Consider the original Festinger and Carlsmith study of forced compliance (1959). Leon Festinger was Elliot's graduate advisor and Merrill's undergraduate advisor. The Festinger and Carlsmith study was actually Merrill's senior honors thesis, and then, as now, graduate students were intimately involved in the training of their advisor's undergraduate students. Elliot helped to design the study, and he had the task of training Merrill, who was not naturally inclined to drama, to give a convincing performance as the distraught experimenter who had to ask for help from the Subject.[1]

The groundwork for the experiment and the dependent variable measure was laid during the first week of the introductory psychology course when the students were told that the psychology department was conducting a study to evaluate the experience of the research Subjects and that some of them would be interviewed by the department after they had participated in an experiment. When the Subject arrives at the lab, he is reminded that the department might want to interview him later, and then set to work on the first task. The Subject is told to fill a tray with 12 spools, one at a time and using one hand, then to take all the spools out one by one, then put them back in, over and over again. After working on this mind-numbing task for half an hour, the Subject moves on to the second task. He is given a board with 48 pegs in it and told to turn each peg a quarter turn clockwise, again using one hand, until he had turned all 48, then go back to the beginning and turn the first one another quarter turn and so on and so on for another half hour. The experimenter watches the Subject, taking notes and doing mysterious things with a stopwatch. After the second half hour, the experimenter explains that the Subject was in the control group and that the purpose of the experiment is to discover whether prior expectations about the task influence performance. In the experimental group another student, posing as the previous Subject, tells the Subject that the task was fun and exciting.

At this point the experimenter hesitates and acts somewhat awkward and embarrassed. He explains that the guy who is supposed to give the ecstatic description to the next Subject just phoned in to say he couldn't make it. What does the experimenter do? "You sweat, you pace up and down, you wring your hands, you convey to the participant that you are in real trouble here—that the next participant is waiting and the goddamn stooge hasn't shown up …" (Aronson, 1999). In desperation you turn to the Subject and beg him to do you a favor and play the role, and you offer him a dollar (or twenty dollars) to do it and to be available in case there's another time when the confederate can't make it. The Subject agrees, the experimenter gives him the money and a sheet listing the main things to say extolling the experiment, then leaves him alone to prepare for a few minutes. Then the experimenter brings the Subject into the waiting room where an undergraduate woman is waiting, and leaves him to describe the experiment to her in glowing terms. The woman is skeptical, forcing the Subject to redouble his praise.

Finally the experimenter takes the Subject to the psychology department office to be interviewed about his experience by a departmental evaluator (who, of course, does not know which condition the Subject was in). It took three people (the experimenter, the "next Subject," and the departmental evaluator) and nearly two hours to run each Subject through this carefully scripted but apparently spontaneous drama.

Not all of the social psychological research of the 1950s, 1960s, and 1970s was so dramatic. The other dominant tradition in social psychology was Carl Hovland's group at Yale; their research was more systematic and more staid. Subjects read newspaper articles supposedly written by highly credible sources (an eminent American scientist, a national research institute) or less credible sources (a Soviet newspaper, a gossip columnist) and filled out attitude questionnaires about the topic of the article. Their research was like most social-psychological research today: Subjects read something and then they answered questions about it. The Yale researchers carefully divided the process of attitude change into Source, Message, Medium, and Audience factors and then created written materials to reflect each one. Dissonance researchers would say, "Hey! We could test dissonance in supermarket shoppers or people placing bets at the race track. Let's try it!" At Yale, even the dissonance research was more systematic and less theatrical. Jack Brehm and Arthur Cohen (1962) replicated the Festinger and Carlsmith experiment by paying Subjects to write counterattitudinal essays. Even in these tamer versions, however, the Subjects actually had to do something and believed that what they did would have consequences for someone else.

Followers of each tradition had a certain contempt for the other kind of research. The Hovland people regarded the Lewinians as wild and crazy guys who valued flamboyance over substance. The Lewinians regarded the Yale group as mechanical and dull. But social psychology was a unified field in those days, and both traditions were taught in all courses (McGuire, 1969).

Methodologically, the Hovland tradition is alive and well, though their systematic theoretical approach is less common. The Lewinian methods are on the endangered list (Baumeister, Vohs, & Funder, 2007). To understand why this is a problem for the field, it is important to understand what these methods were, why they were so great, and what we risk losing by forsaking them.

THE ELEMENTS OF ELLIOT
Real Situations

People are constantly evaluating their environment emotionally and cognitively, they make choices, they *act* on those choices, and their actions change the environment for themselves and often for other people. Sometimes they have the luxury of sitting back and considering these choices in the abstract, weighing the alternatives, but often they are caught up by the situation, driven by motivations and pressures they do not fully recognize, and they act anyway. That is what life is about, that is what Elliot's experiments were about, but that is not what most of today's research is about.

Researchers in the Lewinian tradition wanted to study people coping with real situations. Sometimes they sought out natural settings where theories could be tested. *When Prophecy Fails* (Festinger, Riecken, & Schachter, 1956) was an early example. Festinger and his colleagues heard of a group of people who had staked everything on the belief that the world would come to an end on a specific night in the near future and all would perish except for the true believers, who would be rescued at midnight by a spaceship. These researchers immediately saw that an ordinary night in which nothing special happened at the appointed hour would disconfirm a belief for which the group members had sacrificed everything, which would create massive cognitive dissonance, and so they joined the group so that they could be around on the fateful night to see how the people dealt with the dissonance. Donald Dutton and Arthur Aron (1974) tested Schachter's hypothesis about the spillover of emotional arousal from one situation to another by having a sexy woman approach men who had just made their way across a deep gorge on a shaky suspension bridge: Their anxious arousal turned into attraction to the women. Men who had walked across a solid bridge were not so attracted. Anthony Doob and his colleagues, building on Aronson and Mills's (1959) laboratory finding that people liked their group better if they had undergone a severe initiation to get into it, used a supermarket chain to test the hypothesis that an introductory high price offer would create more brand loyalty than the usual introductory low price offer (Doob, Carlsmith, Freedman, Landauer, & Tom, 1969). It did.

Rather than finding suitable settings, Elliot created them. He moved to natural settings later on, with the Jigsaw Classroom work, but that was because he was interested in classrooms. For testing conceptual variables, Elliot preferred to create them in a controlled laboratory setting, and his genius in pulling this off was his first great contribution to the field. He believed that "virtually all variables are manipulable in the laboratory" (Aronson, 1999, p. 88) and that it was possible to "invent a procedure that would get at the essence" of virtually any hypothesis (Aronson, 2007, p. 17). He showed the world that these beliefs were no idle fantasies. Although the research was conducted in the laboratory and the Subjects were college students, something happened that mattered to them and made them forget that they were participants in an experiment. They had to improvise a lie and mislead an unsuspecting person (Festinger & Carlsmith, 1959); they had to read a steamy passage from *Lady Chatterley's Lover* to a young male experimenter (Aronson & Mills, 1959); after repeatedly failing at a task and deciding that it was not the sort of task they were good at, they suddenly aced it for no apparent reason (Aronson & Carlsmith, 1962).

In Aronson and Carlsmith's revolutionary chapter on "Experimentation in Social Psychology" (1968) there was a section called "Setting the Stage," which was later expanded into a full chapter in our methods book (Aronson, Ellsworth, Carlsmith, & Gonzales, 1990; Carlsmith, Ellsworth, & Aronson, 1976). Creating an experiment was like writing and directing a little play, with the Subject as a major character. It had to have a plot that captured and maintained the Subject's full attention; a plot with unity, coherence, and emphasis, in which the manipulation of the independent variable and the measurement of the dependent variable were elements of the unfolding story. It usually had a cast of characters—not just the Subject and the experimenter, but one or more confederates, who were carefully trained to act their parts. Sometimes it had an elaborate setting, as in Schachter's 1959 experiments on fear and affiliation. The independent variable was fear, operationalized by the threat of electric shock. Schachter could have just told the Subjects that they were going to get shocks, but instead he created what appeared to be a medical laboratory featuring a large, threatening shock apparatus. The experimenter appeared in a white lab coat and introduced himself as a doctor with a vaguely ominous foreign name. He explained that the shocks would be painful and further frightened the Subjects by "reassuring" them that the shocks would cause "no permanent tissue damage." Albert Ax (1953) used an even more extreme fear induction, actually hooking the Subject to a fake polygraph machine that then seemed to malfunction and sent smoke and sparks flying into the air while the Subject was still attached to it.

Designing experiments in the Aronson tradition created a sense of excitement that is far less common in graduate students today than it was for us and our Lewinian advisors. Although some procedures (such as the work on forced compliance or free choice in cognitive dissonance) led to dozens of replications, much of the time when we designed an experiment we started from scratch, looking for new contexts in which a theoretical prediction could be tested. We sat around a table and argued about how to create an event that would make our independent variable real to the Subjects, how to work that event seamlessly into an involving situation, and how to build the measure into the situation so that the subjects would not recognize it as The Measure This Experiment Is About. We argued, we were competitive, our initial thoughts were mercilessly mocked by our advisors and one another, but little by little ideas would emerge that seemed promising, and if one of them was ours we would feel like a genius and be willing to put in all the time in the world to make the study cohere and come alive. We'd develop the idea, working all the parts into an integrated and compelling whole, then try it out, again and again, fixing the problems and adjusting the procedure until it was right. It was exhausting and it was exhilarating.

The Independent and Dependent Variables: Events and Behaviors

In Elliot's experiments and others in the Lewinian tradition, the independent variable was rarely something the Subject read. Often it was an event, something that happened to the Subject (Aronson et al., 1990). Smoke pours under the door of the laboratory (Latané & Darley, 1968). In a boring experiment about perceptual judgments of the lengths of lines, one by one all seven of the other Subjects confidently gives the same obviously wrong answer, and then it's your turn (Asch, 1951). A tourist couple asks you to take their picture and you break their camera (Regan, Williams, & Sparling, 1972). Sometimes the event appears to be an accident, completely unrelated to the experiment. Sometimes a confederate, usually posing as another Subject, delivers the treatment. Sometimes the Subject does not even know that she or he is in an experiment at all. Sometimes the treatment is clearly part of the experiment, but the Subject cannot help being swept up by it: The task seems impossible to solve; the experimenter asks you to walk around campus wearing an idiotic sandwich-brand advertisement (Ross, Green, & House, 1977); the experimenter tells you to give another shock to the man with the heart condition (Milgram, 1963). Typically the Subject is doing things, not reading things or judging things, and typically the Subject is interacting with other people, not sitting in a cubicle with a booklet or a keyboard and a screen.

On the dependent variable side, behavioral measures were much more common than they are today. Subjects were given an opportunity to cheat, or asked to do a favor for someone, or put in a situation where someone cried out for help, and the question was did they do it? Or how much did they do, or how long did it take them to do it, or how much time did they spend doing one thing rather than another? People had to make actual choices. Liking or prejudice was measured by giving the Subject a chair to take into the room and seeing how far from the black or white confederate they chose to sit, or by measuring eye contact. Anxiety was measured by speech disturbances or fidgeting, dominance by interrupting other people who were trying to talk.

We took it for granted that reading about a hypothetical event was not the same as responding to an actual event, and that saying what you *would* do in a situation was not very informative about what you would actually do (Freedman, 1969). Aronson and Carlsmith wrote about the weaknesses of verbal measures in their *Handbook of Social Psychology* chapter (1968), and again at greater length in their research methods book (Aronson et al., 1990; Carlsmith et al., 1976): "There is nothing more likely to produce error variance than a Subject racing through pages of questions, checking without giving much thought, unconcerned about the exact nature or wording of the question" (Aronson & Carlsmith, 1968, p. 57). All of us read *Unobtrusive Measures* by Webb, Campbell, Schwartz, and Sechrest (1966), and learned that the inherent danger of verbal measures is that they are *reactive*: The Subjects almost always know that they are being measured and so are motivated to give answers that look reasonable or normal or smart or good. A decade later Richard Nisbett and Timothy Wilson (1977), in an article that is widely cited but rarely heeded, dramatically illustrated the fallibility of verbal reports in a series of empirical studies: People had no trouble explaining their behavior, and showed high confidence and high agreement, but their explanations were wrong. Their behavior was controlled by the variables manipulated in the experiment, but they had no idea that this was so and gave plausible but false explanations. We thought that people who used verbal manipulations and verbal measures were stupid or lazy. Either they lacked the ingenuity to think up an event that captured the essence of their independent variable (or a behavior that reflected their dependent variable) or they just didn't work hard enough to figure one out. Of course, we used verbal treatments and measures ourselves, but only when we couldn't come up with something better.

The Belief That Subjects Are People

Elliot constantly reminded us that to come up with an experimental situation that meant what you wanted it to mean, you had to look at it through the eyes of the Subject. Subjects were intelligent human beings who came to the lab with human concerns and emotions. They were moved by the inescapable human drive to make sense of what was happening to them and the equally inescapable human drive to seem competent. They were like us, just as complex, just as real. In those days this belief was fairly common. Even William J. McGuire, who was about as far away as possible from Aronson in his methodological style, famously urged us to "observe. But observe people, not data" (1973, p. 452). No matter how advanced our statistics, the computer printout only captures a small fraction of what was going on in the Subject's mind, and it is incumbent upon the researcher to pay attention to what the Subjects are thinking and feeling from the moment the study begins until the moment it ends. In Elliot's words:

> We are investigating the behavior of intelligent, curious, sophisticated adults who have been living in a social world for their entire lives. It goes without saying that, like the experimenters who are studying them, the participants in our experiments have developed their own ideas and theories about what causes their feelings and behavior as well as the feelings and behavior of the people around them ... If we failed to get the participant fully involved in the situation, she would sleepwalk through the procedure and the manipulation simply would not take. (Aronson, 1999, p. 92)

Young researchers nowadays often find that their manipulation didn't take, more often, I think, than they did in the days of high-impact research. They explain their discouraging results by saying that at the end of the semester Subjects aren't paying attention to the treatments or the measures; around midterms students are thinking of other things; after being in several experiments Subjects from the Subject pool are no longer interested; and so on. They don't *know* this, they are just guessing because they neither talked to the Subjects nor watched them during the experiment. Or sometimes they report in frustration that a Subject actually said, "Don't use my data—I was just blowing it off." In any case, bad results are not the Subjects' fault. If they are not paying attention it is because there is nothing in the experiment that seems worth paying attention to, nothing that they care about. Midterms are more interesting. Too many Subjects, in fact, are sleepwalking through the experiment, and the experimenter usually doesn't even know it until it is too late.

The things that matter most to people are usually things that happen to them, individually, and unless the researcher's question involved group behavior (which it more often did in those days), Subjects were run individually. If you were interested in the thoughts or emotions or behaviors of individual people, you studied them as *individuals*: You observed how each one responded to an elaborate scenario in which he or she was the major character. If a Subject interpreted the situation in an unexpected way, or refused to take the study seriously and just drifted off into daydreams and failed to respond, you *knew* it, because in every session of the experiment you were focused on that particular person. If one or two Subjects failed to respond to the treatment, you dropped them; if it happened more often, you redesigned the study.

So, unless we were interested in group behavior, we rarely ran Subjects in groups. First, it would be difficult to create an event that had the same impact on all the individuals in a group, although sometimes it made sense, as in the bystander intervention experiments where the presence of others was actually the independent variable. Second, most treatments would be hopelessly contaminated because the people in the group would influence each other, so the treatment might be different for each person, and the observations would not be independent. Third, this lack of independence has consequences not only for the experience of the Subjects but also for the statistical analysis. We were taught that the correct n for a group study was not the number of people in the group but an n of one: The datum was the group mean. This was the rule even if the group just sits to watch a film or fill out questionnaires (see Raudenbusch & Bryk, 2001, for a more modern view of the appropriate analysis for Subjects run in groups).

One of the benefits of running Subjects individually was that we could debrief them individually, asking them how they felt during the experiment, what surprised them, what confused them, whether anything seemed fishy, whether anything about their experience bothered them. This conversation was valuable for the Subjects, and it was valuable for us. The Subject was able to talk through any lingering concerns and self-doubts, and to really learn about what we hoped to learn from the study and why we conducted it the way we did. We were able to find out whether any Subjects responded to the study in an unexpected way that made it important to assuage their anxieties or to question the validity of the data they had provided. A Subject once told me, for example, that his parents had made him take an IQ test once a month, and that in self-defense he now always answered tests billed as IQ tests by checking A for the first question, B for the second question, C for the third, and so on. And when I looked at his answers, so he had. In another study, where I used a 5-foot-long boa constrictor as a fear stimulus, a Subject told me that she loved snakes and had an even bigger boa constrictor as a pet.

Pilot Testing

In testing theory, Elliot rarely used the same procedure twice. Often he would hear about a real-world situation that seemed like a perfect example of a theoretical construct he cared about, and he would figure out how to re-create that situation in the lab. For example, when he read about how the excruciating adolescent initiation rites in preliterate societies created permanent loyalty to the group (Whiting, 1941), he saw this as a stunning real-life example of dissonance reduction, and looked for a way to bottle it for the lab. What kind of group could you create that would plausibly require an initiation? What would seem like a severe initiation to college women (and, of course, you also needed a weak initiation as a comparison)? How could you make the actual group experience the same for all the Subjects? How could you measure commitment to the group? He and Jud Mills discussed and discarded many ideas, and the more promising ones were tried out and revised and tried out and revised again in pilot testing before the actual experiment was run (Aronson & Mills, 1959; the work that went into creating this study is described in Aronson & Carlsmith, 1969).

We all took pilot testing for granted as part of the research process. Before running the actual study, we did pilot research to see whether the treatments created the psychological state we were interested in, whether the measures captured the process we cared about and whether they showed floor or ceiling effects that required revision, whether the whole sequence of events made sense to people in the way we intended, whether the experimenter and the confederates could play their parts convincingly.

When I ask my current students about pilot testing, some look completely blank, and others tell me that there's a small glitch in E-Prime or some other software that they're still working out, and when I ask them what the treatment, or the measure, or the whole situation *meant* to the Subject, they look at me as though I were a relic of the 20th century, which I am. Pilot testing can often take a long time, often longer than the actual experiment. Occasionally you get it right the first time, and it is exhilarating. More often you don't, and it is frustrating. Time trickles away, and you haven't even started the real experiment.

But moving straight to the real experiment without pilot testing can be even more costly. I've read MA and PhD theses in which the treatment didn't work; the negative mood induction made Subjects laugh because it was too corny, the "popular" CDs that Subjects were given to choose from were 10 years out of date because they were the exact same ones some researcher used 10 years ago and the Subjects never heard of any of them and had no preference, nobody believed your story that the IQ test they were taking was really race neutral. Finding out the answers to questions like these is what pilot testing is all about. It means that when you finally do run the actual study, the treatments mean what you meant them to mean, the measures measure what they are supposed to, and the Subject is involved in the study—not bored, not observing it from the outside, not laughing at it. Like all fine craftsmanship, it takes skill, work, and time, but the effort is worth it because it saves the researcher from running an entire study that gets null results because of flaws that could have been discovered and corrected in advance (Aronson, 1999; Aronson et al., 1990; Ellsworth & Gonzalez, 2003).

Fun

The final words of Aronson and Carlsmith's (1968) groundbreaking chapter are "It's fun." Graduate students often ask me, "What's that supposed to mean?" And at the time, some colleagues from different traditions were uncomfortable with the exuberant enthusiasm of the Lewinians and with the idea that science is fun. They felt that science should be orderly and sober. Women falling off chairs or reading bits of *Lady Chatterley's Lover* out loud, confederates flirting with the Subject or faking epileptic fits, coffee spills and exploding machines seemed like the stuff of farce, not science. Science was counterbalancing and highly controlled sterile laboratory settings and dozens of repetitious trials, not theater. Science was studying a phenomenon the way it was always studied, not thinking up a whole new set of events that would capture it in a different way. Science was no laughing matter. But this attitude is just pointless Puritanism. There is no definition of science that rules out joy.

This is not to say that graduate school in the good old days was an earthly paradise. Like graduate students today, we felt that we were constantly being evaluated by a set of standards that our advisors refused to articulate. Formulating a good research question was hard work and our advisors never seemed to be impressed. No one ever described Leon Festinger as a warm and supportive mentor. Getting the methods right was a frustrating experience, involving many skills and many disappointed returns to the drawing board. The control groups had to rule out alternative explanations, the independent variable had to be real to the Subjects and to mean what we wanted it to mean, the measures had to blend naturally into the procedure and to measure what we cared about, the whole situation had to fully absorb the Subject's attention. But because it was so difficult and so complicated, we were ecstatic when we finally pulled it off.

When Elliot said that research was fun, he meant that it was exhilarating:

> This was a challenging and exciting combination of science and art that electrified my interest and brought out abilities in me that I never knew I had. The challenge always left me tingling. (Aronson, 1999, pp. 91–92)

And deeply satisfying:

> I was enchanted by every part of the process: Getting the idea, designing the experiment, writing the script, rehearsing the performance, training my assistants so that their performance was precise and convincing to the participants, debriefing the participants (explaining why we did what we did), analyzing the data, and writing up the experiment. I loved doing all of it, and I was beginning to allow myself to accept the fact that I was good at it. (Aronson, 2010)

WHY ARE HIGH-IMPACT STUDIES SO RARE TODAY?

The kind of research that Elliot and the Lewinians pioneered has become less common. Roy Baumeister, Kathleen Vohs, and David Funder (2007) document the decline in the use of behavioral measures, but treatments that consist of events that mean something to the Subjects, dramatic procedures with exciting plots and often several characters, close attention to each individual Subject, and all the other elements of "high-impact methodology" have also become increasingly rare, replaced by what Elliot calls "judgment-type experiments" (Aronson, 1999). Subjects read vignettes and answer questions about them, sit in cubicles with a keyboard and a screen, and rarely interact with anybody. Research is less exciting for the experimenter, less involving for the Subjects, and less interesting for the reader. People look back at the heyday of high-impact research somewhat nostalgically and they still assign the old studies to get students interested in social psychology, but they rarely do that kind of research any more. Why? What happened?

The Evil Empire of the IRB

All universities now have committees in place to protect human Subjects and generally insist on reviewing almost all proposed research, whether federally funded or not (although the government does not require this). Almost all researchers complain about their institutional review board (IRB). The common view of IRBs is that they regard human beings as fragile, hypersensitive creatures who must be shielded from any experience that might possibly disturb them or cause them to complain. Their experience as research participants should be an order of magnitude blander than anything they encounter before they arrive or after they leave. If *anyone* complains, the study must be shut down. The IRB is not likely to approve an exciting, high-impact study in the first place, and if it does, the study runs the risk of being terminated before it is finished, so it is pointless to even try.

There may be some truth to this. All of us have stories about the mindless, picky, bureaucratic demands of our IRBs. But I do not remember anyone telling me that they were required to substitute a questionnaire for a behavioral measure, or a verbal description for an event that happens to the Subject. It has probably happened, but far more often researchers complain about delays caused by requests for changes in the details of the boilerplate wording on the consent form or the debriefing description, or having a procedure that was approved a year ago now questioned when the researcher wants to carry out a direct replication or the second wave of a longitudinal study, or having to go through a whole new review cycle because an address or title or sponsor has changed. We complain about time-consuming demands that seem to have nothing to do with the experience or welfare of the Subjects.

Perhaps researchers believe that if IRBs are going to raise such a stink about trivial matters, they'd be apoplectic if they saw a proposal for a lively, event-filled study, and there would be no chance that it would be approved. But I've seen little evidence that this is true. I've certainly bitched about IRBs myself, but it was usually about what I saw as ridiculous or trivial issues in paper-and-pencil studies. For example, once a study I planned to run in Japan was turned back because I included a Kyoto phone number for Subjects to call about their concerns rather than the approved University of Michigan number—which would have required an international call to a person who did not speak Japanese. But at about the same time I was involved in a study of citizens called for jury duty who watched a film of a trial in which a black man was accused of raping two white women, and then deliberated in either all-white or mixed-race juries (Sommers, 2007). That one was quickly approved, and the only changes requested involved exactly the same sort of low-level bureaucratic changes as in the Japanese study. In an addendum, I said I thought we should warn Subjects that the trial involved a rape, in case any of the women had been sexually assaulted and might not want to see the film, and the IRB said, "Good idea!" So my complaint, like many of my colleagues', is not that the IRB is hypersolicitous about the welfare of the Subjects, but that it seems arbitrary. My own intuitions about how disturbing a study might be for the Subjects seem completely uncorrelated with the IRB's demands for changes.

Once I was given the chance to study a complete sample of police interrogations to see whether videotaping made a difference to case outcomes and was allowed to keep copies of all of the recordings for later analysis. I knew this one would be touchy because prisoners are designated as especially vulnerable Subjects, and interrogated suspects are pretty similar to prisoners. So I asked the IRB for guidance before writing the proposal. They were delighted to be treated as professionals with real expertise, rather than as mindless nitpickers, and they went out of their way to help me write an acceptable proposal. If people enlist the IRB as an ally before submitting a proposal for potentially questionable high-impact research, I expect that they may be surprised at how easy the process can be. I sometimes wonder whether IRBs are more an excuse than a reason for the decline in high-impact research.

Still, IRBs may contribute to this decline in other, more indirect ways. Experiments like Elliot's that involve the creation of a little world with a plot and characters, like all good literary works, go through a long pilot stage of revision and improvement. It often takes dozens of small changes—sometimes big changes—before this little world is coherent and convincing. During this period the experimenter talks to each Subject to see how the treatment was interpreted, whether the expected emotions were aroused, whether the measure stood out like a sore thumb. Pilot work doesn't fit well with the requirements of IRBs, which want a complete, unmodifiable description of the research before they will approve it, including the verbatim text of the debriefing. If you're fine-tuning the procedures after every couple of Subjects, you can't write a new proposal every time or pilot testing could take a year. And, if you're going to learn much from the pilot Subjects, you have to have a personal conversation with them about their own individual reactions; an invariant text won't get you very far.

I've already mentioned the importance of pilot work. I believe that experiments fail for preventable reasons more often than they used to when serious pilot testing was the norm. Researchers discover too late that telling college freshmen to recall either a time when they were happy or a time when they were relieved doesn't create the distinction they want—because 80% of the Subjects in both conditions describe the day they found out they got into college. Or that the communal spitting required to take 10 cortisol samples over the course of an hour is so disgusting that the Subjects don't notice anything else about the experiment, including the treatment. These are problems that could easily be discovered and fixed by running a few pilot Subjects, but students rarely do this anymore. They tell me they'd love to pilot test, but they can't, so they don't. This makes for bad research—none of us can get it right the first time by pure intuition very often. IRBs that create obstacles to careful pilot testing promote worthless science.

My own IRB has gone back and forth on this. The last time I tried to argue for pilot testing the IRB said yes you *could* do it, as long as you never talk about it in any publication or colloquium or conference presentation, because if you never describe it professionally, then technically it is not "research" and doesn't fall under its jurisdiction. Silly scholastic compromises like this make researchers wonder whether the welfare of the Subjects is really what the IRB cares about: What happens to the Subject is exactly the same whether or not the researcher ever describes it in public. Also this vow of silence hurts science. Other scientists will learn more from our descriptions of the tribulations of pilot research than from a sanitized publication that makes it look as though the study was perfect from the start. And what if a reviewer asks how you know your manipulation worked? Do you have to say, "I'm afraid it would be unethical to tell you that"?

The usual IRB requirement that we specify the exact words we will say in debriefing the Subjects is also bad for research and, I would argue, for the welfare of the Subjects, because it inhibits any real conversation between the experimenter and the Subject. We used to debrief every Subject at the end of the session (Aronson et al., 1990, chap. 10). The course of those conversations was not always predictable, and only a vague outline could have been provided in advance. Subjects learned a lot more about the nature of psychological research than they do now, and we learned a lot more about what our study meant to them. Now that researchers have to submit a written transcript of the debriefing to the IRB, they figure they might as well just hand the written version to the Subjects and skip the face-to-face conversation altogether. This is what they do, and the Subjects generally toss the piece of paper unread into the wastepaper basket on the way out of the lab. Surely if debriefing is ethically important, this is a problem. It is unlikely that a Subject who is upset is going to turn to the printed sheet for comfort, and the fact that you've given it to him may make him reluctant to try to talk to you.

It doesn't matter if the text of your debriefing has received the IRB seal of approval if no one reads it.

The Demand for Multiple Studies in a Single Article

Half a century ago, Festinger and Carlsmith's "Cognitive Consequences of Forced Compliance" (1959) and Aronson and Mills's "The Effect of Severity of Initiation on Liking for a Group" (1959) appeared in the top journal in the field and electrified the social psychological world. Each of these papers reported just one experiment. They stimulated lines of research that continued for decades, and they are still widely regarded as being among the most important articles in the history of the field. Nowadays the top journals typically require that an article report a whole series of studies. And hiring and promotion committees at top universities typically require a whole series of articles to make an offer or to grant tenure. I tell my students, "If you did a study like Festinger and Carlsmith that was the talk of the field, you'd be in demand." They tell me, "No I wouldn't because it would never *be* the talk of the field because it would never get published." And I can't honestly tell them they're wrong, though I wish I could.

Some journals, like *Psychological Science* and *Social and Personality Science*, have introduced a special category of short articles describing single studies, and I think this is a wonderful idea and should be encouraged. Studies that report a new phenomenon or a new kind of test of a theory—studies that are *news*—deserve quick publication. If a student has a great idea she should not have to grow old before she can tell people about it. Of course, the idea may not stand the test of time; another researcher may follow it up with research that demonstrates a convincing alternative explanation. I suppose the idea behind the multiple-experiment paper was that the hypothesis would be so thoroughly tested that no alternative explanation would be plausible, that it *would* stand the test of time. But I don't see much evidence that the multiple-study articles are any more definitive than the old single-study articles. Experiments 2, 3, and 4 are often second-rate attempts to bolster the original hypothesis, not serious efforts to test alternatives. Karl Popper notwithstanding, nobody wants to disconfirm his own hypothesis before even submitting it (Ellsworth, 2004). Also, debates among researchers about the meaning of empirical results are often among the most fascinating and provocative articles in the field.

Journal editors and reviewers should recognize that some studies require more time and effort than others. If you do a Tversky and Kahneman-type study in which Subjects read paragraph-long puzzles and all the Subjects can be run in one session, it makes some sense for reviewers to ask for more than one study, to demand more precision. Likewise if a study can be run in a few days on the Web, a researcher could easily run 10 of these studies in the time it took Elliot to run one. Requiring multiple studies for a single publication biases the field toward studies that can be run quickly in groups or on the Web, and against carefully crafted high-impact studies. Any policy that limits the available methods that can produce publishable articles is scientifically dubious, especially when these methods create a social psychology that has nothing social about it. Editors and reviewers should not require multiple studies for high-impact studies with Subjects run individually, for studies that involve extensive pilot research, for cross-cultural studies in which Subjects are run in more than one country, or for field research that requires a lot of preparation to establish the context and get permission. They should not force the multiple-study standard on research for which it is not suitable because to do so would lead to—*has* led to—a narrowing of the methods we use (see Cialdini, 2009).

The demand for multiple studies has several bad consequences. First, it discourages pilot work. Any Subject hour that will not be part of the publication seems like a Subject hour wasted. Some of us are clever enough to package our pilot research as "Study 1," and that sometimes works, but it is somewhat of an embarrassing charade. I would rather talk about the pilot research as *pilot* research (if my IRB would let me) and explain how through trial and error I finally managed to come up with a situation that meant what I wanted it to and mattered to the Subjects.

Second, studies in which Subjects are run individually are increasingly rare. Instead, Subjects arrive in groups and are escorted to cubicles where they fill out questionnaires or work on a computer. This is efficient. The instructions and the debriefing are printed. If the experiment is online, the data are instantly ready for analysis; we don't have to be bothered with marginal comments or other extraneous information that might reveal what the Subjects are thinking. One of the central tenets of our field is that people's behavior is strongly affected by their immediate situation, and we should worry that the "situations" we study are increasingly limited to isolation booths. The result is multiple-study articles in an ever-narrowing range of situations.

Occasionally my students do run Subjects individually, and they find these studies strangely interesting. They often come and talk to me after they've run a Subject to tell me how it went. They like it. It's actually fun! They wish they could do more of it. But they really want to get a job.

One consequence of low-impact experiments is that it often takes many more Subjects to get a significant effect. Festinger once told Carlsmith that any study with more than 20 Subjects per cell was not worth doing, because any effect worth bothering about would show up as significant with 20 Subjects, and if you needed more it probably meant that your independent variable wasn't very powerful. Festinger and Carlsmith (1959) had 20 Subjects per cell and some of the early high-impact studies had even fewer. The pilot work took a lot of time, but running the actual experiment took far less time than it would with the larger number of cases typical of today's research. When few Subjects are paying attention, it takes many more to show a significant effect.

The Emphasis on Measuring "Process"

The way the dissonance theorists and other Lewinians reasoned was typically like this: Figure out a situation that would arouse dissonance, then figure out what the Subjects would do to reduce it. Or figure out a situation that would motivate the Subjects to seek social comparison, then create an opportunity for them to seek the company of others and see if they do so. Devise control conditions in which the dissonance or need for social comparison was minimal, but everything else was the same. Run pilot tests to make sure that the independent variable actually did what it was supposed to and the dependent variable measure actually captured the predicted response. There were no direct measures of dissonance or the need for social comparison; the process was inferred. If the theoretical predictions were supported across numerous studies by numerous researchers, their confidence that dissonance or social comparison was really the underlying process was strengthened. Nobody tried to measure dissonance directly.

Richard Nisbett and Tim Wilson (1977) began their classic article about the fallibility of verbal reports with the problem of trying to measure dissonance directly: The Subjects are not conscious of the dissonance or their motivation to reduce it. When asked why they behaved as they did, they came up with plausible answers, but their answers were false. We know from the results that the treatment affected their behavior, but they didn't. When debriefed, they acknowledged that cognitive dissonance was an interesting idea and may even have influenced some Subjects, but not them. My college honors thesis was actually a test of Subjects' explanations of their behavior in the Aronson and Carlsmith performance expectancy experiment (1962). Almost all Subjects had ready explanations, and the vast majority of the explanations did not involve anything like dissonance. This study was never accepted for publication because reviewers unanimously agreed that psychological variables like dissonance could not be measured directly, but must be inferred from the theoretical relationship between the independent and dependent variables. Because Subjects are unable to give a valid answer, asking them about their experience of dissonance is futile. Subjects may also be unwilling to give a valid answer if it makes them look stupid or selfish. It's not necessarily that they consciously lie to the experimenter; more often they deceive themselves (Tavris & Aronson, 2007). Verbal measures are not direct measures of the variables we care about. "There is no necessary correspondence between what the Subjects feel, expect, believe, or do, and what they say" (Aronson et al., 1990, p. 263). We all know this, yet increasingly we require measures of inner processes even though their validity is dubious (Baumeister et al., 2007).

Not all measures of processes (or mechanisms, as they are sometimes called) are verbal. Researchers have used physiological measures, hormone assays, and functional magnetic resonance imaging (fMRI) as measures of inner processes. Although these are better in some ways, they are not simply passive, unobtrusive measures; they may *influence* the process they are supposed to measure. Polygraphs and fMRI scanners are highly salient features of the situation, often frightening. Drawing blood or requiring the Subject to provide spit samples can be the most memorable events that happen in the experiment, much more noticeable than the independent variable. The most elegant methods of getting at underlying mechanisms are often experimental designs that include control groups in which the hypothesized process is impossible. Differences between these groups and the experimental group demonstrate that the process *is* operating in the experimental group. Or the hypothesized process can be established in pilot work so that there is no need to interfere with the flow of the actual experiment by inserting a "direct" (and often obtrusive) measure of the process. If pilot work shows that the treatment arouses fear and no other emotions, then there is no need to ask the real Subjects how scared they are (and to tip them off that what you are interested in is fear).

The demand for process measures has had several unfortunate consequences. First, Baumeister et al. (2007) argue that process measures have tended to replace behavioral measures, not to supplement or explain them. Second, because editors and reviewers want "valid" measures of process, researchers increasingly look for process measures that have been used in previous publications and, therefore, have passed editorial muster: If this measure was acceptable in a recent *JPSP* article, then the reviewers can't criticize it in mine. In any given set of messages sent out over the social and personality psychology listservs, there is usually at least one asking for an off-the-shelf measure of some variable—regret, altruism, adherence to gender norms, whatever. The old measure is used in a new context and the authors bolster their claims by citing the alpha level reported in the original study. This is not good science, not in social psychology. As Richard Gonzalez and I observed, "in social psychology our measures are not valid or invalid *per se*, but are valid or invalid in a particular context ... We are generally interested in situational variables, we expect our measures to be responsive to the particular situation, and therefore we should not expect to find measures that are universally valid or applicable" (Ellsworth & Gonzalez, 2003, p. 35). An alpha level is not an intrinsic property of a scale but is affected by context.

Elliot designed new measures for every experiment. We have now gone to the opposite extreme, using old measures even when they are very unlikely to be valid any more. The Modern Racism Scale is not modern at all. Evolutionary psychologists who study the qualities that men and women look for in a spouse still use measures that were created over 50 years ago (Hill, 1945). Yet in the past 50 years there have been huge changes in race and gender roles and attitudes, and it is ridiculous to assume that these measures measure what they used to. Even pictures go out of date. In pilot testing, I found that commonly used pictures of emotional facial expressions (Matsumoto & Ekman, 1988) no longer elicited high levels of agreement. Just as the method must fit the question, the measure must fit the particular context and the particular sample.

A third unfortunate consequence of the insistence on measures of inner processes is the proliferation of manipulation checks. To demonstrate that the treatment produces the hypothesized mediating process, researchers now feel that they have to measure that process during the actual experiment. Unless the manipulation check is not subject to conscious control (as in some biological measures) or the Subject is unaware that anything is being measured (as in some observational measures), the manipulation check is another event in the Subject's experience, an event that can change the very processes the researcher cares about. Seeing a funny movie and then doing a remote associates task is not the same experience as seeing a funny move, rating how happy/sad/anxious/angry you are, and then doing a remote associates task. Thinking about an emotion can change the emotion (Keltner, Locke, & Audrain, 1993). If there are several independent variables, the situation becomes cluttered with distractions, and possibly with clues to the experimenter's hypothesis. If Subjects are paying any attention at all, they will notice the manipulation checks. Delaying the manipulation checks until the end raises other problems. New events and measures have intervened, which may affect the manipulation check. If Subjects have succeeded in reducing cognitive dissonance, they cannot tell you about it; if the Subjects were frustrated by the remote associates task, they will no longer report happiness. Asking Subjects to report what they felt earlier leads to unreliable answers.

Most measures of psychological processes are self-reports. Given what we know about the biases and weakness of self-report measures (Aronson & Carlsmith, 1968; Aronson et al., 1990; Freedman, 1969; Nisbett & Wilson, 1977; Schwarz, 1999; and many others), it is fair to ask whether we are actually measuring process at all, or whether the substitution of "process" measures for behavioral measures has actually diminished the validity and the explanatory power of our research. As Jerome Kagan (2007), summarizing the evidence, concluded that verbal reports correspond only modestly at best to the behaviors or emotions described. (See also Baumeister et al., 2007.) We know that different people interpret the same question in different ways, that the answers to questions differ greatly depending on the context, and that people are often unable to accurately describe what they have thought or felt, what they have done, what they would think or feel, or what they would do, or why. We have known for decades that multiple methods are necessary to assess a psychological construct (Campbell & Fiske, 1959), but we rarely use them.

Baumeister and his colleagues (2007) claim that "data on behavior without inner processes are regarded as unpublishable by most journals" (p. 401) and report a case in which a reviewer criticized a behavioral study on the grounds that it "lacked psychological variables." I hope this is an exaggeration, and I know that occasionally high-impact studies do sneak by, but the general trend is clear. Not too long ago Larissa Tiedens and I submitted two manuscripts about the influence of power on perceived and experienced emotions. One included (1) a laboratory study in which Subjects were assigned to high- and low-power roles with all the rich trappings of authority for the powerful person and a small shabby corner for the low-power person, (2) a study of bosses and subordinates at an actual company, and (3) a beeper study of people's emotional responses to interactions with more or less powerful others. The other was the standard boring vignette study. The vignette study was published without major complaints (Tiedens, Ellsworth, & Mesquita, 2000). The other study, with three different methods and high-impact settings, was repeatedly rejected and eventually we gave up.

The reasons given for this and similar rejections is typically that the events (on the independent variable side) and the behavioral measures (on the dependent variable side) are ambiguous. They may have multiple meanings, so we cannot be sure of the underlying process. The reviewer speculates that we may have created embarrassment, not dissonance; may have measured aggression, not obedience. But if ambiguity is the issue, why on earth do we trust *verbal* manipulations and measures, where the ambiguity has been studied and documented for decades? We know that hypothetical situations are often poor predictors of what people will do in real situations (Baumeister et al., 2007; Freedman, 1969; Kagan, 2007). We know that questionnaire responses are not a hotline to true underlying psychological processes. So why do we accept the verbal methods and reject the behavioral methods when the only difference between them is that the flaws of the verbal methods are better documented?

The way to validate a method is through triangulation and systematic replication, through pilot testing, and through consideration of the method in the context of the whole study. If we want to use frowning as a measure of anger, we establish *convergent validity* by showing that it is associated with independent variables known to produce anger (such as being insulted or restrained) and with other dependent variables that reflect anger, such as yelling, threatening, or even rating oneself as angry. And to establish *discriminant validity* we have to show that frowning docs not occur with sorrow and mental effort, or, and this is very important, that sorrow and mental effort are extremely implausible in the context of our experiment, and anger is plausible. The same is true if we measure the frown by means of an electrode attached to the corrugator muscle. The same is true if we measure anger with a rating scale: If the Subject is feeling some other negative emotion, for example, and the only negative scale you provide is an anger scale, she can only indicate that she is feeling bad by rating herself as angry. Many of our methods are not valid or invalid per se, but could be perfectly valid in a particular context (Ellsworth & Gonzalez, 2003). No single method can establish the truth of a phenomenon (no matter how many studies are done using the same method) because the phenomenon is confounded with the method (Campbell & Fiske, 1959).

Systematic replication of this sort cannot be done in a single study, but that is no reason that single studies should not be published. Establishing the possibility of a new phenomenon is an important contribution. Extending the generality of a phenomenon by testing it in an entirely different context is an important contribution. Differentiating this phenomenon from another or ruling out alternative explanations is an important contribution. If the hypothesis is interesting enough, systematic replication attempts will follow.

BACK TO THE FUTURE

Although low-impact, computerized, asocial studies are on the rise, the Lewinian tradition is by no means dead. Some social psychologists still manage to conduct beautiful, high-impact studies that engage the Subjects and the readers. Dov Cohen and his colleagues studied the differences in aggressive tendencies in Northerners and Southerners by creating a situation in which the Subject had to walk down a narrow corridor where a confederate was searching the back of a file drawer pulled all the way out so that the corridor was blocked. To let the Subject get by, the confederate had to push the file drawer back in. When the Subject came back down the corridor, the drawer was out again. The confederate grudgingly pushed it in, and as the Subject passed by, glanced at him and muttered, "Asshole!" Southerners responded with anger, Northerners did not (Cohen, Nisbett, Bowdle, & Schwarz, 1996). Dacher Keltner and his colleagues brought groups of fraternity pledges and more senior (high-status) fraternity members to the lab, assigned each one a set of initials (A. D., H. F., etc.) and had them tease each other with nicknames and stories about each other based on the initials. The teasing was generally insulting and hostile, but the pledges held back when it was their turn to tease the high-status members (Keltner, Young, Heerey, Oemig, & Monarch, 1998).

And, of course, Elliot himself has kept the tradition alive. In a study designed to encourage students to conserve water, the experimenter stopped students on their way into the shower room at the gym and asked them to sign a petition promoting water conservation and then asked them a few questions about their own water use. The hypothesis was that they would try to resolve the inconsistency between their endorsement (proconservation) and their past behavior (wasteful) by using water more carefully. A second experimenter, stationed unobtrusively in the shower room with a stopwatch, found that these students took much shorter showers than the students in the control groups (Dickerson, Thibodeau, Aronson, & Miller, 1992).

So it is not impossible to do the kind of research that made Elliot famous. All of these studies were approved by their IRBs and all were published in high-quality journals. As researchers we should do more of this kind of research, and as editors and reviewers we should encourage it, because—as Elliot would say—it is beautiful, because it is rare, and, most important, because it answers questions that cannot be answered in any other way.

NOTE

1. Following the researchers of the golden age of high-impact research, and encouraged by Roediger's excellent article (2004), I refer to the people we study as *Subjects* rather than *participants*. In the typical modern experiment where the Subject works alone at a computer or sits anonymously in a group filling out questionnaires the term *participant* seems inappropriate.

REFERENCES

Aronson, E. (2010). *Not by chance alone: My life as a social psychologist*. New York: Basic Books.

Aronson, E. (2008). *The social animal* (10th ed.). New York: Worth/Freeman. (Original work published 1972)

Aronson, E. (1999). Adventures in social psychology: Roots, branches, and sticky new leaves. In A. Rodrigues & R. Levine (Eds.), *Reflections on 100 years of experimental social psychology* (pp. 82–113). New York: Basic Books.

Aronson, E. (2007). An autobiography. In G. Lindzey & M. Runyan (Eds.), *The history of psychology in autobiography* (Vol. 9, pp. 3–41). Washington, DC: APA Books.

Aronson, E., & Carlsmith, J. M. (1962). Performance expectancy as a determinant of actual performance. *Journal of Abnormal and Social Psychology, 65*, 187–182.

Aronson, E., & Carlsmith, J. M. (1968). Experimentation in social psychology. In G. Lindzey & E. Aronson (Eds.), *Handbook of social psychology* (2nd ed., Vol. 2, pp. 1–79). Reading, MA: Addison-Wesley.

Aronson, E., Ellsworth, P. C., Carlsmith, J. M., & Gonzales, M. H. (1990). *Methods of research in social psychology*. New York: McGraw-Hill.

Aronson, E., & Mills, J. (1959). The effect of severity of initiation on liking for a group. *Journal of Abnormal and Social Psychology, 59*, 177–181.

Asch, S. (1951). Effects of group pressure upon the modification and distortion of judgments. In H. Guetzkow (Ed.), *Groups, leadership, and men* (pp. 177–190). Pittsburgh, PA: Carnegie Press.

Ax, A. F. (1953). The physiological differentiation between fear and anger in humans. *Psychosomatic Medicine, 15*, 433–442.

Baumeister, R. F., Vohs, K. D., & Funder, D. (2007). Psychology as a science of self-reports and finger movements: Whatever happened to actual behavior? *Perspectives on Psychological Science, 2*, 396–403.

Brehm, J. W., & Cohen, A. R. (1962). *Explorations in cognitive dissonance*. New York: John Wiley & Sons.

Campbell, D. T., & Fiske, D. W. (1959). Convergent and discriminant validity by the multitrait-multimethod matrix. *Psychological Bulletin, 56*, 81–105.

Carlsmith, J. M., Ellsworth, P. C., & Aronson, E. (1976). *Methods of research in social psychology*. Reading, MA: Addison Wesley.

Cialdini, R. B. (2009). We have to break up. *Perspectives on Psychological Science, 4*, 5–6.

Cohen, D., Nisbett, R. E., Bowdle, B. F., & Schwarz, N. (1996). Insult, aggression, and the Southern culture of honor: An "experimental ethnography." *Journal of Personality and Social Psychology, 70*, 945–960.

Dickerson, C. A., Thibodeau, R., Aronson, E., & Miller, D. (1992). Using cognitive dissonance to encourage water conservation. *Journal of Applied Social Psychology, 22*, 841–854.

Doob, A. N., Carlsmith, J. M., Freedman, J. L., Landauer, T. K., & Tom, S., Jr. (1969). Effects of initial selling price on subsequent sales. *Journal of Personality and Social Psychology, 11*, 345–350.

Dutton, D. G., & Aron, A. P. (1974). Some evidence for heightened sexual attraction under conditions of high anxiety. *Journal of Personality and Social Psychology, 30*, 510–517.

Ellsworth, P. C. (2004). Clapping with both hands: Numbers, people, and simultaneous hypotheses. In M. R. Banaji & D. Prentice (Eds.), *Perspectivism in social psychology: The yin and yang of scientific progress* (pp. 261–273). Washington, DC: APA Books.

Ellsworth, P. C., & Gonzalez, R. (2003). Questions and comparisons: Methods of research in social psychology. In M. Hogg & J. Cooper (Eds.), *Sage handbook of social psychology* (pp. 24–42). New York and Oxford: Oxford University Press.

Festinger, L., & Carlsmith, J. M. (1959). Cognitive consequences of forced compliance. *Journal of Abnormal and Social Psychology, 58*, 203–210.

Festinger, L., Riecken, H. W., & Schachter, S. (1956). *When prophecy fails.* Minneapolis: University of Minnesota Press.

Freedman, J. L. (1969). Role-playing: Psychology by consensus. *Journal of Personality and Social Psychology, 13*, 107–114.

Hill, R. (1945). Campus values in mate selection. *Journal of Home Economics, 37*, 554–558.

Kagan, J. (2007). A trio of concerns. *Perspectives on Psychological Science, 2*, 361–376.

Keltner, D., Locke, K. D., & Audrain, P. C. (1993). The influence of attributions on the relevance of negative emotions to personal satisfaction. *Personality and Social Psychology Bulletin, 19*, 21–29.

Keltner, D., Young, R. C., Heerey, E. A., Oemig, C., & Monarch, N. D. (1998). Teasing in hierarchical and intimate relations. *Journal of Personality and Social Psychology, 75*, 1231–1247.

Latané, B., & Darley, J. (1968). Group inhibition of bystander intervention in emergencies. *Journal of Personality and Social Psychology, 10*, 215–221.

Lindzey, G., & Aronson, E. (Eds.). (1969). *Handbook of social psychology* (2nd ed.). Reading, MA: Addison-Wesley.

Matsumoto, D., & Ekman, P. (1988). *Japanese and Caucasian Facial Expressions of Emotion and Neutral Faces.* Available from paulekman.com/research-producrs.php

McGuire, W. J. (1969). Attitudes. In G. Lindzey & E. Aronson (Eds.). *Handbook of social psychology* (2nd ed., Vol. 3, pp. 136–344). Reading, MA: Addison-Wesley.

McGuire, W. J. (1973). The yin and yang of progress in social psychology: Seven koan. *Journal of Personality and Social Psychology, 26,* 446–456.

Milgram, S. (1963) Behavioral study of obedience. *Journal of Abnormal and Social Psychology, 67,* 371–378.

Nisbett, R. E., & Wilson, T. D. (1977). Telling more than we can know: Verbal reports of mental processes. *Psychological Review, 84,* 231–259.

Raudenbush, S. W., & Bryk, A. S. (2001). *Hierarchical linear models: Applications and data analysis methods.* Thousand Oaks, CA: Sage.

Regan, D. T., Williams, M., & Sparling, S. (1972). Voluntary expiation of guilt: A field experiment. *Journal of Personality and Social Psychology, 24,* 42–45.

Roediger, R. (2004). What should they be called? *Psychological Science, 17,* 5, 46–48.

Ross, L. D., Greene, D., & House, P. (1977). The "false consensus" effect: An egocentric bias in social perception and attribution processes. *Journal of Experimental Social Psychology, 13,* 279–301.

Schachter, S. (1959). *The psychology of affiliation: Experimental studies of the sources of gregariousness.* Stanford, CA: Stanford University Press.

Schwarz, N. (1999). Self-reports. *American Psychologist, 54,* 93–105.

Sommers, S. (2007). Race and the decision-making of jurors. *Journal of Personality and Social Psychology, 90,* 597–612.

Tavris, C., & Aronson, E. (2007). *Mistakes were made (but not by me).* New York: Harcourt.

Tiedens, L. Z., Ellsworth, P. C., & Mesquita, B. (2000). Stereotypes about sentiments and status: Emotional expectations for high- and low-status group members. *Personality and Social Psychology Bulletin, 26,* 560–574.

Webb, E. J., Campbell, D. T., Schwartz, D., & Sechrest, L. (1966). *Unobtrusive measures: Nonreactive research in the social sciences.* Chicago: Rand-McNally.

Whiting, J. W. M. (1941). *Becoming a Kwoma.* New Haven, CT: Yale University Press.

II

Cognitive Dissonance and Its Descendants

6

DECISIONS, ACTION, AND NEUROSCIENCE

A Contemporary Perspective on Cognitive Dissonance

Eddie Harmon-Jones

Texas A&M University

I first got to "know" Elliot Aronson through his writings, particularly his books, *The Social Animal* (1988) and *Methods of Research in Social Psychology* (Aronson, Ellsworth, Carlsmith, & Gonzales, 1990), and his papers on cognitive dissonance theory (Aronson, 1968, 1969, 1992; Aronson & Carlsmith, 1962; Aronson & Mills, 1959). His writing conveyed a contagious passion for psychological research. So when I first met Elliot in 1997 at the dissonance conference in Arlington, Texas, I told him, "I think you're the best writer in psychology." He leaned over and replied, "You know what, I agree with you." We shared a big laugh, the first of many. Each time I see Elliot, he makes me laugh.

His writing on dissonance inspired me to read everything I could about the theory. And at the time I was reading about dissonance theory, around 1990, it seemed that much of the field had become convinced that the cognitive and behavioral changes caused by "dissonance" manipulations were not due to a motivation to resolve cognitive inconsistency (Festinger, 1957) or self inconsistency (Aronson, 1968). The field appeared to have for the most part accepted that these effects were due to a motivation to avoid feeling personally responsible for producing an aversive consequence (Cooper & Fazio, 1984) or due to a motivation to minimize a general self-image threat (Steele, 1988). But I had the nagging feeling that inconsistency alone was sufficient to cause the cognitive and behavioral changes attributed to dissonance. I believed, along with Leon Festinger (1957), that if I were to walk in the rain and not get wet, I would experience dissonance. And in the remainder of this chapter in honor of Elliot, I will explain why, and will also summarize what we have learned about cognitive dissonance using the tools of neuroscience.

DOES INCONSISTENCY UNDERLIE DISSONANCE OUTCOMES?

Hypocrisy Experiments

A major contribution to the dissonance literature made by Elliot and colleagues was the hypocrisy experimental paradigm (Aronson, 1992, 1999; Aronson, Fried, & Stone, 1991; Dickerson, Thibodeau, Aronson, & Miller, 1992; Fried & Aronson, 1995; Stone, Aronson, Crain, Winslow, & Fried, 1994; Thibodeau & Aronson, 1992). Not only does this paradigm present a novel way to test theoretical predictions with important real-world significance, but it also demonstrates that dissonance can occur even when participants engage in proattitudinal behavior that has positive consequences. This is important because a major revision of dissonance theory, the "new look" by Joel Cooper and Russell Fazio (1984), posited that inconsistency was neither necessary nor sufficient to motivate the cognitive and behavioral changes found in dissonance experiments (see Cooper, this volume). Instead, they proposed that for dissonance to occur, individuals must engage in behavior that has the perceived potential to cause an irrevocable unwanted consequence. Results of several experiments reviewed by Cooper and Fazio (1984) suggested that their new look was correct.

Consider the experiment by Joel Cooper and Stephen Worchel (1970). They posited that individuals who are provided little justification for lying to another person would not experience dissonance if the other person did not believe them, that is, if there were no aversive consequences. To test this idea, they conducted a modified version of the classic experiment by Festinger and Carlsmith (1959), in which participants were paid $1 or $20 to lie to another person. Festinger and Carlsmith found that participants paid $1 (given little justification) for lying to the other person changed their attitudes to be more consistent with their behavior; participants paid $20 did not, because the money justified the counterattitudinal behavior. Cooper and Worchel (1970) suggested that participants in the low-justification ($1) condition in the original experiment changed their attitudes not because of cognitive inconsistency, but instead because they felt personally responsible for producing the aversive consequence of convincing another person to believe that she or he was about to participate in an exciting experiment. Cooper and Worchel found that when low-justification participants were led to believe that they did not convince another person that a boring task was interesting, they subsequently did not rate the task as more interesting. Other experiments have replicated these results by finding that when participants believe that their counterattitudinal statements do not persuade others, they do not change their attitudes (e.g., Cooper, Zanna, & Goethals, 1974; Goethals & Cooper, 1972; Hoyt, Henley, & Collins, 1972; Nel, Helmreich, & Aronson, 1969).

However, it is important to note that the evidentiary basis for the aversive consequences model relies solely on the production of no attitude change in conditions in which aversive consequences do not occur. Because this is a null effect, several alternative explanations can be offered. For example, in these past experiments, participants were encouraged to produce lengthy counterattitudinal statements. These statements may have reduced the likelihood of detecting dissonance-related attitude change, as research has demonstrated that the length of participants' statements is inversely related to the amount of dissonance-related attitude change (Beauvois & Joule, 1996, 1999; Rabbie, Brehm, & Cohen, 1959). This inverse relation may result because longer statements allow for more consonant cognitions that support the counterattitudinal behavior and, hence, reduce the dissonance. Thus, the overall level of dissonance in these experiments may have been rather low, and the addition of aversive consequences was necessary to produce sufficient dissonance to motivate attitude change. Another explanation for the past failures to find attitude change in nonaversive consequences experiments is that dissonance was aroused but reduced in a manner other than attitude change in the no-aversive-consequences conditions. Other alternative explanations have been presented (Harmon-Jones, 1999).

As noted earlier, however, the hypocrisy paradigm is important because it suggests that dissonance can occur even when individuals produce positive consequences, thus supporting the idea that cognitive inconsistency still arouses dissonance. In one experiment representative of the hypocrisy paradigm (Stone et al., 1994), participants either made a persuasive speech about AIDS and safe sex in front of a video camera (allegedly to find the best communicator for a message to be presented about safe sex to high school students) or developed a persuasive message but did not deliver the speech to a video camera. The researchers also manipulated the salience of participants' past failures to use condoms. Participants were either made aware of their past failures to use condoms by publicly writing about instances when they had failed to do so or were not made aware of their past failures. Jeff Stone and colleagues (1994) reasoned that if participants made the pro-attitudinal speech and were then made aware of their past failures to practice what they preached, they would experience dissonance and would attempt to reduce their dissonance by modifying their future behavior. In support of their predictions, participants who were induced to feel hypocritical purchased more condoms than did participants in the other conditions.

Is Inconsistency the Motivating Force in Other Dissonance Experiments?
Although the hypocrisy experiments by Elliot and colleagues provided evidence for inconsistency as a motivating force in dissonance outcomes, they used a new—and very creative—paradigm, and thus left readers to wonder whether inconsistency was a motivating force in the most commonly used framework: the induced compliance paradigm. In addition, Joel Cooper (1992) had taken issue with the hypocrisy experiments, writing, "For some people, acting hypocritically may be devastating to a central core of the self-concept and thus be an extremely aversive event" (p. 322). Although this statement seems to confuse producing an aversive consequence with causing oneself to feel negative affect (i.e., dissonance), it demonstrates that some scientists expressed concerns about the hypocrisy experiments (which I did not share). Nonetheless, the question still remained: Could inconsistency itself motivate dissonance-related outcomes such as attitude change in a standard dissonance paradigm? If this question were not addressed, then one could logically posit that the major experimental paradigms used in dissonance research were producing outcomes driven by a motivation to avoid an aversive consequence rather than a motivation to resolve cognitive inconsistencies.

One morning, Jack Brehm and I were discussing how to create an induced-compliance paradigm in which participants would not produce aversive consequences. We were searching for a minimal-induced-compliance paradigm. We stumbled onto the idea of using a cover story that would tell participants that the study was about influences on memory. During the midst of this discussion over cups of terrible coffee from the Kansas University psychology department, we had to take a bathroom break. While taking this break, we discussed having participants drink an unpleasant tasting beverage while thinking that they would have to recall characteristics of the beverage. In true induced-compliance paradigm form, participants would be asked to write that they liked the beverage, so as to produce a counterattitudinal statement. But our cover story would lead them to believe that the writing was only done to see whether it affected their memory. In fact, before they wrote the statement, we would tell participants that they should throw the statement in the trash once it was written. This would ensure that their counterattitudinal behavior was conducted in private and thus did not produce an aversive consequence.

We piloted the experiment, making sure that the participants disliked the beverage (they did, extremely so), making sure that experimenters remained blind to the beverage type and choice manipulation, and making sure that participants believed that their behavior was truly private. (With pilot participants, we discovered that if no other trash was in the trash can, participants would tell us in debriefing that they thought we would retrieve their statements from the trash, so we added wadded-up "confederate" statements to the trash can. (See Ellsworth's chapter, this volume, for a discussion of the importance of piloting experimental procedures.) Once everything was in order, we conducted the experiment and found that in keeping with predictions supporting an inconsistency model, participants given high choice to write the counterattitudinal statement changed their attitudes to become more consistent with their behavior: They convinced themselves that they liked the beverage better.

Subsequent experiments replicated this basic effect, using different attitude objects such as a boring passage (Harmon-Jones, Brehm, Greenberg, Simon, & Nelson, 1996, Experiment 2). We also used a positive attitude object and had participants write that they disliked the object toward which they previously held very positive attitudes (Harmon-Jones, 2000). We also measured arousal (skin conductance) and found that this counterattitudinal behavior increased arousal (Harmon-Jones et al., 1996, Experiment 3), consistent with past research using the standard induced compliance paradigm (Elkin & Leippe, 1986). Finally, we measured self-reported negative affect and found that this minimal-induced-compliance paradigm also created the subjective experience of negative affect (Harmon-Jones, 2000), consistent with past research using the standard induced–compliance paradigm (Elliot & Devine, 1994).

These experiments strongly suggested that a motivation to reduce cognitive inconsistency does indeed underlie the attitude change observed in induced-compliance experiments. We hypothesized that the aversive state of dissonance resulted because behavior, including verbal behavior, must, in general, be in accord with one's perception of reality. After all, if behavior is not in accord with perceptions of the environment, an organism's most basic welfare is threatened. Hence, people feel uneasy when they say something that is not true, even though the perception (of the original attitude object in our experiments) may be of little importance. The behavior causes dissonance because the person knows that behavior does not match perception, even when no aversive consequence follows that behavior. The aversive state of dissonance then motivates attitude change, so that perception now matches behavior.

Cognitive Inconsistency or Self-Concept Inconsistency?

The aforementioned experiments suggest that cognitive inconsistency even in the absence of aversive consequences can arouse dissonance. However, another question arose. Does the inconsistency need to involve self-conceptions of rationality, morality, or competence as Elliot (Aronson, 1992) has posited? Or might more simple cognitive inconsistencies arouse dissonance? To return to Festinger's example, were I to walk in a downpour and not get wet, would I experience dissonance? In one of the minimal dissonance experiments just reviewed, measures of various forms of self-reported negative affect were included to address this question. If a self-concept violation were motivating dissonance reduction, then we might expect the dissonance-arousing event not only to increase self-reported discomfort, but also to decrease state self-esteem. The results, however, revealed that although the dissonance manipulation increased discomfort, it did not affect state self-esteem (Harmon-Jones, 2000). These results suggest inconsistencies implicating the self-concept are not necessary to arouse dissonance.

One could quibble with whether these self-reported affect and self-esteem results legitimately support such a statement. Although the self-consistency revision is quite similar to the original theory, it restricts dissonance processes to organisms with self-concepts, thus excluding most nonhuman animals and humans under age 2. However, experiments demonstrating that dissonance effects occur in white rats, which presumably lack a self-concept (Lawrence & Festinger, 1962), contradict this revision. In addition, the self-consistency revision restricts dissonance processes to organisms whose self-concepts become accessible as a standard for comparison whenever they encounter self-discrepancies. This restriction would probably omit several situations, as it does not seem plausible that a self-concept would become accessible each and every time an individual encounters a cognitive discrepancy.

In addition, one of the primary predictions derived from the self-consistency revision is that individuals with high self-esteem should respond with more dissonance reduction than individuals with low self-esteem, because dissonance experiments induce individuals to act in ways discrepant from positive views of themselves as moral, rational, or competent people. Studies testing this prediction have produced mixed results: Some showed that individuals with high self-esteem showed greater attitude change, some showed that individuals with low self-esteem showed greater attitude change, and some found no differences between self-esteem groups (see Stone, 2003, for a review). Therefore, the experience of dissonance and the engagement in dissonance-reducing activities does not appear to be limited to discrepancies involving the self-concept.

I suspect, however, that the self-concept has the power to increase the magnitude of dissonance, particularly when the self-concept is in the forefront of working memory (see Stone, this volume). That is, when the self-concept is accessible, inconsistencies that implicate the self likely generate more dissonance than inconsistencies that do not. Given these concerns about the self-consistency model, it seems that several critical theoretical issues remain. Which inconsistencies arouse dissonance? And why does inconsistency arouse dissonance?

THE ACTION-BASED MODEL OF DISSONANCE

The action-based model of cognitive dissonance was proposed to answer the aforementioned questions (Harmon-Jones, 1999). This model concurs with other areas of psychological research in proposing that perceptions and cognitions can serve as action tendencies (Berkowitz, 1984; Gibson, 1966, 1979; McArthur & Baron, 1983). It further proposes that *dissonance between cognitions evokes an aversive state because it has the potential to interfere with effective and unconflicted action*. Dissonance reduction, by bringing cognitions into line with behavioral commitments, serves the function of facilitating the execution of effective and unconflicted action (see also Jones & Gerard, 1967).

The action-based model proposes both a proximal and a distal motivation underlying dissonance processes. The *proximal* motive for reducing dissonance is to reduce or eliminate the negative affective state of dissonance. The *distal* motive is the need for effective and unconflicted action.

Past presentations of the theory of cognitive dissonance have referred to two different constructs as "cognitive dissonance." One is the inconsistency between cognitions. The second is the unpleasant emotional/motivational state that occurs when a person holds two contradictory cognitions. Indeed, Festinger (1957) used the term dissonance to refer to both constructs. To better elucidate the processes of dissonance, the action-based model distinguishes between the two. The model refers to inconsistency between cognitions as *cognitive discrepancy*, and to attempts to reduce the inconsistency as *discrepancy reduction*. It refers to the unpleasant emotive state as *dissonance*, and to the reduction of the unpleasant state as *dissonance reduction*. The unpleasant emotive state of dissonance provides motivation to change one's attitudes or to engage in other discrepancy-reduction processes. As an example of this confusion of constructs, authors often refer to attitude change as dissonance reduction (Stone, 1999), even though attitude change presumably reflects changes in cognitions, or cognitive discrepancy reduction. In most experiments, it is empirically unknown whether dissonance is actually reduced (e.g., a person could change her attitude but still feel uncomfortable if the cognitive discrepancy were large enough).

According to the action-based model, after an individual makes a difficult decision, psychological processing should assist with the execution of the decision. The tendency of participants in dissonance research to view the chosen alternative more favorably and the rejected alternative more negatively after a decision—the spreading of alternatives—may help the individual to follow through, to act on the decision in a more effective manner. The induced compliance situation is just another instance of a difficult decision; in this paradigm, the person must decide whether to act in opposition to his or her attitudes.

To illustrate, consider Sylvia, who has been offered admission to two universities. One university is reputed to be more intellectually stimulating, but most of her friends are going to the other one. One university is located in a city with a pleasant climate, but the other is in a city with a more reasonable cost of living. Sylvia sees both universities as similarly attractive, although they are quite different from each other, and she must decide between them. Once Sylvia makes a decision, she will need to perform actions to follow through with her decision. She will need to relocate, take on new responsibilities, form new social relationships, and perform well socially and academically. After her decision, if she continues to see the two universities as similar in attractiveness, she may experience excess regret, which could inhibit her from effectively following through with her decision. Alternatively, if Sylvia is able to reduce dissonance so that she views the chosen university more positively and the rejected university more negatively, she will likely perform better socially and academically and be more satisfied. In short, she will be better able to convert her decision into effective action.

The action-based model views the experience and reduction of dissonance (and cognitive discrepancy) as adaptive. Of course, functional psychological processes that are adaptive in most circumstances may not be beneficial in all circumstances. Occasionally, discrepancy reduction may cause people to maintain a prolonged commitment to a harmful chosen course of action when it would be better to disengage. Still, when the action-based model predicts that dissonance processes are adaptive, it means that they benefit the organism in the majority of cases.

TESTS OF THE ACTION-BASED MODEL

Action Orientation and Spreading of Alternatives

According to the action-based model of dissonance, individuals who have made a decision are poised for action (Beckmann & Irle, 1985; Gollwitzer, 1990; Kuhl, 1984), such that they are in a mode of "getting things done." Once a decision is made, an organism should be motivated to implement that decision and to do so effectively. After all, an implemental or action-oriented mind-set yields plans for how to execute behaviors that follow from a particular decision (Gollwitzer & Bayer, 1999). When individuals are in this action-oriented state, they are more likely to work to accomplish their goals (Gollwitzer & Bayer, 1999; Gollwitzer & Sheeran, 2006).

The action-oriented state is similar to Ned Jones and Harold Gerard's (1967) concept of an unequivocal behavior orientation. The unequivocal behavior orientation "represents a commitment to action in the face of uncertainty. Such a commitment involves the risks of acting inappropriately, but such risks are assumed to be less grave on the average than the risks of hesitant or conflicted action" (p. 185). Jones and Gerard further posited, "When the time comes to act, the great advantage of having a set of coherent internally consistent dispositions is that the individual is not forced to listen to the babble of competing inner forces" (p. 181).

We proposed that the action-oriented state that follows decision making is equivalent to the state in which dissonance motivation operates and discrepancy reduction occurs (Harmon-Jones & Harmon-Jones, 2002). In other words, following a decision, particularly a difficult one, individuals should be motivated to successfully enact the decision, and this will entail changes in attitudes and other perceptions and cognitions that will assist with executing the decision. Thus, experimentally manipulating the degree of action-orientation that participants experience after they have made a decision should affect the degree of discrepancy reduction (often but not always measured as attitude change in dissonance experiments).

In our first experiment (Harmon-Jones & Harmon-Jones, 2002), we used the decision paradigm developed by Jack Brehm (1956), who asked participants to rate a number of consumer products, to choose between two that they had rated similarly, and then to rerate the products. He found that participants rated the chosen product more positively after choosing it, and the rejected product more negatively after leaving it behind. These attitudinal changes are known as spreading of alternatives because ratings of the chosen and rejected alternatives, which were close to each other prior to the decision, spread apart following the decision. In our first experiment, participants made either an easy decision or a difficult decision about which kind of physical exercise they preferred. As in past research (Brehm, 1956), the easy decision was between a lowly and highly valued alternative, whereas the difficult decision was between two highly valued but different alternatives. They then completed a questionnaire designed to manipulate their postdecision mind-sets. In the neutral mind-set condition, participants listed seven things they did in a typical day; in the action-orientation mind-set condition, participants listed seven things they could do to perform well on the physical exercise they had chosen. Participants then reevaluated the exercises. Compared to participants in the other three experimental conditions, participants who made a difficult decision and who listed what they could do to perform well demonstrated a significantly greater spreading of alternatives, as we say in dissonance parlance: They evaluated their chosen alternative more positively and their rejected alternative more negatively than did other participants.

In our second experiment, we replicated the results of the first experiment using a different manipulation of action orientation (Harmon-Jones & Harmon-Jones, 2002). In this experiment, participants assigned to the action-orientation condition thought about a project or goal that they intended to accomplish, and listed the steps that they planned to use to successfully accomplish the goal (Gollwitzer, 1990). We also included two comparison conditions. In the first, participants wrote about an ordinary day, and in the second, they wrote about a problem on which they were not yet ready to take action. The experimenter told participants that the study examined the relationship between personality characteristics and preferences for different types of psychological research. Participants first read descriptions of nine research projects (e.g., attention, health) and evaluated each one by indicating how desirable it would be to participate in a study similar to the one described. Next, the experimenter gave participants a choice to participate in one of two research projects; the two projects were ones that the participant had earlier rated positively and similarly (e.g., two 7s on a 9-point attitude scale). After this difficult decision, participants completed the above-described action-orientation manipulation. To do this, they completed open-ended "personality questionnaires" about a goal they planned to accomplish, a problem on which they were deliberating, or an ordinary day. Finally, the experimenter returned to the participant's room and told the participant she or he was interested in how familiarity with research descriptions might affect ratings of the research projects. Consequently, participants rerated the nine research descriptions. The participants in the action-orientation condition engaged in more spreading of alternatives following the difficult decision than did participants in the comparison conditions. This study provided stronger support for the action-based model because the action-orientation induction was not directly related to the decision in the experiment. In other words, the action-orientation manipulation in the present study tuned individuals toward action but was not directly tied to their recent decision about the research projects.

Correlational evidence also suggests that action-oriented processing facilitates discrepancy reduction (Beckmann & Kuhl, 1984). In this study, Jürgen Beckmann and Julius Kuhl measured participants' dispositional action orientation using Kuhl's (1980, 1984) action versus state orientation questionnaire, which measures the extent to which people who confront a decision either waiver (state orientation) or take action after deciding quickly (action orientation). For example, participants imagine finding several alternatives when they set out to buy a single item of clothing, then report whether they struggle with the decision ("I often wavier back and forth, trying to decide which I should buy") or make a decision and act relatively quickly ("I usually don't think much about it and make a quick decision"). Participants in their study were actually searching for an apartment, and they were shown information about 16 apartments. As in the standard postdecision–dissonance paradigm, participants rated the attractiveness of the apartments before and after choosing the apartment they preferred. After participants decided which of the 16 apartments they preferred, those who reported that they typically make decisions and act quickly (high dispositional action-orientation) rated their apartment choice more positively than did participants who reported that they typically struggle when making decisions (high dispositional state-orientation). Thus, Beckmann and Kuhl's (1984) correlational results are consistent with the results obtained in the previously mentioned experiments.

Neural Activity Underlying Dissonance Arousal

Our action-based model suggests which neural circuits are involved in dissonance processes, something that no previous model of dissonance has attempted. When dissonance is aroused, it evokes increased sympathetic nervous activity as measured by increased skin conductance (Elkin & Leippe, 1986; Harmon-Jones et al., 1996). Neurally, dissonance should evoke activity in the anterior circulate cortex (ACC), a structure that has been implicated in response conflict on tasks such as the Stroop task (e.g., Carter et al., 1998; Gehring, Goss, Coles, Meyer, & Donchin, 1993). Moreover, recent research has demonstrated increased ACC activity when behavior conflicts with the self-concept (Amodio et al., 2004). David Amodio and his colleagues (2004) found that when individuals who did not view themselves as prejudiced engaged in behaviors that violated their egalitarian self-concept, they evidenced increased activity in the ACC. This suggests that higher-level cognitive conflicts, the type with which dissonance theory has been most concerned, also activate the ACC. More recently, van Veen, Krug, Schooler, and Carter (2009) assessed ACC activation during an induced compliance paradigm, and found that ACC activation increased with dissonance and was significantly associated with attitude change. This prediction of dissonance yielding increased ACC activation is consistent with the action-based model, which suggests that dissonance results from the need for effective and unconflicted action. This ACC prediction could be viewed as compatible with the original theory of dissonance, but is unlikely compatible with other versions of dissonance, given their focus on inconsistencies that implicate the self-concept, a more abstract construct (e.g., self-affirmation processes) and on motivations unrelated to cognitive inconsistencies per se (e.g., the centrality of aversive consequences to dissonance arousal).

Neural Activity Associated with Discrepancy Reduction

Once dissonance is aroused, individuals are immediately motivated to reduce the cognitive inconsistency. Indeed, research has revealed that dissonance-related attitude change can occur immediately after individuals commit to a behavior and before they actually engage in that behavior (e.g., essay writing; Rabbie et al., 1959). The action-based model proposes that discrepancy reduction engages approach motivational processes, as the individual works to successfully implement the new commitment. To our knowledge, only the action-based model makes the prediction that discrepancy reduction following commitment to action involves approach motivational processes, which our model views as part of the distal motive of producing effective and unconflicted behavior.

This increase in approach motivation should activate the left frontal cortex. Several methodologies have suggested that the left and right frontal cortical regions have different motivational functions, with the left frontal region involved in approach motivational processes ("going toward"), and the right frontal region involved in withdrawal motivational processes ("going away"). For instance, Robert Robinson and colleagues (e.g., Robinson & Downhill, 1995) have observed that damage to the left frontal lobe causes depressive symptoms. They have found that for individuals with left hemisphere brain damage, the closer the lesion is to the frontal pole, the greater the depressive symptoms. Additionally, research assessing electroencephalographic (EEG) activity has found that increased left frontal cortical activation relates to state and trait approach motivation (Amodio, Master, Yee, & Taylor, 2008; Harmon-Jones, 2003; Harmon-Jones & Allen, 1997, 1998; Harmon-Jones & Sigelman, 2001; Pizzagalli, Sherwood, Henriques, & Davidson, 2005).

Based on the preceding analysis, we would predict that following commitment to a chosen course of action, left frontal cortical activity should increase relative to right cortical activity, and that this relative increase in left frontal cortical activity should be associated with the degree of change in attitudes in support of the chosen course of action: The greater the amount of left frontal cortical activity, the greater the attitude change. Indeed, past research suggests that the left frontal cortical region may be involved in approach motivational processes aimed at resolving inconsistency on tasks such as the Stroop (1935) task (MacDonald, Cohen, Stenger, & Carter, 2000; van Veen & Carter, 2006).

In one experiment, participants were randomly assigned to a low-versus high-choice condition in an induced compliance experiment. Low-choice participants were *assigned* to write an essay counter to their true attitudes, and high-choice participants were subtly induced to *choose* to write the same counterattitudinal essay. Immediately after participants began their essays, we recorded EEG activity. After participants completed their essays, we measured their attitudes toward the essay topic with which they had earlier disagreed. Results revealed that participants in the high-choice condition evidenced greater relative left frontal activation than did individuals in the low-choice condition (Harmon-Jones, Gerdjikov, & Harmon-Jones, 2008). Moreover, participants given choice over the position to take in their essays reported attitudes more consistent with their essay-writing behavior; this was not the case for participants who were assigned to write the essays. However, in this experiment, relative left frontal activation did not relate to attitudes, perhaps because the attitude measure lacked the needed sensitivity (e.g., it did not tap attitude change from precommitment, but only tapped attitudes following the commitment).

In the previous experiment, when we manipulated the psychological process of interest (commitment to a chosen course of action) and measured the proposed physiological substrate (left frontal cortical activation), commitment to a chosen course of action increased relative left frontal cortical activation (Harmon-Jones, Gerdjikov, et al., 2008). Of course, if we believe that engaging in a counterattitudinal behavior elicits attitude change *because* it causes greater relative left frontal cortical activation, we can strengthen our causal argument by manipulating the physiology and measuring the outcome of interest, in this case, attitude change. In short, if we believe that a given physiological process mediates the relation between an experimental manipulation and a dependent variable, we can make a stronger case by manipulating the proposed mediator directly, and measuring the effect on the dependent variable (see Sigall & Mills, 1998; Spencer, Zanna, & Fong, 2005). In another experiment, my colleagues and I did just that: We manipulated relative left frontal cortical activity after dissonance was aroused to test whether that cortical activity would actually affect attitude change.

To manipulate relative left frontal cortical activity, we used neurofeedback training to teach participants to control EEG activity. This training presents participants with real-time feedback on brainwave activity. When participants' brainwave activity changes in the desired direction, we "reward" them with feedback that they've succeeded; these rewards can be as simple as presenting participants with a tone that informs them that they've changed their brainwaves in the right direction. When participants' brainwave activity does not change in the desired direction, we provide them with either negative feedback or no feedback at all. In essence, we rely on operant conditioning, and the rewarded EEG changes can occur even without participants' awareness (Kamiya, 1979; Kotchoubey, Kübler, Strehl, Flor, & Birbaumer, 2002; Siniatchkin, Kropp, & Gerber, 2000).

In past research, after only three days of training, neurofeedback was effective in teaching participants to decrease the relative activity in the left frontal cortex, and this decrease resulted in fewer approach-related emotional responses (Allen, Harmon-Jones, & Cavender, 2001). Thus, we believed that feedback training would not only enable participants to decrease the relative activity in the left frontal cortex, but more importantly, that this decreased activity would affect the extent to which they changed their attitudes after they had made a difficult decision.

To test these predictions, we used the difficult-decision paradigm described earlier. In our experiment, we provided participants with two days of neurofeedback training designed to increase or decrease relative left frontal cortical activity. On the third day, we first asked them to make a difficult choice among different experiments in which they could participate later in the session. Immediately following their decision, we administered the same neurofeedback training as before. Finally, we measured their attitudes toward their chosen and rejected experiments. We found that participants who learned to decrease relative left cortical activity rated the chosen and rejected experiments more similarly than did other participants; in other words, there was less spread between their (positive) evaluations of the experiment they chose and their (less positive) evaluation of the experiment they rejected. In short, neurofeedback training caused a reduction in relative left frontal cortical activity, which caused an elimination of the familiar spreading-of-alternatives effect (Harmon-Jones, Harmon-Jones, Fearn, Sigelman, & Johnson, 2008). Together with past research showing that commitment to a chosen course of action increases activity in the left frontal cortex (Harmon-Jones, Gerdjikov, et al., 2008), our manipulation of relative left frontal cortical activity, a presumed mediator of the effect of commitment on discrepancy reduction, provides strong support for the role of relative left frontal activity in discrepancy reduction processes.

We designed a follow-up to conceptually replicate the previous experiment. In this experiment, we manipulated action-oriented mental processing following a difficult decision. First, we expected to replicate past research that showed that an action-oriented mind-set would increase discrepancy reduction following a decision. Second, we expected that an action-oriented mind-set would increase relative left frontal cortical activity. Finally, we expected this increase in left frontal cortical activity would relate to discrepancy reduction, as assessed by spreading of alternatives.

To further extend past research, we included a condition to manipulate positive affect that was low in approach motivation (i.e., participants wrote about a time when something happened that caused them to feel very good about themselves, but was not the result of their own actions). We did this to distinguish between the effects of positive affect per se—versus approach motivation—on participants' differential evaluations of chosen and rejected alternatives. Past research suggested that action-oriented mind-sets increase positive affect (Taylor & Gollwitzer, 1995), but we do not predict that positive affect itself causes increased left frontal cortical activity or an increase in spreading of alternatives.

Results from the experiment were consistent with predictions, and revealed that the action-oriented mind-set increased relative left frontal cortical activity and spreading of alternatives, compared to a control condition and the positive affect/low approach motivation condition. These results provide a conceptual replication of past results by using a different operationalization of action-oriented motivational processing. Both experiments revealed that increases in action-oriented processing yielded increased relative left frontal cortical activity. Moreover, both studies revealed that relative left frontal activation correlated positively with the spreading of alternatives.

Increasing Strength of Action Tendencies and Discrepancy Reduction

According to our action-based model of dissonance, dissonance should increase as the press for action increases. More formally, dissonance should increase as the salience of the action implications of dissonant cognitions increases. Several perspectives consider emotions to involve action tendencies (Brehm, 1999; Frijda, 1986). To the extent that an emotion generates an action tendency, as the intensity of that emotion increases and is inconsistent with other information, dissonance should increase.

Research has demonstrated that the emotion of sympathy (empathy) increases helping behavior because it evokes altruistic motivation, that is, the motivation to relieve the distress of the person in need of help (Batson, 1991). We conducted an experiment that tested whether an inconsistency between the emotion of sympathy and knowledge about past failures to act in accord with the sympathy would evoke motivation to reduce this inconsistency (Harmon-Jones, Peterson, & Vaughn, 2003). Our experiment was similar to Elliot and colleagues' research using a hypocrisy paradigm (Aronson, 1999; Stone, Wiegand, Cooper, & Aronson, 1997). However, instead of involving an inconsistency between past behavior (e.g., practicing unsafe sex) and a public speech (e.g., telling others to practice safe sex), our experiment involved an inconsistency between past behavior and a private emotional experience, as described next.

In the experiment, we predicted that when participants experience sympathy for a person in need of help and are reminded of times when they failed to help people in similar straits, they would be more motivated to help. Participants were told that they would be listening to a pilot broadcast for a local radio station and that we were interested in their reactions to the tape. Before listening to the tape, participants were assigned to one of two conditions: one in which they tried to imagine how the person must feel (high-empathy set) or one in which they tried to remain objective as they listened to the tape (low-empathy set). Participants then listened to a tape-recorded message that was purportedly from a person in need of help (an adolescent with cancer). Afterward, they completed self-report questionnaires assessing their emotional responses to and evaluations of the tape-recorded message. Participants then listed times when they failed to help other individuals who were in need of help (in order to induce dissonance) or they completed a demographic survey (control condition). Finally, participants were given an opportunity to help by volunteering time to assist the cancer-stricken teenager by addressing letters that would solicit money from possible donors or by donating money to the person's family. Consistent with predictions derived from the action-based model, results indicated that participants offered significantly more help when they were encouraged to be empathic and were reminded of past failures to come to others' aid.

As noted earlier, this experiment is similar to Elliot and colleagues' research using a hypocrisy paradigm (Aronson, 1999; Stone et al., 1997). However, the present experiment extends the hypocrisy research in an important way. In Elliot and his colleagues' hypocrisy experiments, dissonance was aroused when participants who engaged in a public behavior (i.e., making a videotaped speech) were reminded of past failures to practice what they publicly preached (i.e., they had failed to engage in the same behavior that they were advocating). In our experiment, dissonance was aroused when a private emotional experience was inconsistent with a reminder of past failures to act on a past emotional experience. Thus, hypocrisy-like effects can emerge, even when the dissonance arises in response to a private emotional experience on the one hand, and on the other hand, a reminder of past failures to behave in keeping with that emotional experience. In general, we view past work on hypocrisy as consistent with the action-based model because the conflicting "cognitions" have strong behavioral implications, and because the reduction of the dissonance between these "cognitions" enables individuals to behave effectively with regard to the cognition most resistant to change (i.e., in past studies, the information provided in the speech). We were clearly inspired by Elliot and colleagues' work on hypocrisy in creating this experiment.

A PERSONAL CONCLUSION

Elliot has had a profound impact on psychology through his applied and theoretical research, and through his guidance on the art of methodology. I have been deeply influenced by Elliot's work, and without his influence, I would probably never have joined the field. I greatly appreciate this opportunity to highlight some of Elliot's contributions to dissonance theory and research, and then to review recent research on the action-based model of dissonance. Consistent with Elliot's philosophy of science that champions synthesis of multiple perspectives (Aronson, 1992), the action-based model builds on past dissonance theory research, and offers an analysis that synthesizes dissonance research and theory with developments on perception-action perspectives and the cognitive neuroscience of control and affective neuroscience of motivation. Although even Elliot may not have been prescient enough to predict the role of perception-action perspectives and neuroscience research in the elaboration of cognitive dissonance theory, I hope that he is pleased.

REFERENCES

Allen, J. J. B., Harmon-Jones, E., & Cavender, J. (2001). Manipulation of frontal EEG asymmetry through biofeedback alters self-reported emotional responses and facial EMG. *Psychophysiology, 38*, 685–693.

Amodio, D. M., Harmon-Jones, E., Devine, P. G., Curtin, J. J., Hartley, S., & Covert, A. (2004). Neural signals for the detection of unintentional race bias. *Psychological Science, 15*, 88–93.

Amodio, D. M., Master, S. L., Yee, C. M., & Taylor, S. E. (2008). Neurocognitive components of behavioral inhibition and activation systems: Implications for theories of self-regulation. *Psychophysiology, 45*, 11–19.

Aronson, E. (1968). Dissonance theory: Progress and problems. In R. P. Abelson, E. Aronson, W. J. McGuire, T. M. Newcomb, M. J. Rosenberg, & P. H. Tannebaum (Eds.), *Theories of cognitive consistency: A sourcebook* (pp. 5–27). Chicago: Rand McNally.

Aronson, E. (1969). The theory of cognitive dissonance: A current perspective. In L. Berkowitz (Ed.), *Advances in experimental social psychology* (Vol. 4, pp. 1–34). New York: Academic Press.

Aronson, E. (1988). *The social animal* (5th ed.). New York: W. H. Freeman.

Aronson, E. (1992). The return of the repressed: Dissonance theory makes a comeback. *Psychological Inquiry, 3*, 303–311.

Aronson, E. (1999). Dissonance, hypocrisy, and the self concept. In E. Harmon-Jones & J. Mills (Eds.), *Cognitive dissonance: Progress on a pivotal theory in social psychology* (pp. 103–126). Washington, DC: American Psychological Association.

Aronson, E., & Carlsmith, J. M. (1962). Performance expectancy as a determinant of actual performance. *Journal of Abnormal and Social Psychology, 65*, 178–182.

Aronson, E., Ellsworth, P., Carlsmith, J. M., & Gonzales, M. H. (1990). *Methods of research in social psychology* (2nd ed.). New York: McGraw-Hill.

Aronson, E., Fried, C., & Stone, J. (1991). Overcoming denial and increasing the intention to use condoms through the induction of hypocrisy. *American Journal of Public Health, 81*, 1636–1638.

Aronson, E., & Mills, J. (1959). The effect of severity of initiation on liking for a group. *The Journal of Abnormal and Social Psychology, 59*, 177–181.

Batson, C. D. (1991). *The altruism question: Toward a social-psychological answer*. Hillsdale, NJ: Lawrence Erlbaum Associates.

Beauvois, J. L., & Joule, R. V. (1996). *A radical dissonance theory*. London: Taylor & Francis.

Beauvois, J. L., & Joule, R. V. (1999). A radical point of view on dissonance theory. In E. Harmon-Jones & J. Mills (Eds.), *Cognitive dissonance: Progress on a pivotal theory in social psychology* (pp. 43–70). Washington, DC: American Psychological Association.

Beckmann, J., & Irle, M. (1985). Dissonance and action control. In J. Kuhl & J. Beckmann (Eds.), *Action control: From cognition to behavior* (pp. 129–150). Berlin: Springer-Verlag.

Beckmann, J., & Kuhl, J. (1984). Altering information to gain action control: Functional aspects of human information processing in decision making. *Journal of Research in Personality, 18*, 224–237.

Berkowitz, L. (1984). Some effects of thoughts on anti- and prosocial influences of media events: A cognitive-neoassociation analysis. *Psychological Bulletin, 95*, 410–427.

Brehm, J. W. (1956). Postdecision changes in the desirability of alternatives. *Journal of Abnormal and Social Psychology, 52*, 384–389.

Brehm, J. W. (1999). The intensity of emotion. *Personality and Social Psychology Review, 3*, 2–22.

Brehm, J. W., & Cohen, A. R. (1962). *Explorations in cognitive dissonance.* New York: Wiley.

Carter, C. S., Braver, T. S., Barch, D. M., Botvinick, M. M., Noll, D., & Cohen, J. D. (1998). Anterior cingulate cortex, error detection, and the online monitoring of performance. *Science, 280*, 747–749.

Cooper, J. (1992). Dissonance and the return of the self-concept. *Psychological Inquiry, 3*, 320–323.

Cooper, J., & Fazio, R. H. (1984). A new look at dissonance theory. In L. Berkowitz (Ed.), *Advances in experimental social psychology* (Vol. 17, pp. 229–264). Orlando, FL: Academic Press.

Cooper, J., & Worchel, S. (1970). Role of undesired consequences in arousing cognitive dissonance. *Journal of Personality and Social Psychology, 16*, 199–206.

Cooper, J., Zanna, M. P., & Goethals, G. R. (1974). Mistreatment of an esteemed other as a consequence affecting dissonance reduction. *Journal of Experimental Social Psychology, 10*, 224–233.

Dickerson, C. A., Thibodeau, R., Aronson, E., & Miller, D. (1992). Using cognitive dissonance to encourage water conservation. *Journal of Applied Social Psychology, 22*, 841–854.

Elkin, R. A., & Leippe, M. R. (1986). Physiological arousal, dissonance, and attitude change: Evidence for a dissonance-arousal link and a "don't remind me" effect. *Journal of Personality and Social Psychology, 51*, 55–65.

Elliot, A. J., & Devine, P. G. (1994). On the motivation nature of cognitive dissonance: Dissonance as psychological discomfort. *Journal of Personality and Social Psychology, 67*, 382–394.

Festinger, L. (1957). *A theory of cognitive dissonance.* Stanford, CA: Stanford University Press.

Festinger, L., & Carlsmith, J. M. (1959). Cognitive consequences of forced compliance. *Journal of Abnormal and Social Psychology, 58*, 203–210.

Fried, C. B., & Aronson, E. (1995). Hypocrisy, misattribution, and dissonance reduction. *Personality and Social Psychology Bulletin, 21,* 925–933.

Frijda, N. H. (1986). *The emotions.* New York: Cambridge University Press.

Gerhing, W. J., Goss, B., Coles, M. G. H., Meyer, D. E., & Donchin, E. (1993). A neural system for error detection and compensation. *Psychological Science, 4,* 385–390.

Gibson, J. J. (1966). *The senses considered as perceptual systems.* Boston: Houghton Mifflin.

Gibson, J. J. (1979). *The ecological approach to visual perception.* Boston: Houghton Mifflin.

Goethals, G. R., & Cooper, J. (1972). Role of intention and postbehavioral consequence in the arousal of cognitive dissonance. *Journal of Personality and Social Psychology, 23,* 293–301.

Gollwitzer, P. M. (1990). Action phases and mind-sets. In E. T. Higgins & R. M. Sorrentino (Eds.), *Handbook of motivation and cognition: Foundations of social behavior* (Vol. 2, pp. 53–92). New York: Guilford Press.

Gollwitzer, P. M., & Bayer, U. (1999). Deliberative versus implemental mindsets in the control of action. In S. Chaiken & Y. Trope (Ed.), *Dual-process theories in social psychology* (pp. 403–422). New York: Guilford Press.

Gollwitzer, P. M., & Sheeran, P. (2006). Implementation intentions and goal achievement: A meta-analysis of effects and processes. In M. P. Zanna (Ed.), *Advances in experimental social psychology* (Vol. 38, pp. 69 119). San Diego, CA: Elsevier Academic Press.

Harmon-Jones, E. (1999). Toward an understanding of the motivation underlying dissonance effects: Is the production of aversive consequences necessary to cause dissonance? In E. Harmon-Jones & J. Mills (Eds.), *Cognitive dissonance: Progress on a pivotal theory in social psychology* (pp. 71–99). Washington, DC: American Psychological Association.

Harmon-Jones, E. (2000). Cognitive dissonance and experienced negative affect: Evidence that dissonance increases experienced negative affect even in the absence of aversive consequences. *Personality and Social Psychology Bulletin, 26,* 1490–1501.

Harmon-Jones, E. (2003). Clarifying the emotive functions of asymmetrical frontal cortical activity. *Psychophysiology, 40,* 838–848.

Harmon-Jones, E., & Allen, J. J. B. (1997). Behavioral activation sensitivity and resting frontal EEG asymmetry: Covariation of putative indicators related to risk for mood disorders. *Journal of Abnormal Psychology, 106,* 159–163.

Harmon-Jones, E., & Allen, J. J. B. (1998). Anger and prefrontal brain activity: EEG asymmetry consistent with approach motivation despite negative affective valence. *Journal of Personality and Social Psychology, 74,* 1310–1316.

Harmon-Jones, E., Brehm, J. W., Greenberg, J., Simon, L., & Nelson, D. E. (1996). Evidence that the production of aversive consequences is not necessary to create cognitive dissonance. *Journal of Personality and Social Psychology, 70,* 5–16.

Harmon-Jones, E., Gerdjikov, T., & Harmon-Jones, C. (2008). The effect of induced compliance on relative left frontal cortical activity: A test of the action-based model of dissonance. *European Journal of Social Psychology, 38,* 35–45.

Harmon-Jones, E., & Harmon-Jones, C. (2002). Testing the action-based model of cognitive dissonance: The effect of action-orientation on post-decisional attitudes. *Personality and Social Psychology Bulletin, 28,* 711–723.

Harmon-Jones, E., Harmon-Jones, C., Fearn, M., Sigelman, J. D., & Johnson, P. (2008). Action orientation, relative left frontal cortical activation, and spreading of alternatives: A test of the action-based model of dissonance. *Journal of Personality and Social Psychology, 94,* 1–15.

Harmon-Jones, E., Peterson, H., & Vaughn, K. (2003). The dissonance-inducing effects of an inconsistency between experienced empathy and knowledge of past failures to help: Support for the action-based model of dissonance. *Basic and Applied Social Psychology, 25,* 69–78.

Harmon-Jones, E., & Sigelman, J. (2001). State anger and prefrontal brain activity: Evidence that insult-related relative left-prefrontal activation is associated with experienced anger and aggression. *Journal of Personality and Social Psychology, 80,* 797–803.

Hoyt, M. K., Henley, M. D., & Collins, B. E. (1972). Studies in forced compliance: Confluence of choice and consequence on attitude change. *Journal of Personality and Social Psychology, 23,* 205–210.

Jones, E. E., & Gerard, H. B. (1967). *Foundations of social psychology.* New York: Wiley.

Kamiya, J. (1979). Autoregulation of the EEG alpha rhythm: A program for the study of consciousness. In S. A. E. Peper & M. Quinn (Ed.), *Mind/body integration: Essential readings in biofeedback* (pp. 289–297). New York: Plenum Press.

Kotchoubey, B., Kübler, A., Strehl, U., Flor, H., & Birbaumer, N. (2002). Can humans perceive their brain states? *Consciousness and Cognition, 11,* 98–113.

Kuhl, J. (1980). *Fragebogen zur Erfassung von Handlungs-bzw. Lageorientierung.* Bochum, Germany: Ruhr-Universität Bochum.

Kuhl, J. (1984). Volitional aspects of achievement motivation and learned helplessness: Toward a comprehensive theory of action-control. In B. A. Maher (Ed.), *Progress in experimental personality research* (Vol. 13, pp. 99–171). New York: Academic Press.

Lawrence, D. H., & Festinger, L. (1962). *Deterrents and reinforcement.* Stanford, CA: Stanford University Press.

MacDonald, A. W., III, Cohen, J. D., Stenger, V. A., & Carter, C. S. (2000). Dissociating the role of the dorsolateral prefrontal and anterior cingulate cortex in cognitive control. *Science, 288,* 1835–1838.

McArthur, L. Z., & Baron, R. M. (1983). Toward an ecological theory of social perception. *Psychological Review, 90,* 215–238.

Nel, E., Helmreich, R., & Aronson, E. (1969). Opinion change in the advocate as a function of the persuasibility of his audience: A clarification of the meaning of dissonance. *Journal of Personality and Social Psychology, 12,* 117–124.

Pizzagalli, D. A., Sherwood, R. J., Henriques, J. B., & Davidson, R. J. (2005). Frontal brain asymmetry and reward responsiveness: A source-localization study. *Psychological Science, 16,* 805–813.

Rabbie, J. M., Brehm, J. W., & Cohen, A. R. (1959). Verbalization and reactions to cognitive dissonance. *Journal of Personality, 27,* 407–417.

Robinson, R. G., & Downhill, J. E. (1995). Lateralization of psychopathology in response to focal brain injury. In R. J. Davidson & K. Hugdahl (Eds.), *Brain asymmetry* (pp. 693–711). Cambridge, MA: MIT Press.

Sigall, H., & Mills, J. (1998). Measures of independent variables and mediators are useful in social psychology experiments: But are they necessary? *Personality and Social Psychology Review, 2,* 218-226.

Siniatchkin, M., Kropp, P., & Gerber, W.-D. (2000). Neurofeedback—The significance of reinforcement and the search for an appropriate strategy for the success of self-regulation. *Applied Psychophysiology and Biofeedback, 25,* 167–175.

Spencer, S. J., Zanna, M. P., & Fong, G. T. (2005). Establishing a causal chain: Why experiments are often more effective than mediational analyses in examining psychological processes. *Journal of Personality and Social Psychology, 89,* 845–851.

Steele, C. M. (1988). The psychology of self-affirmation: Sustaining the integrity of the self. In L. Berkowitz (Ed.), *Advances in experimental social psychology* (Vol. 21, pp. 261–302). San Diego, CA: Academic Press.

Stone, J. (1999). What exactly have I done? The role of self-attribute accessibility in dissonance. In E. Harmon-Jones & J. Mills (Eds.), *Cognitive dissonance: Progress on a pivotal theory in social psychology* (pp. 175–200). Washington, DC: American Psychological Association.

Stone, J. (2003). Self-consistency for low self-esteem in dissonance processes: The role of self-standards. *Personality and Social Psychology Bulletin, 29,* 846–858.

Stone, J., Aronson, E., Crain, A. L., Winslow, M. P., & Fried, C. B. (1994). Inducing hypocrisy as a means of encouraging young adults to use condoms. *Personality and Social Psychology Bulletin, 20,* 116–128.

Stone, J., Wiegand, A. W., Cooper, J., & Aronson, E. (1997). When exemplification fails: Hypocrisy and the motive for self-integrity. *Journal of Personality and Social Psychology, 72,* 54–65.

Stroop, J. R. (1935). Studies of interference in serial verbal reactions. *Journal of Experimental Psychology, 18,* 643–662.

Taylor, S. E., & Gollwitzer, P. M. (1995). Effects of mindset on positive illusions. *Journal of Personality and Social Psychology, 69,* 213–226.

Thibodeau, R., & Aronson, E. (1992). Taking a closer look: Reasserting the role of self-concept in dissonance theory. *Personality and Social Psychology Bulletin, 18,* 591–602.

van Veen, V., & Carter, C. S. (2006). Conflict and cognitive control in the brain. *Current Directions in Psychological Science, 15*, 237–240.
van Veen, V., Krug, M. K., Schooler, J. W., & Carter, C. S. (2009). Neural activity predicts attitude change in cogitive dissonance. *Nature Neuroscience, 12*(11), 1469–1474.

7

THE POWER OF THE SELF-CONSISTENCY MOTIVE IN SOCIAL LIFE

Jeff Stone

University of Arizona

I will never forget the evening I came home from a long day of undergraduate instruction to a life-altering message on my answering machine. The caller, in a deep, booming voice, said, "Hello, Jeff, this is Elliot Aronson. I'm calling to say that I would like to admit you to do your graduate work in social psychology with me." I was floored. I had been introduced to the field of social psychology by reading *The Social Animal*, and, inspired by the idea of the Jigsaw Classroom, I had spent my junior and senior years conducting cooperative learning research in schools. I also knew from a quick phone call with Elliot that we were both interested in the AIDS crisis and in finding ways to reduce the transmission of HIV. When I got his call, I was pretty certain that I would carve out a career using social psychology to solve important social problems. I was determined at that time to be the best applied social psychologist on the planet.

But once I got to Santa Cruz and read more of Elliot's research, met with him to design studies, and watched him give talks and lecture in his classes, I became deeply intrigued by the richness of cognitive dissonance theory, and, specifically, by Elliot's views on the power and importance of self-consistency in social life. It seemed true to me then, as it does today, that people have a fundamental desire to know who they are in their social worlds, and that when something shakes this foundation, the dissonance they experience drives them toward restoring a stable and predictable sense of self. One of the most intriguing aspects of this observation is that when self-knowledge is negative, the drive toward a stable and predictable sense of self requires that people accept, and even embrace, their negative self-views. It is not pleasant, but under some conditions, it is absolutely necessary, because self-consistency plays a powerful and important role in the way people navigate their social lives.

Interest in dissonance processes appears to be growing again in journals (e.g., Egan, Santos, & Bloom, 2007), but not many of the studies appear to test predictions derived from self-consistency theory. Elliot would probably say that one reason is that our field tends to have a short memory; instead of "treasuring the old," we keep reinventing it. I agree, but I'd add that another reason is that self-consistency processes can be difficult to capture in the lab. I have actually heard graduate students say something like: "When it takes nine experiments to publish in *JPSP* [*Journal of Personality and Social Psychology*], why spend any time on an elusive phenomenon that I can't produce, let alone, replicate? I need a job!"

My goal in honoring Elliot and his contribution to social psychology is to offer some new insights into the nature of the self-consistency motive. In my view, self-consistency is not as elusive as it seems: It is a powerful motivating force, but like all motivational states, the desire to maintain a consistent and predictable sense of self is determined by factors operating in the immediate social context. To make this case, I will provide a brief overview of the self-consistency perspective, and then provide a detailed analysis of the replication record of the original experiment that Elliot conducted with Merrill Carlsmith (Aronson & Carlsmith, 1962) using the performance expectancy paradigm. I will then present some of my research on self-consistency processes in people with negative and positive self-concepts. By focusing on the conditions under which the self-consistency motive is most likely to emerge, not only can we produce and replicate the process, but we can also generate new hypotheses about how, when, and why the desire for a stable, predictable sense of self influences social behavior.

THE SELF-CONSISTENCY PERSPECTIVE ON DISSONANCE

Elliot first introduced the self-consistency perspective on dissonance processes in a grant application submitted to the National Science Foundation in 1960. In the proposal, he suggested that a common thread ran through most dissonance studies: They involved situations that challenged people's expectancies or beliefs about themselves. To predict when dissonance would occur, dissonance theory needed to take into account the expectations people hold for themselves and their behavior. For example, Elliot argued that the dissonance aroused in Leon Festinger and Merrill Carlsmith's (1959) now-classic experiment was not due to the inconsistency between the thoughts "I believe the tasks were boring" and "I told someone the tasks were interesting." Instead, the dissonance was aroused by the inconsistency between cognitions about the self (e.g., "I am a decent and truthful human being") and cognitions about the behavior (e.g., "I have misled a person who now believes something that is not true"). Elliot later summarized his views in a book chapter, when he concluded that "If dissonance exists it is because the individual's behavior is inconsistent with his self-concept" (Aronson, 1968, p. 23).

Elliot's emphasis on the self-concept shifted the motivational nature of dissonance from one of general psychological consistency to a more specific motive for *self*-consistency. If beliefs about the self are among the most important cognitions that people hold, then dissonance will be greatest when behavior or other cognitions are inconsistent with cognitions about the self. Furthermore, the centrality of cognitions about the self makes them resistant to change. Thus, in the self-consistency formulation, dissonance motivates people to maintain their self-concept by changing their attitudes, behavior, or other relevant cognitions.

The self-consistency perspective also introduced predictions regarding individual differences. Elliot reasoned that many of the successful dissonance experiments reflected the tacit assumption that participants held positive self-concepts and hence positive expectations about their behavior. Would misleading someone about the dullness of a task cause dissonance in people who thought poorly of themselves or who expected their actions to turn out badly? Elliot hypothesized that it would not. Although lying, cheating, or taking a stand against one's own beliefs—the stock in trade of most dissonance experiments—should be self-discrepant for people who think of themselves as honest, ethical, and courageous, such undesirable acts are perfectly consonant for people who hold negative self-concepts. Thus, the self-consistency perspective attempted to refine dissonance theory by specifying the cognitions most likely to underlie dissonance processes, and by considering individual differences that affect both when people experience dissonance and how they resolve it.

In 1962, Elliot and Merrill Carlsmith published the first direct evidence for the self-consistency revision of dissonance theory (Aronson & Carlsmith, 1962). They hypothesized that when an important expectancy about the self is disconfirmed by performance on a task, the inconsistency between the self-expectancy and performance would create dissonance. To reduce this discomfort, people should be motivated to change their performance on subsequent trials to bring their behavior back in line with their self-expectancy. For example, imagine a person who has never taken a professional misstep. Confident in her expectation of future success, she is likely to experience dissonance after an employer criticizes her performance. Once she's licked her wounds and decided that the criticism was appropriate, this dissonance should motivate her to make adjustments so that she can avoid future discrepancies between her positive expectations and behaviors that might fall short. But what are the dissonance implications for those who expect that they will fail or otherwise perform poorly? Elliot and Merrill's great insight was that if self-consistency is more important than self-enhancement, people who hold low self-expectancies should experience dissonance after success, given the discrepancy between their negative expectancies and positive performance. Such is the situation for a person who, through bitter experience, is convinced that she simply cannot do anything right. An unexpected success would generate dissonance between her pessimistic expectations and successful behavior. How might she reduce her dissonance? According to Elliot and Merrill, she might convince herself that her apparent success was not a success at all ("It was a fluke; I'm a fraud"), or she might even try to dodge future success by avoiding a challenging assignment that she expects to botch. Alternatively, if self-enhancement—restoring a positive sense of self—is more important, people with negative self-expectancies should be happy with their good performance and should not be motivated to change their behavior.

Thus, Elliot and Merrill designed a dissonance experiment that was a bold critical test between the motives for self-consistency versus self-enhancement. They led young women to believe that a male experimenter was interested in the relationship between face-to-face interviews and paper-and-pencil measures to assess personality. The experimenter told participants that they would be taking a few short tests, after which they would be scheduled for a follow-up interview. Participants first completed a short self-rating scale followed by the primary experimental task, which was introduced as a measure of social sensitivity. The experimenter explained the social sensitivity measure as being

> highly valid and reliable, ... an excellent measure of how sensitive an individual is to other people; i.e., people who score high on this

test are the same people who, when interviewed, express a good deal of understanding and insight into other people. Participants who score low on this test, on the other hand, tend to express a very superficial understanding of other people when interviewed. (Aronson & Carlsmith, 1962, p. 179)

The social sensitivity test required participants to examine a series of cards containing three photographs of young men and to decide which one of the three men was schizophrenic. The experimenter told the women that it would be difficult for them to assess their own level of social sensitivity while choosing among the faces on the cards, and that "some who think they do very poorly are among the best performers, and vice versa" (Aronson & Carlsmith, 1962, pp. 179–180).

Participants initially viewed four sets of 20 cards and identified which of the photos on each card depicted a schizophrenic. After participants had judged each set of 20 cards, the experimenter reported the participant's score aloud, and then recorded the time elapsed during the trial. To manipulate the women's self-expectancies of social sensitivity, the experimenter told participants in the positive expectancy condition that they did very well, receiving scores of 16 to 17 for each set of 20 cards; he told participants in the negative expectancy condition that they had performed poorly, receiving scores of only 4 to 5 for each set of 20 cards. Thus, feedback on the first four "social sensitivity" trials was designed to convince participants that they were either high in social sensitivity or low in social sensitivity.

To create dissonance, the experimenter manipulated the feedback about performance on a critical fifth and final trial of 20 cards, giving the women scores that were either the same as their previous scores or the opposite of their previous scores. In the crucial experimental conditions, one-half of the participants who were led to expect poor performance on the final fifth task received the same low score on the final trial (i.e., 4 to 5 correct), and the other half received an unexpectedly high score on the final trial (i.e., 16 to 17 correct).

A convincing mistake by the experimenter afforded the dependent measure of dissonance reduction: The experimenter "pretended to be quite chagrined" (Aronson & Carlsmith, 1962, p. 180) at forgetting to time the final trial. While the experimenter pretended to ruminate over his omission, he asked each woman to score her final performance, which he had manipulated to give the positive or negative feedback. After the women calculated their fifth trial score, the experimenter said that to correct his timing error, he would like them to pretend that they did not see the fifth trial pictures and to do the trial over again. This ruse gave participants an opportunity to change their decisions and therefore their scores on the final trial, given that the experimenter had not seen their previous performance.

The number of responses that participants changed when repeating the fifth trial reflected the amount of discomfort they experienced in response to feedback following their first performance on that aborted trial. If participants who were led to expect another low score were uncomfortable after receiving a high score, they would reduce their dissonance by changing their answers—to yield a score more consistent with their low expectancy—when they repeated the final trial. In contrast, if participants who expected another low score were satisfied with an unexpectedly good performance on the final trial, they would leave their initial answers intact when they repeated it.

The results clearly supported the self-consistency prediction: People who came to think of themselves as being poor at "social sensitivity" felt the discomfort associated with dissonance when they received positive feedback, and to reduce it, they changed most of their "correct" responses, effectively sabotaging their positive performance during the final trial. This was compelling evidence that the motive for self-consistency could be more powerful than the motive for self-enhancement.

This experiment led to a flurry of research by other investigators, but many of their studies failed to replicate the self-consistency response among participants with negative self-beliefs. Several reviews of the performance expectancy studies (e.g., Dipboye, 1977; Jones, 1973; Shrauger, 1975) concluded that the vast majority of replication attempts were unsuccessful, and many researchers cite these replication failures as evidence that self-consistency strivings are less powerful than self-enhancement motives (see Baumeister, this volume). For example, citing Robert Dipboye's (1977) review of 17 replications, William Swann (1990) noted that only 4 had successfully reproduced Aronson and Carlsmith's original findings. Based on this "rather dismal track record," Swann concluded that the performance expectancy paradigm simply failed to engender negative self-expectancies in participants. Swann proposed that "the fact that Aronson and Carlsmith's manipulation was ever successful probably says more about the extraordinary skill of those investigators who made it work than it does about the relative ease of manipulating self-conceptions" (p. 413). The assumed low rate of replication led other researchers to characterize Elliot and Merrill's original finding as a fluke or chance event (Dipboye, 1977) or as a function of some unknown artifact of the procedures (e.g., Ward & Sandvold, 1963; Wicklund & Brehm, 1976).

In my view, however, the "dismal" track record of replication had more to do with the degree to which researchers faithfully replicated key elements of the original procedures than with flukes or artifacts. When working with students to design experiments, Elliot often exhorted us to remember that "It's in the details!" I wondered whether the procedural details of replication studies influenced success in capturing the effects of self-consistency pressures. Sure enough, when I took a closer look at the replication studies, starting with the first failure to replicate (Ward & Sandvold, 1963), I found that most of the studies failed to use the original performance expectancy procedures. In fact, few experiments were conducted for the sake of direct replication per se; most were designed to test alternative hypotheses for the original finding regarding those with negative self-beliefs. Some hypotheses focused on procedural problems in the original experiment, including experimenter bias, or demand characteristics, such as informing participants that the test was "highly reliable and valid" (e.g., Ward & Sandvold, 1963). The design in each experiment typically included both a replication of the original low-expectancy conditions and whatever conditions were deemed necessary to test an alternative hypothesis. Thus, the test of each alternative hypothesis relied on replicating the self-consistency effect for low self-expectancies under conditions of positive and negative feedback.

However, with respect to the low self-expectancy conditions that served both as the replication of Elliot and Merrill's study (and as the control group for the test of alternative hypotheses), replications varied on several specific procedures. For example, some researchers excluded many of the original instructions to participants (e.g., Waterman & Ford, 1965); others used an alternative to the original "social sensitivity" photo-judging task (e.g., Maracek & Mettee, 1972; Taylor & Huesmann, 1974; Zajonc & Brickman, 1969); others increased or decreased the frequency of feedback designed to create low self-expectancies (e.g., Brock, Edelman, Edwards, & Schuck, 1965; Taylor & Huesmann, 1974); and in some cases, instead of measuring participants' satisfaction with their final performance, researchers used recall measures after the initial fifth trial (e.g., Brock et al., 1965; Lowin & Epstein, 1965; Moran & Klockars, 1967; Waterman & Ford, 1965). In short, replication studies varied on a number of procedural details, including experimental instructions, participants' tasks, the frequency of performance feedback, and dependent variable measures.

The apparent relation between experimental procedures and the replication record suggests that seemingly minor procedural changes may have tipped the delicate balance between the need for self-consistency and the need for self-enhancement. Why would alterations in experimental procedures affect the replicability of the self-consistency effect? One possibility is that in the performance–expectancy studies, the motivation to maintain a consistent but negative self-view hinged on the successful manipulation of the focal negative self-belief (e.g., Swann, 1990). That is, participants who received negative feedback would not have sabotaged a good final performance unless prior feedback had convinced them that they were indeed low in social sensitivity. If the induction of negative self-beliefs failed, participants would presumably have been left with either an uncertain negative view of themselves, or perhaps with the positive self-beliefs they held prior to entering the study, and they would have embraced positive feedback on the fifth and final trial.

If, as Elliot has reminded us, the devil is in the details, the success of attempts to replicate the self-consistency effect may well pivot on which particular details were directly replicated in later experiments. To test that idea, I conducted a meta-analysis of the performance-expectancy literature (Stone, 1994). In contrast to a qualitative literature review, a meta-analysis enables researchers to precisely quantify the effects of key variables—participant or experimenter characteristics, specific experimental procedures or dependent measures—some of which might account for inconsistent findings across a number of studies (Hunter & Schmidt, 1990; Mullen, 1989; Rosenthal, 1991). In this case, my goal was to document whether later variations on the procedures used in Elliot and Merrill's original experiment might explain the difference between successful and unsuccessful replications.

I found 14 articles that provided 25 tests of the original hypothesis that success would generate dissonance in participants who were led to expect poor performance, whereas failure would not. I trained undergraduate research assistants—blind to my hypothesis—to read and code the method section of each experiment, focusing on differences in such variables as cover story contents, the type of experimental task, the nature and frequency of performance feedback, and dependent measures.

A simple count of results yields six replications of Elliot and Merrill's findings. In addition, in four attempts to challenge Elliot and Merrill's conclusions, researchers proposed that the original participants who expected to fail changed their scores on the do-over of the fifth and final trial because their unexpectedly positive performance on the last trial sabotaged their memory for their original answers. However, in three of the four studies that used memory as a dependent measure, participants who expected to fail but did unexpectedly well showed better recall for their original fifth trial judgments than did participants who received negative feedback on the final trial. This reflects Elliot and Merrill's original assumption and brings the total up to 9 of 25 hypothesis tests (36%) that supported Elliot and Merrill's original findings—five more than the highest number reported in any previous qualitative review (e.g., Dipboye, 1977; Swann, 1990). Not a spectacular record, of course, but a 36% rate of replication is hardly as dismal as other reviewers have claimed.

My results also showed that procedural details made a significant difference: For example, among the task instructions crucial to replication were those that convinced participants that it would be impossible to assess their own performance as they judged the cards. Perhaps such instructions ensured that participants were sufficiently unsure of their ongoing performance, thus enhancing the credibility and persuasiveness of the experimenter's feedback designed to alter their self-views and, consequently, their expectations of future success or failure.

In contrast, use of the original social sensitivity task itself was not crucial to successful replications, but other aspects of the original task were important. Of the five successful self-consistency replications in which expectancies were manipulated (Maracek & Mettee, 1972, measured preexisting expectancies), two appear to have used the original social sensitivity test (Cottrell, 1965; Etgen & Rosen, 1993). Participants in another two successful replications completed a slightly different social sensitivity task. For example, participants in Tim Brock and colleagues' (1965) replications chose the "mentally ill" person from among photographs, although the task was described as a measure of social sensitivity. In the most dissimilar replication (Mettee, 1971), a test of "psychological sensitivity" required participants to look at photos of people's faces and eyes and guess what they were looking at. These variations suggest that participants need not have assessed "schizophrenia" by studying photos; neither were participants required to believe that they were completing a test of "social sensitivity." Still, one necessary ingredient in all of the successful replications appears to be a task that afforded false feedback about performance related to a novel or unfamiliar aspect of the self.

Finally, the amount of performance feedback participants received was important to the replication of the consistency effect. The optimal level appeared to be one piece of performance feedback per 20 trials, the original 5% ratio that Elliot and Merrill used. All of the successful replications that manipulated expectancies used this ratio. Providing participants with either more or less feedback than that led to enhancement strivings, which confirms what Tim Brock and his colleagues (1965) reported when they provided participants with more frequent feedback, such as after every trial. Thus, a key to replicating the self-consistency effect seems to lie in providing just the right amount of performance feedback; too sparse or too frequent feedback undermined replication of the effect.

To summarize, it appears that successful replications of Elliot's first experiment with Merrill Carlsmith were not statistical anomalies, or the result of artifacts or experimenter bias. Of the 25 published hypothesis tests, nine (36%) reported results supporting the original findings. Moreover, of those studies that measured participants' satisfaction with their performance on the final trial, 6 of 21 (28.5%) replicated the consistency effect. Although it might be argued that 28.5% is not a strong track record, my findings do not support an outright dismissal of the performance expectancy paradigm. Instead, it may be more useful to view replication as a function of whether and how experimental procedures tipped the balance between the desire for self-consistency and the desire for self-enhancement in people with negative self-views.

In my view, procedural details mattered because they influenced the *certainty* with which participants embraced performance feedback and the resulting newfound views of themselves on the dimension under investigation. As was the case in Elliot and Merrill's (Aronson & Carlsmith, 1962) original procedure, when experimenters provided highly credible but limited feedback about a novel self-attribute, the procedures activated processes that led participants to develop a relatively certain new view of the self that they were motivated to maintain in the face of inconsistent feedback on the final trial. Studies that failed to replicate the self-consistency effect may have engaged self-enhancement goals in part because the procedures undermined the self-certainty that motivates people to maintain a consistent view of the self. When participants believed that the task assessed a dimension of self about which they already felt certain, used existing self-beliefs to guide their interpretation of the feedback, or received too little or too much feedback, the procedures created a less certain new self-view that was easily dismissed when the inconsistent feedback occurred on the final trial. In his own work, David Mettee (1971; Maracek & Mettee, 1972) offered a similar explanation; he suggested that people can be expected to maintain consistency only when they first "acquire a secure and stable" self-view—one of which they are highly certain. However, when people are "unconvinced" or "uncertain" of the validity of a new self-view, they may direct their efforts toward achievement and reduce uncertainty in a "favorable direction." Mettee (1971) reported direct support for the importance of self-certainty in the performance expectancy paradigm by showing that only participants with low self-esteem rejected the positive feedback on the final trial of a novel "personality" task. My meta-analytic results support this finding.

Still, we can only speculate about the processes by which limited but highly credible feedback about a novel self-attribute activated mechanisms known to instill a strong sense of certainty about a new self-view in the performance-expectancy procedure. For example, performance on a novel task may have been less prone to achievement demands when there were neither clear performance standards nor a clear payoff for a good performance. Given the high personal impact of the task feedback, participants may have been more motivated to think carefully or deeply about that feedback. In addition, when participants were told that they could not rely on previous experience to determine how they were doing, they would engage in little (if any) counterarguing in response to the test feedback, given that the new information did not challenge or threaten a previously held self-view. Thus, successful replications may have induced self-certainty—and the motivation to maintain consistency—when performance feedback compelled participants to elaborate on the information in a relatively objective manner and to conclude that it represented useful new information about the self.

Similarly, there are at least two explanations for why the original ratio of trials to feedback successfully created certain self-views in replications of Elliot and Merrill's findings. First, participants in later experiments that provided a dearth of feedback may have had insufficient information to develop a certain self-expectancy. Alternatively, the deluge of feedback in other studies may have overwhelmed participants' ability to process the information or may have caused them to ruminate, distracting their attention from both the task and experimenter feedback, and precluding the careful thought required to make a self-expectancy memorable (see Demaree, Petty, & Brinol, 2007). The original feedback procedure may have hit the optimal level for making participants' new self-expectancies highly accessible and, therefore, more likely to guide their behavior when they received inconsistent feedback on the final trial of the task.

More broadly, the results of the meta-analysis support Elliot's contention that self-consistency is a powerful motivational force in social behavior. However, in my view, they also show that maintaining a consistent and stable sense of self is not the only concern people have when confronted with a discrepancy between their behavior and self-beliefs; they are often motivated to think and feel good about themselves. What determines which of these competing motives will predominate when behavior conflicts with self-beliefs? Whether people seek self-consistency or self-enhancement depends upon how they construe what they have done—the *meaning* they give to a discrepant act.

EXTENDING THE SELF-CONSISTENCY PERSPECTIVE: A FOCUS ON PROCESS

Precisely 30 years after Elliot and Merrill's classic experiment was published, Elliot and Ruth Thibodeau published an extension of the self-consistency perspective on dissonance processes (Thibodeau & Aronson, 1992). For me, a key element in their paper was the observation that people hold expectancies for competent and moral behavior that they derive from "the conventional morals and prevailing values of society" (Thibodeau & Aronson, 1992, p. 592). For self-consistency motives to operate, people must perceive a discrepancy between their behavior—advocating a counterattitudinal belief (e.g., Festinger & Carlsmith, 1959) or making a questionable decision (e.g., Brehm, 1956)—and their "personal standards" for morality and competence. When people evaluate their own behavior using these personal standards for morality and competence, those with high self-esteem hold positive expectations for moral and competent conduct, and are likely to feel the bite of dissonance arousal when their immoral or foolish behavior falls short of their expectancies. In contrast, people with low self-esteem, who hold less positive expectations for their own conduct, are likely to perceive substandard behavior as confirmation of their low expectations and should, therefore, feel less dissonance. Thus, compared to people with low self-esteem, those with high self-esteem experience more dissonance following acts that deviate from the norms for "lying, advocating a position contrary to their own beliefs, or otherwise acting against one's principles" (Thibodeau & Aronson, 1992, p. 592). Ruth and Elliot's paper presented the results of several studies in which self-esteem and other self-related differences moderated attitude change in the classic dissonance paradigms, as predicted by the self-consistency perspective (e.g., Glass, 1964; Snyder & Tanke, 1974). Several studies published subsequently also support self-consistency predictions about self-esteem as a moderator of dissonance effects (e.g., Gibbons, Eggleston, & Benthin, 1997; Peterson, Haynes, & Olson, 2008; Prislin & Pool, 1996; Stone, 1999).

Nevertheless, contemporary researchers continue to downplay or dismiss the power and importance of self-consistency motives in dissonance arousal and in mental life more generally. As in the case of the performance expectancy paradigm, part of the problem lies in the difficulty replicating self-esteem differences in susceptibility to dissonance arousal. For some scholars, the failure of self-esteem to moderate dissonance effects provides evidence that self-related concerns are not central to dissonance processes (Cooper & Fazio, 1984; Harmon-Jones, Harmon-Jones, Fearn, Sigelman, & Johnson, 2008). Others agree that the self is directly involved, but they prefer to focus on people's motives to seek enhancement rather than consistency, a view first proposed by Claude Steele (1988) in his articulation of self-affirmation theory. According to this "self-resource" model, positive self-related cognitions can serve as resources for people to use in reducing dissonance. The self-resource model predicts that when people reflect on their positive attributes, those with high self-esteem are less motivated than are those with low self-esteem to reduce dissonance following a difficult decision (e.g., Steele, Spencer, & Lynch, 1993) or self-discrepant act (Holland, Meertens, & Van Vugt, 2002; Nail, Misak, & Davis, 2004). The conclusions drawn from such data about the prevalence of self-consistency in dissonance are reminiscent of how the field responded to difficulties replicating findings in the performance-expectancy paradigm: Toss the baby out with the bath water.

Yet, as suggested by my analysis of the performance-expectancy literature, contradictory data should not necessarily lead to the conclusion that self-consistency processes are unimportant. Perhaps dissonance processes do not turn on any single motivation or goal state. All of us may share the desire to feel that we are consistent, moral, and effective, but these different desires are elicited by, and vary with, the immediate social context. Rather than assume that only one of these self-related goals underlies dissonance arousal and attempts to reduce it, we can achieve a more comprehensive understanding of dissonance processes when we investigate and identify the conditions under which each of these goals is activated when people perform a self-discrepant act.

Joel Cooper and I developed the self-standards model (Stone & Cooper, 2001) to describe how the social context can elicit different motivational responses to a self-discrepant act. We propose that when people act, they use existing cognitions—important attitudes, beliefs, or self-knowledge—to make sense of their behavior. The specific cognitive criteria people use, however, depend on what is brought to mind or primed by cues in the immediate situation. Dissonance arises when, after acting, people evaluate their behavior against a standard of judgment that may or may not relate to a cognitive representation of the self. For example, people can evaluate their behavior using a specific attitude or belief (Harmon-Jones, Brehm, Greenberg, Simon, & Nelson, 1996), or by using generally shared, normative considerations of what is most aversive to people (Cooper & Fazio, 1984). However, as Ruth and Elliot (Thibodeau & Aronson, 1992) convincingly argued, people also have idiosyncratic standards of what is foolish or immoral, and these personal standards are linked to expectancies and other cognitions that underlie self-esteem. The self-standards model predicts that when people use relevant personal standards (those that relate to idiosyncratic self-expectancies) in assessing their behavior, those with high self-esteem will bring to mind their positive expectancies for behavior and, as a result, will perceive a relatively large discrepancy between their positive expectancies and questionable behavior. This should lead people with high self-esteem to conclude that they acted in an immoral and incompetent manner, which generates dissonance. In contrast, when people with low self-esteem use their personal self-standards to evaluate their behavior, they should bring to mind their negative expectancies for behavior, which allows them to perceive a relatively smaller discrepancy between their negative expectancies and behavior. Consequently, people with low self-esteem will perceive that their behavior is not inconsistent with what they expect, and this leads them to experience less dissonance. Thus, the self-standards model provides a framework from which to predict *when* and *how* self-esteem will moderate dissonance processes (Stone & Cooper, 2001).

In one direct test of the self-standards model (Stone, 2003), participants wrote a counterattitudinal essay under conditions of high and low choice. Participants completed a sentence scramble task designed to activate concepts related to personal standards for behavior (Bargh & Chartrand, 2000). In control conditions, participants either completed sentences designed to prime normatively held standards or no standards at all (neutral information). As predicted, results showed that priming personal standards for behavior yielded less attitude change among people with low compared to high self-esteem. Further, in a second study, when participants with low self-esteem were primed for either personal standards or for normative standards, those high in self-certainty about their negative self-beliefs who were primed for personal standards reported less self-justifying attitude change compared to those who were less certain about their negative self-beliefs. This finding, based on the more established counterattitudinal advocacy paradigm, conceptually replicates Elliot and Merrill's (1962) original performance expectancy findings. Further, as predicted by the self-consistency perspective, this conceptual replication suggests that when people use personal standards for behavior, those with low self-esteem bring to mind their relatively negative self-views, thereby attenuating their motive to justify questionable behavior. However, both studies also showed that in control conditions in which no standard was directly primed, or in which normative standards were primed, self-esteem did not moderate attitude change. The overall pattern supports the self-standards model claim that the role of the self and self-esteem in dissonance processes depends upon the specific standard people use when making sense of their actions (see also Stone & Cooper, 2003).

According to the self-consistency model, the differential use of positive and negative self-knowledge in the assessment of a counterattitudinal behavior mediates both the perception of a discrepancy and the magnitude of dissonance that is aroused (Aronson, 1999; Stone & Cooper, 2001; Thibodeau & Aronson, 1992). When personal standards are accessible, people with low self-esteem show less evidence of dissonance because they bring to mind more negative and fewer positive self-attributes when interpreting and evaluating their behavior. My students and I (Stone, 2004) tested this hypothesis by priming personal versus normative standards following a counterattitudinal act, and using a self-judgment response task (e.g., Markus & Kunda, 1986), we directly measured the degree to which participants endorsed positive and negative self-cognitions. Specifically, participants who were either very high or very low in self-esteem wrote a counterattitudinal essay under conditions of high choice, and then they completed a sentence-scramble task to prime personal standards, normative standards, or neutral information. Next, using a computer, they indicated the self-descriptiveness of a series of positive and negative traits. They pressed a key labeled "ME" if they thought the trait described them, and pressed a key labeled "NOT ME" otherwise. Positive traits included honest, ethical, capable, and careful; negative traits included phony, untruthful, unreasonable, and careless; and neutral traits included average, ordinary, and restless.

The number of ME responses for each set of randomly presented traits (positive, negative, neutral) was summed to yield three continuous trait descriptiveness ratings for high and low self-esteem participants assigned to each of the three experimental priming conditions (personal or normative standards or neutral information). As predicted, only when primed for their own personal standards, participants with low self-esteem endorsed fewer positive traits and more negative traits as self-descriptive. In contrast, participants with high self-esteem endorsed significantly more positive traits than negative traits, regardless of the standard (personal or normative) primed by the sentence-scramble test.

These findings support the self-consistency perspective on dissonance arousal and attempts to reduce it: Following an objectionable act, people with low self-esteem may feel less dissonance and therefore make fewer attempts to reduce it because they use their negative self-knowledge when attempting to make sense of a potentially self-discrepant act; after all, negative behaviors are less likely to arouse dissonance in those who expect nothing better from themselves. Moreover, the use of negative self-knowledge appears most likely when something in the immediate context causes people with low self-esteem to use their own personal standards for evaluating the meaning of a discrepant act.

Experimental procedures that focus on the accessibility of self-attributes also address the question of whether self-esteem differences in attitude change after a self-discrepant act are due to differences in dissonance *arousal* or to differences in dissonance *reduction* strategies. According to self-consistency theory (Aronson, 1999; Thibodeau & Aronson, 1992), because people with low self-esteem hold negative expectancies for their behavior, counterattitudinal behavior does not generate dissonance in the first place; the immorality and incompetence of such behavior is, after all, consistent with negative self-knowledge, and this consistency attenuates dissonance arousal. Of course, it's possible that even people with low self-esteem feel dissonance when they do something that is incompetent or immoral; perhaps they reduce their discomfort through another strategy, such as trivializing the importance of the discrepancy (Simon, Greenberg, & Brehm, 1995). Indeed, Marie-Amélie Martinie and Valérie Fointiat (2006) showed that when allowed to assess the importance of a counterattitudinal behavior, participants with low self-esteem trivialized the act more than did participants with high self-esteem. Although this finding provides some evidence for the dissonance reduction-strategy explanation for self-consistency effects, it does not appear that people with low self-esteem trivialize potentially problematic behaviors when cues in the situation activate their negative self-expectancies. In fact, they may be less motivated to use trivialization, or any dissonance reduction strategy, if something in the context leads them to use negative self-expectancies to evaluate the meaning of a discrepant act.

My lab examined the use of trivialization by participants with low self-esteem when their negative expectancies were brought to mind in the context of a problematic act (Stone, 2004). Under conditions of high choice, undergraduates with either high or low self-esteem wrote an unsympathetic essay in which they advocated decreased funding for handicapped services at their university. They then completed a task designed to prime either their self-expectancies for compassion or for creativity. They all then completed measures of their attitude toward funding services for the handicapped and a measure of trivialization adapted from Linda Simon and her colleagues' work (Simon et al., 1995).

The results showed that participants with low self-esteem did trivialize the impact of their uncompassionate essay more than participants with high self-esteem, but only when they were primed for expectancies about creativity, a positive trait that was unrelated to their discrepant behavior. Participants with low self-esteem who were primed for expectancies about being compassionate did not trivialize their essay more compared to participants with high self-esteem, who also focused on their expectancies for compassionate behavior. In addition, participants with low self-esteem showed less evidence of attitude change than did participants with high self-esteem when their expectancies for compassion were primed. Overall, the data suggest that when they focused on the self-expectancies directly related to the discrepant act, participants with high self-esteem showed more evidence of dissonance arousal than did those with low self-esteem.

In summary, by directly manipulating the processes by which people evaluate their behavior, we can predict when and how the motivation to maintain a consistent and stable self drives dissonance arousal and reduction. As specified by the self-standards model, when something in their immediate context leads people with low self-esteem to rely on their negative self-expectancies to make sense of what they have done, they bring to mind more negative than positive self-knowledge. In turn, this negative self-knowledge gives them a sense of consistency between their self-knowledge and what would for others be self-*inconsistent* behavior. Because less dissonance is aroused, people with low self-esteem rely less on dissonance-reduction strategies than do people who hold positive expectancies for their behavior.

CONSISTENCY FOR POSITIVE SELF-VIEWS FOLLOWING HYPOCRISY

It is often difficult to untangle self-consistency and self-enhancement motives among people who think highly of themselves because both motives tend to lead to the same responses. However, self-affirmation theory predicts how people reduce threats to their self-esteem. If dissonance arousal motivates people to restore the global positive integrity of the self, then any action that affirms positive self-worth should reduce dissonance, even if that action does not restore the specific positive self-views threatened by the discrepant act. Self-affirmation theory assumes that people are flexible about this; they are motivated to affirm good feelings about themselves by focusing on positive attributes that are unrelated to the specific source of the threat to their sense of self (Sherman & Cohen, 2006). A self-consistency perspective, in contrast, predicts that when behavior is discrepant from a specific positive view that people hold of themselves, they will be motivated to maintain that threatened view, even when other options for self-enhancement are available. Thus, the two theories make opposing predictions for how people who view themselves positively prefer to reduce dissonance when multiple options are available.

Elliot, Andy Weigand, Joel Cooper, and I (Stone, Weigand, Cooper, & Aronson, 1997) examined the preference for self-affirmation versus self-consistency to reduce the dissonance that follows an act of hypocrisy (see also Aronson, 1999; Aronson, Fried, & Stone, 1991). In the hypocrisy paradigm, people are made aware of a preexisting inconsistency between their beliefs and behavior. First, they are asked to publicly advocate for a prosocial behavior that they believe will benefit the welfare of specific individuals or society in general. Their advocacy is designed to be consistent with their current attitudes and beliefs about the activity in question, and as a result they do not feel dissonance. Instead, dissonance is aroused by subsequently inducing them to think about times when they themselves failed to practice what they preached. Once they are made mindful of the inconsistency, people feel the discomfort of cognitive dissonance, which they are motivated to reduce. According to the self-consistency perspective, becoming aware of their "hypocrisy" should motivate people to change their behavior—rather than their attitudes—to reduce the dissonance, so that they can maintain their crucial beliefs about their own honesty and sincerity (Stone et al., 1997).

Initial tests of the dissonance-arousing properties of hypocrisy were designed to motivate sexually active heterosexual college students to adopt the use of condoms to prevent AIDS (Aronson et al., 1991; Stone, Aronson, Crain, Winslow, & Fried, 1994). Participants first made a videotaped speech in which they argued that college students should use condoms with each and every act of intercourse. To induce hypocrisy, participants then generated a list of their previous failures to use condoms during sex. And, in fact, when made aware that they had acted hypocritically, participants reported higher intentions to use condoms in the future (Aronson et al., 1991), and when offered the opportunity, more "hypocrites" purchased condoms, compared to participants who merely advocated the use of condoms, who were made aware of their past failures to use condoms, or who read about the dangers of AIDS (Stone et al., 1994).

Nevertheless, if dissonance activates a goal to affirm a globally positive self, and people can avoid changing their behavior by affirming an important but *unrelated* positive attribute, then a hypocritical discrepancy may not motivate them to resolve the discrepancy by changing their behavior. We predicted that after an act of hypocrisy, when people have an opportunity to affirm the self by performing an unrelated positive action, they might use that dissonance-reduction strategy as a means to affirm the globally positive self, even if it does not restore a sense of honesty and sincerity. However, if an act of hypocrisy arouses dissonance because it threatens people's views of themselves as being honest and sincere in particular, then to restore their sense of integrity and thereby reduce dissonance, participants should be motivated to change the discrepant behavior. Thus, when provided a choice between doing something that would directly reduce their feelings of hypocrisy and restore their integrity, or doing something that would leave the hypocrisy intact but reduce their discomfort by affirming an unrelated positive attribute, most people would choose to do what it takes to reduce the feeling of being hypocritical.

In an experiment designed to test these predictions, some participants who had advocated the use of condoms and been reminded of their hypocrisy were given the opportunity to donate to a homeless shelter; such a prosocial behavior would reduce dissonance via general self-affirmation processes, but would not directly restore their sense of integrity. Other "hypocritical" participants were given the opportunity either to donate to a homeless shelter or to purchase condoms; their preference for condom purchases over donations to the homeless would reflect attempts to restore a consistent sense of self by targeting the dimension of self more closely tied to the source of their hypocritical behavior. Results supported the self-consistency prediction: When offered only the affirmation option, 83% of those in the hypocrisy condition donated to the homeless. However, when the affirmation strategy was offered alongside the opportunity to restore their sincerity by buying condoms, 78% chose to purchase condoms in order to directly restore their integrity, whereas only 13% chose the donation (affirmation) option. A second experiment replicated participants' choice to resolve hypocrisy-induced dissonance directly, even when an indirect affirmation strategy was more central to global self-worth.

Together, the results indicate that when the only dissonance-reduction opportunity available to hypocrites is doing something that affirms their overall good feelings about themselves, they will take advantage of it. After all, people will reduce dissonance by whatever route is most readily available to them. However, when they have a chance to do something that directly resolves the hypocrisy and restores a sense of honesty and sincerity, most people are motivated to reduce dissonance by taking that route (see also Fointiat, 2004). The effect of hypocrisy on prosocial behavior has been replicated in over 20 studies (see Stone & Fernandez, 2008, for a review), including conserving water (Dickerson, Thibodeau, Aronson, & Miller, 1992), participating in a recycling program (Fried & Aronson, 1995), taking action against policies that discriminate against minority group members (Son Hing, Li, & Zanna, 2002), promoting forgiveness (Takaku, 2006), and driving more safely (Fointiat, Grosbras, Michel, & Somat, 2001). These studies indicate that when people *publicly advocate* the importance of an action and are then *privately reminded* of their own *recent personal failures* to do it, hypocrisy motivates a specific form of dissonance arousal and reduction that changes the person's behavior.

AUDACITY, TENACITY, AND SCIENTIFIC PROGRESS

I originally wanted to describe what it was like to work with Elliot to develop the self-consistency interpretation of the hypocrisy paradigm, what it was like to spar with him intellectually during meetings in his office, or what it was like to play tennis against him (and to lose, no matter how hard I tried). But much of what I would say about these experiences is already described in one of my all-time favorite books about social psychology: *A Narrative History of Experimental Social Psychology: The Lewinian Tradition,* written by Shelly Patnoe (1988). Shelly's book documents the dynamic process by which we pass social psychology's theoretical and methodological torch to our graduate students. Because Shelly was teaching at my undergraduate institution, I was able to read her manuscript before I accepted Elliot's offer to study with him. One thing I learned from her interviews, and came to understand more completely through my own experience working with Elliot, is that conducting good experimental research in social psychology requires a high degree of audacity and tenacity—and Elliot used the word *audacity* long before Barack Obama did. To create new theory about the nature of human nature, we must have the audacity to fly in the face of conventional wisdom and to entertain the counterintuitive. And then we need the tenacity to pursue our theory when our studies don't turn out quite the way we predicted, when they succeed but journals reject them, when critics ignore our incontrovertible evidence, or when we need to pay attention to their criticism and to subsequent research in order to improve our theory. Elliot has been an inspiration not only when it comes to scientific social psychology, but also when it comes to audacity and tenacity. And one result of his efforts is that cognitive dissonance theory—now more than 50 years old, with thousands of experiments that have refined it, advanced it, and demonstrated its relevance to our lives—remains vibrant and heuristically valuable. No wonder my students and I continue to find his passion for theorizing and experimental research, and his unflagging efforts to bring social psychology to the "real world," to be infectious.

So I will close my celebration of Elliot's career by drawing attention to a lesson from his professional work that I believe is important for the future of social psychology: how we, as a field, view the relationship between basic research and applied, problem-focused research. This distinction, of course, has always been a source of tension: To what degree should social psychology become more willing to "translate" its theories into real-life application? I hope that social psychologists will become more problem-focused in our approach to testing new ideas derived from theory and better at communicating how our research addresses important social problems. If we want to increase the impact of our research—and continue to secure federal funding to support it—we have to think beyond the lab. As Claude Steele (2008) said in his keynote address at the Association for Psychological Science, "The broader contribution of our research will soon be determined less by the independent variables we artfully create in the laboratory and more by the dependent variables that we carefully measure in the field." Nevertheless, I think many social psychologists view the relationship between theory and application as mutually exclusive: To rigorously test the first, you must sacrifice the second. It's true that most of us are not trained to translate our theoretically derived ideas into solutions to social problems, in part because there are few rewards for doing so (see Pettigrew, this volume), but also in part because we do not understand that basic and applied research can coexist within the same theoretical framework, let alone in the same research laboratory.

I have learned from observing Elliot's research career, and from working directly with him, that conducting theory-driven basic research and addressing social problems are not mutually exclusive. Elliot's applied experimental research has always reflected the highest level of internal validity possible, and there is no substitute for that. But Elliot and his coinvestigators have also striven to ensure—dare I say it?—external validity. His experimental procedures in the laboratory are high in both experimental and mundane realism. And whenever he has ventured into the world outside the laboratory—studying children's dissonance-reduction strategies when they were confronted with mild admonitions to forgo a forbidden toy (Aronson & Carlsmith, 1963), following home energy auditors (Gonzales, Aronson, & Costanzo, 1988), or evaluating the effectiveness of the Jigsaw Classroom—he has conducted carefully controlled experiments while people were going about their everyday lives.

In working with Elliot, I learned to simultaneously carve out new theory in cognitive dissonance and to apply it to problems like reducing the transmission of HIV—in short, I learned that it is possible for research to bridge the gap between theory and application. This is the leap of faith that Elliot taught me to take as a social psychologist. He taught me to have unwavering faith in the enormous utility of social-psychological theory and to maintain faith in the high-impact experimental methodology that he helped to develop. And finally, he taught me to have faith that if we get the study right, our research has the potential to make the world a better place. As a field, we can and should have the same faith in the value of our theories and our research for improving people's lives. In many ways, Elliot's work has always defined the best of what social psychology brings to the table. It seems clear, especially for the current generation of researchers, that it also represents the best of what social psychology can become.

ACKNOWLEDGMENT

Preparation of this chapter was supported in part by the National Science Foundation under Grant No. BCS-0548405.

REFERENCES

References marked with an asterisk indicate studies included in the meta-analysis of the performance expectancy literature.

Aronson, E. (1968). Dissonance theory: Progress and problems. In R. P. Abelson, E. Aronson, W. J. McGuire, T. M. Newcomb, M. J. Rosenberg, and P. H. Tannenbaum (Eds.), *Theories of cognitive consistency: A sourcebook* (pp. 5–27). Chicago: Rand.

Aronson, E. (1999). Dissonance, hypocrisy, and the self-concept. In E. Harmon-Jones & J. Mills (Eds.), *Cognitive dissonance: Progress on a pivotal theory in social psychology* (pp. 103–126). Washington, DC: American Psychological Association.

Aronson, E., & Carlsmith, J. M. (1962). Performance expectancy as a determinant of actual performance. *Journal of Abnormal and Social Psychology, 65*, 178–182.

Aronson, E., & Carlsmith, J. M. (1963). Effect of the severity of threat on teh devaluation of forbidden behavior. *Journal of Abnormal and Social Psychology, 66,* 584–588.

Aronson, E., Fried, C. B., & Stone, J. (1991). Overcoming denial and increasing the use of condoms through the induction of hypocrisy. *American Journal of Public Health, 81,* 1636–1638.

Bargh, J. A., & Chartrand, T. L. (2000). The mind in the middle: A practical guide to priming and automaticity research. In H. Reis & C. Judd (Eds.), *Handbook of research methods in social psychology* (pp. 253–285). Boston: Cambridge Press.

*Beijk, J. (1966). Expectancy, performance and self-concept. *Acta Psychologica, 25,* 381–388.

Brehm, J. W. (1956). Postdecision changes in the desirability of alternatives, *Journal of Abnormal and Social Psychology, 52,* 384–389.

*Brock, T., Edelman, S. K., Edwards, D. C., & Schuck, J. R. (1965). Seven studies of performance expectancy as a determinant of actual performance. *Journal of Experimental Social Psychology, 1,* 295–310.

Cooper, J., & Fazio, R. H. (1984). A new look at dissonance theory. In L. Berkowitz (Ed.), *Advances in experimental social psychology* (Vol. 17, pp. 229–262). Hillsdale, NJ: Erlbaum.

*Cottrell, N. B. (1965). Performance expectancy as a determinant of actual performance: A replication with a new design. *Journal of Personality and Social Psychology, 2,* 685–692.

Demaree, K. G., Petty, R. E., & Brinol, P. (2007). Self-certainty: Parallels to attitude certainty. *International Journal of Psychology and Psychological Therapy. 7(2),* 155–198.

Dickerson, C. A., Thibodeau, R., Aronson, E., & Miller, D. (1992). Using cognitive dissonance to encourage water conservation. *Journal of Applied Social Psychology, 22,* 841–854.

Dipboye, R. L. (1977). A critical review of Korman's self-consistency theory of work motivation and occupational choice. *Organizational Behavior and Human Performance, 18,* 108–126.

Egan, L. C., Santos, L. R., & Bloom, P. (2007). The origins of cognitive dissonance: Evidence from children and monkeys. *Psychological Science, 18,* 978–983.

*Etgen, M. P., & Rosen, E. F. (1993). Cognitive dissonance: Physiological arousal in the performance expectancy paradigm. *Bulletin of the Psychonomic Society, 31(3),* 229–231.

Festinger, L. & Carlsmith, J. M. (1959). Cognitive consequences of forced compliance. *Journal of Abnormal and Social Psychology, 58,* 201–211.

Fointiat, V. (2004). "I know what I have to do, but…" When hypocrisy leads to behavioral change. *Social Behavior and Personality: An International Journal, 32,* 741–746.

Fointiat, V., Grosbras, J.-M., Michel, S., & Somat, A. (2001, May 10–12). *Encouraging young adults to drive carefully. The use of the hypocrisy paradigm.* Paper presented at Promoting Public Health, Chambery, France.

Fried, C. B., & Aronson, E. (1995). Hypocrisy, misattribution, and dissonance reduction. *Personality and Social Psychology Bulletin, 21,* 925–933.

Gibbons, F. X., Eggleston, T. J., & Benthin, A. (1997). Cognitive reactions to smoking relapse: The reciprocal relation of dissonance and self-esteem. *Journal of Personality and Social Psychology, 72,* 184–195.

Glass, D. C. (1964). Changes in liking as a means of reducing cognitive discrepancies between self-esteem and aggression. *Journal of Personality, 32,* 531–549.

Gonzales, M. H., Aronson, E., & Costanzo, M. (1988). Using social cognition and persuasion to promote energy conservation: A quasi-experiment. *Journal of Applied Social Psychology, 18*(12), 1049–1066.

Harmon-Jones, E., Brehm, J. W., Greenberg, J., Simon, L., & Nelson, D. E. (1996). Evidence that the production of aversive consequences is not necessary to create cognitive dissonance. *Journal of Personality and Social Psychology, 70*(1), 5–16.

Harmon-Jones, E., Harmon-Jones, C., Fearn, M., Sigelman, J. D., & Johnson, P. (2008). Left frontal cortical activation and spreading of alternatives: Tests of the action-based model of dissonance. *Journal of Personality and Social Psychology, 94,* 1–15.

Holland, R. W., Meertens, R. M., & Van Vugt, M. (2002). Dissonance on the road: Self-esteem as a moderator of internal and external self-justification strategies. *Personality and Social Psychology Bulletin, 28,* 1713–1724.

Hunter, J. E., & Schmidt, F. L. (1990). *Methods of meta-analysis: Correcting error and bias in research findings.* Newbury Park, CA: Sage.

Jones, S. C. (1973). Self and interpersonal evaluations: Esteem theories vs. consistency theories. *Psychological Bulletin, 79*(3), 185–199.

*Kornreich, L. B. (1968). Performance expectancy as a determinant of actual performance: Failure to replicate. *Psychological Reports, 22,* 535–543.

*Lowin, A., & Epstein, G. F. (1965). Does expectancy determine performance? *Journal of Experimental Social Psychology, 1,* 248–255.

*Maracek, J., & Mettee, D. (1972). Avoidance of continued success as a function of self-esteem, level of esteem certainty, and responsibility for success. *Journal of Personality and Social Psychology, 22,* 98–107.

Markus, H., & Kunda, Z. (1986). Stability and malleability of the self-concept. *Journal of Personality and Social Psychology, 51*(4), 858–866.

Martinie, M. A., & Fointiat, V. (2006). Self-esteem, trivialization, and attitude change. *Swiss Journal of Psychology, 65,* 221–225.

*Mettee, D. (1971). Rejection of unexpected success as a function of the negative consequences of accepting success. *Journal of Personality and Social Psychology, 17,* 332–341.

*Moran, G., & Klockars, A. J. (1967). Dissonance and performance alteration: Critique and empirical re-examination. *Journal of Social Psychology, 72,* 249–255.

Mullen, B. (1989). *Advanced basic meta-analysis.* Hillsdale, NJ: Erlbaum.

Nail, P. R., Misak, J. E., & Davis, R. M. (2004). Self-affirmation versus self-consistency: A comparison of two competing self-theories of dissonance phenomena. *Personality and Individual Differences, 36,* 1893–1905.

Patnoe, S. (1988). *A narrative history of experimental social psychology: The Lewinian tradition.* New York: Springer-Verlag.

Peterson, A. A., Haynes, G. A., & Olson, J. M. (2008). Self-esteem differences in the effects of hypocrisy induction on behavioral intentions in the health domain. *Journal of Personality, 76,* 305–322.

Prislin, R. & Pool, G. J. (1996). Behavior, consequences, and the self: Is all well that ends well? *Personality and Social Psychology Bulletin, 22,* 933–948.

Rosenthal, R. (1991). *Meta-analytic procedures for social research.* Beverly Hills, CA: Sage.

Sherman, D. K., & Cohen, G. L. (2006). The psychology of self-defense: Self-affirmation theory. In M. P. Zanna (Ed.), *Advances in experimental social psychology* (Vol. 38, pp. 183–242). San Diego, CA: Academic Press.

Shrauger, J. S. (1975). Response to evaluation as a function of initial self-perceptions. *Psychological Bulletin, 82*(4), 581–596.

*Silverman, I., & Marcantonio, C. (1965). Demand characteristics vs. dissonance reduction as determinants of failure-seeking behavior. *Journal of Personality and Social Psychology, 2,* 882–884.

Simon, L., Greenberg, J., & Brehm, J. (1995). Trivialization: The forgotten mode of dissonance reduction. *Journal of Personality and Social Psychology, 68*(2), 247–260.

Snyder, M., & Tanke, E. D. (1976). Behavior and attitude: Some people are more consistent than others. *Journal of Personality, 44,* 510–517.

Son Hing, L. S., Li, W., & Zanna, M. P. (2002). Inducing hypocrisy to reduce prejudicial responses among aversive racists. *Journal of Experimental Social Psychology, 38,* 71–78.

Steele, C. M. (1988). The psychology of self-affirmation: Sustaining the integrity of the self. In L. Berkowitz (Ed.), *Advances in experimental social psychology* (Vol. 21, pp. 261–302). Hillsdale, NJ: Erlbaum.

Steele, C. M. (2008, May). *Psychology as a hub science: Three themes for the future.* Paper presented at the 20th Annual Convention of the Association for Psychological Science, Chicago.

Steele, C. M., Spencer, S. J., & Lynch, M. (1993). Dissonance and affirmational resources: Resilience against self-image threats. *Journal of Personality and Social Psychology, 64*(6), 885–896.

Stone, J. (1994). *Self-consistency vs. self-enhancement in the performance-expectancy paradigm: A meta-analytic review.* Unpublished manuscript, Princeton University, Princeton, NJ.

Stone, J. (1999). What exactly have I done? The role of self-attribute accessibility in dissonance. In E. Harmon-Jones & J. Mills (Eds.), *Cognitive dissonance: Progress on a pivotal theory in social psychology* (pp. 175–200). Washington, DC: APA.

Stone, J. (2003). Self-consistency for low self-esteem in dissonance processes: The role of self-standards. *Personality and Social Psychology Bulletin, 29*, 846–858.

Stone, J. (2004). *Investigating the self-standards model of self-justification.* Unpublished data, University of Arizona, Tucson.

Stone, J., Aronson, E., Crain, A. L., Winslow, M. P., & Fried, C. B. (1994). Inducing hypocrisy as a means of encouraging young adults to use condoms. *Personality and Social Psychology Bulletin, 20*, 116–128.

Stone, J., & Cooper, J. (2001). A self-standards model of cognitive dissonance. *Journal of Experimental Social Psychology, 37*, 228–243.

Stone, J., & Cooper, J. (2003). The effect of self-attribute relevance on how self-esteem moderates attitude change in dissonance processes. *Journal of Experimental Social Psychology, 39*, 508–515.

Stone, J., & Fernandez, N. C. (2008). To practice what we preach: The use of hypocrisy and cognitive dissonance to motivate behavior change. *Social and Personality Psychology Compass, 2*(2), 1024–1051.

Stone, J., Wiegand, A. W., Cooper, J., & Aronson, E. (1997). When exemplification fails: Hypocrisy and the motive for self-integrity. *Journal of Personality and Social Psychology, 72*, 54–65.

Swann, W. B., Jr. (1990). To be adored or to be known? The interplay of self-enhancement and self-verification. In R. M. Sorrentino & E. T. Higgins (Eds.), *Motivation and cognition* (Vol. 2, pp. 408–448). New York: Guilford Press.

Takaku, S. (2006). Reducing road rage: An application of the dissonance-attribution model of interpersonal forgiveness. *Journal of Applied Social Psychology, 36*, 2362–2378.

*Taylor, S., & Huesmann, L. R. (1974). Expectancy confirmed again: A computer investigation of expectancy theory. *Journal of Experimental Social Psychology, 10*, 496–501.

Thibodeau, R., & Aronson, E. (1992). Taking a closer look: Reasserting the role of the self-concept in dissonance theory. *Personality and Social Psychology Bulletin, 18*(5), 591–602.

*Ward, W. D., & Sandvold, K. D. (1963). Performance expectancy as a determinant of actual performance: A partial replication. *Journal of Abnormal and Social Psychology, 67*, 293–295.

*Waterman, A. S., & Ford, L. H., Jr. (1965). Performance expectancy as a determinant of actual performance: Dissonance reduction or differential recall? *Journal of Personality and Social Psychology, 2*, 464–467.

Wicklund, R. A., & Brehm, J. W. (1976). *Perspectives on cognitive dissonance.* Hillsdale, NJ: Erlbaum.

*Zajonc, R. B., & Brickman, P. (1969). Expectancy and feedback as independent factors in task performance. *Journal of Personality and Social Psychology, 11*, 148–156.

8

RIDING THE D TRAIN WITH ELLIOT
The Aronsonian Legacy of Cognitive Dissonance

Joel Cooper
Princeton University

When I was an undergraduate at the City College of New York, I commuted from home to school each day by taking a lengthy subway ride on the D train. I was always fortunate to find a seat because I lived near the first station on the run. By the time the train pulled into 125th Street, we were packed like sardines in a can. One needed to plot an exit strategy one or two stops before the college station to successfully exit the train before the doors closed again. This scene repeated itself on a daily basis; the only thing that changed was the path I needed to create to reach the door. Plotting the exit strategy provided the amusement for the dark subterranean ride.

One day, instead of counting stations and plotting strategy, I looked up to find that my train was racing toward Columbus Circle, about 3 miles south of my station. For the first time, I found myself so engrossed in what I was reading that I felt no sense of time or place. The train rocked on its track, the doors opened and closed at 125th street, and I was reading my homework assignment for my social psychology class. I had just finished the procedure section of Aronson and Carlsmith's (1963) study in which children were forbidden to play with an attractive toy and convinced themselves that they did not like the toy very much if the threat had been mild rather than severe. It was a finding artfully derived from a theory called cognitive dissonance. And it was the seminal moment that would drive my own career as a social psychologist.

As we all know, Leon Festinger (1957) created the theory of cognitive dissonance, and his ingenious creativity is unquestioned. However, I would argue that no one was more influential in the development of cognitive dissonance theory as a major force in social psychology than Elliot Aronson. His insight into the nuances of human behavior, his ability to write engagingly and creatively, and his unparalleled ability to stage the ideal experiment have enabled him to carve that indelible niche in the history of the field. Because I have played some part in the development of dissonance theory, it is humbling to be able to reflect on Elliot's contributions to dissonance theory. As is true for most reflections, this one tells a story. It is partly a story about cognitive dissonance, but like most stories, it is at least partly personal. That is where this story begins. No one yet knows where the story will end because the legacy of Elliot Aronson will endure long into the future.

COGNITIVE DISSONANCE: THE EARLY DAYS

Dissonance theory challenged the zeitgeist of the day. Learning theories pervaded what was at that time called experimental psychology, and they reached into social behavior as well. One of the most elaborate and comprehensive approaches of the 1950s was the massive study of attitudes and attitude change by the Yale Communication and Attitude Change Program. The empirical work of that group continues to be an important corpus of work (Hovland & Janis, 1959; Hovland, Janis, & Kelley, 1953). Nonetheless, it was guided loosely by ideas of learning and reinforcement that served more as an underlying foundation and assumption than scrutinized by empirical test. Learning was the key to persuasion. Incentives and rewards facilitate learning, and that simply followed as sunset follows sunrise.

Festinger and Carlsmith (1959) ripped a hole in that logic when their classic study of persuasion showed that, under the proper conditions, attitude change is an inverse function of the magnitude of incentive. Why? Because of the arousal of cognitive dissonance. Elliot and Jud Mills (Aronson & Mills, 1959) widened the hole when they showed that the presumably negative state of suffering led to greater liking of a group and that the more the suffering, the greater the liking. Why? Because of the arousal of cognitive dissonance. And, as they say in the music world, the hits just kept on coming. Dissonance theory predicted all kinds of phenomena that were not predictable from theories that psychologists thought were fundamental. In one of those classic studies, Elliot and Merrill Carlsmith (Aronson & Carlsmith, 1963) showed that children refrained from playing with an attractive toy not when they were threatened with severe punishment, which would be predicted from learning theory, but when they were threatened by a minor admonition. Reading those data when they were published, I missed my stop on the D train. But you already know that.

Disagreement in the Dissonance Camp

As most psychologists know, cognitive dissonance is an aversive state akin to a drive, and it is brought about by the perception that a pair of cognitions is inconsistent. The efficiency of the dissonance statement is undoubtedly one of the aspects that made it so provocative and so useful. With that single notion, great bodies of work were begun and the fundamental assumptions of other theories when applied to social interactions were suddenly open to question. However, the worst kept secret of dissonance analyses is that social life is rarely that simple. There are discrepant cognitions and consonant cognitions. Some are more important than others and some can be changed more easily than others. When dissonance is aroused, it is not always clear how the arousal will be reduced. Which cognition will change? How will we know whether the cognitions are sufficiently discrepant to create a sufficient amount of arousal to force a change? Are there any cognitions that are more special than others in arousing dissonance? As Elliot has remarked on a number of occasions, if you needed to know the answer to these questions in the early days, there was only one way to get it: Ask Leon!

There were some theoretical disagreements that surfaced. Some of us (I had come of data-collecting age by that time) began to look for modifiers of the dissonance effect. Did choice matter? Yes, it turned out that inconsistent cognitions required choice in order for dissonance to be aroused (Linder, Cooper, & Jones, 1967). Did commitment matter? Yes, it turned out that people had to be committed to their counterattitudinal cognitions for the inconsistency to arouse dissonance (Carlsmith, Collins, & Helmreich, 1966; Davis & Jones, 1960).

Elliot (Aronson, 1968) asked a more fundamental question: Did the self matter? Although the import of this question remained dormant for several years, it is typical of Elliot that he raised the fundamental question that propelled an enormous amount of research for the next several decades. The issue began straightforwardly enough. In Festinger's original treatise on dissonance, he delineated a number of examples that he believed were clear instances of dissonance. One was of a person standing in the rain but not getting wet. Elliot once told me that he always found that example perplexing. It did not feel right that someone standing in the rain, but noticing that he or she was dry would experience the same psychological state as someone who had advocated a position inconsistent with his or her attitudes or who had suffered to attain a worthless goal. Although it seemed like dissonance to Festinger and certainly emerged from the notion that inconsistent cognitions create dissonance, it struck Elliot as something other than dissonance. The dry person standing in the rain might be confused, perplexed, bewildered, but not in a dissonant state. The missing element, according to Elliot, was the very special cognition that is crucial to a dissonant state: one's view of oneself.

Elliot was the master of finding the right colloquial expression to create a meaningful portrait. Dissonance, he offered, occurred when people acted like "schnooks." Who but a schnook would try to convince a fellow student that an insufferably boring task was really interesting or convince a dean that tuition should increase at their university? No matter whether readers knew what a schnook was. The New Yorkism was clear from his example. You had to be a schnook to do the things that were requested of you in dissonance experiments, and people do not like to think of themselves as schnooks. Enter, then, the self-concept. Dissonance is aroused for the person making a counterattitudinal speech not because the speech is logically the obverse of the person's opinion, but because he acted schnooky: acting like a schnook was at variance with the actor's generally positive self-concept. That is why the person in the rain would not experience dissonance: He did not act in a way that was at variance with his self-concept. His self-concept was not involved at all. In contrast, make someone feel like a schnook, and then any action that is inconsistent with the schnook's self-concept will be experienced as dissonance (Aronson & Carlsmith, 1962; Aronson, Carlsmith, & Darley, 1963).

To Elliot's credit, his work never broke with Festinger's and he did not describe his self-theory as a renegade model. Rather, his reliance on the importance of the self provided a way of talking about dissonance that helped to make him the most persuasive spokesperson for the dissonance tradition. When serious criticisms were raised about some of the empirical support for and theoretical foundations of the theory, it was typically Elliot's reply that put the issue to rest (e.g., Aronson, 1968). And as Elliot helped us view the world from the vantage point of the decent person acting like a schnook, cognitive dissonance theory made so much sense.

Will the True Cognitive Dissonance Please Rise?

Given that no good theory can remain static for long, researchers began to question the necessary role of inconsistency alone in dissonance arousal. I was one of the culprits in that enterprise. Russell Fazio, my student and colleague, and I produced a new version of dissonance theory that argued that dissonance is aroused when people take responsibility for unwanted consequences of their behavior. This "new look" model (Cooper & Fazio, 1984) argued that people learn to be upset about aversive events for which they were responsible. Attitude change, as one possible dependent measure, is at the service of reducing the aversiveness of the consequence. If an individual acts in such a way as to contribute to, let us say, a tuition increase at his or her university, then deciding that a tuition increase is actually a good idea renders the consequences nonaversive. If you can convince yourself that tuition truly should rise, then you have brought about a positive outcome, not a negative one. Turning the negative outcome into a positive state is what dissonance reduction is all about.

Hypocrisy and Cognitive Dissonance

Although my colleagues and I published numerous studies using the new look paradigm during the ensuing decade, I cannot say that Elliot was ever a fan of this approach. Partly to demonstrate that dissonance occurred independently of aversive consequences, Ruth Thibodeau and Elliot (1992; see also Fried & Aronson, 1995; Dickerson, Thibodeau, Aronson, & Miller, 1992) invented an ingenious dissonance paradigm in which people were induced to make a statement that was consistent with their attitudes and values, but inconsistent with their past behaviors. This novel procedure, of course, allowed people to advocate for a wanted or liked position, with dissonance aroused by the realization that they had acted inconsistently in the past. Dubbed the hypocrisy paradigm, it opened new avenues for research in cognitive dissonance, and it reinvigorated the debate about the importance of the self.

As usual for experiments in which Elliot was involved, the research on hypocrisy had flair and drama. In one study, male college students were asked to deliver a speech to a high school audience, taking the strong position that condoms should always be worn during sex (Stone, Aronson, Cain, Winslow, & Fried, 1994). The students believed this and were happy to videotape their speeches that would be shown in high school classes. However, when the critical experimental group of participants was asked to admit, off camera, to times when they had not used condoms during sex, the conditions for hypocrisy-driven dissonance were met. Because the participants already believed that it was important to use condoms, the usual attitude change measure of most dissonance studies did not seem workable. So, the experimenters devised an interesting behavioral measure: They gave participants the opportunity to purchase condoms before leaving the taping session. Compared to participants who had given no speech and to participants who remained for the moment unmindful of their past risky sexual behaviors, those who had made the procondom speech and who had been reminded of their past (hypocritical) behaviors left the study with more condoms in their pockets.

The one and only time that I had the opportunity to collaborate with Elliot was in the use of the hypocrisy paradigm to solve another mystery that had been brewing in the cognitive dissonance literature. In a well-known and influential series of studies, Claude Steele and his colleagues developed the notion of self-affirmation. Like Elliot, Steele (1988) offered the notion that the arousal of cognitive dissonance was based upon the need to protect the self-concept. However, unlike Elliot, Steele argued that the motivation to affirm the self, thereby restoring a sense of self-worth, was the *primary* reason that people change their attitudes or behavior following inconsistency. If given the opportunity to affirm their self-worth in a different way, they will seize upon it and not deal directly with the inconsistency that produced the initial arousal.

Elliot's former graduate student and my postdoctoral fellow, Jeff Stone, brought us together to collaborate on a new study (Stone, Weigand, Cooper, & Aronson, 1997). We used the hypocrisy paradigm to test the two theories. We viewed dissonance as a primary drive state that people wanted to reduce as effectively and efficiently as possible. Rather than thinking of attitude and behavior change as small battles in a global war for self-affirmation, we viewed the need to reduce dissonance as primary. We reasoned that under some conditions, such as those studied so well by Steele and his colleagues (e.g., Steele & Liu, 1983; Steele, Spencer, & Lynch, 1993), self-affirming actions may be the only way to help reduce the overall impact of dissonance, but when given a choice, people would prefer direct attitudinal or behavioral methods to reduce dissonance-induced aversive states.

In one of our experiments, we asked male students to prepare videotapes advocating the use of condoms, and, in a procedure similar to that used by Jeff Stone and his colleagues (1994), we made them mindful of times when they had not personally used condoms during sex. Our results confirmed that hypocrisy was aroused. Again, following their attitude-consistent videotape, participants who were reminded of past failures to use condoms purchased more condoms than did participants who had not made the speech or who were not reminded of their prior inconsistent behavior.

We added two new wrinkles: The first was to see whether students would use self-affirmation to reduce dissonance, if that were their only way to do it. And indeed they did. Instead of providing the option to purchase condoms, we offered participants a chance to donate money to an important charity—a project to help the homeless—that could bolster their overall sense of self-worth. In the hypocrisy conditions of the study, when giving to the homeless was the only option available, over 80% of participants donated, but only 10% were generous when they had not been made mindful of their past transgressions. So it appears that feeling that you are hypocritical generates a motivation for positive, self-affirming behaviors—when the direct approach to reducing dissonance is unavailable (i.e., there is no opportunity to purchase condoms).

The theoretical importance of our study came from the second new wrinkle. We gave students in the key experimental condition the option of purchasing condoms (direct dissonance reduction) or of donating to the important charity (self-affirmation). When people experienced dissonance via the induction of hypocrisy, 78% chose to spend their money on condoms, whereas only 13% chose the indirect dissonance-reduction technique of making a charitable donation—a whopping preference for the direct route over the indirect route to dissonance reduction. Still, when the only option available to other participants to reduce their dissonance involved the indirect method of donating to the homeless, fully 83% of participants did so. Thus, when self-affirmation is the only way to reduce dissonance, participants will seize the opportunity; but when given the choice between direct and indirect dissonance-reduction strategies, people will choose the former.

I totally respect the ingenuity of the hypocrisy paradigm and the new insights it provides into the arousal of dissonance. Still, I have disagreed with Elliot's assumption that the hypocrisy paradigm undermines my own argument that personal responsibility for the negative consequences of our actions is the prime motivation behind dissonance reduction. Rather, I have argued that it is precisely the recollection of prior attitude-inconsistent behaviors that is necessary for the experience of hypocrisy, and that is also, ipso facto, the aversive consequence of hypocrisy (Cooper, 1992). In the condom studies, the aversive event for which people felt responsible was the risk they took by forgoing safe sex practices. If there ever were a real controversy between Elliot's self-consistency viewpoint and the notion that responsibility for aversive consequences propels the arousal of cognitive dissonance, I think we put it to bed when Jeff Stone and I integrated the two ideas into the self-standards model of cognitive dissonance (see Stone & Cooper, 2001).

EXPANDING THE SELF: THE ROLE OF GROUP IDENTITY

Elliot deserves the credit for recognizing that the self is a critical feature of dissonance arousal, and one of the exciting developments in modern social psychology is a growing understanding that the self is a multiply determined concept that includes group memberships and group identity as key elements. Following that logic to its next step, we should be able to find a role for group identity in dissonance theory and thereby expand the theory beyond the individual focus that characterized its early development. That idea connects Elliot's insights of the 1960s to current progress in dissonance theory.

A basic feature of social life is that people belong to groups. Sometimes their membership is official, the groups have formal boundaries, and members are publicly identified. A child in the Boy Scouts and an adult in Rotary Club are members of such groups. And of course people also belong to many informal groups, some of which come and go seasonally. Being a Bronx resident, I am a New York Yankees fan; Elliot, who grew up near Boston, remains an ardent Red Sox fan. Membership in these groups is informal; I can claim being a Yankee fan or dismiss it. Yet my membership in the group of Yankee fans can play a major role in how I think of myself. If it is baseball season and the Yankees are doing well, I feel better; my self-esteem rises. In the winter, Yankee-fandom is unimportant to my self-esteem. What is important, however, is that the groups I belong to influence my self-esteem. As important as it is for me to have a positive sense of my own achievements, it is also important that I view my social group in a positive and enhancing manner.

Henri Tajfel's (1972, 1982) social identity theory and the concomitant theory of social categorization (Turner, Hogg, Oakes, Reicher, & Wetherell, 1987) argue that people represent social groups in terms of prototypes. We typically think of our own groups in a more positive way than we think of out-groups, and in either case we tend to depersonalize group members—ours or theirs—and lose sight of their idiosyncratic features. From my Bronx perspective, I may imagine that crazy Red Sox fans are all alike; I see a more flattering prototype of "all" Yankee fans, with whom I align myself.

A Little Thought Experiment   Now let's try a thought experiment. You are in a room with fellow group members—let us say, members of your university's faculty—and you overhear one of your colleagues, Harry, agree to make a statement opposing a county ordinance that would have increased funding for recycling. Harry has agreed to argue against the ordinance that you favor, that the faculty at your university favors, and that the faculty member in question most likely favors.

Obviously, Harry should experience cognitive dissonance: He has agreed to make a counterattitudinal statement with high choice and low incentive, and you can predict that he will be motivated to change his attitudes toward recycling. The interesting new question in this thought experiment is: "What about *you*?" You and Harry are members of the same group. Your selves are intertwined by common group membership. According to social identity and social categorization theories, your and Harry's identities are fused as long as your membership as fellow faculty members is salient. Will you also experience dissonance on his behalf, and will you also change your attitude toward recycling?

Recent research indicates that the answer to these questions is yes, as I will show. But I want to acknowledge that Elliot's emphasis on the self as a crucial element in dissonance opened the door to considering the broader question of the influence of one's *social* self on the experience of cognitive dissonance.

The Theory of Vicarious Dissonance

My collaborators and I believe that cognitive dissonance can be experienced on behalf of someone else under three conditions: (1) When people share the same social identity (i.e., are both members of the same social group), (2) the group is important, and (3) group membership is salient and accessible (Cooper, in press; Cooper & Hogg, 2007; Monin, Norton, Cooper, & Hogg, 2004; Norton, Monin, Cooper, & Hogg, 2003). In the earlier example of your fellow faculty member, you will experience dissonance vicariously because you share a salient social identity with Harry and you have observed him act in a way that should cause him to feel dissonance. Because of the fusion of your personal self with the group prototype, you will empathically share his discomfort.

The notion of how to test vicarious dissonance came about with the initiation of a new residency arrangement for freshmen at Princeton, where we conducted our study. All freshmen entering the university are randomly assigned to one of several residential colleges. Students, their parents, and faculty have no say-so whatsoever in where students live. These colleges are social and residential; students live in their colleges, dine together, and have parties there.

The random assignment of incoming students to colleges served as a tailor-made way to operationalize in-groups and out-groups. We designed a cover story, the details of which I will outline because I think that Elliot would have smiled at the procedure. Participants arrived for a study of "linguistic subcultures" in groups of two, although they were taken to separate rooms, each equipped with two-way mirrors. We told them that the purpose of the study was to investigate the way that group cultures create slight but measurable differences in speaking patterns. Just as someone living in Boston develops a pattern of speech that differs from that of someone living in Charlotte, people living in small microcultures can develop unique speech patterns that are different in subtle ways from other microcultures. Our study, we told them, was designed to see whether students living in different residential colleges had developed unique and discernable ways of speaking.

We explained that one of the two students who arrived for the study would randomly be assigned the role of speaker and the other would randomly be assigned the role of listener. The speaker would be given a speech topic, provided with a few minutes to prepare, and then deliver an oral argument that the other student would rate. This provided the opportunity for the listener to overhear a speech, one that would turn out to be a counterattitudinal advocacy of an unpopular, unwanted policy on the university campus. In reality, both participants were independently told that they were assigned to be the listener. Unbeknownst to them, all further interactions with the experimenter were actually piped in on audiotape, as was the counterattitudinal speech that the participants were to hear.

The participants believed that they overheard the experimenter ask their partner some basic demographic questions, one of which was to identify the residential college in which he or she lived. The tape recordings were arranged so that each participant was randomly assigned to learn that the partner (i.e., the student who had been assigned to be the speaker) was either from his or her own college (in-group condition) or from another college (out-group condition). The experimenter was then heard asking the speaker if he or she was willing to make a speech on the topic of why tuition rates should be raised significantly. All participants heard the speaker agree to make this speech. After some perfunctory ratings of the speech patterns of the pro-tuition speech, participants were asked for their own attitudes on the question of whether tuition should be raised significantly.

The predictions of our study follow from our combination of cognitive dissonance and social identity theories. When the speaker was an in-group member, we expected that social identity would facilitate an empathic bond through which the listener would pick up the speaker's emotional experience. In the out-group condition, we expected no such empathic bond to form. But we needed one more element before making a prediction about attitude change. I may value being a Yankee fan, a university professor, and a member of the Association for Psychological

Science, but care less about my membership in other groups, such as the Automobile Club. Consequently, we asked students how important their residential college was to them and how much they identified with their college.

We predicted that participants who feel most identified with their groups should experience dissonance and change their own attitudes after overhearing a fellow in-group member agree to make a counterattitudinal speech in favor of a tuition increase. But when participants do not feel attached to their group, the speaker's counterattitudinal advocacy should not resonate with them, no matter whether the speaker is an in-group member or an out-group member. In short, we predicted a statistical interaction in which dissonance would be experienced vicariously only by students who shared a social identity with the speaker and for whom that social identity was important. The results supported that prediction.

My colleagues and I (Norton et al., 2003) subsequently reported three studies supporting the predictions of vicarious dissonance and showing that vicarious dissonance follows the rules of personal dissonance. For a person to experience personal cognitive dissonance, the attitude-discrepant behavior must be freely chosen; performing the discrepant behavior because one was ordered to do it by an authority does not arouse dissonance. The same is true of vicarious dissonance. Witnessing a fellow group member perform a counterattitudinal behavior because an authority ordered the person to do so does not lead to vicarious dissonance, whereas chosen behavior does. Similarly, unwanted consequences must follow from a counterattitudinal behavior in order for that behavior to lead to personal dissonance; so, too, for vicarious dissonance. Observing a fellow in-group member agree to make a speech that has no unwanted consequence does not produce vicarious dissonance, but observing the same behavior with a negative consequence produces vicarious dissonance and attitude change in the observer.

When an observer witnesses a fellow group member act in a dissonance-producing fashion, the observer experiences what we have called vicarious affect. When we asked observers, "How would you feel if you were in the speechwriter's shoes?" the observers' ratings of discomfort and arousal completely mimicked the results for attitude change. In conditions of high vicarious dissonance, observers changed their attitudes *and* indicated that they felt the speechwriter's pain.

Let's return to our thought experiment in which we pondered the impact of a fellow university faculty member agreeing to make a statement against a proposed recycling program. We have learned some important facts about how you would be affected. If the counterattitudinal statement was made under the conditions that would have caused personal dissonance in your colleague, then it has the potential to cause vicarious dissonance in you. The potential for vicarious dissonance will result in vicarious arousal and attitude change, provided that your self-representation is embedded within the same social group as the speechmaker's—that is, you share in-group membership and your identification with that group is strong. In the thought experiment, if you are not a fellow faculty member or if you do not care about that particular group identity, then vicarious dissonance will be low. However, if you are in the same in-group and strongly identify yourself with that group, you will experience vicarious affect and you will most likely change your attitude about the recycling program.

The Social Self and Culture: Vicarious Dissonance in East and West

One fascinating feature of combining social identity and cognitive dissonance is that it expands the reach of the original theory. When I rode the D train reading Elliot's amazing work, I did not see any need for expanding the impact of dissonance beyond the counterintuitive and theoretically rich work that showed that social life was not all about rewards and punishments. But today, by understanding that dissonance is no longer exclusively personal, but is shared by members of a social group, we also are in a position to examine some of the less obvious ways that dissonance is experienced around the globe. Hazel Markus and Shinobu Kitayama (1991) raised the intriguing question of whether it is wise to assume that cognitive dissonance is a universal phenomenon. Because personal cognitive dissonance relies on the mental representations of a single individual making inferences about the consistency or inconsistency of his or her attitudes and behavior, it seemed reasonable to question whether the same phenomenon is as likely to occur in collectivist cultures that emphasize relationships and interpersonal social bonds as it is in individualistic cultures that rely on individualistic perspectives.

Cognitive dissonance research conducted in cultures that are more collectivist than European and North American cultures suggests that there are limits to the degree to which people in collectivist cultures experience dissonance. Some researchers have suggested that cognitive dissonance does not exist in collectivist cultures (Heine & Lehman, 1997). Other researchers have shown that the arousal of dissonance among East Asians requires attention to the social milieu (Hoshino-Brown et al., 2005). Simply making a dissonance-inducing choice between two consumer items or writing a counterattitudinal essay may be sufficient to arouse dissonance in an individualistic culture, but not in a collectivist one.

Vicarious dissonance, however, is a uniquely social phenomenon. We know that it occurs in social groups in individualistic cultures (Monin et al., 2004; Norton et al., 2003). However, if dissonance arousal depends on social relationships in collectivist cultures, then vicarious dissonance should be an exceedingly powerful phenomenon in those cultures. The strong relationships among members of social groups should enhance the empathic transmission of vicarious dissonance.

Jihye Choye asked students at Korea University in Seoul to participate in a study on the effect of increased tuition rates at their university. The study was conducted in Korean, but was otherwise a faithful replication of our Princeton study (Norton et al., 2003). Again, students were told that they were participating in a study on linguistic subcultures—those small microcultures of linguistic differences that we had described to Princeton students. Instead of using two residential colleges within a university, the alleged speech that supported tuition increases at Korea University was either given by another in-group member from Korea University or by an out-group member, a student from neighboring Yonsei University.

The participants overheard their in-group or out-group partner agree to make the speech advocating a tuition increase and were led to believe that the dean of the university was interested in hearing the content of the speech. As in our previous experiment (Norton et al., 2003), the key variables were the group identification of the speaker and the degree of attachment that the participant felt toward his or her in-group. At the conclusion of the study, participants' attitudes were measured. Was there vicarious dissonance in this East Asian society?

The answer was a resounding yes. The results showed a strong replication of the effects that we had found in the individualistic culture of the United States and that we subsequently replicated in Australia. Highly identified Korea University students changed their attitudes to become more favorable to a tuition increase. In addition, Choye conducted a study in South Korea featuring personal cognitive dissonance. When she asked students at Korea University to write their own counterattitudinal statements endorsing a tuition increase, she found that they did not change their attitudes toward tuition, regardless of the presence of conditions that usually generate dissonance-induced attitude change. Regardless of choice or the presence of aversive consequences, there was no evidence of personal dissonance occurring for this sample of Korea University students. By contrast, vicarious dissonance was alive and well in the South Korean collectivist culture.

THE ARONSON LEGACY: A REPRISE

It is hard to imagine an area of research that has been more prolific and sustaining than cognitive dissonance theory. It is also hard to imagine any area of research within dissonance theory, including the latest work, that has not benefited from Elliot's presence. Controversies about how culture influences dissonance, for example, ultimately come down to controversies about the meaning of the self. And it was Elliot who prompted us to see the central role of the self-concept in dissonance arousal. Moreover, the notion of vicarious dissonance might never have been conceived without Elliot's prior theorizing.

Social psychology in general, and dissonance theory in particular, would have been impoverished without Elliot's contributions. For dissonance theory, he was the scholar who generated theoretically driven hypotheses with counterintuitive predictions. He was the experimenter who conjured up memorable situations that were vivid in participants' and readers' minds alike. Who has ever read Elliot's articles and failed to visualize the look of a 1950s college coed asked to read a list of sexually explicit words or the look of a child gazing longingly at a terrific toy robot after a mild request to play with other less attractive toys instead? Who cannot imagine the look of a student asked to choose the schizophrenic student from an array of yearbook photographs? And Elliot was the master communicator, the writer who made us feel what dissonance felt like by asking us see the world through the eyes of the participant-turned-schnook.

What I always liked about the New York City subway system was that the D train never shut down. There was no hour that marked the beginning of the day and no last train. I think it is fitting that my introduction to Elliot Aronson began on the D train. You can miss your stop if you are engrossed in what you are doing, but it also helps you get to where you need to go. Elliot Aronson's scholarship in social psychology did that for me. It brought me into a new world of social behavior, scholarship, and research, and helped me find my direction. I did not always agree with Elliot, nor did he always agree with me, but the ride was always invigorating. Anyone can ride the D train with Elliot. The train always keeps running.

REFERENCES

Aronson, E. (1968). Dissonance theory: Progress and problems. In R. P. Abelson, E. Aronson, W. J. McGuire, T. M. Newcomb, M. J. Rosenberg, & P. H. Tannenbaum (Eds.), *Theories of cognitive consistency: A sourcebook* (pp. 5–27). Chicago: Rand McNally.

Aronson, E., & Carlsmith, J. M. (1962). Performance expectancy as a determinant of actual performance. *Journal of Abnormal and Social Psychology, 66,* 584–588.

Aronson, E., & Carlsmith, J. M. (1963). The effect of the severity of threat on the devaluation of forbidden behavior. *Journal of Abnormal and Social Psychology, 66,* 584–588.

Aronson, E., Carlsmith, J. M., & Darley, J. M. (1963). The effect of expectancy on volunteering for an unpleasant experience. *Journal of Abnormal and Social Psychology, 66,* 220–224.

Aronson, E., & Mills, J. (1959). The effect of severity of initiation on liking for a group. *Journal of Abnormal and Social Psychology, 59,* 177–181.

Carlsmith, J. M., Collins, B. E., & Helmreich, R. (1966). Studies in forces compliance: 1. The effect of pressure for compliance on attitudes change produced by face to face role playing and anonymous essay writing. *Journal of Personality and Social Psychology, 4,* 1–13.

Cooper, J. (1992). Dissonance and the return of the self-concept. *Psychological Inquiry, 3,* 320–323.

Cooper, J. (in press). Vicarious cognitive dissonance: Changing attitudes by experiencing another's pain. In J. Forgas, W. Crano, & J. Cooper (Eds.), *Sydney Symposium on Social Psychology.* London: Blackwell.

Cooper, J., & Fazio, R. H. (1984). A new look at dissonance theory. In L. Berkowitz (Ed.), *Advances in experimental social psychology* (pp. 229–264). Orlando, FL: Academic Press.

Cooper, J., & Hogg, M. A. (2007). Feeling the anguish of others: A theory of vicarious dissonance. In M. P. Zanna (Ed.), *Advances in experimental social psychology* (Vol. 39, 359–403). San Diego, CA: Academic Press.

Davis, K. E., & Jones, E. E. (1960). Change in interpersonal perception as a means of reducing cognitive dissonance. *Journal of Abnormal and Social Psychology, 61,* 402–410.

Dickerson, C., Thibodeau, R., Aronson, E., & Miller, D. (1992). Using cognitive dissonance to encourage water conservation. *Journal of Applied Social Psychology, 22,* 841–854.

Festinger, L. (1957). *A theory of cognitive dissonance.* Stanford, CA: Stanford University Press.

Festinger, L. & Carlsmith, J. M. (1959). Cognitive consequences of forced compliance. *Journal of Abnormal and Social Psychology, 59,* 203–210.

Fried, C., & Aronson, E. (1995). Hypocrisy, misattribution, and dissonance reduction. *Personality and Social Psychology Bulletin, 21,* 925–933.

Heine, S. J., & Lehman, D. R. (1997). Culture, dissonance, and self-affirmation. *Personality and Social Psychology Bulletin, 23,* 389–400.

Hoshino-Brown, E., Zanna, A. S., Spencer, S. J., Zanna, M. P., Kitayama, S., & Lackenbauer, S. (2005). On the cultural guises of cognitive dissonance: The case of Easterners and Westerners. *Journal of Personality and Social Psychology, 89,* 294–310.

Hovland, C., & Janis, I. (Eds.) (1959). *Personality and persuasability.* New Haven, CT: Yale University Press.

Hovland, C., Janis, I., & Kelley, H. H. (1953). *Communication and persuasion: Psychological studies of opinion change.* New Haven, CT: Yale University.
Linder, D. E., Cooper, J., & Jones, E. E. (1967). Decision freedom as a determinant of the role of incentive magnitude in attitude change. *Journal of Personality and Social Psychology, 6,* 245–254.
Markus, H., & Kitayama, S. (1991). Culture and the self: Implications for cognition, emotion and motivation. *Psychological Review, 98,* 224–253.
Monin, B., Norton, M. I., Cooper, J., & Hogg, M. A. (2004). Reacting to an assumed situation vs. conforming to an assumed reaction: The role of perceived speaker attitude in vicarious dissonance. *Group Processes and Intergroup Relations, 7,* 207–220.
Norton, M. I., Monin, B., Cooper, J., & Hogg, M. A. (2003). Vicarious dissonance: Attitude change from the inconsistency of others. *Journal of Personality and Social Psychology, 85,* 47–62.
Steele, C. (1988). The psychology of self-affirmation: Sustaining the integrity of the self. In L. Berkowitz (Ed.), *Advances in experimental social psychology* (Vol. 21, pp. 261–302). San Diego, CA: Academic Press.
Steele, C., & Liu, T. J. (1983). Dissonance processes as self-affirmation. *Journal of Personality and Social Psychology, 45,* 5–19.
Steele, C., Spencer, S., & Lynch, M. (1993). Self-image resilience and dissonance: The role of affirmational resources. *Journal of Personality and Social Psychology, 64,* 885–896.
Stone, J., Aronson, E., Crain, A. L., Winslow, M. P., & Fried, C. B. (1994). Inducing hypocrisy as a means of encouraging young adults to use condoms. *Personality and Social Psychology Bulletin, 20,* 116–128.
Stone, J., & Cooper, J. (2001). A self-standards model of cognitive dissonance. *Journal of Experimental Social Psychology, 39,* 508–515.
Stone, J., Wiegand, A. W., Cooper, J., & Aronson, E. (1997). When exemplification fails: Hypocrisy and the motive for self-integrity. *Journal of Personality and Social Psychology, 72,* 54–65.
Tajfel, H. (1972). Social categorization. English manuscript of "La categorization sociale." In S. Moscovici (Ed.), *Introduction a la psychologie sociale* (pp. 272–302). Paris: Larousse.
Tajfel, H. (1982). *Social identity and intergroup relations.* Cambridge, UK: Cambridge University Press.
Thibodeau, R., & Aronson, E. (1992). Taking a closer look: Reasserting the role of the self-concept in dissonance theory. *Personality and Social Psychology Bulletin, 18,* 591–602.
Turner, J. C., Hogg, M. A., Oakes, P. J., Reicher, S. D., & Wetherell, M. S. (1987). *Rediscovering the social group: A self-categorization theory.* Oxford, UK: Blackwell.

9

SELF-PERSUASION WHEN IT MATTERS TO SELF

Attitude Importance and Dissonance Reduction After Counterattitudinal Advocacy

Michael R. Leippe and Donna Eisenstadt

John Jay College of Criminal Justice, City University of New York

Among many more exciting and flattering words, *important* often comes to mind for us when we think about Elliot Aronson. To be sure, this is partly because Elliot is a hugely important social scientist who has made important contributions to basic social-psychological knowledge, and has applied it to solving important social problems. But *important* also connects with two other defining qualities of his work and ideas. As the first to openly recognize the essential involvement of the self-concept in cognitive dissonance, Elliot led the way to understanding the critical role of attitude importance (to the self) in the arousal and disposition of dissonance. And, by repeatedly pointing his research programs and methodology at everyday behaviors and attitudes and real-world applications to social issues, Elliot championed the idea that social-psychological research should be important in terms of relating to actual lives, and to producing outcomes—changes in behavior—that have visible effect sizes.

Yet a certain irony arises from these two pillars of importance: We should apply our science to important matters, but the more important the attitude or social behavior we might like to change, the more difficult it will be to change it through dissonance-based techniques. Elliot identified targets with tough hides as important to go after and identified a critical reason—*importance to the self*—why the hides are tough and why dissonance-reducing techniques may be too weak to penetrate those tough hides.

Unfortunately, there has been all too little research on the relation between attitude importance and dissonance, and what research there is offers some mixed results. We will look closely at the matter in this chapter, and present some of our own relevant studies. First, we must trace how Elliot's thinking about self-consistency figures into the attitude-importance factor in dissonance, and also identify the social influence domain and corresponding dissonance-inspired attitude change technique that will be our focus, and why. That would be counterattitudinal advocacy.

THE SELF, ATTITUDE IMPORTANCE, AND COGNITIVE DISSONANCE

Counterattitudinal advocacy occurs when individuals engage in attitude-discrepant behavior, and endorse an attitude position (e.g., about a social policy) that they actually oppose. This inconsistency should create the discomfort of cognitive dissonance, which people should strive to reduce, sometimes by changing their attitude. Elliot effectively revised cognitive dissonance theory in the late 1960s (Aronson, 1968, 1969; Nel, Helmreich, & Aronson, 1969) when he argued that for individuals who engage in counterattitudinal advocacy, it is not attitude-behavior inconsistency per se that arouses the discomfort of dissonance. Rather, dissonance arises from knowing that one's actions, especially if these actions have harmed others, have betrayed one's beliefs and, more important, one's positive self-concept as a person of decency and integrity. This perspective became known as the self-consistency version of dissonance theory and is best known for the prediction that only individuals with reasonably positive self-esteem (which is most of us) experience dissonance following attitude-discrepant behavior, because it is only they for whom self-betrayal contradicts a positive self-concept (see Stone, this volume). For those of us whose careers were developing as "the self" was becoming the hot, central idea in social psychology in the 1980s and 1990s, this take on dissonance dovetailed nicely with other accounts that placed the self at the center of dissonance processes, such as Barry Schlenker's (1982) identity-analytic model, Claude Steele's (1988) work on self-affirmation, and Roy Baumeister's (1982; Baumeister & Tice, 1984) self-presentational view that inconsistencies grate because they spoil the impression we wish to create both for others (our public identity) and for ourselves (our private identity). In addition, and most central to our chapter's thesis, Elliot's identification of the self-concept as the key cognition at the crux of dissonance helped define for us in operational and conceptual terms one of the factors that Leon Festinger (1957) originally maintained was one critical determinant of the magnitude of dissonance, namely, the importance of the dissonant cognitive elements in the dissonance equation. Of course! As we (Leippe & Eisenstadt, 1999) summarized in a chapter that helped celebrate the 40th anniversary of dissonance theory, the attitudes and behaviors that clash in integrity-compromising ways are more important to the extent that they are connected to self-interest, social identity, self-defining values, and other aspects of the self-concept.

Thus, in Elliot's self-consistency approach to dissonance, a cognitive element is important to the extent that it is connected to the positive self-concept. And the self-concept itself is the most important cognitive element of all. The good dissonance historian might note that Festinger posited that it is both the importance and the *number* of dissonant cognitive elements that determine the magnitude of dissonance. Happily, self-consistency theory also subsumes the number variable. Increases in the number of dissonant elements in one's mind, almost by definition, increase the self-relevance of the dissonance, given that more of the self is implicated.

COUNTERATTITUDINAL ADVOCACY, THE QUINTESSENTIAL TECHNIQUE OF SELF-PERSUASION

A half-century and more of research has documented that advocating a position or course of action that is inconsistent with a personal belief often leads to attitude change in the direction of the advocacy. This shift may occur for a number of reasons, including simply talking oneself into the new attitude (Janis & King, 1954; Zimbardo & Leippe, 1991). But the most robust attitudinal consequences of counterattitudinal advocacy occur when advocacy involves subtle "induced compliance" under conditions established by dissonance theory: when advocates perceive their advocacy—their behavior—as feely chosen, feel personal responsibility for its possible negative consequences, and find no sufficient justification for it (Brehm & Cohen, 1962; Cooper & Fazio, 1984; Harmon-Jones & Mills, 1999). Of course, these are precisely the ingredients that should make the attitude-discrepant behavior one that arouses Elliot's self-consistency brand of dissonance. Harmful behavior that one does not even believe in, but "owns" through choice and responsibility, would seem especially likely to be inconsistent with a positive self-concept.

Although it was not Elliot's favorite dissonance domain to study, he did some important research involving counterattitudinal advocacy (e.g., Nel et al., 1969) and was there at Stanford when his mentor, Leon Festinger, conducted the most influential early test of dissonance theory: the counterattitudinal advocacy study in which participants were paid either $1 or $20 to tell a waiting participant that a boring task was really fun and interesting (Festinger & Carlsmith, 1959). Counterattitudinal advocacy is perhaps the most clear-cut and dramatic example of what Elliot has described as the "single unifying thread" in his long and distinguished body of empirical scholarship, namely, *self-persuasion* (Aronson, 1999). What more powerful example of self-persuasion is there than how sharply a person's attitude changes after he or she advocates an attitude directly opposed to it?

Counterattitudinal advocacy also exemplifies the essential message of dissonance theory: Attitudes can follow behavior as readily as they cause behavior. In addition, the counterattitudinal advocacy paradigm is the most popularized demonstration of dissonance (e.g., check out most introductory psychology texts published since the early 1960s) as well as the clearest.

We know a lot about counterattitudinal advocacy, including the conditions under which it leads to attitude change. But one variable that is not very well researched in this domain is, well, you guessed it, the importance of the attitude in question. To be sure, interventions that involve variants of counterattitudinal advocacy have influenced people in important practical domains, ranging from eating disorders (Becker, Smith, & Ciao, 2006; Stice, Marti, Spoor, Presnell, & Shaw, 2008) to age discrimination in employment settings (Gringart, Helmes, & Speelman, 2008). But these interventions are not generally clean and exclusive inducements of counterattitudinal espousals. They usually include other techniques of influence as well. Moreover, it is usually behaviors, and not the espoused attitude, that are the targets of influence. What about the attitude itself? Can *important attitudes* be changed? In general, what is the relation between importance and change in the focal attitude following counterattitudinal advocacy?

In 1994, we introduced our research using counterattitudinal advocacy in the service of reducing racial prejudice, in part by lamenting that social psychologists seem to believe that induced compliance can change superficial attitudes on unimportant topics, but have no effect on deeply held values about important topics (Leippe & Eisenstadt, 1994,

p. 396). Some research had demonstrated shifts on socially significant issues, such as attitudes toward the local police (Cohen, 1962) and the legalization of marijuana in a study coauthored by Elliot (Nel et al., 1969) in which students opposed to legalization warmed up a bit toward their counterattitudinal position when they were provided insufficient justification for advocating legalization to impressionable students. But most induced-compliance studies have targeted attitudes toward minor campus issues (e.g., tuition increases), laboratory tasks, and bad-tasting foods like fried grasshoppers and vinegar-laced drinks. Even when the issue has involved an issue that was important in the investigators' minds, it has not been clear that the issue was important or self-defining to individual participants. All in all, there is not a great deal of evidence that the dissonance created by counterattitudinal advocacy can drive changes in attitudes that people hold dear.

Research on another form of social influence, persuasive communication, does not inspire optimism about changing important attitudes. Because already-formed attitudes are connected to self-defining factors, such as values, reference groups, and vested interests, people tend to resist persuasive appeals directed at those attitudes (Leippe, 1991; see also Boninger, Krosnick, Berent, & Fabrigar, 1995; Johnson & Eagly, 1989; Ostrom & Brock, 1968; C. W. Sherif, Kelly, Rogers, Sarup, & Tittler, 1973; Zuwerink & Devine, 1996). In the face of these persuasion attempts, people counterargue, selectively interpret the message information, or somehow render the information irrelevant in their minds. Other things being equal, there will be less attitude change among recipients for whom the issue is important to their self-concept than among those for whom it is not. Few of us are willing to give up attitudes that are central to our definitions of who we are.

And then we have the larger question of how attitude importance relates to dissonance reduction strategies in general. Is the likelihood of attitude change, which is just one of several means of reducing dissonance, less, greater, or unchanged as attitude importance increases? What factors determine whether the relationship between attitude importance and change is negative or positive? And if and when the relationship is negative, what happens to the dissonance arousal that is not relieved by attitude change? How else do people relieve the discomfort of dissonance if they won't and can't change their minds? In the remainder of this chapter, we describe some of our efforts (and touch on those of a few other investigators) to answer these questions.

THE ROLE OF ATTITUDE IMPORTANCE IN DISSONANCE REDUCTION FOLLOWING COUNTERATTITUDINAL ADVOCACY

Most of our experiments involved college students and used an induced-compliance paradigm. In an elaborate cover story, we told participants that an influential university committee was seeking their ideas about a potential new university policy that would be anathema to most of them. These ideas were to be expressed in an essay or a listing of thoughts about the policy that would be sent to the committee, in some cases with the participant's signature affixed to it. We instructed some participants to write a counterattitudinal essay that favors the proposal; given the absence of choice in this situation, they should experience little dissonance. We informed others, and later reminded them, that the choice of supporting (or not supporting) the proposed policy in the essay was theirs, but we dropped subtle prompts into the instructions emphasizing the bigger need, and our undying gratitude, for propolicy essays; in this way, we nudged participants into writing the counterattitudinal essay, even while assuring them that, indeed, the choice was theirs. These high-choice participants should experience considerable postessay dissonance, as they could find little justification (such as coercion) for betraying their true attitude in their essay. After submitting their essay, we polled the participants privately about their real attitude regarding the policy.

The Prejudice Studies

In the early 1990s, we began a series of studies that used an induced-compliance technique to take aim at prejudice against African Americans. White college students were asked (high choice) or told (low choice) to write a counterattitudinal essay that advocated a scholarship policy of giving more funds to black students at the expense of white ones. Although the essay issue was not by itself intrinsically important, it was connected to the very important attitude domain of prejudice. Prejudice-related matters tend to have symbolic importance because they connect to self-defining values, such as fairness, humanitarianism, and equity, and because they can make salient the link between social identity and the self-concept. In the present case, additional importance was conferred by the economic implications for the advocates themselves, for their racial in-group, or both. Moreover, race issues were highly salient at the time, as the Rodney King beating and other racially tinged events were in the headlines. Attesting to the importance of the attitude issue, resistance to change in these studies was evident early on: Up to 40% of the participants given a choice did not fully comply with the request to write an unequivocal endorsement of the scholarship proposal. These "semi-compliers" endorsed the humanitarian, affirmative-action spirit of the proposal, but simply could not bring themselves to advocate all-out for the local plan to give more to deserving black students and necessarily less to equally deserving white ones.

In several studies, the full-compliers in high-choice conditions showed significant changes in attitudes about the scholarship policy. In fact, many of these counterattitudinal advocates even crossed the neutral point of our scale and moved to the favorable side. But both full- and semi-compliers evinced changes on an additional, arguably more profound, measure. Following the collection of attitude responses, a different experimenter under the guise of a separate study administered to participants a measure of beliefs about black Americans, Katz and Hass's (1988) Pro- and Anti-Black Beliefs Questionnaire. This measure includes pro-black questions in which respondents indicate their degree of agreement with positive, sympathetic statements about blacks (especially those concerning past and current racial discrimination and its unfair and disadvantageous effects), and anti-black questions in which respondents indicate their level of agreement with negative statements based mainly on the belief that blacks have not done enough to help themselves. After advocating a scholarship policy that favored black applicants over whites, high-choice full- and semi-compliers alike espoused more positive beliefs about blacks than did low-choice participants or those in a control group, a clear example of prejudice reduction achieved through counterattitudinal advocacy.

We attributed these positive changes in beliefs about blacks to a need to reduce dissonance created when, as they contemplated the proposal and wrote their essays, high-choice participants generated inconsistent thoughts and sentiments about blacks specifically and prejudice in general. The dissonance was reduced by a restructuring or shifting of their beliefs about blacks (and, in the case of full-compliers, their attitudes about the scholarship policy) in the direction of the pro-black spirit of their essay and, more important, away from prejudiced sentiments toward blacks . We referred to this extension of change to general beliefs as the *generalization of dissonance reduction*. It is evidence that if the matter is important enough, dissonance reduction may not stop with a single change, such as an attitude shift, but rather be more fully accomplished by adjustments in other cognitions related to an attitude-behavior discrepancy.

The reduction of prejudice through counterattitudinal advocacy has been replicated by others using different measures of prejudice (e.g., Gawronski & Strack, 2004) and by ourselves (as we will discuss later). The finding leaves little doubt that the dissonance energy (Leon Festinger's term) created by counterattitudinal advocacy can be unleashed to change an attitude of substantial importance. Yet it says little specifically about the importance–change *relation*.

Importance and Change When the Source of Importance Is Personal Cost or Relevance

The original formulation of dissonance implied a positive relation between attitude importance and attitude change: Importance was seen as a magnifier of dissonance-induced distress, which, in turn, should serve to ratchet up the motivation to reduce it by changing something in the dissonance equation. The answer to the positive or negative relation question may depend on the *type*, or *basis*, of attitude importance, in terms of how the attitude issue is connected to the self. One type of importance is the personal cost associated with the attitude. Personal cost has clear relevance to the self, at least in a utilitarian way. Higher personal-cost relevance might compel more change by motivating counterattitudinal advocates to invest more thought and effort into their advocacy, much as people do when they receive personally relevant persuasive messages (Petty & Cacioppo, 1986). In both cases, they thereby "own" the behavior and have more cognitions that support both the advocacy and a change in attitude.

To investigate this possibility, we did a study involving a prejudice-related issue, varying the personal importance of the advocated counterattitudinal policy in terms of economic costs, from trivial to substantial (Eisenstadt, Leippe, Rivers, & Stambush, 2003). In response to a cover story emphasizing their free choice in the matter, white college students wrote an essay endorsing a proposed university policy that would raise their annual tuition either a measly $100 or a rather daunting $2,000, all in the service of providing more scholarship funds to black students. Afterward, participants answered questions about their own opinions about the policy and listed the thoughts they had about the proposal. Participants who engaged in the high-importance, more costly advocacy were more likely to change their attitudes than were those who advocated the less personally costly proposal. Indeed, full- and semi-compliant participant-advocates in the high-importance condition reported significantly more positive attitudes than did participants in a control condition who did not compose an essay, whereas participant-advocates in the low-importance condition did not differ from control participants. Apparently, the amount of dissonance created in the low-importance condition was not sufficient to motivate participants to reduce it. In short, this study found that attitude importance was *positively* related to attitude change.

Some other results of this study add interesting twists to our plot line. We also manipulated distraction during essay writing, thereby simulating a classic method of disrupting the all-critical cognitive responses to the message that determine attitude change in persuasion settings (e.g., Petty, Wells, & Brock, 1976). As they were writing their essays, distracted participants, but not undistracted ones, were asked to keep track of the high-pitched tones among the variously pitched piano tones emanating at random from a tape recorder. This task had no influence on how much or strongly the written essays advocated for the scholarship policy. But distraction had substantial effects on both post-essay attitudes and listed thoughts. Participants who complied with essay task instructions changed their attitude less when they had been distracted while writing and listed a smaller percentage of thoughts that were favorable to the proposal. Moreover, their thoughts mediated the impact of distraction on attitude change. This finding suggests that it is the cognitive effort of generating counterattitudinal thoughts—a kind of mental attitude-discrepant behavior that was freely chosen—that drives attitude change following counterattitudinal advocacy. And because personal relevance reliably increases attitude-relevant thinking when individuals confront messages and other attitude-relevant information (cf. Leippe & Elkin, 1987; Petty & Cacioppo, 1986), it is reasonable to expect more attitude change when the advocated position becomes increasingly important.

In a subsequent study, we varied two forms of an attitude's importance (Eisenstadt & Leippe, 2005). High *personal* relevance was established when participants learned that a policy to fund scholarships by increasing tuition by $2,000 could take effect during the very next academic year, if the committee that would be reading the students' essays so recommended. In the low-personal-relevance condition, we told participants that any approved policy would not take effect for six years. We also systematically varied the racial symbolism of the policy. To vary *symbolic* importance, we informed half of our white participants that the $2,000 tuition hike would benefit "deserving students" and the other half that it would benefit "deserving black students."

The essential results can be seen in a comparison of the differences between the postadvocacy attitudes of participants who wrote an essay endorsing the policy under high choice in each of the four importance conditions and the attitudes of participants who received equivalent importance information, but were told they were not needed to write an essay (and so did not). Let us consider first the effect of increasing each type of importance with the other type held constant on the low side. Consistent with what we found in the distraction study, participants changed their attitudes significantly more in the direction of their counterattitudinal essays when the personal relevance of the scholarship policy was high (if adopted, the tuition hike would take effect during the following academic year) than they did when personal relevance was low (the hike would take effect six years hence). Further, when racial symbolism was high (the scholarship policy would benefit deserving black students), participants changed their attitudes more than when racial symbolism was low (the policy would benefit all deserving students). In sum, both forms of importance alone were positively related to attitude change. However, when relevance and symbolism were both high, there was no statistically significant effect on attitudes. Counterattitudinal advocate-participants changed their attitude toward the advocacy issue significantly less when both forms of importance were high than when just one was. More, it seems, is less.

So we have a hint that the importance of an attitude has a curvilinear effect on attitude change. Why might this be? One reasonable account is that two forces are at work and that they eventually come to oppose one another: the motivation to reduce the dissonance and the motivation to protect the self. With increasing importance comes increases in the magnitude of the dissonance involved in the attitude-betraying behavior, and hence increases in the motivation to reduce dissonance by changing the attitude to match the counterattitudinal behavior. But something else also comes with increasing attitude importance, and that is an increase in the connections of the attitude to more central aspects of the self, to beliefs and cognitions on which one's positive self-concept rests. The more connected the attitude is to the self, the more a change in that attitude implicates the veracity of other self-relevant beliefs and, by extension, the integrity of the self. At some point on the continuum of escalating attitude importance, the amount of change required in the self should exceed what individuals will tolerate, and the motivation to avoid self-implicating attitude change should trump the growing motivation to reduce dissonance through attitude change. At that point, the positive importance/attitude-change function should turn negative. In this light, we can understand a little better the participants in the high-relevance/high-symbolism condition in which the immediate hefty tuition increase they advocated would benefit only black students, yielding negative consequences for themselves and their in-group in ways that likely violated self-defining values such as fairness, equity, and support and protection of their white peers, not to mention financial resources. There is good reason to resist the attitudinal implications of one's own behavior and to somehow distance oneself from the advocacy and to justify it in some way other than by saying, "Well, I guess I agree with it." To do the latter would require too many adjustments in beliefs about oneself and one's world. People will resist changes that would challenge self-definition too much.

In another study, we used the prejudice-relevant issue paradigm to test the downward side of the curve (Eisenstadt, Leippe, Stambush, Rauch, & Rivers, 2005, Experiment 1). We left symbolic importance in terms of race high across all conditions, such that all policies would benefit black students, and varied personal relevance/cost from small or indeterminate to considerable. Because the advocated policy always involved the hot-button issue of race, the net total importance of the attitude issue probably ranged from moderate to pretty high. Under high choice, our white, Hispanic, and Asian–American college participants, all of whom were freshmen and sophomores, were asked to write a list of arguments supporting a proposal to increase tuition by $2,000 next year for scholarships for black students (high importance), to wait six years to increase tuition by $2,000 for such scholarships (moderate importance), or to double the percentage of scholarship funds that go to black students (lower importance, given the apparent absence of a tuition increase). In a control condition, participants were asked to endorse the utterly acceptable policy of doubling scholarship funds that go to all students.

Ostensibly, as part of different studies, we collected data on participants' preadvocacy attitudes, postadvocacy attitudes, and postadvocacy racial beliefs (as assessed by the Katz–Hass scale). We also changed the induced-compliance procedure, which was designed to increase participant compliance with essay-writing instructions and to help us generalize to a highly social setting for counterattitudinal advocacy. In the "induction" phase, individual participants worked alongside a second participant, who was actually our confederate. The experimenter delivered his spiel about how—although the side of the issue to be written on was voluntary—it would be a real help if the participants would write pro-proposal arguments. Then he looked beseechingly at the two and said, "I wonder if you wouldn't mind writing in favor of the tuition [scholarship] increase, okay?" After a brief pause, the confederate responded with an earnest and chirpy, "Sure, I'll do it," and received a heartfelt thanks from the experimenter, who then turned to the participant and asked, "Would you also mind writing in favor of the proposal?" Trapped like a lab rat! This sly seduction through social comparison was quite successful, as 93% of our participants handed in a list of arguments supporting the counterattitudinal proposal, yet ascribed at least a modest level of freedom to choose their side.

As we expected, attitude change was negatively related to importance, a significant trend that showed up on both the specific attitude scale and on an "evaluation index" reflecting participants' ratings of the policy on a number of relevant dimensions (e.g., good–bad, wise–unwise"). These results fill out the downward side of the curvilinear importance/attitude-change function. Whereas the distraction study showed that attitude change increased when importance was increased up to the modest level represented in the doubling-for-blacks-but-no-tuition-increase condition, we see in this study, as in the one that preceded it (Eisenstadt & Leippe, 2005), that as the importance of the issue addressed in essays increased beyond this level, attitude change following counterattitudinal advocacy actually decreased.

Big news also came from participants' reports of their racial beliefs. We compared beliefs in the three experimental conditions involving counterattitudinal advocacy on behalf of black students to the beliefs of participants in the control condition in which advocacy was proattitudinal and unrelated to race. Despite the differences between conditions in importance and in the amount of attitude change, participants' racial beliefs were equivalently positive and were significantly more positive than were racial beliefs in the control condition. Generalization of dissonance reduction to racial beliefs was ubiquitous. That is, for white students, the experience of reducing dissonance by becoming more positive toward blacks in general was evident in all importance conditions, and even when participants could not bring themselves, owing to importance, to change their specific attitude toward the pro-black counterattitudinal policy they had advocated.

Eisenstadt et al. (2005), in a second study, established that this generalization occurs because of the favorability of the thoughts that participants recalled having as they endorsed the pro-black policy. Prejudice reduction redux! Dissonance-driven change in the specific attitude associated with the advocacy may be stymied when the attitude is highly important; still, the drive to reduce dissonance remains, and, as we also demonstrated in our first studies, this drive finds its way into changes in related cognitive elements and structures assessed by the Katz–Hass scales. This result suggests that dissonance about an important attitude can be reduced through means other than direct attitude change.

Personal Relevance and the Trivialization Mode

Through what other means can dissonance about an important attitude be reduced? A step toward identifying an answer came from our former student, Mark Stambush, as part of his dissertation (Stambush, 2006). In this experiment, he manipulated personal relevance in one of the good old-fashioned ways of persuasion researchers: He told college students that their university was considering a requirement that students pass a "senior comprehensive exam" in their major as a condition of graduation; further, the exams could be put in place either in six years (low relevance) or in the very next academic year (high relevance). Yikes! Now that's counterattitudinal. Participants received the usual cover story that a university committee sought their input about this proposal in the form of an essay, followed by instructions that encouraged a counterattitudinal, proexams essay written under the illusion of free choice. In the conditions of the study that concern us here, participants who believed that the exam requirement would take effect after they had graduated (thus rendered irrelevant) shifted their attitudes appreciably toward a more favorable view of required senior exams. And the high-relevance folks who advocated for a senior exam to be imposed on *themselves*? Their attitude change was trivial, significantly lower than that of participants for whom the exam was personally irrelevant. Importance, in the form of personal relevance, once again mitigated attitude change following freely chosen attitude-discrepant behavior.

But what happened to the dissonance? This study included a way to examine whether the high-relevance participants, if given the chance, would drop their dissonance on another doorstep. Following the attitude measure, Stambush (2006) asked participants additional questions about their advocacy, including the following: How significant is it for you to write something positive about senior comprehensive exams? How likely is it that the committee will consider your arguments when deciding on an exams policy? Responses revealed where the dissonance went. Compared to low-relevance advocates (who had changed their attitudes), high-relevance advocates (who had not changed their attitudes) rated their counterattitudinal advocacy as a less significant action and tended to report that the committee was less likely to take their arguments into account. In other words, high-relevance participants made light of their transgression. Apparently, they reduced their dissonance by adding a consonant cognition, namely, that their behavior was unimportant, inconsequential, and no big deal. The dissonance field has come to refer to this mode of dissonance reduction as trivialization.

Trivialization has been observed in several studies of counterattitudinal advocacy. Generally, regardless of an attitude's importance, when advocates have an opportunity to trivialize their act of self-betrayal before being confronted with an attitude measure, they grab the chance and dismiss their act as trivial (Simon, Greenberg, & Brehm, 1995). Doing so seems to provide sufficient relief from dissonance distress, in that no attitude change is evident later. The reverse is also true when the attitude issue is not terribly important. Individuals who take the opportunity to change their attitude first are less likely to then trivialize; they don't need to, having already reduced their dissonance. In Stambush's study (2006), owing to the attitude's importance, high-relevance advocates did not use the opportunity to alter their attitude, leaving them still in the throes of dissonance. Their greater trivialization compared to low-relevance advocates suggests that the motive to resolve an important self-discrepancy does not simply dissolve through forgetting or avoidance.

Changing Attitudes That Stem from Caring and Values

So far, the manipulations of importance in our studies have mainly involved *making* the attitude more or less important to individuals for whom the attitude issue is new and for which there is no preexisting thought-out, committed position. People, of course, walk around with attitudes that they have held for a long time, that are shared by their friends and peers, that are related to issues that are personally important to them, and that they feel they know something about. Attitudes likes these, variously known to be ego involving (M. Sherif & Hovland, 1961) and values-relevant (Johnson & Eagly, 1989), are notoriously resistant to change. As Patricia Devine and her colleagues found (Devine, Tauer, Barron, Elliot, &, Vance, 1999), individuals who took a counterattitudinal position on a personally important issue did not change their attitude about it one iota when given an opportunity to do so.

In a second experiment for his dissertation, Mark Stambush (2006) endeavored to replicate and expand on this finding. College participants filled out a questionnaire that probed for their feelings about the environment and being green, and how central these feelings were to their core values. Participants were then divided into high-, medium-, and low-importance groups on the basis of their questionnaire responses. Then they answered questions about numerous campus and social issues, including one that asked them to indicate on a rating scale their degree of agreement that "the university should do more to protect the environment by updating its recycling procedures." Not surprisingly, practically all students agreed that the university should indeed do more. But then, under the usual "high dissonance" conditions involving high choice, public personal responsibility, and the undesirable consequence of having an instrumental committee read their work, participants were cajoled into writing an essay opposing a specific environment-friendly university proposal that would greatly improve and expand the university's recycling procedures. After writing that the university should not embark on new and improved recycling practices, would participants still hold to their attitude that the university should do just that? Yes, indeed—if protecting the environment was an important issue for them. Participants for whom being green was of little or moderate personal importance changed their attitudes significantly more in the direction of their counterattitudinal advocacy than did those to whom caring for the environment was highly important. In fact, those to whom being green was important didn't change their attitudes at all.

A twist in this study was that the participants completed the postadvocacy attitude measure either before or after they answered questions designed to give them the opportunity to reduce dissonance by trivializing or otherwise recasting the nature of their attitude and attitude-inconsistent essay. Interestingly, it was only individuals to whom caring for the environment was personally important who showed an order effect, and they showed it on only one trivialization item. When they had already reported their attitude, high-importance participants rated the importance of expressing positive views about recycling higher than did their low- and medium-importance counterparts. This certainly is to be expected; after all, caring for the environment matters a great deal to them.

However, when this question of the importance of expression preceded the attitude item, high-importance people downplayed the importance of expressing positive views about recycling; their ratings were the same as those for whom the environment was less important. It seems as if dissonance about the essay written on the wrong side of being "green and clean" was reduced by high-importance people through a subtle bit of trivialization: "I'm for a university recycling update, and it's important, but expressing a positive view on the matter here (which I didn't do in the essay) is not such a big deal."

Notice that this little cognitive adjustment did not occur when the attitude question was asked first. This is probably because attitude-first participants had already expressed a pro-recycling-plan attitude, in spite of having written an anti essay, making salient to themselves their inconsistency and making it difficult to now call the attitude expression unimportant. These attitude-first, high-importance advocates would need to find another way to reduce their dissonance. This pattern resembles findings obtained by Starzyk, Fabrigar, Soryal, and Fanning (2009), who reported that counterattitudinal advocates eschewed a chance to trivialize their attitude when the high personal importance of their attitude on the matter was made salient to them.

When trivialization—an easy alternative to attitude change— was available as a dissonance-reduction strategy before the attitude change opportunity, those to whom being green was important used it. Interestingly, a chance to trivialize the significance of expressing their true proenvironmental attitude seems to have had a surprising and potentially significant additional effect on participants: It seems to have softened their staunch commitment to their true attitude just enough for that attitude to budge a little. All participants, including those to whom being green was highly important, changed their proenvironmental attitudes more when they had the opportunity to trivialize the importance of attitude expression before actually reporting those attitudes. When they had the chance to trivialize first, high-importance participants changed their attitudes; of course, they did not cross the line to oppose the university recycling plan—as they did in their counterattitudinal essays—but they did shift their true attitudes to a more moderate position.

But why did it happen? Some research on dissonance reduction suggests that once dissonance is reduced by one strategy, it is over and done with. No need to make any additional changes. Indeed, several studies have found that people are less likely to change their attitudes following attitude-discrepant behavior when they have first used other dissonance-reduction strategies, such as trivialization of a counterattitudinal act (Simon et al., 1995), denial of responsibility for a counterattitudinal act (Gosling, Denizeau, & Oberle, 2006), self-affirmation (Steele, 1988), and derogation of the source of self-discrepant news (Gotz-Marchand, Gotz, & Irle, 1974). Other studies, however, have not found this on–off switch, via which one strategy fully eliminates the dissonance that follows an attitude-discrepant act. Josh Aronson, Hart Blanton, and Joel Cooper (1995), for example, observed attitude change following counterattitudinal behavior even after individuals had made other dissonance-reducing cognitive shifts. We believe that the post-attitude-change restructuring that we found in our prejudice-reduction studies is evidence of a *hydraulic model* in which dissonance reduction flows into multiple paths of change, depending on how a previous mode of change has altered the cognitive and emotional landscape. Although a single change may eliminate dissonance under some circumstances, it may not be enough when more important self-discrepancies are involved and are salient (Leippe & Eisenstadt, 1999).

Generalization Redux, in the Light of Learning About Importance

We now describe two final studies in our journey. The first, we think, illustrates the power and reach of the social influence that can result from counterattitudinal advocacy in a domain that is important and relevant to people. The second points to a critical and theoretically revealing condition for the generalization effect that dovetails nicely with what we have learned so far about importance and modes of dissonance reduction.

Dissonance on Trial
This is a study that Elliot should love. It marries the dramatic high-impact elaborate cover-story study (which Elliot has championed; see Aronson, Ellsworth, Carlsmith, & Gonzales, 1990), in the form of the induced-compliance paradigm, with a livened-up variety of paper-and-pencil simulation study (about which he is less keen, if unlivened up) in the form of a written trial. College students, mostly white, Latino, and Asian, and a few blacks, were ushered through a procedure that ostensibly involved two independent surveys. The first involved our familiar counterattitudinal advocacy situation, described to participants as involving a proposal to "at least double the percentage of available scholarship money that is given to deserving African American students," about which a university committee was seeking student input. In the *advocacy* condition, participants were induced under high-choice conditions to write a proscholarship essay for the committee's consideration. Afterward, they handed their signed essays to the experimenter and indicated their degree of agreement with the proposal. In the *no-advocacy* condition, the first survey asked only about participants' attitudes toward the scholarship proposal. All participants then were introduced to the second (allegedly unrelated) survey, a "trial simulation" involving a computer presentation of a robbery/murder trial. The first computer screen presented photographs of the principal trial participants. The defendant was either black or white; the others—lawyers, judge, witnesses—were all white or Hispanic. This screen was followed by a transcript that included attorneys' opening and closing arguments; direct and cross-examination of several witnesses, including the defendant; and judge's instructions. In the course of the trial, several pieces of incriminating evidence and testimony were presented, but so were some indications that made it reasonable to conclude that the defendant was actually innocent. Finally, participants cast individual verdicts, and rated the strength of the prosecution evidence, the defendant's believability, and the likelihood of guilt.

Why did we put the students through all of this? Because we were looking to see how far generalization of dissonance reduction might actually extend. You may recall that in our first studies of prejudice reduction, we argued that the postadvocacy changes in racial beliefs occurred because counterattitudinal advocacy got the advocates thinking about the many inconsistencies of attitudes, beliefs, and behaviors within their prejudice-relevant belief system. Attitude change is insufficient for resolving—and may even add to—the myriad cognitive inconsistencies that resulted, so dissonance is further reduced by adjusting racial beliefs in the direction of the advocacy. We hypothesized that these adjustments, reflecting more favorable views of blacks in general, would extend to a specific instance of the racial category—the black defendant in the trial—and that, ultimately owing to dissonance reduction, advocates would be more lenient toward the black (but not necessarily the white) defendant in their interpretation of the imperfect trial evidence.

We also reasoned that additional adjustments and restructuring might be part of the flow of this long-reach generalization of dissonance reduction. What we did not tell you earlier is that the "pro-black" beliefs that were adjusted in these studies are not related solely to attitudes about the advocated helpful-to-blacks policy. As Irwin Katz and Glen Hass (1988) carefully documented in research with the instruments they developed, and as we confirmed in our paradigm (Leippe & Eisenstadt, 1994), pro-black beliefs are also intimately associated with the personal values of egalitarian fairness and humanitarianism—in essence, a concern for helping the disadvantaged who have historically been treated unfairly. Given this connection, it seemed reasonable to expect that attitude-discrepant behavior related to the scholarship policy would activate these humanitarian values and thoughts, and that this activation, along with churned-up racial concerns, would yield defendant-friendly processing of the trial evidence.

Results of the study supported our hypothesis and then some. We found reliable effects of advocacy on numerous trial outcome measures. When the defendant was black, mock-jurors in the scholarship advocacy condition rated the evidence against the defendant as weaker, rated the defendant's believability as higher, and reported more not-guilty verdicts, compared to those in the no-advocacy condition. It was interesting, however, that precisely the same results were found when the defendant was white—lower ratings of evidence, higher ratings of the defendant's believability, and more not-guilty verdicts—when mock-jurors previously had been asked to advocate for the scholarship program than when they had not. Surprised? We were, but only a little, because we had realized that the white defendant in this case was also a disadvantaged underdog as a criminal defendant in a trial involving evidence that truly could support the conclusion of innocence. We are convinced that in both the black and white defendant cases, the advocacy effect represents a generalization of dissonance reduction, itself a by-product of the cognitive restructuring necessitated by an attitude-behavior self-discrepancy (the counterattitudinal advocacy) within a larger system of attitudes, beliefs, and values.

If the attitude is embedded in a domain replete with connections to beliefs, values, and other attitudes, and if the attitude, the attitude domain, or both, are important and self-relevant, the generalization effect—this spreading of cognitive changes through the domain in the service of achieving a more satisfying level of dissonance reduction—appears to be a reliable and robust outcome of counterattitudinal advocacy. It holds promise for creating important changes on important matters through dissonance techniques. But what makes it tick and what might stall it?

Curtailing Generalization
In the final experiment we will describe, college students engaged in the same high-dissonance counterattitudinal essay-writing procedure as in the previous study and later completed the Katz–Hass racial beliefs scales as a measure of generalization. What varied was what happened between the two steps. Participants either received or did not receive an attitude question on the essay topic. When they completed the attitude item, it was either followed or not followed by questions that allowed them to trivialize the importance of their behavior. Thus, following advocacy, participants received both an attitude-change and trivialization opportunity, an opportunity for attitude change only, an opportunity to trivialize only, or an opportunity for neither. If you guessed that we were interested in whether trivialization would short-circuit generalization, you are correct. But we also wondered how the opportunity to change attitudes might factor in, as this opportunity had been provided in all of our previous studies of dissonance-reduction generalization.

As it turned out, the trivialization opportunity did not matter, and the attitude change opportunity not only mattered but was crucial. Having the opportunity to change their attitude toward the scholarship proposal they wrote about in their essay made all the difference in participants' beliefs about blacks as expressed on the Katz–Hass scales, which were significantly more positive when participants had previously considered and expressed their attitude than when they had not done so. This was true whether or not they also had the opportunity to trivialize the importance of their essay-writing behavior.

Trivialization apparently does not derail generalization. Instead, it seems that the path to more cognitive restructuring ends when counterattitudinal advocates do not first pay a postadvocacy visit to their attitudes toward the topic of their advocacy. The channeling of dissonance reduction into the kind of cognitive restructuring that leads to reduced prejudice requires counterattitudinal advocates to confront their behavioral self-transgression in some conscious way. The attitude change question appears to be the necessary confrontation in this case, essentially forcing advocates to continue to think about both the issue at hand and the implications for their other thoughts and beliefs.

The necessity of the attitude-change opportunity is reminiscent of a finding reported by the first author and his former student, Roger Elkin, more than 20 years ago. Elkin and Leippe (1986) conducted two induced-compliance studies that demonstrated that individuals become physiologically aroused upon engaging in a counterattitudinal advocacy under high-choice, high-dissonance conditions. We also observed that unless an attitude-change opportunity or some other reminder of the transgression occurred, the arousal merely dissipated. We dubbed this the "don't remind me effect," and speculated that people will just as soon forget about their dissonance, and need reminders or an occasion to stay "on task" with the work of dissonance reduction.

The general upshot is that the multifaceted repercussive cognitive gymnastics of dissonance reduction that often follow dissonance-arousing behaviors like counterattitudinal advocacy require situational stimuli that keep the dissonance salient, and even increase it by prompting cognitive changes that require still more cognitive changes. Interestingly, among the studies we have reported in this chapter, there may be at least one other example of this principle: the facilitating effect on attitude change that a prior opportunity to trivialize had on even high-importance participants in Mark Stambush's (2006) recycling study. The trivialization questions may have kept participants' attention on their attitude-discrepant behavior, and provided an opportunity to recast it, add a new cognition, and find a place for attitude change in the attitude system.

CONCLUSIONS AND IMPLICATIONS

We believe we have demonstrated that Elliot's trust in self-persuasion as a basis for meaningful social influence is trust well placed. Let's summarize, with four points and a call to application.

First, consistent with the original formulation of dissonance, and with Elliot's view that the experience of dissonance requires that an inconsistency include some threat to a positive self-concept, dissonance arousal and subsequent attitude change seem to require that the behavior-discrepant attitude have a modicum of importance, which is to say some relevance to the self. As importance increases—up to a point—attitude change increases.

Second, the relation is curvilinear. Beyond that point of modest importance, importance impedes attitude change. This finding makes sense. It is consistent with audiences' resistance to persuasive appeals that target key attitudes and with the basic conceptualization that important attitudes, by definition, connect more to self and identity than do less important attitudes. Changing an important attitude requires questioning the self in ways that we are for the most part unwilling and unprepared to do. As Anthony Greenwald (1980), a student of Elliot's and mentor of the first author, observed in describing the totalitarian ego, the self is inherently conservative and resists tinkering, let alone major renovation.

Third, people's resistance to changing important attitudes following counterattitudinal advocacy may not be the insurmountable barrier that we may have feared. Unresolved dissonance does not simply or immediately go away. Research has not yet fully answered the question of whether people spontaneously and actively seek out ways to reduce their dissonance. Most often, they probably do not, and gradually let it go in the course of the arousal dissipation seen by Elkin and Leippe (1986). After all, as Elliot pointed out years ago, attitude-discrepant behavior and the dissonance it arouses are common, daily experiences (Aronson, 1968). We can't possibly deal mindfully with all of them and are probably happily distracted by the next daily event that comes along.

But our studies, and others as well, suggest that when we make the consequent discomfort salient to those whose behavior compromises their values, they will be motivated to make cognitive adjustments that serve to reduce their dissonance and to promote a new cognitive order in the system of attitudes and beliefs that was disrupted by their counterattitudinal advocacy. Some platform—such as questioning about the relevant attitude or the behavior—may be required to create the necessary salience. But once that happens, counterattitudinal advocates may employ any number of paths afforded by situations, tasks, and interactions to work out the self-discrepancies caused by their counterattitudinal advocacy, from changing their beliefs about the significance and relevance of behaviors (e.g., on trivialization measures) to changing their beliefs about people in general (e.g., on racial beliefs measures), and even changing their assessments about specific people (e.g., the defendant in our trial simulation).

Fourth, and finally, this more extended, generalization process may be more likely when the attitude targeted by counterattitudinal advocacy is very important, even if specific attitude change is less likely. The motivation and ability to cognitively restructure around an attitude that is contradicted by behavior clearly should be greater as attitude importance increases (Festinger, 1957; Hardyck & Kardush, 1968; Leippe & Eisenstadt, 1999).

All of this is heartening news to those scientist-practitioners who, like Elliot Aronson, make it a habit to think about ways of applying the social-scientific knowledge they and others create. It should not be too difficult to incorporate counterattitudinal advocacy or role-playing procedures into educational, public-service, and questionnaire-survey venues in the real (and really important) world, and to couple these procedures with social interactions and other situations in which dissonance may be channeled into changed perceptions and beliefs. As Elliot has suggested about the central theme of his wonderful career of science and application, what really works to move people is the power of self-persuasion—if you can capture and channel it. We think it can be done, even if, and perhaps especially because, the matter of change matters to people.

REFERENCES

Aronson, E. (1968). Dissonance theory: Progress and problems. In R. P. Abelson, E. Aronson, W. T. McGuire, T. M. Newcomb, M. J. Rosenberg, & P. H. Tannenbaum (Eds.), *Theories of cognitive consistency: A sourcebook* (pp. 5–27). Chicago: Rand-McNally.

Aronson, E. (1969). The theory of cognitive dissonance: A current perspective. In L. Berkowitz (Ed.), *Advances in experimental social psychology* (Vol. 4, pp. 1–34). New York: Academic Press.

Aronson, E. (1999). The power of self-persuasion. *American Psychologist, 54,* 875–884.

Aronson, E., Ellsworth, P. C., Carlsmith, J. M., & Gonzales, M. H. (1990). *Methods of research in social psychology* (2nd ed.). New York: McGraw-Hill.

Aronson, J., Blanton, H., & Cooper, J. (1995). From dissonance to disidentification: Selectivity in the self-affirmation process. *Journal of Personality and Social Psychology, 68,* 986–996.

Baumeister, R. F. (1982). A self-presentational view of social phenomena. *Psychological Bulletin, 91,* 3–26.

Baumeister, R. F., & Tice, D. M. (1984). Role of self-presentation and choice in cognitive dissonance under forced compliance: Necessary or sufficient causes? *Journal of Personality and Social Psychology, 46,* 5–13.

Becker, C. B., Smith, L. M., & Ciao, A. C. (2006). Peer-facilitated eating disorder prevention: A randomized effectiveness trial of cognitive dissonance and media advocacy. *Journal of Counseling Psychology, 53,* 550–555.

Boninger, D. S., Krosnick, J. A., Berent, M. K., & Fabrigar, L. R. (1995). The causes and consequences of attitude importance. In R. E. Petty & J. A. Krosnick (Eds.), *Attitude strength: Antecedents and consequences* (pp. 159–189). Mahwah, NJ: Erlbaum.

Brehm, J. W., & Cohen, A. R. (Eds.) (1962). *Explorations in cognitive dissonance.* New York: Wiley.

Cohen, A. R. (1962). An experiment on small rewards for discrepant compliance and attitude change. In J. W. Brehm & A. R. Cohen (Eds.), *Explorations in cognitive dissonance* (pp. 73–78). New York: Wiley.

Cooper, J., & Fazio, R. H. (1984). A new look at dissonance theory. In L. Berkowitz (Ed.), *Advances in experimental social psychology* (Vol. 17, pp. 229–266). New York: Academic Press.

Devine, P. G., Tauer, J. M., Barron, K. E., Elliot, A. J., & Vance, K. M. (1999). Moving beyond attitude change in the study of dissonance-related processes. In E. Harmon-Jones & J. Mills (Eds.), *Cognitive dissonance: Progress on a pivotal theory in social psychology* (pp. 297–323). Washington, DC: American Psychological Association.

Eisenstadt, D., & Leippe, M. R. (2005). Dissonance and importance: Attitude change effects of personal relevance and race of the beneficiary of a counterattitudinal advocacy. *Journal of Social Psychology, 145,* 447–467.

Eisenstadt, D., Leippe, M. R., Rivers, J. A., & Stambush, M. (2003). Counterattitudinal advocacy on a matter of prejudice: Effects of distraction, commitment, and personal importance. *Journal of Applied Social Psychology, 33,* 2123–2152.

Eisenstadt, D., Leippe, M. R., Stambush, M. A., Rauch, S. M., & Rivers, J. A. (2005). Dissonance and prejudice: Personal costs, choice, and change in attitudes and racial beliefs following counterattitudinal advocacy that benefits a minority. *Basic and Applied Social Psychology, 7,* 127–141.

Elkin, R. A., & Leippe, M. R. (1986). Physiological arousal, dissonance, and attitude change: Evidence for a dissonance-arousal link and a "don't remind me" effect. *Journal of Personality and Social Psychology, 51,* 55–65.

Festinger, L. (1957). *A theory of cognitive dissonance.* Stanford, CA: Stanford University Press.

Festinger, L., & Carlsmith, J. M. (1959). Cognitive consequences of forced compliance. *Journal of Abnormal and Social Psychology, 58,* 203–211.

Gawronski, B., & Strack, F. (2004). On the propositional nature of cognitive consistency: Dissonance changes explicit, but not implicit attitudes. *Journal of Experimental Social Psychology, 40,* 535–542.

Gotz-Marchand, B., Gotz, J., & Irle, M. (1974). Preference of dissonance reduction modes as a function of their order, familiarity, and reversibility. *European Journal of Social Psychology, 4,* 201–228.

Gosling, P., Denizeau, M., & Oberle, D. (2006). Denial of responsibility: A new mode of dissonance reduction. *Journal of Personality and Social Psychology, 90,* 722–733.

Greenwald, A. G. (1980). The totalitarian ego: Fabrication and revision of personal history. *American Psychologist, 35,* 603–618.

Gringart, E., Helmes, E., & Speelman, C. (2008). Harnessing cognitive dissonance to promote positive attitudes toward older workers in Australia. *Journal of Applied Social Psychology, 38,* 751–778.

Hardyck, J. A., & Kardush, M. (1968). A modest modish model for dissonance reduction. In R. P. Abelson, E. Aronson, W. T. McGuire, T. M. Newcomb, M. J. Rosenberg, & P. H. Tannenbaum (Eds.), *Theories of cognitive consistency: A sourcebook* (pp. 684–692). Chicago: Rand-McNally.

Harmon-Jones, E. & Mills, J. (Eds.) (1999). *Cognitive dissonance: Progress on a pivotal theory in social psychology*. Washington, DC: American Psychological Association.

Janis, I. L., & King, B. T. (1954). The influence of role-playing on opinion chance. *Journal of Abnormal and Social Psychology, 49,* 211–218.

Johnson, B. T.,& Eagly, A. H. (1989). Effects of involvement on persuasion: A meta-analysis. *Psychological Bulletin, 104,* 290–314

Katz, I., & Hass, R. G. (1988). Racial ambivalence and American value conflict: Correlational and priming studies of dual cognitive structures. *Journal of Personality and Social Psychology, 55,* 893–905.

Leippe, M. R. (1991). A self-image analysis of persuasion and attitude involvement. In R. C. Curtis (Ed.), The relational self: Theoretical convergences in psychoanalysis and social psychology (pp. 37–63). New York: Guilford.

Leippe, M. R., & Eisenstadt, D. (1994). The generalization of dissonance reduction: Decreasing prejudice through induced compliance. *Journal of Personality and Social Psychology, 67,* 395–413.

Leippe, M. R., & Eisenstadt, D. (1999). A self-accountability model of dissonance reduction: Multiple modes on a continuum of elaboration. In E. Harmon-Jones & J. Mills (Eds.), *Cognitive dissonance: Progress on a pivotal theory in social psychology* (pp. 201–232). Washington, DC: American Psychological Association.

Leippe, M. R., & Elkin, R. A. (1987). When motives clash: Issue involvement and response involvement as determinants of persuasion. *Journal of Personality and Social Psychology, 52,* 269–278.

Nel, E., Helmreich, R., & Aronson, E. (1969). Opinion change in the advocate as a function of the persuasibility of his audience: A clarification of the meaning of dissonance. *Journal of Personality and Social Psychology, 12,* 117–124.

Ostrom, T. M., & Brock, T. C. (1968). A cognitive model of attitudinal involvement. In R. P. Abelson, E. Aronson, W. T. McGuire, T. M. Newcomb, M. J. Rosenberg, & P. H. Tannenbaum (Eds.), *Theories of cognitive consistency: A sourcebook* (pp. 373–389). Chicago: Rand-McNally.

Petty, R. E., & Cacioppo, J. T. (1986). The elaboration likelihood model of persuasion. In L. Berkowitz (Ed.), *Advances in experimental social psychology* (Vol. 19, pp. 123–205). New York: Academic Press.

Petty, R. E., Wells, C. L., & Brock, T. C. (1976). Distraction can enhance or reduce yielding to propaganda: Thought disruption versus effort justification. *Journal of Personality and Social Psychology, 34,* 874–884.

Schlenker, B. R. (1982). Translating actions into attitudes: An identity-analytic approach to the explanation of social conduct. In L. Berkowitz (Ed.), *Advances in experimental social psychology* (Vol. 15, pp. 193–247). New York: Academic Press.

Sherif, C. W., Kelly, M., Rogers, H. L., Sarup, G., & Tittler, B. I. (1973). Personal involvement, social judgment, and action. *Journal of Personality and Social Psychology, 27,* 311–328.

Sherif, M., & Hovland, C. I. (1961). *Social judgment: Assimilation and contrast effects in communication and attitude change.* New Haven, CT: Yale University Press.

Simon, L., Greenberg, J., & Brehm, J. (1995). Trivialization: The forgotten mode of dissonance reduction. *Journal of Personality and Social Psychology, 68,* 247–260.

Stambush, M. A. (2006). Examining the role of value-relevance and outcome-relevance in dissonance reduction strategies (Unpublished doctoral dissertation). St. Louis University, MO.

Starzyk, K. B., Fabrigar, L. R., Soryal, A. S., & Fanning, J. J. (2009). A painful reminder: The role of level and salience of attitude importance in cognitive dissonance. *Personality and Social Psychology Bulletin, 35,* 126–137.

Steele, C. M. (1988). The psychology of self-affirmation: Sustaining the integrity of the self. In L. Berkowitz (Ed.), *Advances in experimental social psychology* (Vol. 21, pp. 261–302). New York: Academic Press.

Stice, E., Marti, C. N., Spoor, S., Presnell, K., & Shaw, H. (2008). Dissonance and healthy weight eating disorder prevention program: Long-term effects from a randomized efficacy trial. *Journal of Counseling and Clinical Psychology, 76,* 329–340.

Zimbardo, P. G., & Leippe, M. R. (1991). *The psychology of attitude change and social influence.* New York: McGraw-Hill.

Zuwerink, J. R., & Devine, P. G. (1996). Attitude importance and resistance to persuasion: It's not just the thought that counts. *Journal of Personality and Social Psychology, 70,* 931–944.

III

Research and Applications

10

A TILLER IN THE GREENING OF RELATIONSHIP SCIENCE

Jeffry A. Simpson
University of Minnesota

Elliot Aronson is my academic grandfather and my connection to Kurt Lewin, and those two facts have always been a source of pride. Though I never worked with Elliot, I almost feel as if I did through contacts I have had with some of his former students (e.g., Ellen Berscheid, Marti Hope Gonzales) and with his colleagues over the years at Minnesota, Texas, and Santa Cruz.

My first "contact" with Elliot was similar to the experience of many people in our field. During my junior year of high school, I took a psychology course as a break from the drudgery of physics, chemistry, and math. The textbook was a typical one—thorough to the point of being encyclopedic, but stale and awfully dry. During the first week of class, our teacher, who happened to be getting a PhD in social psychology, pulled three of us aside and asked us to read a "new book" along with the regular text. It was something called *The Social Animal*. Mind you, I was not a slacker, but neither was I a sucker, and I wasn't eager to tackle two dry encyclopedias. The thought of having to read yet another textbook alongside the regular book seemed a bit excessive—until I read the first page of that new book. Whoa! I had never seen or heard of a textbook that read like an intriguing and suspenseful novel. It was fascinating to realize that one could do interesting and important scientific experiments with participants who occasionally behaved in some pretty strange and unexpected ways. And the unique way in which Elliot set the stage and recounted the unfolding drama as people struggled to rationalize and justify their actions, especially in stressful or socially difficult situations, was mesmerizing. I was 17, and I was hooked.

When I ventured to the University of Minnesota for graduate school in the fall of 1981, Elliot entered my life once again. In the 1960s, he had spent several years on the faculty at Minnesota, where he helped define the "Minnesota tradition" in social psychology. Compelling stories of Elliot, his imaginative experiments, and his lively lab meetings were, of course, part of the lore at Minnesota, and many of us felt a direct and personal connection to that history. While in graduate school, I developed three indelible impressions of Elliot. First and perhaps foremost, he was the consummate experimental social psychologist who, unlike anyone before or since, fused art and science in his work. We didn't need to read the author line on a paper to know when Elliot was its ingenious mastermind; the style, flair, stage direction, and drama of the research gave him away. Second, Elliot was a devoted applier in the Lewinian tradition. In our courses, many of us teach our students that behavior depends on both the person and the current environment, and that one should ultimately use theory and experimental methods to solve important societal problems. What most of us teach, however, is not always what many of us practice. Throughout his career, Elliot lived Lewin's creed that nothing is as practical as a good theory, that tackling tough, applied social problems was a central mission of our field, and that what is learned in field settings can and should be used in reciprocal fashion to inform and refine our theories. Third, Elliot was one of the first great communicators and public ambassadors of social psychology. Not only did he introduce many of us to the wonders of our field, but, years before it became fashionable to do so, he took the time to communicate to the wider public all that social psychology had to offer.

Elliot also taught all of us some valuable principles about how rigorous and psychologically engaging research can and should be conducted. We all learned, for example, that studies ought to be high in experimental realism if not always high in mundane realism (Aronson, Brewer, & Carlsmith, 1985; Aronson, Carlsmith, & Ellsworth, 1976; Aronson, Ellsworth, Carlsmith, & Gonzales, 1990; also see Ellsworth, this volume). When individuals participate in studies, they need to be engaged in the unfolding experimental procedures, script, and drama. (We actually have an informal rule in our research lab: No participant should *ever* be thinking about lunch or what she or he will do after the study ends. Everyone should be completely engrossed in—and perhaps trying to make it through—the next 45 minutes.) And when done right, social situations in experiments unfold like well-scripted plays in which different people assume different roles, and everyone, including the experimenter, has an important part to enact. To this day, my students and I still draft detailed scripts before we conduct every experiment.

PREPARING THE GROUND FOR RELATIONSHIP SCIENCE

Many people who know Elliot and the field of social psychology know about these accomplishments. What many people may not know, however, is that Elliot Aronson was an important tiller in the greening of relationship science (see Berscheid, 1999). He was *not* a gardener, mind you, because he did not actually plant the seeds that became the green fields—the foundation—of modern relationship science. But the field might not have become as lush and verdant as it did without his initial inspiration.

To begin with, Elliot motivated and inspired the first generation of relationship researchers to do creative studies and to think outside the box. Indeed, one of Elliot's earliest graduate students, my former coadvisor Ellen Berscheid, played a pivotal role in launching and nurturing the relationships field. Second, Elliot gave the study of interpersonal phenomena credibility both within and beyond social psychology. He did so through his masterful prose and storytelling in *The Social Animal*. He did so through the types of issues and problems he chose to study, particularly during the early part of his career. He did so through the clever studies he conducted, several of which generated extremely interesting and counterintuitive findings. And he did so through occasional excursions out of the lab to tackle important social problems, such as how to integrate classrooms (the Jigsaw Classroom) and how to promote energy efficiency (Aronson & Gonzales, 1990; Gonzales, Aronson, & Costanzo, 1988) and safe-sex practices (Aronson, Fried, & Stone, 1991; Stone, Aronson, Crain, Winslow, & Fried, 1994), long before it was either common or fashionable to do so.

Third and even more important, some of Elliot's early research gave the seeds of relationship science fertile ground in which to grow. For example, his early investigations into the sources of interpersonal attraction granted legitimacy to the study of relationships at a time when social psychology was dominated by laboratory-based experimentalists, and when some public figures (such as William Proxmire, the former senator from Wisconsin) were arguing that an understanding of relationships was better left to poets or Dear Abby than to science and theory testing. Just when attraction and relationship research was beginning to be viewed as frivolous, Elliot was *validating* the study of attraction, intimacy, and the ties that bind people together. His actions had an important impact on senior scholars within social psychology, many of whom held the opinion that "if Elliot thinks it's worthwhile, it probably is." With this foundation, Ellen Berscheid and Elaine Walster (Hatfield) wrote a seminal book on interpersonal attraction (Berscheid & Walster, 1969), which solidified the study of interpersonal relationships and was a precursor to relationship science.

Elliot's early research on cognitive dissonance also drew the attention and imagination of young psychologists who otherwise might never have ventured into social psychology or the scientific study of relationships. During the early 1980s, I was one of those people. Elliot's early dissonance work shifted theoretical attention away from simple exchange or reinforcement explanations of social behavior toward Lewin-inspired *motivational* approaches (e.g., cognitive consistency models). Beginning with his famous "severity of initiation" experiment (Aronson & Mills, 1959), in which people who had to "suffer" to join a boring discussion group actually liked the group better than those who didn't suffer, Elliot moved interpersonal attraction away from cut-and-dried reinforcement-centered models of the resources that are exchanged in relationships (see Byrne, 1961; Homans, 1961) toward more dynamic, motivational models that addressed how deep-seated motives, needs, and dispositions sometimes alter perceptions and behavior in rationalizing (but not always rational) ways.

In doing so, Elliot documented some interesting boundary conditions of several important attraction effects. This included his groundbreaking work on gain–loss theory (Aronson & Linder, 1965), which proposed that the pattern of positive and negative events experienced across time is more important in determining attraction to another person than is the total number of positive and negative events. In this research, participants ("subjects" in those days) interacted with an experimental accomplice (a "confederate") in a series of seven brief conversations. After each interaction, the participant overheard the confederate sharing her impressions of the participant with the experimenter. In keeping with the manipulation of the independent variable, participants overheard the confederate expressing either a positive attitude toward the participant after each of the seven brief interactions, a negative attitude after each of the interactions, a negative attitude that gradually became positive across the series of seven interactions, or an initially positive attitude that gradually became negative as the interactions progressed. This study had all the features of a classic high-impact experiment: high experimental realism, real and engaging social interactions, an elaborate and carefully crafted script, and artful and appropriate deception. Contrary to predictions derived from reinforcement theory, Elliot and

Darwin Linder predicted that the least attractive individuals should be those with whom things start out positively but end negatively, whereas the most attractive people should be those who have little laudatory to say at the outset but gradually come around. This is precisely what was found: Attraction is not based on the total amount of positive or negative feedback we receive from others; instead, it depends on the specific pattern of positive versus negative feedback.

This initial gain–loss research inspired other important research on what happens when two people directly vie for the attention and affection of a third individual. Testing the "law of infidelity" derived from gain–loss theory, Ellen Berscheid, Tom Brothen, and William Graziano (1976) found that when two people compete for the affection of another individual and one suitor expresses consistently positive attitudes and the other expresses a "gain" in positive attitudes (i.e., moving from initially negative to positive), the consistently positive evaluator is liked more. This study was one of the first to highlight the context-dependent nature of attraction in settings that resemble typical, real-world interactions, and to show that competition was the key to their contrary findings. When two people compete for the attraction of another, they question the motives of a potential suitor who becomes increasingly flattering over time, and their suspicion undermines his or her personal appeal. Romantic competition can undermine the gain–loss effect when "infidelity" is at stake.

Another example of how Elliot shifted the theoretical focus of relationship research is his clever work on the pratfall effect (Aronson, Willerman, & Floyd, 1966), which demonstrated that small foibles (pratfalls) can make highly competent people even more likeable. Along with research revealing that the most attractive people are not necessarily those we choose to date (Walster, Aronson, Abrahams, & Rottman, 1966), Elliot's pratfall research confirmed that slight imperfections in others are both reassuring and endearing, most likely because occasional slip-ups make those to whom we are drawn—including our partners—seem more approachable and within our grasp.

Elliot also infused the self-concept into major theories in social psychology, especially cognitive dissonance theory (Aronson, 2003). He did so by showing that cognitive dissonance theory makes the clearest predictions when an individual's self-concept is threatened by his or her troublesome behaviors. He demonstrated, for instance, that people who have low self-esteem behave differently from those with high self-esteem in standard dissonance-inducing situations because dissonance is more strongly aroused in people with low self-esteem when they freely engage in actions that reflect positively on them (Aronson & Carlsmith,

1962). Elliot's experiment with Merrill Carlsmith was the first and most compelling demonstration that people who expect to perform poorly on a test, but who then are told that they performed well, actually change their correct answers in order to align their performance with their negative self-views. These initially counterintuitive findings were important in part because they laid the groundwork for the development of later *interpersonal* theories, including self-verification theory (e.g., Swann & Ely, 1984). According to self-verification theory, people should prefer to receive feedback that is consistent with their self-concepts, and when their self-concepts are negative, they should prefer negative over positive feedback. Though Bill Swann and his colleagues rarely cite Elliot and Merrill's classic study, they should. Even today, this study remains one of most powerful and vivid demonstrations of the need for self-consistency.

Elliot's early self-esteem findings also prepared the stage for Sandra Murray and her colleagues' research on self-esteem and dependency regulation processes (Murray, Holmes, & Collins, 2006). To be happy in relationships, people with low self-esteem must believe that their partners have foibles, too, so that the perceived gap between their negative self-evaluations and their evaluations of their partners remains sufficiently small (Murray et al., 2006). If they want to feel good about their relationships, those who have low self-esteem do not benefit from putting their partners on pedestals. Instead, they need to acknowledge their partners' shortcomings and pratfalls, which keeps their partners "in their league" and stabilizes their relationships.

THE TILLER'S LASTING INFLUENCE

Throughout his illustrious career, Elliot always followed his nose, conducting ingenious experiments that were designed to answer questions of deep interest to him. He did not concern himself with whether studying attraction might be viewed as strange or frivolous, even in the eyes of his close social psychologist colleagues. He tackled topics and issues because he found them challenging, fun, and highly relevant, and this motivation is of course reflected in his classic work in the areas of cognitive dissonance and attraction. Elliot's primary interest in intrapersonal processes, including the motive to reduce dissonance, resonated with scholars who were interested in the deeply interpersonal nature of our social lives. Moreover, the intrapersonal dynamics of consistency pressures that Elliot was so fond of investigating were eventually revealed to be important interpersonal dynamics, as documented by Bill Swann and colleagues in their research on self-verification processes. Elliot tilled these fields because that was his passion. As he did so, he had little if any inkling that he was preparing the ground for the seeds of relationship science.

One of the primary indicators of influence in a field is how many careers and research programs an individual has affected, either directly or indirectly. On that indicator alone, Elliot scores several standard deviations above the mean. So thank you, Elliot, for drawing so many of us into social psychology. Thank you for inspiring us to think creatively and to conduct studies that are scientifically rigorous and psychologically meaningful and engaging to participants. Thank you for showing us how to take theories and findings born in the lab and to apply them in novel and insightful ways to address significant real-world problems. Thank you for showing us how to be complete academics. Thank you from the vibrant, verdant pastures of relationship science.

REFERENCES

Aronson, E. (2003). Drifting my own way: Following my nose and heart. In R. Sternberg (Ed.), *Psychologists defying the crowd: Stories of those who battled the establishment and won* (pp. 3–31). Washington, DC: American Psychological Association.

Aronson, E., Brewer, M., & Carlsmith, J. M. (1985). Experimentation in social psychology. In G. Lindsey & E. Aronson (Eds.), *The handbook of social psychology* (3rd ed., Vol. 1, pp. 441–486). New York: Random House.

Aronson, E., & Carlsmith, J. M. (1962). Performance expectancy as determinant of actual performance. *Journal of Abnormal and Social Psychology, 66,* 178–182.

Aronson, E., Carlsmith, J. M., & Ellsworth, P. C. (1976). *Research methods in social psychology.* Reading, MA: Addison-Wesley.

Aronson, E., Ellsworth, P. C., Carlsmith, J. M., & Gonzales, M. H. (1990). *Methods of research in social psychology* (2nd ed.). New York: McGraw-Hill.

Aronson, E., Fried, C. B., & Stone, J. (1991). Overcoming denial and increasing the use of condoms through the induction of hypocrisy. *American Journal of Public Health, 81,* 1636–1638.

Aronson, E., & Gonzales, M. H. (1990). Alternative social influence processes applied to energy conservation. In J. Edwards, R. S. Tindale, L. Heath, & E. J. Posavac (Eds.), *Social psychological applications to social issues: Vol. 1. Social influence processes and prevention* (pp. 301–325). New York: Plenum Press.

Aronson, E., & Linder, D. (1965). Gain and loss of esteem as determinants of interpersonal attractiveness. *Journal of Experimental Social Psychology, 1,* 156–172.

Aronson, E., & Mills, J. (1959). The effect of severity of initiation on liking for a group. *Journal of Abnormal and Social Psychology, 67,* 31–36.

Aronson, E., Willerman, B., & Floyd, J. (1966). The effect of a pratfall on increasing interpersonal attractiveness. *Psychonomic Science, 4,* 227–228.

Berscheid, E. (1999). The greening of relationship science. *American Psychologist, 54,* 260–266.

Berscheid, E., Brothen, T., & Graziano, W. G. (1976). Gain-loss theory and the "law of infidelity": Mr. Doting versus the admiring stranger. *Journal of Social and Personality Psychology, 33,* 709–718.

Berscheid, E., & Walster, E. H. (1969). *Interpersonal attraction.* Reading, MA: Addison-Wesley.

Byrne, D. (1961). Interpersonal attraction and attitude similarity. *Journal of Abnormal and Social Psychology, 62,* 713–715.

Gonzales, M. H., Aronson, E., & Costanzo, M. (1988). Using social cognition and persuasion to promote energy conservation: A quasi-experiment. *Journal of Applied Social Psychology, 18*(12), 1049–1066.

Homans, G. C. (1961). *Social behavior: Its elementary forms.* New York: Harcourt Brace & World.

Murray, S. L., Holmes, J. G., & Collins, N. L. (2006). Optimizing assurance: The risk regulation system in relationships. *Psychological Bulletin, 132,* 641–666.

Stone, J., Aronson, E., Crain, A. L., Winslow, M. P., & Fried, C. B. (1994). Inducing hypocrisy as a means of encouraging young adults to use condoms. *Personality and Social Psychology Bulletin, 20,* 116 128.

Swann, W. B., Jr., & Ely, R. J. (1984). A battle of wills: Self-verification versus behavioral confirmation. *Journal of Personality and Social Psychology, 46,* 1287–1302.

Walster, E. H., Aronson, V., Abrahams, D., & Rottman, L. (1966). The importance of physical attractiveness in dating behavior, *Journal of Personality and Social Psychology, 4,* 508–516.

11

LIES, *DAMNED* LIES, AND THE PATH FROM POLICE INTERROGATION TO WRONGFUL CONVICTION

Deborah Davis

University of Nevada, Reno

What I warn you to remember is that I am a detective. Our relationship with the truth is fundamental but cracked, refracting confusingly like fragmented glass. It is the core of our careers, the endgame of every move we make, and we pursue it with strategies painstakingly constructed of lies and concealment and every variation on deception. The truth is the most desirable woman in the world and we are the most jealous lovers, reflexively denying anyone else the slightest glimpse of her. We betray her routinely, spending hours and days stupor-deep in lies, and then turn back to her holding out the lover's ultimate Mobius strip: "But I only did it because I love you so much." ... This is my job, and you don't go into it—or, if you do, you don't last—without some natural affinity for its priorities and demands. What I am telling you, before you begin my story, is this—two things: I crave the truth. And I lie.

Detective Robert Ryan
(Tana French, In the Woods, *2007, pp. 3–4)*

On December 10, 1984, University of California, Berkeley student Bradley Page falsely confessed[1] to the murder of the girl he loved, Roberta "Bibi" Lee, and to the later rape of her dead body. Page was led to false confession in the usual way: through an unconscionably long police interrogation in which he was isolated, relentlessly accused of having killed his lover, made to feel guilty and distressed, and lied to—about why he was there, about the nature of evidence against him, about his interrogators' motives and intentions, and about what would happen to him if he refused to confess. But unlike countless false confessors before him, Page soon turned to an expert on social influence to explain to the trial jury how police interrogation tactics could influence a person of normal intelligence and mental health to falsely confess to such a heinous crime. Thus, it was that on March 30, 1988, Elliot Aronson, then teaching at nearby University of California, Santa Cruz, became the first psychologist in the United States to testify as an expert witness on causes of false confession (Fulero, in press).

As Elliot's testimony would soon illustrate, the dynamic conflict between the goal of finding the truth and the pursuit of that goal through lies, concealment, and misdirection is nowhere more evident than in the police interrogation room. Criminal interrogation is directed toward one goal—the elicitation of incriminating statements, preferably a full confession of guilt and detailed account of the crime—from a criminal suspect whose guilt is presumed. Since confession is rarely, if ever, in the suspect's best interest (even if guilty), the interrogator must first and foremost convince the suspect of his biggest and most overarching lie—that confession actually is in the suspect's best long-term legal interests—a lie openly acknowledged in popular interrogation manuals: "Psychologically speaking, a successful interrogation is analogous to selling a resident of the Yukon air conditioning in January; for a suspect to acknowledge a criminal act involving negative consequences requires that the suspect believe a confession is in his best interest" (Jayne & Buckley, 1999, p. 207).

To successfully convince his target of this "biggest lie," the interrogator must endeavor to mislead the suspect in at least four crucial ways: (1) to falsely cast the interrogation as a negotiation in which the interrogator will have significant influence on whether and what charges are filed against the suspect; (2) to minimize resistance to the interrogator by falsely casting him as a benevolent ally; (3) to take the possibility of establishing innocence off the table through claims of incriminating evidence and/or false characterizations of guilt as established and inevitable, having thereby turned the suspect's attention away from establishing innocence toward attempts to minimize the consequences of the crime; (4) to offer misleading or wholly false arguments regarding the relative advantages of confession versus denial. In this way, the interrogation functions, in effect, as an extended "anti-Miranda warning"

(Davis & Leo, 2006a) designed to mislead the suspect to believe that if he exerts his Miranda rights and refuses to submit to interrogation or demands an attorney, this will be held against him, but that everything he admits to will work to his long-term legal benefit—in other words, lies and *damned* lies.

The very nature of the dynamic conflict between the goal of truth and its pursuit through lies and deception raises the issue of how the "truth" that emerges from such procedures might be affected—perhaps at best distorted or at worst replaced entirely by falsehood and forever lost. Is it really so strange that a suspect would do something as apparently "crazy" as offering a false confession if the information he uses to make that decision is all (or mostly) false?

The target of an American police interrogation must make a series of fateful decisions under severe stress and without time for reflection. Faced with relentless demands from the interrogator to perform a specific set of actions—"Talk to me!"; "Confess that you are the perpetrator of this crime!"; "Tell me exactly how and why you did it!"; "And do it *now*!"—he must make the decision of whether to comply with these demands, what, if any, story to tell. And, in making that decision, he is faced with implicit and explicit arguments and information that contradict much of what he thinks he knows.

If the suspect is guilty, the contradictory information may simply surround the wisdom of confession and some of the details of the evidence, criminal acts, and motivations. But if he is innocent, the contradictions are much greater. Most striking, of course, is the contradiction between his knowledge that he is innocent and his concept of himself as someone who not only *didn't*, but also *wouldn't*, commit such a crime, versus the absolute conviction of his interrogators that he is guilty, and the many arguments and items of "evidence" they present supporting his guilt. Sometimes led to doubt his own senses and memory, as was Bradley Page, he may also have to try to sort out what actually happened and whether there is any chance he may have committed the crime without remembering. Added to these conflicts is that between the suspect's own needs—to protect himself, to be true to himself, to tell the truth (if innocent)—versus the needs and demands of the interrogator.

How does he make such decisions and pursue his own goals in the context of these multiple contradictions and conflicts? How might these contradictions and conflicts lead an innocent person to conclude that he may have committed a heinous crime he didn't remember and didn't think he was capable of? And how might they lead him to conclude that false confession would be the best choice under the circumstances? Is such an apparently senseless decision really so crazy or unlikely when the information it's based on is so completely false, but conveyed by a powerful and apparently sympathetic, credible source? These were the difficult and fascinating issues addressed by Elliot Aronson when he began his pioneering journey into the American legal system.

BRADLEY PAGE AND THE MURDER OF BIBI LEE

Elliot's journey to the courtroom began with the disappearance of Bibi Lee on the morning of November 4, 1984, while she jogged in Redwood Regional Park in the Oakland Hills. Lee, Bradley Page (her boyfriend), and another UC Berkeley student, Robin Shaw, began their jog together, but Page and Shaw became separated from Lee when they reached a picnic area in Roberts Park. After continuing their jog for a few minutes, Page and Shaw returned to look for Lee at the point where they had become separated. Failing to find Lee there, they walked two miles back to the parking lot in case she had returned to the car. Again failing to find her after waiting a few minutes, Page left Shaw in the parking lot in case Lee returned, then drove slowly, looking for Lee between the parking lot and the picnic area where they had become separated. He returned after approximately 15 to 20 minutes, once again having failed to locate Lee. It was during this interval that police later claimed he had actually somehow located, killed, and hidden her.

Page and Shaw left the park a few minutes after Page's return. Page called Lee's house during the afternoon, asking for her. Having been told she wasn't there, Page carried on with his plans to visit San Francisco for the afternoon, returned to the co-op around 6 p.m., where he had dinner, then called again to see if Lee had gotten home. Page's whereabouts between this phone call and 11 p.m. on November 4 was disputed, and it is in this window of time that he was alleged to have returned to the crime scene, had sex with Lee's dead body, then buried her, using a hub cap from his car as a shovel.

During the following weeks, Page spent much or all of his free time searching for Lee, again to no avail. It was not until Sunday, December 9, 1984, almost five weeks later, that Lee's body was discovered in a small clearing amid a clump of low shrubs in the park where the three had been jogging. Page and Shaw were told to come to the Oakland Police Department on the morning of December 10, when Page was about to begin his own fractured and distorted relationship with the truth—and with the detectives who pursued that truth through lies and deception.

Simply because he was Lee's boyfriend, Sergeants Jerry Harris and Ralph Lacer had presumed him guilty as soon as they heard of Lee's death, as Detective Lacer later explained on national TV (*Eye to Eye with Connie Chung,* 1994). Though Page had been told he was coming to the station to help them solve the crime, the detectives clearly had other intentions, namely, to extract a full confession from a target whose guilt they believed was certain. Page was interviewed repeatedly throughout the day and evening, into the wee morning hours—a total of more than 16 hours. The first interview began at 10:12 a.m. and lasted approximately an hour, but was not taped. The detectives described this interview as covering background information and the events of the morning Lee disappeared, but as not meant to be "probing." A second interview began shortly under an hour later at 11:50, the first of four taped statements taken from Page. In it, Page gave a more detailed account of his relationship with Lee, some tensions that existed the night before and the day of the run, and of his reasons for leaving the park without Lee. At 1:10, Sergeant Harris asked Page if he would take a polygraph. Page agreed, and following a polygraph examination by Sergeant Furry, Page was returned to the interrogation room at 3:15 and left alone for about 25 minutes while the polygraph examiner informed the detectives that Page had been deceptive (an erroneous reading of his results, as later shown at Page's trial).

Unfortunately, neither the polygraph session nor the interrogation to come was taped. But according to Page (appellant's opening brief, *California v. Page;* postconfession statements), when the detectives resumed the interrogation after the polygraph, they insisted that Page had something to do with Lee's death, citing his failure of the polygraph, and falsely claiming to have evidence connecting him to the crime: eyewitnesses who allegedly saw him kill Lee, and his fingerprints at the crime scene (see Leo & Ofshe, 2001; Pratkanis & Aronson, 2001, p. 176). Page reported that no matter what he said, the detectives continued to accuse him of killing Lee and to tell him he was lying. When reminded that the polygraph indicated that he was lying, he insisted that he had no memory of hurting Lee and that if anything happened he would have had to "black it out." Pressed to imagine how he might have hurt her—*if* he had hurt her—Page's first apparent admission came at about 4:10 p.m., about six hours after the interrogation began, when he made a statement to the effect of having *an image* of hitting and kicking Lee, and of "wailing on her or going off on her." But Page still talked about blacking out and did not admit to any actual memory of harming Lee.

At 4:30 p.m., Detective Harris began to lie in earnest. He first told Page that his fingerprints had been found at the crime scene and that this was one way the detectives knew Page was lying. He later told Page that a witness had seen Page's car south of the entrance to the park on the day of Lee's disappearance, though Page denied having been in that area. For the next 2.5 hours, although he never claimed to remember finding or harming Lee, Page reported that detectives relentlessly confronted him with their "concerns" about his story and continued to demand that he tell them how he found her, killed her, and later raped her. When he made "mistakes" in his story that were inconsistent with the evidence, the detectives corrected him and got him to try again. They suggested that the crime might not be as serious as it seemed: that it might not be cold-blooded murder but rather an accidental killing arising from a quarrel (*California v. Page,* 1991, p. 173)—a scenario much like the false confession Page eventually constructed. At about 5:45, almost eight hours after his interrogation began, Page began to construct a story of how he actually killed Lee. Page reported that the officers would suggest something, and he would imagine their suggestion, or they would ask if something happened and he would put it into the scenario (such as if he had a branch or rock, or she had hit her head on something—things the detectives would have expected based on what they knew of the location of the body and the nature of her injuries). Page later described the process as using his imagination to construct a story, much like making a movie, recounting how he *would have* killed her *if he had* killed her.

Detectives reported that they turned off the tape recorder during this time because they had learned from experience that it can inhibit a suspect when he is approaching readiness to confess. But once they had shaped the initial story to their satisfaction, at 7:07 p.m. they turned the tape recorder on again, asking Page to tell the story again on tape. In this taped account, Page described having located Lee during the 15 to 20 minutes he left Robin Shaw to search for her. He described getting out of the car and leading Lee up a slope into some trees, where, in response to her rebuff of his attempts to hold and kiss her, he ended up backhanding her and causing her to fall by a tree, hitting her head and becoming unconscious. He reported leaving her unmoving and apparently unconscious to return to the parking lot to find Shaw. Page recounted how he went back later that evening and found Lee dead. He reportedly picked her up, dragged her over to a rock, propped her head up on the rock, and lay down with her underneath a blanket he had gotten from his car—where he cried, caressed her, and made love to her dead body (though rigor mortis would have made this impossible). He then used a hubcap from his trunk to scoop up material to bury her.

The taped confession ended at 7:33, at which point Page agreed to talk to a district attorney. When the district attorney arrived, just after 9:00 p.m., still with no advice of an attorney, Page offered the first of two taped statements, lasting until 2:15 the next morning, in which he retracted his confession and explained why and how he had made up the story for the detectives. Page explained that the relentless demands of his interrogators led him to try to help by imagining how he could have done it. Page claimed that police tactics had temporarily convinced him that he might have killed her, leading him to essentially concoct a confession from a combination of what he knew, feared, or imagined.

Although Page had retracted his confession immediately after he had given it, it was too late to convince the detectives or the district attorney that his confession was false. He was charged with first-degree murder, and his first trial began on February 10, 1986. Though the first jury seemed to experience sufficient doubt to find him not guilty of the most serious charges of first- or second-degree murder, and to hang on the charge of manslaughter, in his second trial Page was convicted of the remaining charge of manslaughter—a verdict that was upheld on appeal. The appellate judges, despite a wealth of evidence disputing his guilt, stated in their published opinion that the verdict was supported by substantial incriminating evidence in addition to his confession (see *California v. Page*, 1991, p. 161).

Why did Bradley Page confess falsely to such a legally serious and morally heinous crime? Was Page cognitively impaired or mentally ill? If not, what police tactics could convince a mentally "normal" person to falsely confess? And, given the many discrepancies between Page's confession and the evidence, and the existence of substantial additional exculpatory evidence available to police, prosecutors, juries, and appellate judges, why did none of them recognize his innocence or admit it if they did? What could a social influence expert offer, then and now, to address these questions?

The task, of course, is a difficult one. Strongly held commonsense notions fly in the face of the idea that a person would falsely confess to a heinous crime he didn't commit (see Chojnacki, Cicchini, & White, 2008; Henkel, Coffman, & Dailey, 2008). Reflecting the difficulty of overcoming such assumptions, studies of proven-false confessors have shown that those whose cases were taken to trial were found guilty 73% to 81% of the time (Drizin & Leo, 2004; Leo & Ofshe, 1998). In view of this risk, many (perhaps most) innocents who have falsely confessed are pressured by their own defense attorneys to plead guilty. When there has been a confession, falling prey to the same commonsense assumptions, these attorneys may fail to believe their clients' claims of innocence or, recognizing the pervasiveness of such assumptions in others, may view attempts to establish innocence at trial as hopeless and as risking a more serious sentence, perhaps even death (for reviews, see

Leo, 2008; Leo & Davis, 2009; Redlich, in press). But Bradley Page took his case to trial, not once, but twice. To succeed, Page would have to make the jury understand why anyone, and specifically why Page himself, would falsely confess to a crime so heinous as the murder and posthumous rape of the woman he claimed to love. How then, to explain the apparently incomprehensible?

THE CONTEXT OF THE DAY

The year 1988, when Elliot undertook this task, was the dawn of what later became psychologists' widespread interest in false confessions. Though there had been several previous analyses of police interrogation-induced false confessions (e.g., Bem, 1966, 1967; Driver, 1968; Kassin & Wrightsman, 1985; Munsterberg, 1908; Wrightsman & Kassin, 1993; Zimbardo, 1967), experimental studies of the phenomenon had only just begun around the time of Bradley Page's false confession. But these studies began with questions about individual vulnerability to interrogative influence (by clinical psychologist Gisli Gudjonsson, 1984a, 1984b), and examination of the effects of confession evidence on juror reactions (e.g., Kassin & Wrightsman, 1980). It was not until the early 1990s that researchers began to conduct experimental tests of the influence of interrogation tactics on confessions, and of the mechanisms through which they exerted their influence (e.g., Kassin & McNall, 1991; see review by Wrightsman & Kassin, 1993). It was still later, well after Page's case had gone to trial, that the first experimental study of the impact of interrogation tactics on false confession was published (Kassin & Keichel, 1996). By the time of Page's second trial in 1988, still lacking an experimental science of interrogation-induced false confessions, Elliot could only testify as to scientifically documented principles of social influence and how they might apply to the interrogation of Bradley Page.

A further barrier for Elliot and Page was the lack of a full recording of the two crucial sections of Page's interrogation: the polygraph session and the interrogation that followed. Elliot had to rely on the less informative recordings of the sessions preceding the polygraph and the recording of the "confession" *after* it had been shaped by the accusatory stage of the interrogation, and on the recordings of Page's interviews with the district attorney and his interrogators, during which he explained how and why he developed and recounted his false story.[2] Since the subsequent accounts of Page and the detectives differed with respect to what happened during the interrogation, no indisputable record of the police tactics existed.

Notwithstanding these difficulties, Page's own explanation of his false confession, as well as Elliot's 1988 testimony, anticipated much of what experts now testify to in court regarding common interrogation tactics and the causes of police-induced false confession. In the 20 years since Elliot's 1988 testimony in the Page case, a burgeoning social science literature has provided increasingly sophisticated theoretical analyses of the mechanisms of influence in police interrogations, as well as experimental tests of these mechanisms. Concurrently, a rising tide of DNA exonerations highlighted the role of false confession in proven-wrongful convictions (for reviews, see Garrett, 2008; Leo, 2008). The resulting increased awareness of the role of false confessions within the legal system, along with the exponential increase in legal and scientific publications examining the causes of false confessions, has fueled the growth of a cohort of social science experts providing expert testimony on interrogation-induced false confessions to courts in the United States and abroad. Though the scientific basis of their testimony is vastly expanded since Elliot's pioneering appearance in the courts, these experts still testify to many of the same causes of false confession as Elliot pointed to 20 years ago. Moreover, in discussing Page's confession itself, Elliot anticipated now common recommendations for how to recognize a potentially false confession.

LIES AND *DAMNED* LIES: WHAT ARE THEY AND WHAT ARE THEIR EFFECTS?

In a pretrial hearing on March 30, 1988, Elliot provided his first general summary of how a person might be led to falsely confess, pointing heavily to the role of deception:

> When a trusted person in authority misleads or lies to another person or puts that other person under stress or makes that other person feel particularly guilty or arranges a situation so that that other person begins to believe that he can't trust his own perceptions or his own memory, it throws that person off balance, it makes him increasingly suggestible, and it temporarily makes him very vulnerable to persuasion. What the person tries to do when he's confronted with what seems like incontrovertible evidence that contradicts the evidence of his own sense or own memory is what most of us try to do is we try to cope with that in the best way we can. We try to make sense of it. We try to put things together in ways that make sense, and in so doing we are sort of

grabbing at straws to try to make sense out of that situation. In my judgment, that's not the best way to get a reliable statement or a reliable confession out of anyone. (Transcript of proceedings, Wednesday, March 30, 1988; *California vs. Page*, No. 81366).

In other words, in this summary and throughout his testimony, Elliot noted that the detectives had taken an already stressed boy, one who trusted them, who took their lies at face value, and who wanted to help and please them, added to his stress by subjecting him to an unconscionably long interrogation, played on his feelings of guilt, and lied to him throughout the interrogation—about their own motivations, about the evidence against him, and about the choices available to him and the implications of those choices. And, quite rightly, Elliot pointed to the risks of relying on statements given by a person whose thinking is compromised by physical and emotional distress, and who offers them in the context of trying to resolve his own true experiences with a set of dramatically discrepant falsehoods from an apparently credible source. As Elliot recognized with respect to Page, lies, big and small, play an integral role in producing a false confession.

But what else would Elliot have seen had a complete transcript of Page's interrogation been available? What other deceptions do interrogators employ? How do they unfold during the typical interrogation? And how do such lies and misdirection continue to affect the suspect *after* he confesses—during the postconfession investigation and through the procedures to come, as he faces prosecutors, judges, and juries?

Lies to the Suspect: The Interrogation

A police interrogation is a very carefully orchestrated, multifaceted strategy to induce the target to do three things: to talk to police without an attorney, to admit guilt, and to provide a comprehensive narrative explicating the causes and enactment of the crime. Toward this end, almost everything about American police interrogations can be deceptive, with each misleading cog in the wheel carefully designed to convince the suspect that compliance is in his best long-term legal interest. Modern psychological interrogation methods are truly brilliant psychology—insofar, that is, as they so effectively accomplish this goal. But, they're also not so brilliant, in that they're billed as the way to *get the truth*, reflecting no recognition that these powerful weapons of influence elicit compliance with demands to tell a particular story, sometimes one completely at odds with the truth.

In my own initial foray as a psychologist writing about interrogation, I relied heavily on Elliot's book with Anthony Pratkanis, *Age of*

Propaganda (Pratkanis & Aronson, 2001), to consider how and why police interrogation tactics so effectively induce compliance. I was astonished to see how thoroughly police tactics incorporate the many principles of social influence social psychology has documented and tested. As the next sections illustrate, essentially every verbal and nonverbal action incorporates known principles of influence (see Davis, 2008; Davis & O'Donohue, 2004; Davis & Leo, 2006a, 2006b; Leo, 2008, for more extensive explication and documentation of police strategies and their incorporation of psychological principles of influence; and Cialdini, 2008; Pratkanis & Aronson, 2001; Pratkanis, 2007, for general reviews of social influence techniques).

Most detectives in the United States are trained to use the Reid nine-step method of interrogation as described by Fred Inbau, John Reid, and their colleagues (Inbau, Reid, Buckley, & Jayne, 2001; the fourth edition of their training manual) and in their many training seminars offered in the United States and abroad (see Reid.com), or similar methods. An interrogation following their recommended strategies will take place largely as follows.

Setting the Stage

The suspect may enter the interrogation already vulnerable to influence, already stressed and fatigued by the incident in question and its aftermath. This distress and fatigue can be further enhanced by a lengthy and aversive interrogation, as was certainly true in Bradley Page's case. A mentally compromised suspect offers fertile ground for deception, and indeed, Inbau and his colleagues (2001) suggest that anxiety can motivate confession. Hence, interrogators may aim to capitalize upon existing anxiety and distress, as well as to exacerbate them through aversive tactics. As noted by the Supreme Court in *Miranda v. Arizona* (1966, p. 465): "The entire thrust of police interrogation there, as in all the cases today, was to put the defendant in such an emotional state as to impair his capacity for rational judgment." Distress resulting from such tactics enhances the likelihood that the suspect may confess just to escape the duress of the interrogation, and also renders him less capable of attending to, remembering, and analyzing relevant information to form reasonable conclusions, particularly when isolated from others who might help him think more clearly (see Follette, Davis, & Leo, 2007; Kassin, Drizin, Grisso, Gudjonsson, Leo, & Redlich, 2010, for analysis of effects of mental capacities on decision making in interrogation). Recognizing such vulnerabilities, once police identify a suspect, they may attempt to interview him as quickly as possible after the crime to capitalize on his existing distress (among other reasons).

Page pointed to the impact of his emotional state in explaining his confession. He began the interrogation in considerable distress. After a month of unrelenting worry and efforts to search for Lee, Page had just learned of the discovery of her dead body the day immediately preceding the interrogation. Moreover, he felt considerable guilt for not having done more to find her on the day of her disappearance, which the detectives encouraged by their many comments, questions, and suspicions about the fact that Page had left Lee without more effort to find her. "It's been a hard, a hard month and I came in and was questioned and everything kind of led up to my guilt that I would have had for not helping Bibi," Page said to Lacer and Harris (1 a.m. statement, p. 2). Page also referred to the additional distress posed by the detectives' unrelenting accusations and challenges to his story: "Every time I was telling the truth you, you were giving me this really negative feedback and every time I was leading on and saying, you know, don't you feel better now that you're telling me this. I was feeling better that I was telling you this because it was relieving the pressure from you" (1 a.m. statement, p. 28).

A distressed suspect, as Page clearly was, is already vulnerable to influence. But the interrogator soon engages in a number of additional stage-setting tactics designed to render the suspect ever more vulnerable to his primary goal of persuading the suspect that confession is in his best interests.

The First Lie: Why Are You Here?

Though suspects are sometimes arrested before interrogation, very often police ask criminal suspects to come to the police station voluntarily, with their own transportation, ostensibly to help police with the investigation. Quite rightly, police know that if the person realizes he is a suspect, he is likely to be less forthcoming from the outset. Moreover, if the person is not placed under arrest, police are not obligated to administer Miranda warnings and to obtain a waiver of rights. Hence, as the interrogation begins, many suspects—and particularly innocent suspects—have no idea that they are actually being interrogated. Indeed, some are never offered Miranda warnings or waivers until after they have offered a full confession.

Finessing Miranda—Just a Formality to Get Out of the Way

If Miranda warnings are administered before the accusatory interrogation, they are widely misunderstood by suspects (see Kassin et al.,

2010, for review), and detectives often further mislead suspects as to the nature, function, and significance of their rights. For example, they might say something like: "We really need to talk to you to get 'this thing' straightened out. But before we can talk to you, we have to have you read and sign this." Notice the many levels of deception inherent to this statement. As a whole, it is a strong statement of the desire and intention of the police to talk to the suspect, making it more difficult for the suspect to refuse those in authority what they clearly want. It also implicitly challenges the notion that the suspect is actually free to refuse to talk to the interrogator. And, as interrogation manuals teach (e.g., Inbau et al., 2001), references to the crime itself are designed to mislead. The use of such words as "this thing" rather than "this rape" or "this murder" distracts the target from careful contemplation of the serious criminal nature of the offense under discussion. And "get this straightened out," or another favorite, "get this cleared up" promote the hope of a noncriminal resolution. The goal, of course, is to get the confession needed to get the person convicted, not to get the matter cleared up and done with during the interrogation—at least not to do so in a manner favorable to the suspect.

Though four out of five suspects waive Miranda rights and submit to questioning (Kassin et al., 2010; Leo, 1996a, 1996b), innocent suspects are especially prone to do so. In an experimental demonstration of this vulnerability of innocents, Kassin and Norwick (2004) randomly assigned participants to commit or not to commit a mock crime before being interrogated. When asked to waive their rights, innocent persons were more likely to do so than the guilty. In several studies with my colleagues Richard Leo and William Follette (Davis, Leo, & Follette, 2008, in press), participants were asked to read an interrogation of an innocent suspect. They then recommended whether he should invoke his rights and demand an attorney, continue to talk to police without confessing, or falsely confess to child molestation. In open-ended responses explaining their choices, participants who recommended that the suspect should continue to answer questions but not confess overwhelmingly explained either (1) that the person could potentially prove his innocence or show that he had nothing to hide by continuing to talk, or (2) that he would look guilty should he refuse to talk.

Indeed, it was the latter reasoning that Brad Page referred to in his interrogation. During one of several readings of Miranda rights, Page was asked if he understood his right to an attorney and the fact that one would be provided to him free of charge. He responded, "Yeah, I guess. Maybe—I mean, somehow it seems—it feels to me that if I ask for a lawyer that I'm admitting guilt and I know I'm not, but ..." (9:09 p.m. statement to district attorneys, p. 4). Indeed, police promote this perception. If a suspect does ask for an attorney, the detective may say something like: "Well, we can get you an attorney, and that's your right. But I have to tell you, people are going to have to wonder why you think you need one. You might as well just point a finger at yourself and let everyone know you have something to hide." This and other implicit and explicit messages of the interrogation can be so strong and pervasive as to make the suspect doubt that he actually can invoke his rights, or afraid of the consequences should he do so.

The Preinterrogation Interview
As suggested in common interrogation manuals, the interrogator may begin his questions with a preinterrogation "interview" in which he gathers as much background and incident-relevant information as possible before accusing the suspect of involvement in the crime. Then, immediately prior to the accusatory interrogation, he will ask a series of "behavior analysis" questions designed to assess deceptiveness. If the detective concludes that the suspect is guilty (which, in fact, tends to already be assumed), he will proceed to the accusatory part of the interrogation. Unfortunately, commonly taught techniques for detecting deception at this stage have been shown to *reduce accuracy*, while *increasing detectives' confidence* in their judgments of deception. Further, law enforcement personnel manifest a "guilt bias," such that misclassifications are more likely to be toward belief that the suspect is lying (for reviews, see Kassin et al., 2010; Vrij, 2008). Thus, innocents are unlikely to be recognized as such, and the interrogator is likely to proceed to interrogation.

As Elliot and Anthony Pratkanis (2001) point out, proper "landscaping" or "pre-persuasion" will undermine resistance and smooth the way for persuading a target. A central component of this process is to define the nature and purpose of the interaction, the roles of the participants, and the agenda for carrying it out. This process begins during the preinterrogation interview, but takes shape in earnest during the earliest stages of the interrogation, when the interrogator communicates five crucial lies to the suspect: (1) "I know you're guilty; your guilt has been established beyond any doubt"; (2) "Nevertheless, there may be a resolution that doesn't involve serious consequences"; (3) "I have the authority to affect what happens to you"; (4) "I like you and want to try to help you"; and (5) "I can't help you unless you explain what happened, now, before we finish here." Throughout the interrogation, the interrogator also attempts to undermine resistance to himself and his attempts to influence by enhancing his own likeability and rapport with the suspect.

The Set-Up Question
Toward the end of the behavior analysis interview, just before the accusatory state of the interrogation, the interrogator will ask a question such as, "Tell me Jack, what do you think should happen to the person who did this thing? Should he just go straight to jail? Or, are there circumstances where he would deserve a second chance, maybe to get counseling, not go to jail ...?" This is the first misleading hint to the suspect that the alleged crime would not necessarily result in criminal charges or jail, and the first implication that the detective may have the authority to achieve the ideal resolution for the suspect. My colleagues and I have shown in our research that participants who read an interrogation transcript including such a set-up question believe that the detective has significantly more options in deciding what to do with the suspect, should he confess, than those reading an interrogation transcript without the set-up question—including the option to send the suspect home with no charges (Davis, Follette, & Leo, 2007; Davis et al., 2008, in press; Davis, Leo, Knaack, & Bailey, 2006).

The Borg Maneuver: Taking Innocence Off the Table
Clearly, among the most powerful sources of resistance to confession, whether true or false, is the hope or expectation that the suspect will be proven innocent. The first step of the nine-step accusatory stage of the interrogation, positive confrontation, is designed to eliminate this resistance. Toward this end, the suspect is confronted with the accusation that he committed the crime, with the interrogator's claims of absolute confidence in this guilt, and with true and/or false "evidence" of that guilt. The intention is to convince the suspect that "resistance is futile" (the favorite saying of the Borg, the nemesis of *Star Trek*'s United Federation of Planets), that there is overwhelming evidence of guilt, and that he will not be able to convince anyone of his innocence. Without hope of exoneration, the suspect's attention will turn to how to minimize the consequences, thereby setting the stage for the detective to convince him that this can best be accomplished through confession. Confession can seem the best alternative to innocent and guilty suspects alike if they are sufficiently convinced that they cannot hope for exoneration. The essentials of the Borg maneuver begin with the initial accusations

and confrontation with "evidence" of guilt, but continue throughout as necessary to shut down protestations and claims of innocence from the suspect.

Lies About Evidence: The Engine of False Confession
Part and parcel of the positive confrontation stage of the interrogation is presentation of "evidence" against the suspect. When the suspect is innocent, such evidence is necessarily wholly or largely false—whether deliberately deceptive or not. The detective may knowingly and falsely claim to possess evidence such as fingerprints, DNA, or incriminating witnesses against the suspect, or may refer to evidence presented in good faith, but mistaken nonetheless—such as a mistaken (but honest) witness or the account of an alleged co-perpetrator who has previously falsely confessed when subjected to coercive interrogation.

Prominent among the false or misleading information presented to criminal suspects are polygraph results, typically misrepresented as infallible assessments of deception. Hoping to prove their innocence, criminal suspects—particularly innocent suspects—often ask to take a polygraph. If not, the interrogator may ask him to take a polygraph (or "voice stress analysis"), suggesting that it is simply for the purpose of "eliminating" the person as a suspect. In fact, interrogators use the polygraph primarily as a tool to facilitate confession (Lykken, 1998). Whether suspects pass or not, they are often told they failed—a tactic Lykken referred to as "the fourth degree," and one I've found in my research to lead subjects to recommend higher rates of false confession for known innocents (Davis, Weaver, & Leo, 2007). (Also see the National Research Council Committee to Review the Scientific Evidence on the Polygraph, 2003 warning of the risk of polygraph-induced false confessions.)

Such false or mistaken evidence can cause a suspect to confess falsely because he has become hopeless about the prospects of exoneration. Moreover, as clearly occurred with Bradley Page, some suspects, faced with apparent "proof" of their guilt, may be caused to doubt their own innocence and to believe (however temporarily) that they may have actually committed the crime (see Kassin, 2007, for review of such "internalized" false confessions). Page stated that he constructed his false story in part because he began to doubt his own memory and to wonder if he had somehow committed the crime ("right now my whole concept of reality is shocked"; "To think that I could black out at any time and do those kind of things … right now my mind is so shocked and topsy-turvy, you know …"; "I was shocked. I was distraught, shocked past the belief that yes, … there is a possibility"; 9:09 statement to district attorney, pp. 7, 13). Page said they needed to find out why he had killed Lee, for his own sake and theirs. Convinced that he might well have killed Lee and suffered traumatic amnesia as a result, Page explained, "I had to find a plausible story that I could have killed her—my girlfriend—and it had to be so outrageous that I wouldn't remember it" (1 a.m. statement to detectives, p. 19).

The polygraph was particularly instrumental in convincing Page that he may have actually committed the crime. "I was so open to everything right then. ... I do not have any barriers up and when, so this polygraph said I was lying and I went, God, you know, maybe I lied. Maybe there is something I can't remember. I don't recall and then you guys were insistent in 'No, you're lying, you're lying, we know, you have, you know, fingerprints ...' and everything's topsy turvey and, I mean I was at the point where you, I was going crazy by, by the, by the pressure and, yes, I believe that I, there is a possibility that somehow I would've blocked out ..." (1 a.m. interview, p. 25).

The "Pretext" for the Interrogation

If the Borg maneuver is successful in convincing the suspect that evidence of guilt is overwhelming, this raises the question of why the interrogation should continue. Of course, the interrogator has a ready answer! This interrogation is not about "investigating guilt," it's about "deciding what to do about it." In other words, the interrogation is cast as a negotiation in which the interrogator has the authority to determine what will happen to the presumably guilty suspect, and in which what the suspect says can affect this decision.

To promote the perception that the interrogation is not about whether the suspect is guilty, interrogators are advised to "argue against self-interest," telling the suspect that they don't need a confession from the suspect, since guilt is already proved. Instead, the reason for continuing the interrogation is to find out *why* the suspect committed the crime, and *what kind of person* he is—which the interrogator describes as often more important (see Inbau et al., 2001, pp. 225–226). This clearly (and falsely) implies that the motive for the crime and the character of the suspect will affect the likelihood and seriousness of criminal charges. The detective will shortly take advantage of these mistaken assumptions by offering various scenarios for the commission of the crime, answering these questions in ways that appear to put the suspect in the most favorable light.

Meanwhile, the detective invokes the reciprocity principle of persuasion by emphasizing his own effort and sacrifice in continuing the interrogation. He may point out that he has no need to be there (arguing against self-interest) and that he could go home to his family and relax instead, but that he is "concerned" about the suspect and what will happen to him if he doesn't "explain this thing" and tell "his side of the story" before "it's too late." This alleged sacrifice can encourage the suspect to reciprocate by complying with the interrogator's demands to confess. Page seemed to fall prey to the feeling that he was helping the detectives by trying to produce a story explaining the crime. Referring to his construction of the false confession as "helping," Page described the tendency to be helpful as central to his personality: "I like to make people happy ... I feel like that is my attribute. My main attribute" (9:09 p.m. statement to district attorneys, p. 9).

The "Sympathetic Detective With a Time-Limited Offer"
Once it is clear to the suspect that he is not being interviewed as a witness, but rather interrogated as a suspect, the natural inclination would be to distrust the interrogator as an enemy. Interrogators will often work to overcome this resistance by falsely presenting themselves as benevolent allies. They are friendly, nonthreatening, and engaging during the preinterrogation interview, attempting to establish rapport with the suspect, projecting similarity and common ground. This sympathetic demeanor is maintained into the accusatory stage of the interrogation, sometimes by one detective playing "good cop" to another's more hostile "bad cop," an attempt to focus resistance on the bad cop and thereby lessen resistance to the good cop.

The misperception that the detective has the suspect's best interests at heart is promoted both implicitly, through friendly demeanor, and explicitly, through statements of desire and intentions to help. The detective might say, "Listen Jack, I think you're a nice guy—a stand-up guy—and I'd like to help you. But I can't do anything if you don't tell me the truth." "I can't do anything for you once you leave here. Once the DA gets you, he's not going to be interested in what you have to say anymore. The wheels are gonna grind, and what happens happens. This is your chance to tell your side of the story. I hate to see you waste it." Invoking the scarcity principle of influence, also called the "deadline technique" (Cialdini, 2008), the "sympathetic detective" has made a "time-limited offer" to help the suspect get the best legal outcomes.

Such statements promote two misperceptions: that the detective *can* help the suspect (that he has "authority") and that he *wants* to help the suspect (that he is "beneficent"). My research has shown that compared to participants who read an interrogation transcript without the sympathetic detective tactic, those who read one including the sympathetic detective tactic believed the detective had greater choice of what to do should the suspect confess, and that he liked the suspect more, wanted to help him more, and would be more likely to try to get him the best legal outcomes. Further, they were more likely to recommend false confession for an innocent suspect accused of child sexual abuse (Davis et al., 2006, 2008, in press; Davis et al., 2007).

Page clearly fell for the sympathetic detective's story. Explaining why he confessed, he stated that in part he wanted to help the police ("I was trying to be so open and willing. I want to help"; 1 a.m. statement to detectives, p. 5), who he thought were trying to help him ("...said they were my friends ... they were there to help me"; "I thought you were here to help"; 9:09 statement, p. 5; 1 a.m. statement, p. 29).

Making the Sale: Lowering the Relative Costs of Confession
The initial stages of the interrogation set the stage for the detective to convince the suspect of his biggest lie. But arguably the most important goal remains to be achieved: to convince the suspect that confession actually will result in the best relative outcomes.

> *Constructing the Story of the Crime: Theme Development and Self-Justification*
> Have you ever rationalized or justified your own questionable behavior? That same justification process is developed in the mind of the criminal offender ... We can therefore develop a strategy of how to present to the offender his own justifications and rationalizations in a morally, legally acceptable manner, with the primary goal of obtaining the truth—typically a full confession or admission of guilt.
>
> **—Louis Senese**
> (Anatomy of Interrogation Themes, *2005, pp. 10–11*)

Just as Elliot's self-justification expansion of dissonance theory would suggest, interrogation manuals recommend that guilty criminals will be naturally motivated to justify their criminal acts. Thus, Step 2 of the Reid method, theme development, is designed to play upon such natural needs for self-justification by suggesting apparently relatively justifiable scenarios for the motivation and commission of the crime. For example, the detective may suggest that the crime was the fault of the victim—who started the fight, dressed provocatively, or had committed a crime against the suspect or his family first. Or, he may suggest admirable motives for the crime—such as the need to feed one's children versus greed. The interrogator may also attempt to minimize the seriousness of the act by normalizing it—suggesting that anyone would have done the same thing in similar circumstances, or that he himself has had similar needs or motives in the past. Interrogation manuals contain long lists of such self-justifying themes, categorized and tailored according to the specific crime (e.g., Senese, 2005).

The detective pursues this process of theme development, leading up to the alternative question (Step 7 of the Reid technique), in which the detective contrasts an apparently more serious with a less serious version of the crime, and asks the suspect which it was. For example:

> Listen Jack, I don't believe this was something you ever intended to happen. She probably just yelled at you and started throwing things, and got you so upset you didn't realize what you were doing. You just pushed her away, and she fell and hit her head. If that's what happened, I can understand that. It's "no big deal." But if this is something you planned and did on purpose, that's completely different. Which was it, Jack? Was this just an accident, something that got out of hand? Or was it deliberate?

In contrast, the accidental scenario seems even less serious, often not criminal at all (such as an alternative question involving self-defense versus premeditated murder), and frequently leads to a first admission of any involvement. Even though interrogators recognize that the initial admission of involvement in the crime is likely to be inaccurate, at least in details, they view theme development as part of a "stepping stone" approach to eventually eliciting the full and true story. Unfortunately, this expectation is unrealistic. At minimum, the interrogator has been strongly suggestive, essentially telling the suspect how and why he believes the crime was committed, offering false evidence to support these constructions, and refusing to accept any claims from the suspect that are inconsistent with the story—at least until the suspect first agrees to it. Then, as he further shapes the suspect's narrative to come closer and closer to his notion of the real truth, the interrogator may offer many suggestions, arguments with the suspect's position, and perhaps more "evidence" that can irretrievably contaminate the suspect's narrative and lead him even further from the truth—particularly if he is innocent.

Theme development, or minimization, is often supplemented by the complementary use of maximization, or raising fears of more serious consequences that may result from failure to confess (see Kassin et al., 2010). The interrogator may raise issues of how judges and juries are likely to react to those who refuse to take responsibility for their crimes or may emphasize the severity of the crime, and the serious risks facing the suspect. In some cases, the interrogator may explicitly threaten more serious legal consequences if the person refuses to confess, although such explicit threats may be grounds for suppression of any resulting confession. Indeed, Bradley Page referred to such maximization in his explanation of his false confession, reporting that detectives threatened that he would "not be able to live" and would "rot away from the inside" and that he would spend the rest of his life in jail as a murderer if he didn't "explain" what happened. When he did come up with a story of how he might have committed the crime, he described an apparently unintended and accidental scenario consistent with common interrogator themes—that is, a fight in which Lee rejected his advances and he accidentally caused her to fall and hit her head. Explaining his story, Page noted that detectives had suggested that it might not be so serious if it were an accident: "I had been led to believe that if I, it was an accident and stuff ..." (1 a.m. statement to detectives, p. 18).

Interrogators do not recognize the use of either maximization or minimization as communicating threats of harsh punishment or promises of leniency. Minimization, for example, is described by interrogators as using the suspect's need to morally (rather than legally) justify himself to allow him to save face while still confessing. But substantial research has shown that such "themes" also serve to lower the perceived costs of confession—implicitly suggesting that the act, if committed for the reasons and in the manner suggested, would result in less serious criminal charges or even none at all. Further, laboratory studies have shown that the use of minimization leads to higher rates of false confession (see Kassin et al., 2010, for review).

When the Initial Interrogation Fails: Widening the Net of Deception

What we do is crude, crass and nasty. A girl gives her boyfriend an alibi for the evening when we suspect him of robbing a north-side Centra and stabbing the clerk. I flirt with her at first, telling her I can see why he would want to stay home when he's got her ... Then I tell her we've found marked bills from the till in his classy white tracksuit bottoms, and he's claiming that she went out that evening and gave them to him when she got back. I do it so convincingly, with such delicate cross hatching of discomfort and compassion at her man's betrayal, that finally her faith in four shared years disintegrates like a sand castle and through tears and snot, while her man sits with my partner in the next interview room saying nothing except: "Fuck off, I was home with Jackie," she tells me everything from the time he left the house to the details of his sexual shortcomings. Then I pat her gently on the shoulder and give her a tissue and a cup of tea, and a statement sheet.

—**Detective Robert Ryan**
(French, 2007, p. 3)

The Reid tactics are often successful in eliciting admissions from criminal suspects during the interrogation and have been implicated in most known false confessions (Leo, 2008). But if they don't work, police may choose to engage in other elaborate and deceptive ruses to get a confession, spreading their net of deception far beyond the interrogation room. They may plant jailhouse informants to try to elicit incriminating statements under the guise of friendship, or enlist the aid of friends and family, lying shamelessly to them and destroying relationships in the process. In a particularly tragic example, police, who suspected Billy Wayne Cope of raping and killing his daughter, lied to Cope's wife, telling her that Cope's DNA matched that found in their daughter. They planned to send her into the jail, wired, to try to elicit a confession from him. Though Cope was actually innocent, his wife died of natural causes shortly thereafter, believing her husband had raped and killed their own daughter (see account in Kassin, 2007).

Taking the Confession and Making it Stick

Getting a confession is only the beginning. After that you need to waterproof it, second guess defense lawyers and juries.

—**Detective Robert Ryan**
(French, 2007, p. 377)

Once the suspect begins to admit culpability and tell the story of how and why the crime was committed, the last task of the interrogator is to get the confession in writing or on video. At this stage, the goal is to elicit a sufficiently detailed and compelling narrative to survive any claims of coercion and to convict the suspect in court. A confession taken by a skilled interrogator is a very carefully constructed attempt to persuade, not an uncontaminated item of evidence.

Recognizing the preeminence of narrative in our ability to comprehend and in our tendencies to be persuaded, detectives know the confession should contain basic elements of a compelling story to be convincing to the prosecutors, judges, and juries to come. Thus, as Leo (2008) describes in detail, detectives work to ensure that the confession contains at least five elements: "(1) a coherent, believable story line, (2) motives and explanations, (3) crime knowledge (both general and specific), (4) expressions of emotion, and (5) acknowledgements of voluntariness" (p. 168). Together, these elements yield a credible story of the crime, one incorporating elements and behaviors that promote the perception that the suspect is telling the truth (such as the use of detail, intense emotional expression of anger, sorrow, shame or remorse, and statements of apology to the victims or their families) and that he has done so without coercion (such as asking the suspect to include an explanation of why he is confessing, for example, with respect to his feelings of guilt or need for forgiveness). With the inclusion of such elements, even false confessions may be very compelling, sometimes entailing elaborate acting out and demonstrations of the crime by the false confessor.

But the Reid method goes even further, including recommendations for deceptive actions to enhance the appearance of validity and voluntariness. For example, the manual (Inbau et al., 2001) recommends that a woman should be in the room (to minimize the credibility of claims of physical coercion). Further, it recommends that the suspect should be led to write the confession in his own handwriting (to promote the perception that it did come from the suspect), and, if it must be typed, to deliberately make mistakes that the suspect must correct and initial in his own handwriting. These and other recommendations are designed for the sole purpose of persuasion rather than of authenticity, and are among the many features of false confessions that make them very difficult to recognize, as the next sections illustrate.

From False Confession to Wrongful Conviction: The Damndest Lies We Tell Ourselves

The path from police interrogation to false confession is clearly strewn with lies, big and small. But what about the path from false confession to wrongful conviction? Do lies still play a role? My colleague Richard Leo and I have recently enumerated seven deadly pathways from false confession to wrongful conviction (Leo & Davis, 2009). Prominent among them are the lies that law enforcement personnel tell themselves—that they're objective; that they didn't do anything that could cause an innocent person to falsely confess; that they can tell when a suspect is lying to them and when he's telling the truth; that they don't interrogate innocent people; that they didn't make a mistake; that they've got the true perpetrator, no matter the arguments or evidence to the contrary; that no matter what evidence appears to dispute the suspect's guilt, it really doesn't, for there's another explanation (see Davis & O'Donohue, 2004; Kassin et al., 2010; Lassiter & Meissner, in press; Leo, 2008; Leo & Davis, 2009; Vrij, 2008).

These, of course, are the sort of lies to oneself that have been the (intellectual) love of Elliot's life—dissonance; self-justification; and selective, biased information-processing and judgment. Though he had no official role in explaining why "mistakes were made," but not discovered by law enforcement, judges, or juries in the Bradley Page case, Elliot and Carol Tavris returned to the general issue in their book, *Mistakes Were Made (But Not by Me)* (Tavris & Aronson, 2007). They aptly chose the words of Rob Warden (2003) to point to these self-justification processes:

> You get in the system and you become very cynical ... People are lying to you all over the place. Then you develop a theory of the crime, and it leads to what we call tunnel vision. Years later, overwhelming evidence comes out that the guy was innocent. And you're sitting there thinking "Wait a minute. Either this overwhelming evidence is wrong or I was wrong—and I couldn't have been wrong because I'm a good guy." That's a psychological phenomenon I have seen over and over. (Tavris & Aronson, 2007, pp. 130–132)

In part, detectives' self-deception begins at the outset of an investigation, and entails a set of faulty assumptions concerning the accuracy and objectivity of police judgment. Police may believe they have targeted a suspect rationally and objectively, based on a quality investigation, an accurate profile of the type of suspect likely to have committed the crime, or on incriminating evidence pointing to the suspect; in fact, the "profile" may be wholly inaccurate, the suspect may be targeted simply because he happened to be available to gain the attention of investigators, and the "evidence" may be misleading, not probative of guilt (Davis & Follette, 2002; Leo, 2008). Once targeted, the suspect is likely to be subject to the police "tunnel vision" referred to in Warden's description, whereby even as their investigation seems subjectively objective, police attention is focused on the suspect to the exclusion of other potential suspects, and self-confirming biases direct the selective search for and interpretation of evidence.

Self-deception and self-aggrandizement likewise pervade the interrogation room, where interrogators' overconfidence in their own abilities to detect deception and to accurately reconstruct the details of the suspect's motivations and criminal actions impairs their ability to overcome confirmation biases and recognize their mistaken assumptions. Too often, detectives simply do not recognize innocence when they see it. Interrogation training includes a method for detecting deception that is billed as producing a rate of accuracy of 85% or more. In fact, such training actually *reduces* accuracy below that of untrained college student controls, but simultaneously *inflates* confidence in judgments of accuracy—a dangerous combination indeed (see Kassin et al., 2010). Interrogators are trained to assess the subject's credibility during the preinterrogation "behavior analysis interview" and to proceed to interrogation only with suspects they judge to be guilty. Thus, interrogators are firmly convinced of the suspects' guilt before beginning the accusatory interrogation, when they are no longer interested in searching for the truth, but rather are determined to induce the suspect to confess. Any search for truth is confined to learning the full details of how and why the crime might have been committed, not to learning whether the suspect was the one who committed it. Prominent interrogators have claimed proudly that they simply "do not interrogate innocent people" and that the techniques recommended in their manuals will not cause an innocent person to confess (Inbau et al., 2001).

Once convinced of his target's guilt, the interrogator can subject his suspect to his armament of powerful weapons of influence with no concern that they might lead an innocent person to confess. The interrogation becomes a guilt-presumptive process in which no denial is accepted as true, all evidence is interpreted as confirming guilt, and the interrogator falls prey to self-fulfilling expectations whereby he himself causes the very behaviors he interprets as indicating guilt. His aversive tactics, for example, can cause anxiety in the suspect, which he then interprets as evidence of deception. Interrogators engage in these processes with no awareness that the pressures they exert can be the primary cause of any statements the suspect makes, and with no awareness of the potential of these pressures to cause their targets to offer false statements ranging from inaccurate details among the guilty to fully concocted elaborate "confessions" among the innocent (Leo & Davis, 2009).

Lacking awareness of the biasing impact of interrogation tactics, interrogation-elicited confessions seem valid and compelling to the police who elicit them and to later observers. And, lacking recordings of many interrogations, as in the Page case, prosecutors, judges, and juries have no access to the details of the interrogation. Only the tape-recorded or written confession is available, a final product recorded only after it was fully developed—one, as noted earlier, that has been carefully developed during the unrecorded interrogation to include all elements necessary to render it thoroughly incriminating and powerfully compelling enough to make it invulnerable to any later attempts to refute it. As such, the "confession" can be deceptively compelling—a very *damning damned lie*.

Thus, it is no surprise that neither detectives nor lay judges can perform better than chance when they try to distinguish between confessions known to be true versus those known to be false (for review, see Kassin et al., 2010; Vrij, 2008). Sadder still, even the detectives who actively shape confessions, who challenge any account that doesn't fit their preconceptions, who feed suspects the evidence and storylines to include in their confessions, and who refuse to accept anything but their own preconceived version of the story, can fail—often spectacularly—to recognize the fundamental invalidity of the story and the innocence of the suspect, even when incontrovertible evidence later shows the confession to be false (see Wells & Leo, 2008, for examples).

Such was the case for Bradley Page. Recall, he retracted his "confession" immediately after it was given, first to the district attorney, and then to the detectives who had taken it. The bulk of Page's fourth taped interview with his interrogators, Harris and Lacer, was consumed with their questions about why Page had incorporated various elements into his confession, if, as he claimed, they weren't true. Essentially, Page explained that he went on two facts that he "knew"—that Lee's body had been found approximately ¼ mile south of Roberts Park, where they had become separated, and that the bottom of the body was clothed. He then tried to make up a story that might have actually happened, that detectives would accept, and that might result in them "going easy" on him. Page explained that he chose specific elements of his story based on how events might have logically unfolded given what he already knew or assumed, given how he could imagine himself and Lee acting, and based on information provided by the detectives and the questions they asked. He explained his inclusion of the postmortem sex with Lee, for example, by noting that he had assumed Lee was molested, based on the detectives' questions and "leading" comments: "there was a lot of leading on about how much I loved this person, and I do" (1 a.m. interview, p. 20). When asked why he admitted to using a hubcap to bury Lee, Page explained that he knew he had one in his car, and "I thought of a shovel at one time and then you guys said 'no, there was no shovel' and I said okay there's no shovel" (1 a.m. interview, p. 23).

Page's confession included many now commonly noted hallmarks of false confessions. First, Elliot noticed the "tentativeness" with which Page recounted what happened (transcript of preliminary hearing). Indeed, false confessors often confess tentatively and hypothetically "I must have..." "I might have..." "I would have..." " I think I..." and so on. Second, as many false confessors do, Page confessed to things police thought happened at the time of the interrogation, but later proved to be false. Third, his confession pointed to no new evidence unknown to police (manifesting no unique knowledge that could be available only to the perpetrator), and fourth, it was contradicted by substantial exonerating evidence (see *California v. Page*, 1991, appellate brief; Leo & Ofshe, 1998, 2001). For example, Page confessed to having sex with Lee's dead body, even though this was deemed impossible due to rigor mortis, and even though no semen was found during the autopsy. Further, an exonerating witness, Karen Marquardt, reported seeing a man abducting a woman into a van shortly after noon, when Page was still with other witnesses. She described the woman as dressed similarly to Lee, in jogging shorts and a long sleeved T-shirt-type top. And, when shown a photo of Lee, she identified Lee as the person she had seen struggling with her abductor.

But these explanations and inconsistencies were to no avail. Page failed completely to convince the detectives that they could have "fed'im and led'im" in the construction of a false narrative. Nor did he convince anyone to come. Page was still charged and convicted, inconsistencies between his confession and the evidence were explained away, and his conviction was upheld on appeal, by appellate judges convinced by the compelling detailed narrative of his confession. "Page was very specific regarding many of the details of the assault. He remembered kissing Bibi on the top of her head before he backhanded her with his left hand. He remembered that she fell on her backside by a tree, and that she had a bloody nose. He remembered that when he returned to the crime scene he parked in the same place, but facing the correct direction this time. He remembered propping Bibi's head on a rock when he lay down with her to make love. Finally, he remembered using his hubcap to cover her body with pine needles and a big branch" (*California v. Page*, 1991, p. 175). (See Leo, 2008, and Leo & Davis, 2009, for reviews of the effects of such "misleading specialized knowledge" [details incorporated into a confession that would seemingly be unavailable to any but the true perpetrator] on failures to recognize false confessions.)

As Page's experience illustrates, once the confession is in, it overwhelms other evidence, creating a powerful presumption of guilt that provides context for interpretation of all other facts and evidence. The potential to detect inconsistent facts typically comes to a screeching halt, as the conviction that the crime is solved terminates the search for any additional evidence, save, of course, for evidence that corroborates the confession. But, even if contradictory evidence should surface, any dissonance between the confession and other apparently inconsistent facts is likely to be resolved in favor of the confession. Even DNA evidence, which to some would seem the gold standard of evidence, can be explained away in favor of a confession (see Findley & Scott, 2006; Hirsch, 2007). It was contaminated! There was a coperpetrator! There's *some* explanation, *whatever!* It *has* to be misleading, the guy confessed!

The tendency to resolve dissonance via the path of least resistance would suggest that the most credible or powerful evidence would be least likely to change. But as Rob Warden wisely noted in his description of the detective's motivations, and as Elliot has consistently pointed out in his self-justification theory and research, the most resistant belief is the concept of oneself as competent and good (e.g., Tavris & Aronson, 2007). A detective who has investigated a case, interrogated a suspect and taken his confession, aided the district attorney with his prosecution, and therefore has been instrumental in sending the suspect to prison (perhaps even to his death) will resist new evidence or reinterpretations of evidence that would question the suspect's guilt. His behavioral commitment to this guilt escalates from the moment the person is targeted as a suspect, and builds with every action the detective takes to promote the suspect's prosecution and secure his conviction. Self-justifying and self-protective motivations become ever more likely to override even the most compelling evidence of innocence as the behavioral commitments of investigators, prosecutors, and judges escalate.

As our self-admitted liar—Detective Robert Ryan of our opening quote—described it, has the truth become so fractured, so obscured, and so inaccurately reflected in the broken shards of the surviving record that it can no longer be found? Can psychologists, as expert witnesses for the courts, offer testimony that will aid jurors in finding the truth? Or, if not, can we at least provide understanding that will help them more effectively consider and properly weight a potentially coerced confession?

WE SHALL OVERCOME! ... OR WILL WE?

As we've seen, interrogation practices are complicated, multifaceted, carefully orchestrated combinations of the most powerful weapons of influence mankind has to offer—short of the overt threats, promises, or physical coercion deemed unacceptable by the courts. And they are clearly effective. The majority of real-life suspects subject to police interrogation confess (e.g., Leo, 1996), including a growing number of convicted persons subsequently proven innocent (for reviews, see Garrett, 2008; Kassin et al., 2010; Leo, 2008); and laboratory experiments have successfully induced false confession to a variety of offenses (for reviews, see Kassin et al., 2010). There can be no question that false confessions do exist, in greater numbers than widely suspected, and that they are induced by common police interrogation practices. Further, there exists extensive documentation of the nature of interrogation training and common interrogation practices, and extensive science supporting the effectiveness of such practices in inducing compliance with demands of all kinds, as well as in eliciting false statements ranging from the mundane (such as political polls) to the extreme (such as reports of alien abduction).

Yet those who would testify as expert witnesses on police interrogation practices and false confession face an imposing challenge—one of teaching and persuasion (Davis & Leo, in press). First, if called in support of a pretrial motion to suppress a confession, the expert must try to explain to the trial judge how and why interrogation tactics can be sufficiently coercive as to render the confession involuntary and therefore inadmissible. Elliot was not asked to testify in a suppression hearing, and thus didn't face this challenge. But experts today find this to be perhaps the greatest challenge of the three, as judges seem reluctant to consider the coercive force of interrogation tactics that eschew overt threats, promises, or physical coercion in favor of more sophisticated psychological tactics sufficient to render a confession involuntary (Kassin et al., 2010).

If, as is most likely, the confession is deemed admissible (Kassin et al., 2010), the expert may yet face a second challenge in the form of a hearing to determine whether she or he will be allowed to testify at trial to explain the possibility and causes of false confession to the jury. In this respect, Elliot's experience in the Page case seems truly remarkable, in light of current treatment by U.S. courts of expert testimony on interrogations and confessions. That is, even with no precedent for such testimony in any state, but with precedents denying it, Elliot was allowed to testify to the jury in Page's trial (see Fulero, in press). The judge held a pretrial hearing to determine whether to admit Elliot's testimony, in which Elliot explained his opinions in the case and what he proposed to say before the trial jury to the judge—a procedure many of us go through in other states today. But unlike many trial judges and many states today, Judge Martin Pulich did allow Elliot's testimony. Through the appeal of Page's case, Elliot's testimony set a precedent in California case law (*California v. Page*, 1991) that allows many of us to testify in California without the necessity of pretrial hearings. Though testimony on false confession has been allowed in many jurisdictions since that time, it is still denied in some state and federal courts and admitted in others. Unfortunately, most experts have had the experience of having some trial judges deny their testimony (for review, see Chojnacki et al., 2008; Fulero, in press).

If the expert is allowed to testify to the jury, his or her goal is to impart understanding to judges or juries that will help them evaluate the voluntariness or validity of the confession in question—that is, that will (1) unfreeze preconceptions that false confessions simply don't occur, particularly for serious crimes, (2) promote understanding of the conditions that increase the risk of false confessions, and (3) increase the ability to distinguish true from false confessions. He or she must present this testimony in a way that will be truly understandable, and that will explicate what police tactics are, how they could convince an innocent person to falsely confess, and how that confession could incorporate elaborate detail and information seemingly unavailable to anyone but the true perpetrator.

Whether at pretrial hearings or before the jury, the teaching task is formidable. Confession evidence is extremely powerful and intuitively compelling to judges and juries alike—more likely to ensure a conviction than other compelling evidence. Confession evidence alone is extraordinarily convincing. But as we discussed earlier, it creates a powerful presumption of guilt that biases interpretation of other evidence or overwhelms it. How, then, to fight the natural tendency to simply believe the confession? The subtlety and sophistication of the persuasive weapons incorporated into police tactics may be difficult to grasp at all and may seem unlikely to matter if grasped (as reflected in judiciary rulings on voluntariness or admissibility of expert testimony; see Fulero, in press; Kassin et al., 2010; Leo, 2008).

But even if judges and juries were to understand the nature of police interrogation tactics, their power to influence and their role in the elicitation of false confessions and their task of evaluating the voluntariness or validity of a particular confession is made more difficult by their lack of other important relevant knowledge and case facts. These information deficits create a restricted context for evaluation of a claim of false confession. Judges and juries don't know everything they need to in order to render the most accurate judgment—and though some missing or inaccurate knowledge can be corrected by the expert, other things cannot.

Some false assumptions affect the evaluation of the confession itself and can be addressed by the expert. Overconfidence among judges and juries in their abilities to assess truthfulness combine with false assumptions about which cues do and do not reflect truth or deception. These further combine with lack of understanding of situational causes of behavior to misinform their judgments, and to render observers unable to distinguish between true and false confessions (see Leo & Davis, 2009). If the suspect manifests anxiety, shows powerful emotion while confessing, or reenacts the crime physically, observers may falsely conclude that these behaviors reflect guilt. But such judgments are also undertaken in a progressively restricting context as the case moves from detectives to prosecutors to trial judges and juries to appellate judges. All must rely on the restricted information presented by their predecessors. That is, potentially exonerating evidence may be forever lost when investigators focus "tunnel vision" on the targeted suspect and miss evidence pointing to others. With this broader context lost, the targeted suspect may appear in hindsight to be the inevitable choice and the clearly guilty party, both to investigators and to later fact-finders.

Elements of context surrounding the crucially important interrogation can also be lost. The condition of the suspect when he enters interrogation—such as existing sleep deprivation, fatigue, or distress—may go undocumented, as may factors affecting his condition as the interrogation progresses (such as food, water, bathroom privileges, rest, and others). Such factors are crucial to understanding why a person might suffer enhanced suggestibility or susceptibility to influence.

Some or all of the interrogation may be unrecorded, leaving the memories of detectives and the suspect as the only surviving windows to the many and varied weapons of influence observers must know of and understand to explain *why* the suspect might have falsely confessed, and *how* he could have come up with such a compelling story if innocent. Memory, as we know, may itself be an "honest liar" subject to mistakes, distortions, and fully confabulated constructions (for reviews, see Brainerd & Reyna, 2005; Davis & Follette, 2001; Schacter, 2001). And, in particular, memory for conversations broadly, and for interviews specifically, is subject to failure and distortion in ways posing dangers for those trying to reconstruct the content and crucially the *order* of statements in an interrogation (see Davis & Friedman, 2007; Davis, Kemmelmeir, & Follette, 2005, on memory for conversation in legal contexts). But, as our Detective Ryan colorfully notes, "Most people have no reason to know how memory can turn rogue and feral, becoming a force of its own and one to be reckoned with" (French, 2007, p. 211).

Honest failures of memory for the content and order of lengthy interrogations can be supplemented by deliberate and knowing distortions by officers determined to deny any and all behaviors that could lead the confession to be suppressed (see Leo, 2008, for explication and examples). The simple requirement of recording all interviews and interrogations, as widely recommended by interrogation experts, would protect both parties against false or mistaken claims and memories of the other, and significantly aid judges and juries attempting to evaluate the causes of a specific confession.

How difficult to confront the available and salient evidence with the unavailable and unretrievable! It is clear that these missing features of the context of an interrogation strongly bias those who judge the suspect toward findings of voluntariness and guilt. Even with access to a full recording, the extent of access to views of the faces of the suspect and interrogator is crucial. Those watching a camera angle focusing only on the suspect (as is typically the case) are more likely to judge the confession as voluntary and true than those seeing an equal focus on both, whereas those whose view focuses only on the interrogator are least likely to do so (for review, see Lassiter, Ware, Lindberg, & Ratcliff, in press). If such a minor aspect of context exerts such significant effects, how much stronger is the difference between full access to the details of the interrogation versus none at all?

For judges, an additional source of resistance arises when the expert testifies in support of a motion to exclude the confession as involuntary. That is, explicit threats regarding the legal consequences of refusal to confess or explicit promises regarding the legal benefits of confession are grounds for suppression. But, as many have argued, the entire interrogation is designed to indirectly or implicitly convey exactly such threats and promises (Davis & Leo, in press). Were U.S. judges to recognize the impact of these indirect or implicit messages, the number of confessions that would have to be suppressed as a result would be unacceptable. Perhaps in part for this reason, confessions are rarely suppressed, with or without expert testimony (Kassin et al., 2010).

In this and in our other tasks of teaching and persuasion, we experts have often failed. Judges allow clearly coerced (in our view) confessions into evidence, and they sometimes refuse to allow us to testify, failing, despite our detailed presentations of research, to believe in the adequacy of the science supporting the role of interrogation tactics in creating false confessions. And, despite our testimony, juries sometimes convict a clearly innocent defendant. A prominent challenge for all of us is to develop effective presentations of our evidence and conclusions to judges and juries. It is there that, if he was to engage these challenges, Elliot, as one of psychology's most successful teachers and communicators, and as an author of one of our most accessible books on persuasion and social influence (Pratkanis & Aronson, 2001), would surely have valuable insights to offer.

As Elliot's work on dissonance theory has shown, most of us rarely, if ever, fundamentally change our minds about issues of importance—even scientists, when it comes to their own theories and research. It takes extraordinary circumstances to make extraordinary changes. And the changes we as experts are asking of judges and juries are indeed extraordinary—nothing less than fundamental changes in their understanding of the causes of behavior, and of themselves as capable and accurate judges of others. We're asking them to fight much of what they think they know; to replace it with sophisticated, nuanced, and often counterintuitive understanding of human judgment and behavior (in short, to become sophisticated social psychologists); and to skillfully apply this newfound understanding to the confession at hand—all based on the single "lecture" of our limited trial testimony.

What a challenge for all of us! In light of my successes and (too frequent) failures, as I invent and reinvent my presentations of this material for classes and courts, I often try to imagine how Elliot—a much better communicator than I—might find a better way to explain it clearly, to make it interesting and personal to the audience, and to draw analogies and comparisons that make it instantly and easily ring true.

ACKNOWLEDGMENTS

I would like to thank Richard A. Leo and G. Daniel Lassiter for providing me with materials regarding the Bradley Page case that were necessary to write this chapter (transcripts of the interrogations of Bradley Page and of Elliot's testimony in the pretrial hearing, and official documents such as pleadings and appellate decisions). I also thank Carol Tavris and Marti Hope Gonzales for their editorial comments, and Richard Leo and Elizabeth Loftus for their comments on previous drafts of the chapter.

NOTES

1. Bradley Page's confession cannot be definitively proven false. However, there was *no evidence* connecting Page to Lee's murder other than his confession, whereas a great deal of evidence existed to dispute the validity of his confession (see Leo & Ofshe, 1998, 2001, for detailed accounts of this evidence).
2. Page's case was very unusual in that he retracted his confession in an interview with the district attorney immediately after his "confession" before speaking with an attorney. And, as is even less typical, the district attorney and his interrogators immediately interviewed him extensively, while his memory of the interrogation was fresh and before he was subjected to any external influence, about why he had falsely confessed and how he had come up with the various elements of his false story. In his postconfession statements, Page listed a number of causes of his false confession.

REFERENCES

Bem, D. J. (1966). Inducing belief in false confessions. *Journal of Personality and Social Psychology, 3,* 707–710.

Bem, D. J. (1967, June). When saying is believing. *Psychology Today, 1*(2), 21–25.

Brainerd, C. J., & Reyna, V. F. (2005). *The science of false memory.* New York: Oxford University Press.

Chojnacki, D. E., Cicchini, M. D., & White, L. T. (2008). An empirical basis for the admission of expert testimony on false confessions. *Arizona State Law Journal, 40,* 1–45.

Cialdini, R. A. (2008). *Influence: Science and practice* (5th ed.). Upper Saddle River, NJ: Pearson.

Davis, D. (2008). Selling confession: The interrogator, the con man, and their weapons of influence. *Wisconsin Defender, 16*(1), 1–16.

Davis D., & Follette, W. C. (2002). Rethinking probative value of evidence: Base rates, intuitive profiling and the *post*diction of behavior. *Law and Human Behavior, 26,* 133–158.

Davis D., & Follette, W. C. (2001). Foibles of witness memory for traumatic/high-profile events. *J. Air Law Commerce* 66:1421–549.

Davis, D., Follette, W. C., & Leo, R. (2007, September). *Effects of interrogation tactics on recommendation of false confession for the innocent.* Paper presented at the Interrogations and Confessions, El Paso, TX.

Davis, D., & Friedman, R. D. (2007). Memory for conversation: The orphan child of eyewitness researchers. In M. P. Toglia, J. D. Read, D. R. Ross, & R. C. L. Lindsay (Eds.), *Handbook of eyewitness psychology: Vol. 1. Memory for events* (pp. 3–52). Mahwah, NJ: Erlbaum.

Davis, D., Kemmelmeier, M., & Follette, W. C. (2005). Conversational memory on trial. In Y. I. Noy & W. Karwowski (Eds.), *Handbook of human factors in litigation* (pp. 12–29). Boca Raton, FL: CRC Press.

Davis, D., & Leo, R. (2006a). Strategies for prevention of false confessions. In M. Kebbell & G. Davies (Eds.), *Practical psychology for forensic investigations and prosecutions* (pp. 121–150). New York: John Wiley & Sons.

Davis, D., & Leo, R. A. (2006b). Psychological weapons of influence: Applications in the interrogation room. *Nevada Lawyer, 14,* 14–18.

Davis, D., & Leo, R. A. (in press). Confessions, judiciary, and the fundamental attribution error: Preference for disposition versus situation based expert analyses of causes of false confession. *Journal of the American Academy of Psychitry and the Law.*

Davis, D., Leo, R., & Follette, W. C. (in press). Selling confession: Setting the stage with the Sympathetic Detective with a Time-Limited offer. *Journal of Contemporary Criminal Justice.*

Davis, D., Leo, R. A., & Follette, W. C. (2008, May). *Recommending false confession for the innocent.* Paper presented at the annual meeting of the American Psychology-Law Society, Jacksonville, FL.

Davis, D., Leo, R. A., Knaack, D., & Bailey, D. A. (2006, May). *Sympathetic detectives with time limited offers: Effects on perceived consequences of confession.* Paper presented at the Association for Psychological Science, New York.

Davis, D., & O'Donohue, W. T. (2004). The road to perdition: Extreme influence tactics in the interrogation room. In W. T. O'Donohue & E. Levensky (Eds.), *Handbook of forensic psychology* (pp. 897–996). New York: Elsevier/Academic Press.

Davis, D., Weaver, T., & Leo, R. A. (2007, August). *Effects of failed polygraph results on perceived wisdom of true and false confessions.* Paper presented at the American Psychological Association, San Francisco.

Driver, E. D. (1968). Confessions and the social psychology of coercion. *Harvard Law Review, 82,* 42–61.

Drizin, S. A., & Leo, R. A. (2004). The problem of false confessions in the post-DNA world. *North Carolina Law Review, 82,* 891–1007.

Eye to Eye with Connie Chung [Television news broadcast]. (1994, January 13). New York: CBS Broadcasting Inc.

Findley, K. A., & Scott, M. S. (2006). The multiple dimensions of tunnel vision in criminal cases. *Wisconsin Law Review, 40,* 14–29.

Follette, W. C., Davis, D., & Leo, R. A. (2007). Mental health status and vulnerability to police interrogation tactics. *Criminal Justice Magazine, 22* (3), 42–49.

French, T. (2007). *In the woods.* New York: Viking.

Fulero, S. M. (in press). Tales from the front: Expert testimony on the psychology of interrogations and confessions five years later. In G. D. Lassiter & C. A. Meissner (Eds.), *Police interrogations and false confessions: Current research, practice, and policy.* Washington, DC: American Psychological Association.

Garrett, B. (2008). Judging innocence. *Columbia Law Review, 108,* 55–142.

Gudjonsson, G. H. (1984a). Interrogative suggestibility comparison between "false confessions" and "Deniers" in criminal trials. *Medicine, Science, and the Law, 24,* 56–60.

Gudjonsson, G. H. (1984b). A new scale of interrogative suggestibility. *Personality and Individual Differences, 5,* 303–314.

Henkel, L. A., Coffman, K. A. J., & Dailey, E. M. (2008). A survey of people's attitudes and beliefs about false confessions. *Behavioral Sciences and the Law, 26,* 555–584.

Hirsch, A. (2007). Confessions and harmless error: A new argument for an old approach. *Berkeley Journal of Criminal Law, 12,* 1–28.

Inbau, F. E., Reid, J. E., Buckley, J. P., & Jayne, B. C. (2001). *Criminal interrogations and confessions* (4th ed.). Gaithersburg, MD: Aspen.

Jayne, B. C. & Buckley, J. P. (1999). *The investigator anthology.* Chicago: John Reid Assoc.

Kassin, S. M. (2007). Internalized false confessions. In Toglia, M. P., Read, J. D., Ross, D. F., Lindsay, R. C. L. (Eds.), *The handbook of eyewitness psychology, Vol. I: Memory for events.* Mahwah, NJ: Lawrence Erlbaum Associates, 2007. pp. 175–192.

Kassin, S. M., Drizin, S. A., Grisso, T., Gudjonsson, G. H., Leo, R. A., & Redlich, A. D. (2010). Police-induced confessions: Risk factors and recommendations. *Law and Human Behavior, 34,* 3–38.

Kassin, S. M., & Kiechel, K. L. (1996). The social psychology of false confessions: Compliance, internalization, and confabulation. *Psychological Science, 7,* 125–128.

Kassin, S. M., Leo, R. A., Meissner, C. A., Richman, K. D., Colwell, L. H., Leach, A.-M., & La Fon, D. (2007). Police interviewing and interrogation: A self-report survey of police practices and beliefs. *Law and Human Behavior, 31,* 381–400.

Kassin, S. M., & McNall, K. (1991). Police interrogations and confessions: Communicating promises and threats by pragmatic implication. *Law and Human Behavior, 15,* 233–251.

Kassin, S. M., & Norwick, R. J. (2004). Why people waive their *Miranda* rights: The power of innocence. *Law and Human Behavior, 28,* 211–221.

Kassin, S. M., & Wrightsman, L. S. (1980). Prior confessions and mock juror verdicts. *Journal of Applied Social Psychology, 10,* 133–146.

Kassin, S. M., & Wrightsman, L. S. (1985). Confession evidence. In S. M. Kassin & L. S. Wrightsman (Eds.), *The psychology of evidence and trial procedure* (pp. 67–94). Beverly Hills, CA: Sage.

Lassiter, G. D., & Meissner, C. (in press). *Police interrogations and false confessions: Current research, practice, and policy recommendations.* Washington, DC: American Psychological Association.

Lassiter, G. D., Ware, L. J., Lindberg, M. J., & Ratcliff, J. J. (in press). Videotaping custodial interrogations: Toward a scientifically based policy. In G. D. Lassiter & C. A. Meissner (Eds.), *Police interrogations and false confessions: Current research, practice and policy.* Washington, DC: American Psychological Association.

Leo, R. A. (1996a). Inside the interrogation room. *The Journal of Criminal Law and Criminology, 86*(2), 266–303.

Leo, R. A. (1996b). Miranda's revenge: Police interrogation as a confidence game. *Law and Society Review, 30,* 259–288.

Leo, R. A. (2008). *Police interrogation and American justice.* Cambridge, MA: Harvard University Press.

Leo, R. A., & Davis, D. (2009). From false confession to wrongful conviction: Seven psychological processes. *Journal of Psychiatry and the Law, 37,* 332–343.

Leo, R. A., & Ofshe, R. J. (1998). The consequences of false confessions: Deprivations of liberty and miscarriages of justice in the age of psychological interrogation. *The Journal of Criminal Law and Criminology, 88*(2), 429–496.

Leo, R. A., & Ofshe, R. J. (2001). The truth about false confessions and advocacy scholarship. *The Criminal Law Bulletin, 37*(4), 293–370.

Lykken, D. T. (1998). *Tremor in the blood: Uses and abuses of the lie detector.* New York: Plenum.

Miranda v. Arizona, 384 U.S. 436 (1966).

Munsterberg, H. (1908). *On the witness stand.* Garden City, NY: Doubleday.

National Research Council Committee to Review the Scientific Eviendence on the Polygraph (2003). *The polygraph and lie detection.* Washington, DC: National Academies Press.

Pratkanis, A. R. (2007). *The science of social influence: Advances and future progress.* New York: Psychology Press.

Pratkanis, A. R., & Aronson, E. (2001). *Age of propaganda.* New York: W. H. Freeman.

Redlich, A. (in press). False confessions, false guilty pleas: Similarities and differences. In G. D. Lassiter & C. A. Meissner (Eds.), *Police interrogations and false confessions: Current research, practice, and policy.* Washington, DC: American Psychological Association.

Schacter, D. L. (2001). *The seven sins of memory: How the mind forgets and remembers.* New York: Houghton Mifflin.

Senese, L. (2005). *Anatomy of interrogation themes: The Reid technique of interviewing and interrogation.* Chicago: John E. Reid and Associates.

Tavris, C., & Aronson, E. (2007). *Mistakes were made (but not by me).* New York: Harcourt.

Vrij, A. (2008). *Detecting lies and deceit: Pitfalls and opportunities* (2/e). Chichester, England: John Wiley & Sons, LTD.

Warden, R. (2003). *The role of false confessions in Illinois wrongful murder convictions since 1970.* Chicago: Center on Wrongful Convictions, Northwestern University School of Law.

Wells, T., & Leo, R. A. (2008). *The wrong guys: Murder, false confessions, and the Norfolk four.* New York: New Press

Wrightsman, L. S., & Kassin, S. M. (1993). *Confessions in the courtroom.* Newbury Park, CA: Sage.

Zimbardo, P. G. (1967). The psychology of police confessions. *Psychology Today, 1*(2), 17–20, 25–27.

Bradley Page References

California vs. Bradley Nelson Page, Appellant's opening Brief; No. A Crim. AO43127; Alameda County Superior No. 81366.

California v. Page, 2 Cal. App. 4th 161 (1991).

Statement of Bradley Page: Oakland Police Department, by Sgts. Jerry Harris and Ralph Lacer, 12-10-1984, 11:50 a.m.

Statement of Bradley Page: Oakland Police Department, by Sgts. Jerry Harris and Ralph Lacer; 12-10-1984, 7:07 p.m.

Statement of Bradley Page: Oakland Police Department by Kevin Leong, Inspector, Office of the District Attorney and Aaron Payne, Deputy District Attorney; 12-10-1984, 9:09 p.m.

Statement of Bradley Page: Oakland Police Department by Sgts. Ralph Lacer and Jerry Harris; 12-10-1984, 12:59 a.m.

Transcript of proceedings taken Wednesday, March 30, 1988; *People vs. Bradley Nelson Page*, no. 81366.

12

GIVING PSYCHOLOGY AWAY TO ENERGY POLICY

Paul C. Stern

National Research Council

In the summer of 1980, I was working on a project at the Institution for Social and Policy Studies at Yale, where I had gone on a National Science Foundation postdoc almost two years before to work on social science and energy policy. When my postdoc ended after a year, I had managed to stay on by helping write research grants under the names of real Yale faculty who could hire me as a research associate. Early one afternoon, my colleague Jerry Gardner picked up the ringing phone and called me: "Paul," he said, "it's for you. It's Elliot Aronson."

"Sure," I thought. "Fat chance Elliot Aronson is calling me." Of course I knew of him. Not only was he one of the leaders of social psychology, but I had used his book, *The Social Animal*, as a required text in my social psychology course at Elmira College since I had first heard of it several years earlier. I had built the whole course around it because I knew instantly how attractive it would be to my undergraduates. There was no way Elliot Aronson would be calling me. It must be some kind of practical joke.

I kept my cool and picked up the phone to see who it really was. The voice at the other end identified himself as Elliot Aronson. He said he was calling to invite me to Santa Cruz in August to participate in a summer study run by the American Council for an Energy-Efficient Economy (ACEEE). The ACEEE wanted to include the social sciences in its summer study for the first time that year, and had called on Elliot,

Tom Pettigrew, Dane Archer, and a few other Santa Cruz faculty to help bring in the social sciences. Elliot knew that I had written a review article on psychological research and energy policy, and he said it would be very helpful to have me at the summer study.

Of course I agreed to go. It seemed like an incredible opportunity for me, and I needed one. I had been turned down for tenure at Elmira College—the autocratic president had made a policy decision not to grant anyone tenure until there were more retirements—and my only hold on an academic career was to have gotten that postdoc and then to have worked my way into a soft-money research associate position, dependent on the good will of tenured faculty. Who knew how long I would be able to go on doing that?

It was an odd coincidence that had put my review in Elliot's hands. When I got to Yale in the fall of 1978, I set out to write the review article, which was to be my project for the postdoc. I put a notice in the *APA Monitor* saying I was writing the review, would have it finished in the spring, and would send it out to anyone who wanted a copy. Energy was a hot topic in 1979, and I got about 60 requests for copies. Sometime in the 1979–1980 academic year, Elliot (who had not requested my paper) was invited by his former Stanford student, Dick Katzev, to give a talk at Reed College. Elliot had become interested in energy by then and must have mentioned that to Dick, who had requested my paper. Dick made him a copy. I would like to think that Elliot knew a good thing when he saw it and that is why he invited me to Santa Cruz.

I had never been to Santa Cruz before. It was an incredibly beautiful place just to walk around, and there were very interesting sessions to attend and people to talk to. After a couple of days, it was decided that the social scientists would write a statement together, and as a young and eager member of the group, I took on a big chunk of the work. I thought it went well, chalked it down as a great opportunity that might lead somewhere someday, and went home to New Haven and my research project.

THE COMMITTEE ON BEHAVIORAL AND SOCIAL ASPECTS OF ENERGY

Meanwhile, in Washington, an official of President Carter's Department of Energy (DOE) had the idea that the behavioral and social sciences might be useful in helping solve the nation's energy crisis. DOE was not quite sure what forms this help might take, so it asked the National Academy of Sciences to convene a committee of leading behavioral and social scientists to study the problem and offer advice. The staff at the National Research Council (NRC)—the part of the academy that conducts such studies—developed a long list of leading scientists who might be asked to serve on the committee of distinguished volunteers who would be the authors of the study. The Assembly of Behavioral and Social Sciences (ABASS)—the NRC advisory group for these sciences—met and considered the list. Elliot's adviser, Leon Festinger, was a member of the assembly and knew that Elliot had recently taken an interest in energy issues. He suggested that Elliot be asked to chair the new committee, and it was agreed to ask Elliot.

As Elliot tells me the story, he was reluctant to take on this role. He had never served on an NRC committee before, so he didn't know what to expect. Moreover, he was new to the energy field and certainly no expert. He told the executive director of ABASS that he would agree to be the chair only if they hired me as staff director of the study. He thought I had the knowledge needed, and he knew he could work with me.

The NRC had already begun looking for a study director and a research associate for the study. They ran ads in a number of places, including the *APA Monitor*. I had seen the ad in the *Monitor* and decided to apply, not sure which position I might be considered qualified for. Elliot contacted me to see if I was interested in directing the study, and of course I was. With Elliot in my corner, I got the job.

The new Committee on the Behavioral and Social Aspects of Energy Consumption and Production, with Elliot as chair and me as study director, held its first meeting December 5–6, 1980—just a month after Ronald Reagan had been elected president on a platform that included eliminating the DOE, my source of funding, and getting the social sciences out of government. Despite these bad omens, the civil servants in DOE managed to transfer the money for our study and we were able to proceed. We had the luxury of great freedom to define our task. The National Academy of Sciences normally provided that, but in addition, the sponsor did not want to listen to us. We were pretty much guaranteed that whatever advice we offered to DOE would be ignored at the highest levels.

The panel was very interdisciplinary. Along with its three social psychologists (Elliot, John Darley, and Sara Kiesler), we had distinguished members from economics, sociology, anthropology, organizational research, political science, game theory, statistics, and the physical sciences. Our first report, *Energy Use: The Human Dimension* (National Research Council, 1984a), showed many of these influences. Thanks to the sociologist Allen Schnaiberg, the report noted the importance of the social construction of energy: Energy has multiple meanings in society (it is a commodity, an ecological resource, a social necessity, and a strategic material), and policy debates and conflicts can turn on who is using which meaning. We showed that the invisibility of energy use made it difficult for households to make wise choices, for example, if they wanted to reduce their consumption. We reviewed the existing behavioral studies aimed at changing individuals' energy use, including early studies of feedback and financial incentives, studies of information and persuasion campaigns, and Elliot's experimental work at Santa Cruz.

Elliot and I worked very well together on the study. He ran efficient meetings, negotiated around the potential conflicts that might have emerged among strong personalities with very different intellectual perspectives, and helped us all keep our sense of humor. I kept in touch with committee members between meetings, saw to it that their contributions all found a place in the draft report and that the report maintained coherence despite the diversity of ideas contributed, and I did a lot of synthetic writing. I think the process was greatly enjoyable for both of us and for many of the committee members as well.

NRC studies are typically at their most integrative when the committee chair and the staff director come from different fields. Still, although Elliot and I both came from the same subfield of psychology, we complemented each other very well within the committee. He was a master of social relationships and contributed concepts from psychology, while I focused more on integrating ideas from across many disciplines and presenting an interdisciplinary contribution to understanding energy use from a behavioral and social standpoint.

An important contribution of the energy use study, resulting from its interdisciplinary character, was that it began to identify and move beyond some of the limitations of the idea that energy use is a straightforward technical activity or economic choice—what is now called the physical–technical–economic model (PTEM) of energy use (Lutzenhiser et al., 2009). We identified some barriers to behavioral change in households and organizations that were not well recognized by engineers or economists. We began to show, for example, how attributes of energy such as its "invisibility" and the cognitive difficulty of estimating the benefits of particular energy-saving actions could lead people to take actions that look irrational if one assumes that cost minimization alone should explain energy use. We believed that we were on the way to producing significant advances in energy analysis and policy that moved beyond the PTEM (also see Stern, 1986). A leading economist who reviewed the report in draft for the NRC showered us with faint praise:

"The National Academy of Sciences will not be embarrassed to release this report."

The committee produced two more reports before it went out of business in 1985: *Improving Energy Demand Analysis* (National Research Council, 1984b), which integrated analytic approaches from economics and psychology, and *Energy Efficiency in Buildings: Behavioral Issues* (National Research Council, 1985). The latter provides what is still the best available analysis of how much the effectiveness of financial incentives depends on nonfinancial factors. It documented the fact that the proportion of households that actually takes advantage of a particular financial incentive for home weatherization typically varies by a factor of 10 or more depending on program implementation. For example, when the Bonneville Power Administration offered a very strong financial rebate for home weatherization through seven participating utility companies, the most successful company program was able to retrofit 32.3% of the homes in its service area over the 20 months of the program, whereas the least effective two programs retrofitted only 2.3% and 3.2%. This variation in effectiveness depends on a number of nonfinancial factors, such as how well the programs are marketed, how easy the process is for its clients to use, and how much is done about quality assurance through such actions as certifying home improvement contractors and inspecting their work (Gardner & Stern, 2002; National Research Council, 1985; Stern et al., 1986). This insight has still not penetrated into energy policy circles, where economic incentives are usually believed to be a straightforward policy tool that has an effect predictable by an empirical constant known as the price elasticity of demand. I continued to cite this research in papers and in talks to policy audiences (e.g., Dietz et al., 2009).

The three NRC reports offered a major early statement of the contributions that psychology and the other noneconomic social sciences could make. They convinced a small number of policy makers and a few natural scientists that energy conservation was a people issue as well as a technical and economic one. But in the larger picture, neither the federal government nor the public was interested in energy policy in the mid-1980s. The "energy crisis" was past and the country was more concerned with recovering from a major recession and dealing with continuing national security threats from the Soviet Union. Our report went on a shelf—though it became something of a touchstone for a small collection of behavioral and social science researchers and a few policy analysts who continued to work on energy use. By the time the committee closed shop, Elliot had moved on to other research interests.

I moved on to other projects, too, as there was no financial support for continuing our work.

PROBLEM-DRIVEN VERSUS PSYCHOLOGY-DRIVEN PERSPECTIVES

Elliot's and my division of labor on the NRC committee partly reflected the fact that we came to the topic of energy use from fundamentally different intellectual perspectives. My perspective was shaped in the early 1970s when the first Earth Day and the publication of books like *The Limits to Growth* (Meadows, Meadows, Randers, & Behrens, 1972) focused my attention on the major environmental "problematique" of exponential growth of human activities on a finite planet. I saw this as probably the preeminent problem of my time, and wanted to do something to promote what became called environmental sustainability.

At the time, I was working on my dissertation, which had become an albatross for me. In my first semester teaching at Elmira College, fall 1971, I collected the data for a test of cognitive dissonance theory against self-perception theory that became the basis for the dissertation. But teaching took most of my attention and I did not complete writing the dissertation until the spring of 1975. By then, I was beyond bored with the topic and saw those particular theoretical issues as insignificant compared with the great global problems.

Freed from the dissertation and with a denial of tenure looming, I spent the summer of 1975 reading, talking, and thinking about the future of my career. At first, I saw a stark choice: stay in psychology and seek out work I thought worth doing—probably teaching undergraduates at another college—or throw aside all my painful graduate work and start in a brand new field. Neither option excited me.

I came across an article in *Science* by the entomologist David Pimentel and his students at nearby Cornell University, which analyzed changes in the energy inputs used to grow an acre of corn in the United States (Pimentel et al., 1973). I thought the article tackled an important environmental problem in an interesting and interdisciplinary way. I invited myself to Ithaca to meet David to learn about his work. He told me that his colleagues in the entomology department had not been very supportive. They thought he should be studying the behavior of insects, not farmers. But he pressed on and he encouraged me to do the same— to follow my interests and not my discipline.

Sometime in midsummer I found a way out of my dilemma while rereading Garrett Hardin's (1968) famous article, "The Tragedy of the

Commons." I realized that his account of the environmental problematique, which pitted individual against collective interests and short-term against long-term benefits, was in fact a social-psychological model that I could simulate in the laboratory. Hardin argued that individual interests and short-term benefits would always win out and that the environment was doomed unless coercive solutions were applied. I realized I could test that idea as a hypothesis and simulate noncoercive interventions that could prove it wrong. I set to work designing a model and an experiment, which led to my first publication, one of the earliest social dilemma simulations in the psychological literature (Stern, 1976). More important, I proved to myself that it was possible to use my psychological training to work on environmental problems.

Ever since, my priority has been the problem first, the psychology second. I came to judge psychological research on the environment by its usefulness for understanding or addressing problems defined in environmental terms. That is, I judged research findings primarily in terms of potential environmental impact rather than in terms of impact on environmental attitudes, intentions, or even behavior. I judged my own simulation harshly by that standard. Although it produced interesting and statistically significant results, I did not find the results believable. It was far too easy to change resource-depleting behavior by explaining to the research participants how the resource depletion worked in the simulated world. I concluded that a half-hour small-group interaction just could not adequately simulate global environmental degradation that takes place globally and over decades. I wanted to find a way to do something of more potential value than what I saw possible by continuing my laboratory simulation work. That led me to my literature review project, to Elliot, and to the NRC. I have continued to put problem ahead of discipline. I am much more interested in research that addresses behaviors with important environmental impacts than in studies of low-impact behaviors, no matter the quality of psychological understanding. In my mind, the relevance of the latter kinds of studies has to be demonstrated, not assumed.

My impression is that Elliot has proceeded from quite a different perspective: He is a social psychologist first, shaped by the Lewinian tradition of action research, which advocated scientifically rigorous testing of theory to enhance our understanding of significant social problems, all the better to solve them. His approach is evident in two studies he conducted in the shower rooms at Santa Cruz. In one, student assistants modeled the practice of taking short showers to influence others to save energy by doing the same (Aronson & O'Leary, 1983). And in another, he and his colleagues took advantage of people's motivation to reduce cognitive dissonance. They induced "hypocrisy" by convincing students to make a public commitment after being reminded that they sometimes wasted water while showering, and found that students reminded of the discrepancy between their current positive attitudes toward water conservation and past water-wasting behaviors took shorter showers (Dickerson, Thibodeau, Aronson, & Miller, 1992).

Because Elliot is interested in giving psychology away to address social problems and because he is so creative, he has found ways to test theory and to demonstrate the applicability of social-psychological principles to a variety of important problems. In the case of energy, his shower studies were clever field experiments that demonstrated social-psychological principles in a topical context. But I questioned their importance. As I saw it, showers account for a very small proportion of personal energy use (Gardner & Stern, 2008; Stern & Gardner, 1981), and it was hard for me to see how this kind of in-person modeling or dissonance induction would affect actions that had a greater impact on energy use, such as purchases of home insulation or fuel-efficient cars.

I do not want to overdraw the difference between our views on how psychology should relate to energy problems. In his time working on energy issues, Elliot published analyses of energy issues that put problems first but analyze them from a social-psychological perspective (Coltrane, Archer, & Aronson, 1986; Costanzo, Archer, Aronson, & Pettigrew, 1986). And in at least one study, he applied social-psychological concepts to a high-impact behavior—weatherizing homes (Gonzales, Aronson, & Costanzo, 1988). In the 1980s, the Pacific Gas and Electric Company was conducting home energy audits as a qualifying step for households to take advantage of a zero-interest loan program and a partial rebate program that covered recommended investments in energy efficiency. Elliot's group trained auditors to use psychological principles of persuasion—using vivid examples, eliciting commitment, framing energy conservation as avoiding financial losses rather than as saving money, and so on—in the hope that these techniques would make the auditors into more effective marketers of energy efficiency. The study produced very promising results: 61% of the homes in the experimental group took advantage of the incentives and retrofitted their homes, compared with 39% of the control group.

The difference in approach I see between Elliot's work and mine is that I tend to analyze problems in terms of the full range of influences on behavior, to seek the most promising approaches for solving them, whereas Elliot tends to look first for their main social-psychological elements. With energy use, I have put more emphasis on the economic, institutional, and technical barriers to behavioral change than Elliot has, and I have found that these barriers are often more important than the psychological ones (Black, Stern, & Elworth, 1985; Gardner & Stern, 2002). Moreover, the most promising applications of social-psychological processes are often in combination with other forces, such as with financial incentives, as shown in the Bonneville program. I believe that the strong behavioral effect of the psychological manipulations in Elliot's study of energy auditors would have been much weaker if the utility company had not also been offering financial incentives for retrofitting homes.

PSYCHOLOGY AS PART OF AN INTERDISCIPLINARY, PROBLEM-ORIENTED APPROACH TO POLICY

Elliot stayed with psychology and eventually turned his attention away from the energy field. He continued, of course, to contribute to social-psychological theory and to its application to important practical problems. Thanks in part to the NRC job that he helped me get, I went in a different direction. The job suited my problem-driven perspective much better than a job in a university psychology department ever would have. NRC projects are almost always interdisciplinary and problem oriented. Study committee members tend to come from every discipline that is potentially relevant, as well as from the world of practice. They have to find a common language and learn to work together, and are motivated to do so by a shared practical interest. Everyone applies the test of problem relevance to whatever ideas or research someone else brings to the table.

This work environment—collaborating on real-world problems with top researchers from across the social sciences and beyond—taught me a lot about the problems we studied, confirmed for me the value of my problem-first orientation, and greatly broadened my thinking about energy and the environment, as well as about other problems I took on over the years as a study director at the NRC.

When the energy committee shut down, I was able to stay at the NRC and to lead a series of interdisciplinary studies on other important problems, including the prevention of nuclear war (National Research Council, 1989a, 1989c, 1991, 1993), nationalism (Comaroff & Stern, 1995), international conflict resolution (National Research Council, 2000), environmental risk (National Research Council, 1989b, 1996), the use of polygraph testing to detect spies (National Research Council, 2003), and the human dimensions of global environmental change (e.g., National Research Council, 1992, 1999b). In each case, psychology has something of value to contribute, but its value increases through integration with ideas from other disciplines and fields. Working across disciplines on the human dimensions of global change led me to develop interdisciplinary analyses of important environmental issues that are partly psychological, such as environmentally significant consumption (National Research Council, 1997), risk analysis (National Research Council, 1996), and environmental decision making (National Research Council, 2005a, 2008, 2009a). It also led to a broader approach to the problem of the commons (Dietz, Ostrom, & Stern, 2003; National Research Council, 2002)—one that incorporates psychological work (e.g., Kopelman, Weber, & Messick, 2002), but that is strongly influenced by the integrative interdisciplinary framework of Elinor Ostrom (1990), and enriched by the field work of anthropologists and human ecologists and the institutional studies of political scientists and economists.

I continued to work on problems of energy and the environment, first outside my day job (Kempton, Darley, & Stern, 1992; Stern, 1986, 1992a, 1992b; Stern & Oskamp, 1987) and then, with the establishment of the Committee on the Human Dimensions of Global Change (CHDGC) in 1989, alongside it. The CHDGC became an important standing committee of the NRC and a strong voice for the social and behavioral sciences in the worlds of environmental science and policy. It has continued to define agendas for integrated research on human–environment interactions (National Research Council, 1992, 1999b, 2005a; Stern & Wilbanks, 2009) and to demonstrate the value of knowledge and concepts from the social and behavioral sciences to understanding and solving environmental problems (National Research Council, 1997, 1998, 1999a, 2002a, 2002b, 2005b, 2008, 2009b). I have had opportunities to bring psychological perspectives into interdisciplinary investigations and they have broadened my perspective in return.

In my research on energy use, I have emphasized the need to characterize the behaviors and analyze their importance in energy terms. In early analyses, Jerry Gardner and I distinguished what we called efficiency and curtailment behaviors (Stern & Gardner, 1981). Efficiency actions (such as adding insulation; installing more efficient windows, furnaces, and appliances; or getting a more fuel-efficient car) tend to be infrequent and to cost money at first. Curtailments (such as turning out lights, lowering winter thermostat settings, or driving more slowly on the highway) tend to have no first cost and to be frequently repeated. Efficiency actions provide the same goods and services at lower energy cost, whereas curtailments reduce service and are therefore likely to be seen as entailing sacrifice of well-being. When President Carter personified energy conservation by sitting in his sweater in front of a fire, he defined conservation as curtailment, and probably contributed to equating conservation with sacrifice in the public mind. The impact of efficiency actions tends to be maintained automatically because energy-efficient equipment continues to save throughout its useful life, whereas curtailment, which usually involves frequently repeated behavior and takes continual effort, can more easily backslide.

We have found continually over many years that efficiency actions can generally produce greater energy savings than curtailments of the same energy service (Gardner & Stern, 2002, 2008; Stern & Gardner, 1981). In the average U.S. home, about twice as much energy can be saved by upgrading attic insulation as by lowering winter temperatures by 4°F during the day and 7°F at night, and five times as much by upgrading to a high-efficiency vehicle as by combining errand trips to reduce travel for errands by half (Gardner & Stern, 2008). These findings shaped my view that behavioral scientists should pay a lot of attention to the determinants of efficiency actions.

This sort of behavioral analysis can be carried further to help us understand the barriers to behavioral change and to identify the highest-impact strategies for behavioral change in environmental terms. In recent work, my colleagues and I divided actions that can reduce household direct energy use into five categories and estimated the amount of carbon dioxide emissions reduction that could be achieved if the most effective, documented, nonregulatory policies were applied nationwide (Dietz, Gardner, Gilligan, Stern, & Vandenbergh, 2009). We divided efficiency into two categories: W (for weatherization, but also including home heating and cooling equipment), which involves adoption of household technologies whose main product attributes are cost and energy savings; and E (for equipment), which involves household equipment with more complex sets of important product attributes, such as cars, refrigerators, and washers. We identified three other classes of action by their behavioral attributes. M (maintenance) includes infrequent, low-cost actions such as replacing filters in home furnaces and cars. A (adjustment) involves changes in equipment usage that are typically maintained for long periods automatically, such as changing thermostat settings on furnaces or water heaters. Finally, D (for daily) actions must be repeated to achieve their potential. These include driving and accelerating more slowly in cars, using the lowest feasible temperature setting on washers, and drying clothes on the line. We analyzed the potential for reducing carbon emissions from household energy use from 17 actions of these types and found that the greatest potential savings by far was from E (equipment) actions, followed by W, D, M, and A (weatherization, daily actions, maintenance, and adjustment, respectively). The potential savings from efficiency (weatherization and equipment) was more than three times the potential from curtailment (adjustment and daily actions). We also found that the most effective interventions differ with the category of action.

Our emphasis on efficiency differs from psychologists' most common approach to energy use. The great majority of psychological research aimed at reducing energy use, beginning with early work on feedback (e.g., Geller, Winett, & Everett, 1982), modeling (e.g., Aronson & O'Leary, 1983), and personal commitment (Katzev, 1986), has focused on daily actions and one-shot adjustments to equipment: changing frequently repeated, zero-cost behaviors involving the use of home (and occasionally vehicle) technology. Very few researchers have investigated the infrequent, often expensive actions, such as choosing the size of one's home, insulating attics and walls, and purchasing motor vehicles and major appliances that make much more difference in household energy use.

It is easy to see why psychologists focus on frequently repeated behaviors—they are much easier to measure and to statistically document change. But it does not necessarily follow that the principles that change these behaviors have wider applicability. It is sometimes claimed, for example, that the foot-in-the-door effect applies—that changes in low-impact behaviors will lead to changes in higher-impact behaviors. But the available evidence does not support that claim (Crompton & Thøgerson, 2009).

Focusing on problems and developing psychological theory is not an either–or choice. I believe that new problems create a need for new or refined theory that is more useful than past theory for addressing those problems. An example from my work involves attitudes about global environmental change, including climate change. Attitudes presumably affect action, but in the 1980s and early 1990s few people had formed attitudes about "global environmental change" because it was a new idea—what I call an emergent attitude object. I didn't think existing attitude theory very helpful for understanding attitude formation with such objects. Over several years, I worked with Tom Dietz and other colleagues in sociology at George Mason University to develop a theory based on the idea that people constructed attitudes to emergent objects by considering how those objects would affect their most important values. We adapted previous work by Shalom Schwartz on personal norm activation (Schwartz, 1977) and on universals in values (Schwartz, 1992) to develop and test what we came to call the value–belief–norm theory of attitude formation (Stern, Dietz, Abel, Guagnano,

& Kalof, 1999). This formulation has proved useful to many researchers in accounting for variation in attitudes, and sometimes behavior, in relation to environmental attitude objects.

I see most of the great societal problems as requiring broadly interdisciplinary approaches. An important part of my work at the NRC over the years has been to demonstrate the value of the behavioral and social sciences to addressing problems that are usually handed over to physical and biological scientists, to engineers, or to narrowly disciplinary economists. Environmental problems in particular require not only the well-known interdisciplinary environmental science enterprise that integrates various disciplines from the physical and biological sciences, but also an interdisciplinary science of human–environment interactions (Stern, 1993). Progress is being made in this direction. More of the influential natural scientists are coming to understand the need for approaches to environmental problems that integrate the social and natural sciences (e.g., National Research Council, 2009b), and policy makers may follow their lead.

Psychology, of course, should be part of the emerging interdisciplinary environmental science. In my view, though, psychological ideas are most useful when integrated into a broad analysis of the human element of the problem at hand, as Elliot and I did in the 1984 report. To contribute effectively, psychologists need to question our disciplinary biases, focus on aspects of environmental issues for which the discipline has relative strengths, and work collaboratively across disciplines (Stern, 2000a, 2000b). When psychology contributes, it may not be the aspect of psychology that first comes to mind. For example, in seeking ways to understand and reduce environmentally destructive individual behavior, social psychologists often look first to attitude theory for answers. But attitude–behavior relationships have limited importance for high-impact consumer behaviors such as the choice of the size of a home or car, the mode of transportation that one uses to get to work or school, or the energy efficiency characteristics of homes. These choices usually depend more on contextual than personal factors (Black et al., 1985; Costanzo et al., 1986; Guagnano, Stern, & Dietz, 1995). Attitudes have no discernible direct effect on most of these actions, and they are often unrelated even to low-cost energy-saving actions (e.g., Costanzo et al., 1986).

The most effective ways to induce change in a high-impact action such as investment in home weatherization combine financial incentives, social marketing, and careful program design to overcome barriers to behavioral change, for instance, by reducing the cognitive effort needed to take the target action and assuring the quality of the retrofit (Gardner & Stern, 2002; National Research Council, 1985; see also Coltrane et al., 1986). Psychology can contribute by helping to understand the choice environment from the consumer's perspective, identifying barriers to action, applying knowledge about social influence and trust to the design of social marketing efforts, and applying understanding of cognitive heuristics to the problem of making behavioral change simpler for people. Environmental attitudes tend to have little direct effect on the most environmentally important consumer behaviors because other influences dominate. Attitudes are likely to be more influential in relation to the less environmentally significant frequently repeated behaviors (Black et al., 1985) and to support environmental organizations and proenvironmental public policies (Stern et al., 1999).

In the search for answers to practical problems, psychology (like other academic disciplines) can be an impediment. Prestige in the disciplines, career advancement, and publication in leading journals depends on linking one's work to current theoretical perspectives or controversies in the discipline or a subdiscipline. An early-career researcher who develops and tests concepts for their practical value for solving problems is swimming against the disciplinary current and can have a hard time making a career in psychology departments, especially top-rated ones (see Pettigrew, this volume). Publishing research in *Energy Policy* or *Climatic Change* does not usually help one get tenure in a psychology department. I hope that the creation of new interdisciplinary programs on energy and environmental problems can bring psychology into the new environmental science by cross-training psychologists and providing career paths for psychologists who put problems first. Increased research funding for problem-oriented environmental social science and integrated natural-social science, if it becomes available, will also help. I think that this kind of work will also benefit the discipline by bringing in new ideas, and posing new and compelling research questions. These are outcomes toward which I continue to work.

EPILOGUE: THE HUMAN DIMENSION OF ENERGY AFTER 25 YEARS

My work with Elliot in the 1980s was a great boon to my career. Elliot pulled me out of a very shaky career path onto a productive and satisfying one. In broader terms, Elliot's work has left a lasting legacy through the three NRC reports and their influence on other researchers, myself included. *Energy Use: The Human Dimension* continues to be read and is increasingly cited by researchers. If humanity is to significantly alleviate the threat of climate change in the coming decades, decision makers will need to make use of that work and on the later work that it inspired.

From the 1980s until quite recently, though, energy use was very low on the policy agenda in the United States, and little attention was paid to our work. Even when scientific and policy interest began to focus on climate change and other global environmental change in the early 1990s, neither energy use nor behavioral science was prominent on the research agenda. The NRC Committee on the Human Dimensions of Global Change got few opportunities to follow up on the earlier NRC energy work, even though energy use is undeniably a critically important human dimension.

Recently, of course, the country has been reawakening to energy as a problem. The new interest is spurred by growing dependence on imported oil, a large jump in oil prices in 2008 followed by a sharp economic recession, and increased awareness of the accelerating effects of energy use on the global climate. There are some signs that this time there will be greater recognition that new technology and economic incentives alone will not be enough to achieve the needed behavioral change. California and New York are commissioning behavioral studies to inform their states' energy policies. A new series of international Behavior, Energy, and Climate Change (BECC) conferences began in the United States in 2007 and spread to Europe by 2009, bringing together psychologists, other social researchers, engineers, and policy people from all levels of government, the utility industry, and nonprofit organizations. ACEEE continues to involve social scientists in its activities, and the European Council for an Energy-Efficient Economy (ECEEE) featured behavioral work at its 2009 summer study for the first time. In Europe, which reawakened to the behavioral aspects of energy use before the United States did, psychologists and other researchers have been publishing behavioral studies on energy and training graduate students in the field for the past decade. And in Washington, both Congress and the Department of Energy are contemplating creating a social and behavioral science research program in the department.

Academic interest is also increasing in the United States. In 2008, the American Psychological Association named a Task Force on the Interface between Psychology and Climate Change, which has produced a report (2009) to the profession summarizing what we have learned and showing what we might contribute. And our work from the 1980s is getting increased attention—citations of the 25-year-old *Energy Use* report have more than doubled in Google Scholar in less than two years since summer 2007.

The reemergence of interest in energy use has given me a series of Rip Van Winkle experiences. Energy colleagues and friends I have not seen since the days of the Santa Cruz conferences and the energy committee have reappeared as organizers of the BECC and ECEEE conferences and in state and federal agencies, ready to pick up the threads of the field that Elliot and I and the others on the NRC committee tried to synthesize in the early '80s. And as someone who has continued to work in this field over the years, I have been getting multiple invitations in the past year or two to talk to policy audiences about energy and behavior. I talk about our findings from the 1980s, which seem like fresh insights to people in these audiences.

Still, at this writing, it is too soon to tell whether national policy initiatives will draw on the lessons of the earlier behavioral research. The problem is still being treated primarily as one of technology and economics. The main energy policy debates are still about which major new energy technologies to invest in and which economic policy instrument (an energy tax or a cap-and-trade regime) to rely on as the main motivator for reducing greenhouse gas emissions. The leaders in U.S. energy policy still come predominantly from physics and engineering, and the analysts predominantly from economics. The role of behavioral factors in energy use is still an afterthought or a nonthought to many. But because of the work we did in the 1980s, there are more voices to point out the lessons of past behavioral work, and there is documentation of how behavioral factors matter. We can point out that technologies do not save energy unless people use them, and we can cite studies explaining why people do or don't. We can show that the effect of financial incentives is not straightforward and we can offer empirically based advice on how to make incentives more effective. It continues to be a struggle, but more people are beginning to understand. This time, when we try to give psychology away, we may find policy makers more willing to take it.

REFERENCES

American Psychological Association Task Force on the Interface between Psychology and Climate Change. (2009). *Psychology and global climate change: Addressing a multi-faceted phenomenon and set of challenges.* Washington, DC: American Psychological Association.

Aronson, E., & O'Leary, M. (1983). The relative effectiveness of models and prompts on energy conservation: A field experiment in a shower room. *Journal of Environmental Systems, 12,* 219–224.

Black, J. S., Stern, P. C., & Elworth, J. T. (1985). Personal and contextual influences on household energy adaptations. *Journal of Applied Psychology, 70,* 3–21.

Coltrane, S., Archer, D., & Aronson, E. (1986). The social-psychological foundations of successful energy-conservation programmes. *Energy Policy, 14,* 133–148.

Comaroff, J. L., & Stern, P. C. (Eds.). (1995). *Perspectives on nationalism and war.* Newark, NJ: Gordon & Breach.

Costanzo, M., Archer, D., Aronson, E., & Pettigrew, T. (1986). Energy conservation behavior: The difficult path from information to action. *American Psychologist, 41,* 521–528.

Crompton, T., & Thøgerson, J. (2009, February). *Simple & painless? The limitations of spillover in environmental campaigning.* Godalming: WWF-UK.

Dickerson, C. A., Thibodeau, R., Aronson, E., & Miller, D. (1992). Using cognitive dissonance to encourage water conservation. *Journal of Applied Social Psychology, 22,* 841–854.

Dietz, T., Gardner, G. T., Gilligan, J., Stern, P. C., & Vandenbergh, M. P. (2009). Household actions can provide a behavioral wedge to rapidly reduce U.S. carbon emissions. *Proceedings of the National Academy of Sciences of the United States of America, 106*(44), 18452–18456.

Dietz, T., Ostrom, E., & Stern, P. C. (2003). The struggle to govern the commons. *Science, 302,* 1907–1912.

Gardner, G. T., & Stern, P. C. (2002). *Environmental problems and human behavior* (2nd ed.). Boston: Pearson Custom Publishing.

Gardner G. T., & Stern, P. C. (2008). The short list: The most effective actions U.S. households can take to curb climate change. *Environment, 50*(5), 12–24.

Geller, E. S., Winett, R. A., & Everett, P. B. (1982). *Preserving the environment: New strategies for behavior change.* New York: Pergamon Press.

Gonzales, M. H., Aronson, E., & Costanzo, M. (1988). Using social cognition and persuasion to promote energy conservation: A quasi-experiment. *Journal of Applied Social Psychology, 18,* 1049–1066.

Guagnano, G., Stern, P. C., & Dietz, T. (1995). Influences on attitude-behavior relationships: A natural experiment with curbside recycling. *Environment and Behavior, 27,* 699–718.

Hardin, G. (1968). The tragedy of the commons. *Science, 162,* 1243–1248.

Katzev, R. (1986). The impact of commitment in promoting consumer energy conservation. In E. Monnier, G. Gaskell, P. Ester, B. Joerges, B. LaPillone, C. Midden, & L. Puiseux (Eds.), *Consumer behavior and energy policy: An international perspective* (pp. 280–294). New York: Praeger.

Kempton, W., Darley, J. M., & Stern, P. C. (1992). Psychological research for the new energy problems: Strategies and opportunities. *American Psychologist, 47,* 1213–1223.

Kopelman, S., Weber, J. M., & Messick, D. M. (2002). Factors influencing cooperation in commons dilemmas: A review of experimental psychological research. In E. Ostrom, T. Dietz, N. Dolsak, P. C. Stern, & E. U. Weber (Eds.), *The drama of the commons* (pp. 113–156). Washington, DC: National Academy Press.

Lutzenhiser, L., Cesafsky, L., Chappells, H., Gossard, M., Moezzi, M., Moran, D., Wilhite, H. (2009, April). *Behavioral assumptions underlying California residential sector energy efficiency programs.* Oakland, CA: California Institute for Energy and Environment.

Meadows, D. H., Meadows, D. H., Randers, J., & Behrens, W. W. (1972). *The limits to growth.* New York: Universe Books.

National Research Council. (1984a). *Energy use: The human dimension* (P. C. Stern & E. Aronson, Eds.). New York: Freeman.

National Research Council. (1984b). *Improving energy demand analysis* (P. C. Stern, Ed.). Washington, DC: National Academy Press.

National Research Council. (1985). *Energy efficiency in buildings: Behavioral issues* (P C. Stern, Ed.). Washington, DC: National Academy Press.

National Research Council. (1989a). *Behavior, society, and nuclear war, Vol. 1.* (P. E. Tetlock, J. L. Husbands, R. Jervis, P. C. Stern, & C. Tilly, Eds.). New York: Oxford University Press.

National Research Council. (1989b). *Improving risk communication.* Washington, DC: National Academy Press.

National Research Council. (1989c). *Perspectives on deterrence* (P. C. Stern, R. Axelrod, R. Jervis, & R. Radner, Eds.). New York: Oxford University Press.

National Research Council. (1991). *Behavior, society, and nuclear war, Vol. 2.* (P. E. Tetlock, J. L. Husbands, R. Jervis, P. C. Stern, & C. Tilly, Eds.). New York: Oxford University Press.

National Research Council. (1992). *Global environmental change: Understanding the human dimensions.* (P. C. Stern, O. R. Young, and D. Druckman, Eds.). Washington, DC: National Academy Press.

National Research Council. (1993). *Behavior, society, and international conflict, Vol. 3* (P. E. Tetlock, J. L. Husbands, R. Jervis, P. C. Stern, & C. Tilly, Eds.). New York: Oxford University Press.

National Research Council. (1996). *Understanding risk: Informing decisions in a democratic society* (P. C. Stern & H. V. Fineberg, Eds.). Washington, DC: National Academy Press.

National Research Council. (1997). *Environmentally significant consumption: Research directions* (P. C. Stern, T. Dietz, V. R. Ruttan, R. H. Socolow, & J. L. Sweeney, Eds.). Washington, DC: National Academy Press.

National Research Council. (1998). People and pixels: Linking remote sensing and social science. D. M. Liverman, E. F. Moran, R. R. Rindfuss, & P. C. Stern (Eds.), Washington, DC: National Academy Press.

National Research Council. (1999a). *Human dimensions of global environmental change: Research pathways for the next decade.* Washington, DC: National Academy Press.

National Research Council. (1999b). *Making climate forecasts matter* (P. C. Stern & W. E. Easterling, Eds.) Washington, DC: National Academy Press.

National Research Council. (2000). *International conflict resolution after the cold war* (P. C. Stern & D. Druckman, Eds.). Washington, DC: National Academy Press.

National Research Council. (2002a). *The drama of the commons* (E. Ostrom, T. Dietz, N. Dolsak, P. C. Stern, & E. U. Weber, Eds.). Washington, DC: National Academy Press.

National Research Council. (2002b). *New tools for environmental protection: Education, information, and voluntary measures* (T. Dietz & P. C. Stern, Eds.). Washington, DC: National Academy Press.

National Research Council. (2003). *The polygraph and lie detection.* Washington, DC: National Academy Press.

National Research Council. (2005a). *Decision making for the environment: Social and behavioral science research priorities* (G. D. Brewer & P. C. Stern, Eds.). Washington, DC: National Academy Press.

National Research Council. (2005b). *Population, land use, and environment: Research directions* (B. Entwisle & P. C. Stern, Eds.). Washington, DC: National Academy Press.

National Research Council. (2008). *Public participation in environmental assessment and decision making* (T. Dietz & P. C. Stern, Eds.). Washington, DC: National Academies Press.

National Research Council. (2009a). *Informing decisions in a changing climate* (Panel on Strategies and Methods for Climate-Related Decision Support, Committee on the Human Dimensions of Global Change). Washington, DC: National Academies Press.

National Research Council. (2009b). *Restructuring federal climate research to meet the challenges of climate change* (Committee on Strategic Advice to the U.S. Climate Change Science Program). Washington, DC: National Academies Press.

Ostrom, E. (1990). *Governing the commons: The evolution of institutions for collective action.* Cambridge, UK: Cambridge University Press.

Pimentel, D., Hurd, L. E., Bellotti, A. C., Forster, M. J., Oka, I. N., Sholes, O. D., & Whitman, R. J. (1973). Food production and the energy crisis. *Science, 182,* 443–449.

Schwartz, S. H. (1977). Normative influences on altruism. *Advances in Experimental Social Psychology, 10,* 221–279.

Schwartz, S. H. (1992). Universals in the content and structure of values: Theoretical advances and empirical tests in 20 countries. *Advances in Experimental Social Psychology, 25,* 1–66.

Stern, P. C. (1976). Effect of incentives and education on resource conservation decisions in a simulated commons dilemma. *Journal of Personality and Social Psychology, 34,* 1285–1292.

Stern, P. C. (1986). Blind spots in policy analysis: What economics doesn't say about energy use. *Journal of Policy Analysis and Management, 5,* 200–227.

Stern, P. C. (1992a). Psychological dimensions of global environmental change. *Annual Review of Psychology, 43,* 269–302.

Stern, P. C. (1992b). What psychology knows about energy conservation. *American Psychologist, 47,* 1224–1232.

Stern, P. C. (1993). A second environmental science: Human-environment interactions. *Science, 260,* 1897–1899.

Stern, P. C. (2000a). Psychology and the science of human-environment interactions. *American Psychologist, 55,* 523–530.

Stern, P. C. (2000b). Toward a coherent theory of environmentally significant behavior. *Journal of Social Issues, 56*(3), 407–424.

Stern, P. C., Aronson, E., Darley, J. M., Hill, D. H., Hirst, E., Kempton, W., & Wilbanks, T. J. (1986). The effectiveness of incentives for residential energy conservation. *Evaluation Review, 10,* 147–176.

Stern, P. C., Dietz, T., Abel, T., Guagnano, G. A., & Kalof, L. (1999). A value-belief-norm theory of support for social movements: The case of environmentalism. *Human Ecology Review, 6,* 81–97.

Stern, P. C., & Gardner, G. T. (1981). Psychological research and energy policy. *American Psychologist, 36,* 329–342.

Stern, P. C., & Oskamp, S. (1987). Managing scarce environmental resources. In D. Stokols & I. Altman (Eds.), Handbook of environmental psychology (Vol. 2, pp. 1043–1088). New York: Wiley.

Stern, P. C., & Wilbanks, T. J. (2009). Fundamental research priorities to improve the understanding of human dimensions of climate change. In National Research Council, Restructuring federal climate research to meet the challenges of climate change. (pp. 167–202). Washington, DC: National Academies Press.

13

UNDER WHAT CONDITIONS DOES INTERGROUP CONTACT IMPROVE INTERGROUP HARMONY?

Anthony G. Greenwald
University of Washington

This chapter is about Elliot Aronson and also about Gordon Allport, both of whom I met in the fall of 1959 when I became a new graduate student in Harvard's Department of Social Relations. Elliot would surely have been my PhD advisor had he not moved to Minnesota in 1962. That was when Gordon Allport took pity on me because not only Elliot but everyone else with whom I had worked during my first few years at Harvard had departed to other academic pastures.

My starting motivation for PhD training was to avoid being drafted into the U.S. Army. America was not then at war, but the Cold War fueled an active military draft. By national policy, student deferments were used to encourage men toward socially useful careers. If there had been a draft deferment for aspiring bebop trumpet players, I would not now be writing this chapter. (What, I wonder, would have been the societal and scientific effect if there had been a draft for women, who would then have sought the deferment shelter of graduate schools at a rate similar to men?)

Harvard's Social Relations Department reflected an interdisciplinary spirit that took similar form at several other universities, combining sociology, social anthropology, social psychology, and clinical psychology. (That combination existed as a Harvard department from 1946 until the early 1970s, at which time the partnering disciplines gave up and reidentified with their respective primary disciplines of sociology, anthropology, and psychology.) In 1959, Social Relations was distributed widely across the Harvard campus. Elliot had been given office and research space in a Social Relations outpost at 9 Bow Street, a three-story frame building about three blocks from Harvard Square and outside the Harvard Yard. Probably the most influential coincidence of my Harvard career was that, shortly after arrival, I was given a desk at 9 Bow Street, even though my primary research activity was assisting Richard L. (Dick) Solomon in studies of avoidance conditioning in dogs, in a lab in the fourth-floor attic of Emerson Hall in the Yard.

Elliot was fresh from Stanford, where he had assimilated so much of the spirit of his mentor and PhD advisor, Leon Festinger, that he eventually was expected to channel that spirit after Leon left social psychology in the mid 1960s. Preceding Elliot to Harvard by one year was someone who was close to Elliot and also influential to me—Merrill Carlsmith, who had also worked with Leon at Stanford, but as an undergraduate. Merrill was the becoming-famous coauthor of what social psychologists ever since have simply called "Festinger and Carlsmith 1959," the article that directly confronted cognitive principles of Festinger's (1957) dissonance theory with the reward and incentive concepts of Hull–Spence behavior theory. In my professional naiveté, I did not immediately understand the revolutionary importance of Merrill's work with Leon, nor the similar importance of the already published affirmation of dissonance theory's effort-justification principle—pulled off by Elliot as an empirical tour de force, working together with Jud Mills at Stanford (Aronson & Mills, 1959).

Thankfully, Merrill was not overly taken with his own achievements. He took me under his wing, nurturing what eventually became a finely honed ability to read almost anything critically (except my own work, of course), and also beating me mercilessly in games of Go. Merrill's kindness made it impossible for me to be jealous of his achievements or even of the fact that Elliot obviously loved Merrill more than he loved me. Working incredibly productively in just a few years at Harvard, Elliot and Merrill produced the studies that established the empirical basis for Elliot's self-concept interpretation of dissonance theory, which I settled on as my favorite form of the theory after several competing interpretations had appeared in the 1960s and 1970s.

I felt very privileged to have been adopted by the small group that included Elliot, Merrill, and another new Harvard faculty member, Walter Mischel. At Bow Street I began to learn how to read my own work critically. I was shown how to do this by Elliot and Walter, who would take all opportunities to make fully clear to me just how much my writing could be improved. Combining sarcastic humor with their writing suggestions, they taught me the irreplaceable value of having teachers and colleagues who care enough to devote a portion of their waking hours to telling you just how you can improve yourself. I am still blessed with colleagues who will do that for me, including a few for whom I am prepared to do likewise by modeling toward them my approximation of the style that Elliot and Walter modeled for me. Elliot and Walter remain ready to straighten me out whenever I provide the opportunity. It is sad that Merrill, who died so young in 1984,[1] no longer participates in those tradeoffs and does not have the chance to reflect, along with the other contributors to this volume, on how Elliot's work touched his life.

My reflection about Elliot's work focuses on the contact hypothesis, which holds that under the right conditions, interactions between members of two initially hostile groups can overcome preexisting antipathy. The important question is: What are those "right conditions"?

Elliot's development of interest in intergroup contact came in the 1970s. That was during the first of several extended episodes in Elliot's career when he turned his attention to using social psychology to solve a societal problem. Elliot might never have mentioned the contact hypothesis in my presence at Harvard. However, in effect, he mentioned it to me annually for most of the quarter century during which I taught undergraduate social psychology courses at Ohio State and the University of Washington, using Elliot's *The Social Animal* as the main course text. Elliot's "Prejudice" chapter made the contact hypothesis very familiar to me and also brings Gordon Allport into the story.

Gordon Allport was a formal man. Alas, I never got to call him "Gordon." Over 40 years later, the closest I can get to treating him familiarly is to use his initials (GWA), a liberty I shall take for the remainder of this chapter. By my present standards, GWA was relatively young (in his early 60s) while I was at Harvard, but he was more than 40 years my senior and had a greater aura of elderly eminence than any other Harvard professor I encountered. Tom Pettigrew, who knew GWA far better than I did, tells me that this impression was created by GWA's shyness, something that never occurred to me.

I have been asked quite a few times what it was like to work with GWA and how he influenced me. There is irony here. In my career, I have taken up three major topics that GWA contributed to: attitudes, the self, and prejudice. He was the authority on attitudes in the 1930s, on the self in the 1940s, and on prejudice in the 1950s. I took those topics up in the same order, respectively, in the 1960s, the 1980s, and close to 2000 (yes, it took me longer to work through each). The irony:

In my years at Harvard, GWA was no longer interested in those topics and I was only just beginning to be interested in attitudes. When I later began working on those topics, his published work of three to five decades earlier was still definitive and shaped my approach in each case. His scholarly attention to detail and accuracy also resonated and stayed with me—although some of my advisees have been inclined to see this as compulsiveness.

I have wondered what GWA would have thought of my work on the topics to which he had made such major contributions. My first answer is not encouraging, because he apparently had no sympathy for the experimental social psychology movement that was inspired by Leon Festinger and in which I was being indoctrinated by Elliot, Walter, and Merrill. GWA's disdain for experimental social psychology never appeared in anything that he published or anything I ever heard him say. However, I did discover a note that he, as my dissertation chair, had sent with a copy of my dissertation to one of my dissertation committee members. I treasure that note, which I later found between pages of the copy of my dissertation that came back to me from that committee member. The adjectives "constipated," "rigid," and "fashionable" all appeared in immediate proximity to "experimentation." GWA was a scholar of the first order and had great respect for data, but little fondness for the highly creative and sometimes deceptive methods that Elliot and Merrill (Aronson & Carlsmith, 1969) later described as "experimental realism."

I hope nevertheless that GWA would find something of value in the recent work in which I have tried to bring together the topics of attitudes, self, and prejudice, even though that work is rooted in the methods of experimental social psychology. GWA died in 1967. Were he alive today, he could not help but notice how much I was influenced by his work. If he could spot his parental influence on me, perhaps that would be enough to give him a positive (implicit, of course) attitude.

My repeated exposure to the contact hypothesis through *The Social Animal* became valuable background when, relatively recently, the Implicit Association Test took my career on an unpredicted journey into research on prejudice. In the rest of this chapter I try to merge Elliot's and GWA's insights about the contact hypothesis, along with those of other students of the contact hypothesis, especially Tom Pettigrew (e.g., Pettigrew & Tropp, 2006). Because of my come-lately interest, I am much less expert than these others. What prompts me, nevertheless, to take up the topic is the growing evidence that intergroup relations are impaired by implicit attitudes and stereotypes that are far more pervasive than are their parallel overt forms (cf. Dovidio,

Glick, & Rudman, 2005; Greenwald, Poehlman, Uhlmann, & Banaji, 2009; Nosek, Greenwald, & Banaji, 2007). These recent demonstrations of the pervasiveness of implicit biases necessarily challenge aficionados of the contact hypothesis to find ways to increase the effectiveness of intergroup contact in producing intergroup harmony.

GWA'S RECIPE

In the 1954 case of *Brown v. Board of Education of Topeka, Kansas*, the United States Supreme Court found that racial segregation of American public schools violated the United States Constitution's Fourteenth Amendment. The *Brown* decision led many to expect that desegregation of schools would soon follow and, furthermore, that there should follow a rapid warming of black–white race relations in America.

The expected warming did not occur. American federal courts went slowly (described ironically as "all deliberate speed," with "deliberate" being the operative word) in obliging school districts to implement desegregation programs. In a preface to the 1958 edition of *The Nature of Prejudice*, GWA wrote: "The delay has given time … for fierce disagreement to arise among authorities occupying strategic roles in the hierarchy of law enforcement" (reprinted in Allport, 1979, p. xxi).

In the late 1960s, more than a decade after *Brown*, American courts at last started to order implementation of school desegregation in communities that had not already achieved desegregation on their own. Here is what Elliot observed in Austin, Texas, shortly after federal court orders had produced the start of school desegregation efforts there in 1971:

> Because Austin had always been racially segregated, white youngsters, African-American youngsters, and Hispanic youngsters found themselves in the same classrooms for the first time. Within a few weeks, long-standing suspicion, fear, and distrust between groups produced an atmosphere of turmoil and hostility. Fist-fights erupted in corridors and schoolyards across the city. (Aronson, 2000–2009, para. 1–2)

The contact hypothesis, of course, suggested the contrary—that desegregation would produce a thaw in race relations (see Stephan, 1978). The intuition underlying the contact hypothesis is that face-to-face contact between mutually distrustful groups should allow members of each group to discover that their counterparts are also ordinary human beings. Through direct experience with the other group, contact should dispel stereotypes and erroneous expectations. Stereotypes should be replaced by recognition that the other group's members are normal people, fundamentally similar to those in one's own group.

Historical roots of the contact hypothesis are reviewed in the opening pages of Tom Pettigrew and Linda Tropp's (2006) comprehensive meta-analytic study. The following statement by GWA in *The Nature of Prejudice* (Allport, 1954) is often quoted as *the* definitive statement of the contact hypothesis:

> To be maximally effective, contact and acquaintanceship programs should lead to a sense of equality in social status, should occur in ordinary purposeful pursuits, avoid artificiality and if possible enjoy the sanction of the community in which they occur. The deeper and more genuine the association, the greater its effect. While it may help somewhat to place members of different ethnic groups side by side on a job, the gain is greater if these members regard themselves as part of a team. (p. 489)

Later writers distilled this statement by GWA into what is widely accepted as a recipe for effective intergroup contact, having four ingredients:

1. Members of the contacting groups should have *equal status*. For example, in contact between two nations that are in conflict, the representatives of each nation should have similar status in their respective governments. It is interesting that GWA's first sentence said that the contact situation "should *lead to* [emphasis added] a sense of equality in social status." This led me to wonder whether GWA was more willing than were later writers to consider the effects of contact in situations that did not start with equal status. I am grateful to Tom Pettigrew for pointing out to me that GWA's prior statements did indeed specify equal status as a starting condition (e.g., Allport & Kramer, 1946).
2. Members of the contacting groups should have *shared goals*. For example, both nations might desire peaceful and economically prosperous relations.
3. Contact should be *authority sanctioned*. For example, leaders of major international powers or of international organizations such as the United Nations might make clear their approval of the negotiations.

4. Contact should occur in the context of *cooperation* rather than competition. For example, representatives of two conflicting nations should see that they have more to gain by working together with each other than by remaining opposed.

Of course, negotiating an international conflict bears almost no resemblance to the situation that Elliot found in the schools of Austin, Texas, in 1971. After he had visited and observed classrooms in several of Austin's schools, Elliot saw that three of the four ingredients of the contact recipe were generally missing. In particular (1) there was nothing approaching equal status of white, black, and Latino students; (2) there were no important shared goals; (3) yes, there was authority sanction, but it may have been more the authority of federal courts than the enthusiasm of local school authorities; and (4) rather than cooperation among white, black, and Latino students, those groups were more likely to be competing and fighting with one another.

Particularly telling were Elliot's observations in the routine classroom situation in which teachers ask questions and students are called on to answer—a situation in which students compete for the teacher's attention and praise. (Elliot's description of this can be found in the "Prejudice" chapter in all editions of *The Social Animal*.) Minority students, who were newly arrived from less challenging classrooms, frequently lost those competitions. They could lose either by hesitating to raise their hands or, when called on, by failing to give correct answers.

Elliot responded to these multiple deviations from optimal contact by inventing a new format for classroom work that supplied the missing ingredients. In his invention, the Jigsaw Classroom (Aronson & Patnoe, 1997), students were organized into racially mixed small teams that worked together on assignments. The need to complete assignments provided the shared goals ingredient. The jigsaw name came from the device of giving each team member a different piece of the material needed for the team to complete the assignment. The group task thus became the equivalent of completing a puzzle for which all team members had equal shares of the needed information. The need for all team members to contribute to the solution provided the cooperation ingredient. The equal status ingredient came from preparing each student to provide contributions to the group project that were equally essential.

In introducing the Jigsaw Classroom in Austin, Elliot and his collaborators showed that the jigsaw method not only improved intergroup harmony but also improved performance by minority students, even when it was used for as little as an average of one hour out of the classroom day. These initial successes in Austin were rapidly followed by successes in other cities.

Despite the repeated demonstrations of its success in field experiments, the Jigsaw Classroom now has only limited adoption in American school systems. (Unfortunately, there are no good data on the Jigsaw Classroom's penetration of American schools. When I recently asked Elliot about this, he told me that he has never encountered an authoritative survey of the extent of its use.) Perhaps one reason for the limited adoption is that few current American schools have the types of racially mixed classrooms that initially motivated Elliot's invention. Why do present-day American schools have so few classrooms with more than token racial mixture? The explanation can be found in actions of American courts after 1980. After a period of court-mandated integration efforts between 1970 and 1980, American courts started making decisions that allowed a gradual return to levels of racial segregation approximating those of 1970 (Orfield & Lee, 2004, 2006). Many Americans now seem content with this retreat from active desegregation. Part of the reason is that there was (and still is) wide dislike—by school administrators and by parents of both majority and minority children—for programs that oblige children to be bussed for long distances to attend an integrated school. Segregation of schools will likely not disappear until residential segregation disappears.

FOUR CASES OF CONTACT

My tribute to GWA's and Elliot's work on contact attempts to advance their shared cause by considering the (at least mildly puzzling) juxtaposition of four well documented illustrations of successful intergroup contact. Only the first illustration included all four ingredients of GWA's recipe. For the other three, the challenge is to understand whether their sometimes striking deviations from GWA's recipe were merely exceptions that prove the rule or, alternately, clues to possible alternative recipes for effective contact.

Prototypical Equal-Status Contact

In 1971, C. P. Ellis was a white labor union official and also an avowed racist who was a leader of Durham, North Carolina's, Ku Klux Klan. Ann Atwater, also of Durham, was a black civil rights activist. When Ellis died in 2005 at age 78, a *New York Times* obituary described Atwater and Ellis as "the unlikeliest of friends." Like Austin, Texas, in 1971 Durham was experiencing turmoil surrounding school desegregation. Along with several other community leaders, Atwater and Ellis participated in a series of meetings that were organized to solve

Durham's school desegregation difficulties. After 10 days of meetings, Atwater and Ellis developed a friendship that eventually led Ellis to renounce both his Klan membership and his racist beliefs. In later years, Ellis and Atwater often appeared together publicly as advocates of racial harmony.

The meeting of Ann Atwater and C. P. Ellis appears to have been a perfect convergence of the four ingredients of GWA's recipe: equal status, shared goals, support from authorities, and cooperation. It was also a striking instance of contact leading not only to personal friendship but to a broader acceptance of the other's racial group.

The most remarkable feature of the Atwater–Ellis friendship may have been the attention that it received at Ellis's death, including coverage in the *New York Times* (November 11, 2005) and on National Public Radio (November 8, 2005). There must have been many other communities in which pairs as initially antagonistic as Atwater and Ellis were similarly brought together to manage difficulties of desegregation. If the contact recipe worked even 10% of the time, shouldn't friendships such as that between Atwater and Ellis have been commonplace enough not to merit the national attention occasioned by Ellis's death? Does that attention tell us that effective operation of the contact recipe may not be so routine? A related observation at the international level is that there have been many occasions on which Palestinian and Israeli representatives have met with all four ingredients present. Why did this not, long ago, produce peace and amity in the Middle East?

Two Bank Robberies

On August 23, 1973, during an attempted bank robbery in Stockholm, Sweden, a police officer was shot and injured by the lone robber. The robber proceeded to keep police at bay by threatening to harm four hostages inside the bank. Hoping for a speedy resolution, the police allowed a friend of the robber to enter the bank. However, once inside the bank the friend became a second captor. After five days of standoff, the police tear-gassed the bank, the two captors surrendered, and the hostages were freed without injury. The Stockholm bank robbery survives in our memories because of a surprising observation that emerged in later news reports: The hostages came to like their two captors.

In early 1974 in Berkeley, California, heiress Patricia (Patty) Hearst was kidnapped by a group that identified itself as the Symbionese Liberation Army (SLA). Two months later, she was photographed during a bank robbery, holding a rifle. Hearst then informed the press that she was an active member of the SLA, henceforth to be known as "Citizen Tania." Occurring so close in time, the Stockholm robbery and the Hearst kidnapping prompted popular belief that there might be a general phenomenon of captives becoming attached to captors. The label "Stockholm syndrome" has since been widely attached to this circumstance.

What about the recipe? Which ingredients were present? This is answered more easily for the Stockholm robbery, which was more in the public eye than the Hearst kidnapping. Two of the ingredients of GWA's recipe were absent. There was no equal status. Captors and captives do not have equal status. There was also no authority sanction. The captivity was illegal and the police sought to end it. What about shared goals and cooperation? At the start, there were no shared goals. The captors wanted to escape and the hostages wanted to be rescued. The fourth ingredient, cooperation, was also missing at the start. However, by the end things may have changed if the hostages concluded that they would be in the same danger as their captors if the police invaded the bank (which they did). The captors and hostages may have begun to see themselves as potentially cooperating allies with a very important shared goal of survival.

The Loan of a Book

In 1736, 30-year-old Benjamin Franklin arranged to borrow a book from a member of the Pennsylvania Assembly who had opposed Franklin's aim to become clerk of the assembly. Franklin was without doubt displeased with the legislator, whom he described as having given "a long speech against me, in order to favour some other candidate [i.e., for the position of clerk]." The following paragraph is Franklin's description of what followed.

> Having heard that he had in his library a certain very scarce and curious book, I wrote a note to him, expressing my desire of perusing that book, and requesting he would do me the favour of lending it to me for a few days. He sent it immediately, and I return'd it in about a week with another note, expressing strongly my sense of the favour. When we next met in the House, he spoke to me (which he had never done before), and with great civility; and he ever after manifested a readiness to serve me on all occasions, so that we became great friends, and our friendship continued to his death. (Eliot, 1909, pp. 94–95)

Brief as it is, Franklin's remarkable story challenges our understanding of the conditions of friendship formation. Two of the contact recipe's four ingredients were lacking. There was no sanctioning authority and status was unequal. The Pennsylvania Assembly member had high status by position and clearly had the power to influence an important outcome for Franklin. Franklin also put himself in the lower status role of help seeker. Why did the simple act of requesting a loan of the book so dramatically improve the relationship? The distinctive characteristic of Franklin's story was helping. Franklin arranged for an enemy to help him by lending a book.

After writing all of this, I made the welcome discovery that I must first have encountered the story of Franklin's borrowed book in *The Social Animal*. Elliot had used the story in his chapter on interpersonal attraction to illustrate a nonstandard means of producing liking (e.g., Aronson, 1992, p. 351). That placement delivers a useful message: Rather than thinking that special methods are needed to reduce prejudice, why not apply the full armory of methods known to be effective in increasing interpersonal attraction to the task of reducing prejudice?

Helping is fundamental to many human relationships, such as parent–child relationships and charitable giving. Helping is likewise central to situations in which professionals such as nurses and teachers give assistance that often far exceeds the expectations of the help-giving jobs for which they are paid. On the surface, it may appear that the benefits of these helping relationships go entirely to those who receive help. However, an enduring bond may develop between help giver and recipient. That bond can be as cherished by the help giver as by the receiver.

A Remarkable Second Baseman

In 1947, Branch Rickey was president of the Brooklyn Dodgers. Rickey had a plan to combine a benefit to professional baseball (racial desegregation) with a substantial economic benefit to the Dodgers. He had the prescience to believe that a young ballplayer from the segregated Negro League, Jackie Robinson, could be the key to two profitable outcomes for the Dodgers—a possible league championship and an increase in ticket sales.

The success story of Branch Rickey's hiring of Jackie Robinson has been told many times (see especially Pratkanis & Turner, 1994a, 1994b). That success must have depended partly on Robinson's personal characteristics. Robinson endured and tolerated abuse from many white baseball fans in Brooklyn who were not ready for "their" team to have a black player. Robinson likewise tolerated what must have seemed an endless stream of insults from supporters of Brooklyn's opponents, both on and off the field, as he traveled to play in other cities. On the baseball field, Robinson was simply outstanding. He received Major League Baseball's Rookie of the Year award in 1947 and the National League's

Most Valuable Player award in 1949. His on-field performances helped the Brooklyn Dodgers to become National League champions in 6 of his 10 years with the team.

The story of the integration of Major League Baseball is a story of successful intergroup contact that lacks the main ingredient of GWA's recipe. Was there authority sanction? Yes. Rickey and other baseball officials provided it. Were there shared goals? Yes. Robinson's teammates wanted to win and other teams in the league must have appreciated the increased audiences that he helped to attract. Was there cooperation? Although some resisted, Rickey was able to get many others to support the integration effort. Also, Robinson and Rickey were certainly cooperating. The missing ingredient was equal status. In 1947, Robinson's first year with the Dodgers, there must have been few settings in which he had status equal to others. In his most important relationship—with Rickey—Robinson was clearly lower in status. On the baseball field, the reverse may have been true. By virtue of his ability, Robinson was ultimately higher in status than most others. But, as the only one of his race on the field, his status was different from all others and not equal. In off-field settings, because of the generally poor treatment of blacks in American society, Robinson was often very visibly lower in status than others. During his first year with the Brooklyn Dodgers, it could not have been possible for Robinson to feel that he had status equal to others on the team.

Do the Four Cases Prove Anything?

In the case of Atwater and Ellis the four-ingredient contact recipe worked perfectly. In the other three cases, contact succeeded despite one missing ingredient (Robinson and Rickey) or two missing ingredients (the two bank robberies and Franklin's borrowed book). Although these cases offer no scientifically adequate basis for drawing conclusions, they encourage us to think that there may be useful alternatives to GWA's four-ingredient recipe for effective intergroup contact.

ANOTHER RECIPE? (HELPFUL CONTACT)

With a long and distinguished past, the contact hypothesis and GWA's recipe will certainly continue to guide scientific thinking about how to improve intergroup relations. But GWA's recipe may have achieved such stature as to have blocked attention to other effective strategies. Still, occasional voices have suggested that alternatives to GWA's recipe warrant serious consideration. In their review of more than 500 reports of investigations of the contact hypothesis, Pettigrew and Tropp (2006) described the broad support achieved by the contact hypothesis, but also concluded that "Allport's conditions should not be regarded as necessary for producing positive contact outcomes" (p. 766). In similar spirit, John Dixon, Kevin Durrheim, and Colin Tredoux (2005) pointed out that there are relatively few situations of natural intergroup contact in which all four ingredients of the recipe can be found.

In wondering about other recipes, I found it difficult to resist focusing on a characteristic that was prominent in the successes of Franklin's borrowed book and Rickey's integration of Major League Baseball—the act of one person helping another. Perhaps this is the basis for another effective recipe, which might be called *helpful contact*. This almost certainly is not a single-ingredient recipe. Besides helping, other possibly necessary ingredients are (a) that the recipient welcomes the help and (b) an expectation by both helper and recipient that the recipient will benefit enough so as not to need help indefinitely. These additional ingredients may separate effective forms of helpful contact from acts of help that are condescending or patronizing, or acts in which the recipient is coerced to accept help, such as in an abusive relationship (see Fisher, Nadler, & Whitcher-Alagna, 1982, for a theoretical interpretation of negative responses to help by recipients).

Some instances of what appears to be helpful contact have occurred on a massive scale in recent history. Consider the difference between international relations following World War I and those following World War II. Policies pursued by the victorious Allies after World War I left Germany downtrodden. Would Germany's pre-World War II international stance have been different had the United States and its allies pursued policies that took a more helpful approach toward their defeated enemy? After World War II, the United States did just that. In the form of the Marshall Plan, America took the lead in assuring the reconstruction of Germany and took similar steps to assist Japan. In the decades following World War II, America's relations with its recently defeated Japanese and German enemies were, remarkably, much more favorable than were its relations with the Soviet Union, which was the geopolitical descendant of America's wartime ally, Russia.

A region of more recent hostilities is the Middle East. Might the current atmosphere differ from its present instability and tenseness if Israel had instituted major aid programs for its defeated enemies after the Arab–Israel wars of 1948, 1967, and 1973?

Helpful contact has certainly existed for millennia as an effective strategy for establishing interpersonal friendship and favorable intergroup relations. Nevertheless, social psychologists have not identified helpful contact as a distinct strategy for achieving intergroup harmony nor has helpful contact received any fraction of the half-century of sustained scholarly research attention received by the equal-status contact recipe.

CODA

In closing, I cannot resist noting that one sustained instance of helpful contact, provided by Elliot—along with Walter and Merrill—to me, a lower status would-be member of their group in 1959, produced warm relationships that have now lasted more than half a century.

NOTE

1. A warm remembrance of Merrill Carlsmith by several Stanford faculty colleagues can be found at http://histsoc.stanford.edu/pdfmem/CarlsmithJM.pdf.

REFERENCES

Allport, G. W. (1954). *The nature of prejudice*. Oxford, UK: Addison-Wesley.
Allport, G. W. (1979). *The nature of prejudice* (25th anniversary ed.). Cambridge, MA: Perseus.
Allport, G. W., & Kramer, B. M. (1946). Some roots of prejudice. *Journal of Psychology, 22,* 9–39.
Aronson, E. (1992). *The social animal* (6th ed.). New York: W. H. Freeman.
Aronson, E. (2000–2009). *History of the jigsaw: An account from Professor Aronson*. Retrieved from http://www.jigsaw.org/history.htm
Aronson, E., & Carlsmith, J. M. (1969). Experimentation in social psychology. In G. Lindzey & E. Aronson (Eds.) *Handbook of social psychology* (2nd ed., Vol. 2, pp. 1–79). Reading, MA: Addison-Wesley.
Aronson, E., & Mills, J. (1959). The effect of severity of initiation on liking for a group. *Journal of Abnormal and Social Psychology, 59,* 177–181.
Aronson, E., & Patnoe, S. (1997). *The jigsaw classroom*. New York: Longman.
Dixon, J., Durrheim, K., & Tredoux, C. (2005). Beyond the optimal contact strategy: A reality check for the contact hypothesis. *American Psychologist, 60,* 697–711.
Dovidio, J. F., Glick, P., & Rudman, L. A. (Eds.). (2005). *On the nature of prejudice: Fifty years after Allport* (pp. 1–15). Malden, MA: Blackwell.
Eliot, C. W. (1909). *The autobiography of Benjamin Franklin* (pp. 94–95). New York: P. P. Collier & Son.
Festinger, L. (1957). *A theory of cognitive dissonance*. Stanford, CA: Stanford University Press.
Festinger, L., & Carlsmith, J. M. (1959). Cognitive consequences of forced compliance. *Journal of Abnormal Social Psychology, 58,* 203–211.

Fisher, J. D., Nadler, A., & Whitcher-Alagna, S. (1982). Recipient reactions to aid. *Psychological Bulletin, 91,* 27–54.

Greenwald, A. G., Poehlman, T. A., Uhlmann, E., & Banaji, M. R. (2009). Understanding and using the Implicit Association Test: III. Meta-analysis of predictive validity. *Journal of Personality and Social Psychology, 97,* 17–41.

Nosek, B. A., Greenwald, A. G., & Banaji, M. R. (2007). The Implicit Association Test at age 7: A methodological and conceptual review. In J. A. Bargh (Ed.), *Automatic processes in social thinking and behavior* (pp. 265–292). New York: Psychology Press.

Orfield, G., & Lee, C. (2004). *Brown at 50: King's dream or Plessy's nightmare?* Cambridge, MA: The Civil Rights Project at Harvard University.

Orfield, G., & Lee, C. (2006). *Racial transformation and the changing nature of segregation.* Cambridge, MA: The Civil Rights Project at Harvard University.

Pettigrew, T. F., & Tropp, L. R. (2006). A meta-analytic test of intergroup contact theory. *Journal of Personality and Social Psychology, 90,* 751–783.

Pratkanis, A. R., & Turner, M. E. (1994a). The year Cool Papa Bell lost the batting title: I. Mr. Branch Rickey and Mr. Jackie Robinson's plea for affirmative action. *Nine: The Journal of Baseball History and Social Policy Perspectives, 2,* 260–276.

Pratkanis, A. R., & Turner, M. E. (1994b). Nine principles of successful affirmative action: II. Branch Rickey, Jackie Robinson, and the integration of baseball. *Nine: The Journal of Baseball History and Social Policy Perspectives, 3,* 36–65.

Stephan, W. G. (1978). School desegregation: An evaluation of predictions made in *Brown v. Board of Education. Psychological Bulletin, 85,* 217–238.

14
JIGSAW AND THE NURTURE OF HUMAN INTELLIGENCE

Joshua Aronson
New York University

Educational romantics of the Left focus on race, class, and gender. It is children of color, children of poor parents, and girls whose performance is artificially depressed, and their academic achievement will blossom as soon as they are liberated from the racism, classism, and sexism embedded in American education [yet] … a massive body of evidence says that reading and mathematics achievement have strong ties to underlying intellectual ability, that we do not know how to change intellectual ability after children reach school, and that the quality of schooling within the normal range of schools does not have much effect on student achievement.

> —**Charles Murray (coauthor of *The Bell Curve*)**
> *in* "The Age of Educational Romanticism" (2008a)

We must fight the doctrine of *The Bell Curve* both because it is wrong and because it will, if activated, cut off all possibility of the proper nurturance of everyone's intelligence.

> —**Stephen J. Gould**
> *The Mismeasure of Man (1996)*

People who do crazy things are not necessarily crazy.

> —**Elliot Aronson**
> *The Social Animal (1972/2008)*

In an important and penetrating essay titled "The Age of Educational Romanticism," Charles Murray (2008a) called me an educational romantic. The slur was actually directed at my research on reducing the racial achievement gap, the *Bell Curve* coauthor assigning it a place in the educational dustbin, next to other tantalizing but supposedly bankrupt constructs such as the "Pygmalion" effect, self-esteem, and "multiple intelligences." I was pinched by the characterization. Granted, I am an educational romantic. I believe we can accomplish great things in schools, much more than we are accomplishing now. But I base this on the evidence of science and of real life—first as a student, later as a teacher and a researcher, next as a parent, as now as all of these at once. I like to think that I'm optimally romantic about the science. That is, if I'm positive that *The Bell Curve* (Herrnstein & Murray, 1994) doctrine is wrong, it is not because I have stars in my eyes, but because I've been examining the science on both sides of the issue, and see great promise in harnessing constructs from social psychology for improving human intelligence and achievement. The evidence on improving intelligence is mixed, of course, which only means I'd be a romantic fool to be too strident about it. But there is enough solid evidence to disprove some of the more gloomy implications of Murray's doctrine. Even so, because the data are mixed, I know I will never convert Murray (who is a friend) to my way of thinking or convince him to invest resources in school reform. But I would still be happy if I could get him to appreciate the possibility that he might have missed something; that there are sound reasons to believe in the power of interventions to improve human learning and reduce the disparities that plague our schools.

Extreme romanticism is indeed a scourge worthy of Murray's scorn and everyone's concern. At best, it makes for bad and boring science. At worst, it's dangerous. For example, for the past eight years, our educational system has been suffering from blind faith in such romantic notions as thinking that all children can become academically proficient (with not a one left behind!) just by passing laws that force schools to try harder. Or the equally "romantic" delusion that teaching abstinence to teenagers curbs premarital sex, despite years of data that just keep saying no. This sort of romanticism is destructive. I'm with Murray on that. But in its nondelusional form, educational romanticism can be a force for good and a wellspring for good science. I know this because my father is Elliot Aronson. I became aware of psychology during the stretch of my father's career when he began doing fewer of his laboratory experiments to test theory and more field experiments to test theory and improve human behavior. To have been introduced to psychology by this particular body of work and by my father was to learn at an early age that a great scientist can also be a great romantic, so long as he's as enamored of the truth as he is of good news.

My father's scientific disposition is the result, I believe, of the fact that he was the child of two great but parallel traditions in psychology, epitomized by his two significant mentors, Abraham Maslow and Leon Festinger. Whereas the softhearted Maslow modeled an exuberant faith in man's potential for growth and "self-actualization," Festinger, the hardheaded experimentalist, ingrained in him an equally strong zeal for scientific rigor, and an abiding impatience with sloppy thinking, imprecise operationalizations, and correlation coefficients. Years of exposure to this combination of scientist and humanist in my father have left me with a deep-seated optimism about the possibilities of education, if done right. Call it educational romanticism if you like.

Behavioral geneticists tell me that, like all traits, the traits that make my father such a uniquely terrific scientist are heritable, and that they will increasingly manifest in me as I age. I hope so. I will never know, because scientific talent and integrity, coupled with optimism about human growth, were so impeccably modeled by both my parents that nature and nurture are hopelessly muddled; both undoubtedly shaped my experiences as a son, a student, a father, teacher, and researcher. Whatever the precise origin of my educational romanticism, I cannot believe in the *Bell Curve* doctrine. What follows is why.

THE SCIENTIST AND THE SCHOOL

Many years ago, a middle-aged scientist visited a school near his home to observe a group of children who, without knowing it, were subjects in an important social experiment. Young, black, and uneducated, the children had been picked at random from the community to receive schooling, mainly in the form of Bible study, spelling, and, for the girls, household skills like embroidery. The premise of the experiment was to see whether the children could be educated and Christianized, and whether this could be done without provoking a backlash from members of the white community who opposed educating black people. The scientist's wife was first to see the experiment unfold, and she returned so enchanted with the children that she urged her husband see for himself. When he went to the school he had quite the same reaction as his wife, but he also had a special epiphany of his own. He wrote to the director of the society that created the school to report being "much pleased" by his visit and to confess the unexpected effect of what he had seen:

> I have conceived a higher opinion of the natural capacities of the black race than I had ever before entertained. Their apprehension seems as quick, their memory as strong, and their docility in every respect equal to that of white children.

That was Benjamin Franklin writing in 1763. It is unfortunate that he never followed up on this experiment; American racial attitudes might have evolved more quickly had the country's premier scientist and celebrity replicated his experiment and convinced others that blacks were the intellectual equals of whites. The Philadelphia school and others like it closed down at the start of the revolution, and Franklin became too consumed with other matters to turn an experiment in Christian philanthropy into a program of research on race and intelligence. But clearly something happened in that school to create conditions that allowed a keen observer to glimpse in those children the innate intelligence hidden by the conditions of their everyday life as slaves.

To be sure, the school experiment was imperfect. For one thing, there was no formal control group of average white children; that group existed only as a simulation in Franklin's head. Nonetheless, it was persuasive enough a demonstration to change Franklin's mind for good. For instance, 12 years earlier in his role as demographer, Franklin had written a report called *Observations on the Increase of Mankind*. In it he warned against a growing black population. "Why," he had asked, "increase the sons of Africa by planting them in America, where we have so fair an opportunity by excluding all blacks and Tawneys, of increasing the lovely white and Red?" His chief arguments echoed the genetic thinking of the times; black people were innately immoral, untrustworthy, and stupid. This attitude was most explicit in a line that read "almost every slave, *being by nature a thief* ..." That was in 1751.

In his 1769 revision of the report, published six years after his epiphany in the school, his change of heart shows up in an elegant stroke of editing: "Almost every slave," he wrote, "being from *the nature of slavery* a thief ..." Later still, in 1789, he wrote about the "Negro, who has long been treated as a brute animal, too frequently sinks beneath the common standard of the human species. The galling chains that bind his body, do also fetter his intellectual faculties, and impair the social affections of his heart."

Franklin thus became the first American, certainly the most famous, to recognize that the flaws of black people were rooted not in their inherent characteristics, but in their maltreatment—the first to convert from naturism to nurturism. He went on to become the most ardent abolitionist of the Founding Fathers.

This little-known educational experiment raises obvious questions for anyone who has pondered the doctrine of *The Bell Curve*. Something so spectacular happened in that classroom that Franklin reversed a lifetime of thinking. What did he see that day that Charles Murray, in a lifetime of thinking, still seems unable to see?

THE MYSTERIOUS MISS A

In the 1950s a second, more systematic experiment was conducted with even more eye-opening results. This time the subjects were 6-year-old children living in a forlorn section of an industrial city in the Northeast. The site was a gloomy, low-slung building with bars on its windows, an elementary school attended by poor and working-class children. Garbage was strewn about the streets, and many of the children who walked to school had to pass by a brothel, a sanitation dump, and other unsavory sights on their way each morning. As measured by IQ tests the children took frequently, they were the lowest performing children in the district, which meant they were widely considered to be the dumbest children in the city.

The experiment couldn't have been simpler. The children were merely assigned at random to receive one of three first-grade teachers who differed markedly in quality and teaching style. The children's IQ test scores and academic progress were followed over time; the teachers recorded their impressions of the children, how smart and well behaved they were. In their own way, the results were even more stunning than Ben Franklin's. One of the teachers, whom the researchers named "Miss A," consistently produced huge IQ gains in her students. This, in and of itself, is surprising enough, but Miss A's first graders maintained those gains—some in excess of 30 IQ points—regardless of what happened to them in the later grades. The children were followed into adulthood, and 25 years later their careers were noted, the researchers sorting them into high, low, and medium status. Mirroring the IQ scores, Miss A's children were wildly successful compared to their peers who got the other teachers. None of her students ended up in low-status careers; most had jobs that required brains and skill, and most earned excellent salaries. Years after spending just one year as Miss A's students, they had escaped the destiny to which the school, the neighborhood, and their families seemed likely to consign them. The students assigned to Miss B and Miss C did not fare so well. Some actually lost IQ points over the years, and most ended up in low-status, low-paying jobs, continuing the cycle of poverty and dim prospects of their parents and community. Imagine: Somebody in your elementary school office flips a coin and you are assigned to receive a terrific teacher like Miss A. As a result, you turn out vastly smarter and more successful than if you had been assigned a more ordinary teacher like Miss B or Miss C. One tiny decision—one that burns less than a calorie—and you grow up to become a college professor or a lawyer or a doctor. Meanwhile the unlucky but no less innately intelligent child assigned to a lesser teacher ends up managing the late shift at Burger King. There is no provision in the *Bell Curve* doctrine for this kind of result (which may explain why the study is not cited in *The Bell Curve*). This kind of thing is not supposed to happen, but apparently it can.

In addition to refuting a central tenet of *The Bell Curve*, the Miss A experiment answers many of the questions that are still debated by social scientists: Do teachers matter? Can intelligence be raised lastingly? Can schools overcome the disadvantages of class and race? This experiment says yes to all three.

Sadly, the research report (Pedersen, Faucher, & Eaton, 1978) is virtually mute on the subject of how Miss A pulled off this spectacular feat. The report was able to offer only scant clues about the stylistic differences among the three teachers or to the classroom dynamics they created, because the experiment, it turns out, was unplanned and only recognized as an experiment decades after the random assignment was done. Was this a replicable effect of something Miss A did, or some rare alchemy between a charismatic teacher and her students?

THE SOCIAL PSYCHOLOGIST AND THE SCHOOL

Miss A died many years ago, taking with her the secrets of her success and leaving psychologists (see, for example, Judith Rich Harris, 1998/2009) to ponder another Benjamin Franklin mystery: What exactly happened in Miss A's classroom to make her children so smart? It is likely that we will never know. But the good news is that a trail of research findings from psychology and education in the last half-century leads to the conclusion that what happened in Miss A's classroom and in Ben Franklin's school cannot be written off as flukes.

For the past few years I have been sorting through these clues and findings, in addition to doing research of my own, to gain an understanding of how schools and teachers impact their students, and how we might reproduce the wondrous effects produced in those classrooms. Research shows that if certain conditions are met in a classroom, children can become considerably smarter than people would otherwise assume. Conversely, it is clear that maltreatment, neglect, and other social influences can make people measurably dumber (Aronson &

Steele, 2005; Ceci & Williams, 1997; Nisbett, 2009). In other words, like other human traits, human intelligence can be suppressed or enhanced by social-psychological circumstances. The nature of intelligence is that it is both fragile and elastic. It needs to be nurtured or it will be suppressed. If it is nurtured in the right way, it can grow considerably.

A landmark on the path to this understanding occurred in Texas in 1971, in a scene that bears a striking resemblance to Ben Franklin's school visit two centuries earlier. A young scientist named Elliot Aronson was summoned to observe schools near his home, this time by a perplexed former student named Matt Snapp, who was now the assistant superintendent for the Austin schools. Facing a crisis at work, Snapp found his mind drifting back to things he'd learned in Aronson's introductory social psychology course some years before. Aronson was a scientist who took teaching as seriously as laboratory work and publishing, and his courses became so popular that enrollment had to be determined by lottery. His lectures, stirring narratives about human nature, were based on hard science by social psychologists, but they were also infused with the softer side of psychology and the humanities—Sigmund Freud, Abraham Maslow, Edward Albee, Franz Kafka, Kurt Vonnegut, J. D. Salinger, and others—all woven into a passionate case for man's potential for both good and evil. In Aronson's class, students were introduced to the scary things that nice, ordinary people could do to one another under extreme circumstances. He showed a movie in which people delivered (apparently) fatal levels of shock to an innocent-looking man in the Milgram experiment and a nearly unbearable documentary about the horrors of Nazi Germany. There was also a movie in which a social psychologist with a funny beard rounded up nice and normal college students in their neighborhoods and locked them up in a mock prison in the psychology department with other nice and normal students acting as guards. In just a short time spent in this "Stanford Prison Experiment," their behavior degenerated to levels one might expect from real prisoners and real guards.

Yet Aronson argued that the ultimate message of these dark experiments—indeed the big message of social psychology—was an optimistic one. By understanding the power of the situation to corrupt human behavior, one could ultimately use this power for good. Get the situation right and people would treat one another better. (Snapp was hard pressed to remember many data on this second point; social psychologists at the time tended to dwell on the problems—prejudice, conformity, aggression, rationalization, and the like. There was, for example, no "Stanford Charity Experiment" movie to show in class.)

When he called Aronson, Snapp reminded him of his lectures on the power of social psychology for doing good and challenged his former professor to prove it by helping him out. Hell was breaking loose in the Austin schools. He and his colleagues were ordered to carry out the desegregation plan mandated by the Supreme Court in the 1954 *Brown v. Board of Education*, the ruling that declared unconstitutional the practice of separate-but-equal schools for black and minority children. In Austin, as in much of the South, desegregation was not going well. Instead of yielding the hoped-for harmony, softening of racial prejudice, and improved learning and self-regard of minority students, the schools were descending into violence and chaos. Fights were commonplace, often bloody, and once in a while (among the students in junior high and high school) nearly fatal. Among these older students, an atmosphere of danger and apprehension had engulfed the classrooms, the students' attention to learning largely subverted by the more pressing goal of getting safely through the day. The Austin schools thus perfectly exemplified the disappointing results of desegregation efforts across the country (e.g., Gerard, 1983; Gerard & Miller, 1975; Stephan, 1978).

It was not hard to comprehend the problem. Typically two years behind the white students in academic skills, the minority students were plucked from their neighborhoods to attend schools far on the other side of town. Each day they had to wake two hours before the white students to board buses to take them to the comparative splendor of Austin's west side. Sleepy and underprepared, they were dropped into this unfamiliar place to compete with students who were better off, better educated, and better rested, and who considered their new classmates to be—in every respect but physically—inferior. What's more, the predominantly white faculty didn't respect these newcomers either, didn't expect much of them, and didn't really want them there. Faced with this humiliation, many of the minority students disengaged during class; some became quiet and withdrawn, others unruly and loud. Between classes, they would frequently turn the tables—in the corridors, the cafeteria, the restrooms, or on the playgrounds, where street smarts and toughness reigned, and where there was strength in numbers. It was, simply put, a recipe for disaster. The superintendents were no fools: They could see all this. But what could they do about it?

The superintendent canceled school for a cooling off period, and when the schools reopened, Aronson and a group of graduate students came in to observe. The research team fanned out in an elementary school and observed some fifth-grade classrooms, with Aronson's instruction to go in without preconceptions, "like visitors from Mars." What they saw was a troubling mirror image of the environment Ben Franklin had observed 200 years earlier:

> Observing the classrooms, it didn't take long for us to realize that the typical classroom was an intensely competitive, high stakes environment. The children were vying for the respect and even love of their teacher. There were clear winners and losers in these classrooms; there was an uneven playing field, and the black and Latino kids were guaranteed to lose. (E. Aronson, 2008)

Because you are reading this book, you probably know what happened next. Aronson devised an elegant intervention, a method of getting children to stop competing and excluding one another, to cooperate, to like one another, and, in so doing, to unleash the natural capacities of the minority students. The Jigsaw method was born.

JIGSAW

To be sure, Aronson didn't pull Jigsaw out of thin air; it was a deft application of earlier theory, most directly of Gordon Allport's (1954) intergroup contact theory, which proposed the importance of common goals, equal status contact, reduced competition, and sanction from authority as a means of establishing harmony between racial groups. It was also, in a sense, a conceptual replication of the second half of Muzafer Sherif's famous Robbers Cave experiment (Sherif, Harvey, White, Hood, & Sherif, 1961). In that experiment, boys at a summer camp were first divided into two groups, and by way of a series of competitions and conflicts engineered by the experimenters, the groups were set against each other to the point of enmity. Then, in the second half of the experiment, the two groups were led to like one another by having to cooperate to pursue a series of common goals, such as pushing a stalled truck up a hill. Thus, Aronson may not have invented cooperative education (that designation probably belongs to Morton Deutsch), nor did he conduct the most research on its parameters (see Robert Slavin, or Roger and David Johnson). But no one developed a more elegant incarnation of the idea, nor wrote or spoke about it with as much charm and passion. Tom Pettigrew (this volume) says that Aronson is the ultimate Lewinian. Jigsaw perfectly exemplifies this Lewinian spirit and approach, drawing upon Aronson's talents as an experimentalist, his training (at NTL in Bethel, Maine) as a sensitivity group leader, and a certain democracy-makes-the-world-a-better-place optimism manifested in much of Lewin's empirical work (e.g., Lewin,

Lippitt, & White, 1939). Capping a decade of seminal research studies on dissonance and interpersonal attraction, inventing Jigsaw also established Aronson as the consummate experimental social psychologist, a master of both laboratory and field.

In the first Jigsaw experiments, fifth-graders were assigned to five-person groups. Lessons were cut into five discrete pieces, with each student in a group assigned a piece of the lesson to learn and rehearse with the help of students in an "expert group," each of whom had the same piece to learn. After learning this individual lesson, each student would then move to a Jigsaw group, where he or she taught it to the four others, each of whom had a different part of the lesson. For students to have any hope of learning the overall lesson (and thereby scoring well on a test given later), he or she would have to both teach and learn from each of the members in the Jigsaw group. Everyone thus possessed an equally valuable piece of the overall puzzle, and therefore had to be taken seriously, encouraged by the others, and brought into the group as a valued member (E. Aronson, 2002; E. Aronson, Blaney, Sikes, Stephan, & Snapp, 1978).

Once the children adjusted to the novelty of this arrangement, things changed markedly in the Jigsaw classrooms. After a few weeks, prejudice and racial tensions eased, liking between children increased, and the minority students gained self-esteem, liked going to school more, and improved their academic performance. They were measurably smarter. All of the students—white and minority—became more *socially* intelligent as well. For example, as measured by formal tests of perspective taking, the children who had participated in Jigsaw learning groups made significant gains in the ability to drop their own egocentric point of view and see the world through the eyes of others—an ability typically thought to develop on its own through normal maturational processes (Bridgeman, 1981). In short, Jigsaw induced growth in the children's capacities for compassion and empathy, putting them at a level typically observed among older students. Given this bouquet of important effects, it is not surprising that the Jigsaw technique is considered to be among the most elegant, constructive, and important applications of social-psychological theory in the history of the discipline. But it is not simply one of the most important innovations for the reduction of prejudice, which is how it is typically discussed. It is also a landmark piece of research on the production of intelligence, one that answers questions raised by such stories as Franklin's school and Miss A's children: You make children smarter by recognizing and acting on the fact that they are, first and foremost, social animals who need to belong and be respected.

A VIEW FROM THE CONTROL GROUP

When asked to tell their history and that of their mentor—as in a book like this—most psychologists can point to a few big moments when things turned them in a new direction, taught them lasting lessons, forged their character, and so on. Most *wise* psychologists know too much about the foibles of human memory to give much causal weight to these moments. Still, some events are so big, so temporally linked with change that we can be pretty sure they were pivotal. Jigsaw had that kind of effect on both my father and on me.

I admire all of my father's work. Indeed, I cannot remember reading an article of his that isn't interesting; or that doesn't bear his trademark wit and charm; or his uncanny knack for getting an experiment just right, whatever the topic, whatever the methodological challenge. But for me, Jigsaw is on a different plane altogether, something that inspires a sense of reverence. This appreciation clearly arises from my training in developmental and educational psychology, and, in particular, from my interest in social factors that contribute to the achievement gap between minority and white students. Jigsaw drew me to psychology in general and to educational romanticism in particular. My father was never an official mentor; we never did research together. But it's clear to me that I wouldn't have delved into this profession or these particular research topics had I been someone else's son. For one thing, I wouldn't have lived in Austin and attended those troubled schools, and would have missed the opportunity of witnessing the promise of Jigsaw from the vantage point of a student in that environment. I saw firsthand how bad environments can stunt intellectual development and how good environments can nurture it. I remember classmates in school in Austin who were both black and brilliant, but whose brilliance was frequently obscured inside the classroom, stolen from them by the situation of being black in an overtly racist environment.

Of course, a full appreciation of this fact would elude me until adulthood, long after I read *The Social Animal* and *The Jigsaw Classroom*, when I began working with Claude Steele and conducting my own research on "stereotype threat." In 1971, I was just another fifth-grader going to school during the time of the first Jigsaw experiment. Unhappily for me, my schools were not among those participating in the Jigsaw experiments. I was in the control group.

Things began well enough. In fact, in the early grades I was a happy, high-functioning kid. Third grade was the apex. In that year, the Beatles released "Hey, Jude," and one of my fondest memories is of sitting atop my father's shoulders as the entire family and a house full of friends danced and romped around and around the house as the great, long song played over and over. At school, two girls in my class had crushes on me and sent me love notes, my friends were the coolest kids in class, and I was picked early when choosing teams for sports. I was smart, cute, surrounded by friends, and on top of it all, Mrs. Williams, my teacher, loved me. She was the best teacher I would ever have and in her classroom I performed very well. I won the spelling bee three times that year. But then we moved to California for a year and that glorious period ended abruptly.

I will not go into great detail here, but the major events unfolded like this: In my new school my teacher took an instant dislike to me. He didn't like the length of my hair, the clothes I wore, or, it seemed, anything else about me. On the first day of school he publicly humiliated me, mocking my "hippie" appearance and intimating that I deserved physical punishment that he would be only too happy to administer, if only the rules would allow it. My new classmates found this very amusing, laughing openly at me. At the same time, my teacher was openly complimentary to many of the other children, so it was clear to me that he wasn't simply a mean person. He seemed always to be sneering when he spoke to me. It was a tough year academically. Very much like those black and Latino kids in Austin, I would seek to reclaim my pride on the playground by adopting a tough attitude and menacing weaker children.

Returning to Austin for fifth grade, I was placed into the low track, where my new teacher was a towering authoritarian, and my classmates were either stupid, unruly, or both. Within this class, we were assigned (on some unknown basis) to ability groups; mine was called the "Tortoises," the better students the "Hares." My old friends from the third grade were no longer in my life; I'd see them from a distance on the playground but we were like strangers in different worlds. I was with new kids, most of them bad influences. I took up with a dynamic but wild classmate named Michael. One day, to impress me, Michael brought a loaded revolver to school wrapped in a brown paper lunch bag. At lunch, he cocked the gun, still in the bag, and pointed it at the principal, who was sitting at a nearby table. Thank God he wasn't crazy enough to pull the trigger. Later, he and I took the gun to a wooded area near the playground, where the plan was to fire off a few shots, but we were caught on our way and brought to the principal's office. That ended of my friendship with Michael, but it was the beginning of a new identity in school: Teachers never looked at me quite the same. I was pegged as a bad kid.

I don't remember liking school after that. I was frequently absent, either at home with a "stomach ache," or later during junior high and high school, on the streets or in the woods near my home—whatever it took to escape the boredom and psychological discomfort awaiting me in the classroom, and the growing threat of physical danger in the restrooms, the corridors, or the shower room before and after gym class. There was no Jigsaw or anything like it in my schools, and every day I faced the threat of being beaten up. Junior high was the worst; some of the students were three times as big as I was and for the most part, the teachers didn't teach; classes were frequently little more than an extension of the playground, a free-for-all with adult supervision. I would just try to get through the day.

My parents were concerned about me, of course. They could tell I didn't love school, and they knew about most of the big trouble I'd get into. My father knew how bad the schools could be, and he was very attentive to the negative possibilities, and both my parents cared a lot. But the irony is that they didn't know about the countless social-psychological melodramas of which I couldn't or wouldn't speak, the very kinds of difficulties that Jigsaw would have helped. Teachers who didn't teach or who were cold, unsupportive, or abusive; the exclusion by and teasing from peers; the low expectations and boredom: These things frequently go undetected by parents, unless something compels the school to say something. Such are the daily trials that students suffer in silence—and over time, simply take as normal—that erode a child's self-concept, motivation, and intellectual development (see J. Aronson, 2002, for reviews).

In the 10th grade I took a standardized aptitude test, one that purports to measure your abilities and suggests a suitable career path. The report came in an official envelope, professionally scored with analysis of my intellectual worth and career prospects. Two words on the bottom of the page summed up the results of my six years of miseducation: POSTAL WORKER. Needless to say, I never told my parents about the test results. I managed to get into college (no doubt with affirmative action of the son-of-professor variety), and, with the help of inspiring teachers, helpful parents, and peers who cared about learning, was able to do pretty well there. But I don't think I've ever fully shaken that succinct and damning verdict on my intellectual worth, or the aftershocks of going from such a lofty place in third grade to the low status of fourth grade and beyond. At times I still feel like a tortoise. But on balance, I think those experiences have served me well. After all that, who *wouldn't* appreciate the role of social psychology in school achievement?

LETTER FROM A STUDENT

During one of my visits home from college, my father showed me a typewritten letter he had received from a student:

Dear Professor Aronson,

I am a senior at U.T. Today I got a letter admitting me to the Harvard Law School. This may not seem odd to you, but let me tell you something. I am the 6th of 7 children my parents had—and I am the only one who ever went to college, let alone graduate, or go to law school. By now, you are probably wondering why this stranger is writing to you and bragging to you about his achievements. Actually, I'm not a stranger although we never met. You see, last year I was taking a course in social psychology and we were using a book you wrote, *The Social Animal,* and when I read about prejudice and jigsaw it all sounded very familiar—and then, I realized that I was in that very first class you ever did jigsaw in—when I was in the 5th grade. And as I read on, it dawned on me that I was the boy that you called Carlos. And then I remembered you when you first came to our classroom and how I was scared and how I hated school and how I was so stupid and didn't know anything. And you came in—it all came back to me when I read your book—you were very tall—about 6½ feet—and you had a big black beard and you were funny and made us all laugh. And, most important, when we started to do work in jigsaw groups, I began to realize that I wasn't really that stupid. And the kids I thought were cruel and hostile became my friends and the teacher acted friendly and nice to me and I actually began to love school, and I began to love to learn things and now I'm about to go to Harvard Law School. You must get a lot of letters like this but I decided to write anyway because let me tell you something. My mother tells me that when I was born I almost died. I was born at home and the cord was wrapped around my neck and the midwife gave me mouth to mouth and saved my life. If she was still alive, I would write to her too, to tell her that I grew up smart and good and I'm going to law school. But she died a few years ago. I'm writing to you because, no less than her, you saved my life too.

Sincerely, Carlos

The Carlos letter had a big effect on both my father and on me. For him, it was, of course, gratifying to have touched the life of a student in that way and he saw that Jigsaw could have lasting effects. Carlos gave a voice to the data. Thereafter, when he gave lectures about the power of social psychology to improve people's lives, my father didn't have to talk about other people's work, extrapolate from laboratory studies, or speak about hypothetical kids. Here was a real kid whose life had changed, who had made a gains as impressive as any of Miss A's first graders because his classroom was designed according to social-psychological principles.

During this time, my father was working in the sensitivity-training groups, which was also revealing the transformative power of group work. These influences, in addition to the ethos of applied psychology at Santa Cruz, changed his orientation to psychology by giving him a close-up view of its real-world possibilities. I don't think he was ever the same. His work was no longer conducted primarily in the laboratory. He continued to test theory, such as in his research on hypocrisy, which clarified the necessary conditions for dissonance induction. But, after Carlos, his work was increasingly conducted in the context of encouraging adaptive behavior, such as conserving water during a drought (e.g., Thibodeau & Aronson, 1992) or encouraging condom use during an AIDS epidemic (Stone, Aronson, Crain, Winslow, & Fried, 1994). Carlos helped cement my father's orientation toward doing good by doing good research.

As for me, I had mixed feelings after reading that letter. First, I felt that conducting important applied research is among the noblest and most spiritually rewarding of professions. I still feel that way. I also felt incredibly proud of my father and his work. I still feel that way, too. But I must confess to a third feeling: I was jealous of Carlos. Where was Jigsaw when *I* needed it?

REAL EDUCATION?

Research on the achievement gap between minorities and whites lies at the crossroads of sociology, economics, education, and public policy, and several branches of psychology. As such, there is a surplus of opinion about the roots of school success. Some say high achievement requires good teachers, others emphasize economic stability, others focus on good parenting, still others say you need a combination of these things. Given the vast mosaic of findings on the topic and the primarily correlational nature of much of the research, people can find ample support for whichever theory they like. I've found no better Rorschach for political and racial attitudes than the evidence on group differences in intelligence or achievement. Charles Murray believes that school and life success are determined primarily by how much intelligence you have, which is largely a function of how much you inherit from your parents. Malcolm Gladwell (2007) calls this "IQ fundamentalism." From this perspective you can take a smart kid, put him into horrible circumstances, and it will make little difference to how he turns out. By the same token, no amount of intervention can really raise people's intelligence to any significant degree. Thus, social policies that seek to level the playing field—by redistributing wealth, or by providing high quality teachers, nurturing environments, and so on—will mostly succeed in wasting time and money, because intelligence is impervious to circumstance; those who have it will succeed and those without it will fail, no matter what.

If Murray ever read about Jigsaw or Miss A, he either forgot or simply ignored the obvious implications. He has sent forth a stream of op-ed pieces and a book (Murray, 2006, 2008a, 2008b), all arguing that too many people are going to college who really don't belong there. Too dumb to capitalize on higher learning, they lower the standards and spoil the educational environment for the intellectually elite. There is surely some wisdom in this argument, particularly if we can return to a time when there was no shame—and decent pay—attached to work that does not require a college degree. And anyone who has ever taught a college course comprising students who range widely in sophistication or motivation can surely sympathize with the argument that not everyone is college material. But here's the rub: How are we to determine who will benefit from college? Give children an aptitude test? Find out early how smart your students are and usher them toward the appropriate station—college for the smart, trade school for the below average? This is the system one would have to adopt to create the system Murray envisions.

And given what we know about schooling and IQ, it sends a cold shiver down my spine to even contemplate it. After all, such a scheme would have consigned me to a future of sorting letters and fantasizing about gunning down coworkers. I'm quite sure academia could have borne losing me. But what about Robert Sternberg? As a child, the noted psychologist and intelligence expert couldn't pass a bubble test and felt like a dummy. But he got lucky; with the help of a compassionate teacher who believed in him, he went on to a brilliant career, publishing more papers and books than anyone else I have met. And what of Neil de Grasse Tyson, the brilliant and beloved astrophysicist who directs the Hayden Planetarium? With barely average SATs and no encouragement from teachers, he got to college on a basketball scholarship and there discovered astronomy. So many great minds elude early detection by tests and teachers, and these would be wasted under Murray's plan. Yet George W. Bush would still been guaranteed a place at Yale and

Harvard under this arrangement (he had very respectable SAT scores and impeccable connections). One need only look at a scatterplot of any aptitude test predicting academic or life success to appreciate how frequently and far individual cases fall off the diagonal. IQ may be one of the best predictors of life success, but it doesn't predict terribly well.

To be sure, aptitude tests have their place. Had only school grades been considered, my father would not have been admitted to college and you'd be reading a different book. The SAT served its intended purpose beautifully; it identified him as the brilliant, if undermotivated, diamond in the rough that he was, a smart kid stuck in a bad circumstance of a lousy, uninspiring school, with uneducated parents who didn't push him to excellence or bring books into the house, and peers who were not intellectually engaged. For students like my father the standardized test can be a lifeline. But for untold numbers of individuals the "real education" plan Murray advocates would be a disaster. And many of the losers would be minority students, like Carlos or Miss A's low-income students, who tend not to test well.

PREJUDICE, SOCIAL EXCLUSION, STEREOTYPE THREAT, AND THE FRAGILITY OF INTELLIGENCE

Why such students fail has been a central interest in my own research for the past 15 years. The field has unearthed a great deal of evidence to suggest that minority students' intellectual performances, even in the modern era, manifest some of the same dynamics on display in Franklin's Philadelphia, interracial dynamics strong enough to suppress intelligence. Slavery's "galling chains" may be long gone, but in their place are more subtle and nuanced forms of constraint, what Gustav Ichheiser (1949) called the "invisible jails" that surround people, which was his way of describing the power of the situation. Two situations in particular fit this invisible jail description and have been implicated in the low test scores and school achievement of black and Latino students, who typically score a full standard deviation below their white counterparts—social exclusion and stereotyping. Being looked down upon or excluded by peers and adults exacts a toll on cognitive and emotional functioning. This has been demonstrated in a number of experiments over the years.

Although never written up formally, the classroom experiments conducted by the Iowa teacher Jane Elliott in 1968 captures how easy it is to make students mean and stupid, how little it takes to simulate the conditions of the Jim Crow South or Benjamin Franklin's Philadelphia.

Bothered by her white third graders' prejudice toward black children (revealed by their apathy following the assassination of Martin Luther King, Jr.), Elliott devised an experiment designed to teach her class what it felt like to be Negro. She divided her class into two groups determined by eye color, informing them that the blue-eyed children were superior to their brown-eyed classmates. She made the brown-eyed children wear a special collar designating inferiority and denied them privileges she publicly extended to the blue-eyed children, such as drinking from the water fountain, getting seconds at lunch, and extra time at recess. She explicitly told the students that science had indicated that brown eyed-students were not as smart as blue-eyed children, and she openly praised the blue-eyed children for their intelligence and hard work. In very short order, a dramatic change in classroom dynamics occurred: "I watched what had been marvelous, thoughtful, cooperative children turn into nasty, vicious, discriminating little third graders—in the space of 15 minutes" (Peters & Cobb, 1985).

Because Elliott wanted her students to experience both inferiority and superiority, she then reversed the roles, telling the children that she had lied about which group of kids was superior. This allowed her not only to give all her children the full experience of prejudice, but also to give intelligence tests to the same children under different psychological circumstances. And from this informal experiment, a telling finding emerged: When the children were given the test but thought they belonged to the inferior group, they took five and a half minutes to correctly work through a set of flash cards. The next day, after being informed that they actually belonged to the "superior group," they took 3 minutes less to complete the same task. The only thing that had changed (other than the specific items on the test) was their artificially induced stigmatized status. In other words, Jane Elliott had effectively created a measurable achievement gap merely by decreeing one. Over many years of repeating her experiment, Elliott has found consistently that the students' test scores would go up on days when they were assigned to the superior group and down when assigned to the inferior group (Peters, 1986). Overt prejudice can make you stupid.

In a similar but more subtle vein, Claude Steele and I (Steele & Aronson, 1995) found we could enable African–American college students to perform significantly better on difficult standardized tests by convincing them that we were not interested in measuring their intelligence. We reasoned that performing tests of ability makes African Americans apprehensive about confirming the widely known and accepted stereotypes about their intellectual inferiority, an apprehension that can interfere with their ability to think clearly and calmly during a test. We called the apprehension "stereotype threat" and argued that it plays a role in the longstanding underperformance of certain groups in society. Over 300 subsequent experiments have confirmed what we found; individuals targeted by such stereotypes perform worse in situations that make those stereotypes salient or when nothing is done to counter assumptions about their inferiority. These experiments corroborate earlier experiments by psychologists like Irwin Katz (e.g., 1964) and Edward Zigler (e.g., Zigler & Butterfield, 1968), who found that minority test takers were very sensitive to the psychological conditions of testing. Zigler and Earl Butterfield (1968) showed, for example, that children in Head Start classes obtained remarkably higher IQ test scores if they could simply spend a few minutes playing a game with a man in a white lab coat before being tested by a different man in a white lab coat. The play session seemed to reduce their apprehensions about having their intelligence probed by a stranger.

Roy Baumeister and his colleagues (Baumeister, Twenge, & Nuss, 2002) have added importantly to this literature, showing that when students are led to believe that they will be socially excluded, they perform significantly worse than control test-takers on an IQ-like test of reasoning. These studies show that intellectual test scores are surprisingly fragile and malleable, that, in a sense, mental tests measure not only the grey matter in a student's head, but also the quality of the environment in which the test is taken.

My independent work in this area was much influenced by two lines of my father's work—his success in boosting the achievement of minority students with Jigsaw, and his success in changing people's attitudes and behavior by getting them to make public statements advocating a particular point of view. This work also drew upon Carol Dweck's (e.g., 1999) studies on individual differences in theories of intelligence and their effects on achievement. Dweck finds that students who believe that intelligence is something that can grow respond better to task difficulty and failure than do students who believe that intelligence is finite and fixed. My reasoning was straightforward: If minority students are troubled by the cultural expectations that they are unintelligent, changing what they think about intelligence should help make these expectations less unnerving. So, in a series of experiments ranging from one-shot lab studies (J. Aronson & Good, 2009; J. Aronson, McGlone, & Doyle, 2009) to long-term randomized field interventions (e.g., J. Aronson, Fried, & Good, 2002; Good, Aronson, & Inzlicht, 2003), we have found that convincing students that they can "grow" their intelligence—by getting them to preach to others about the malleability of intelligence— has all kinds of positive effects. For example, when we place them under evaluative scrutiny (a standard stereotype-threatening situation), they perform better than students who are under no threat at all. In essence, by changing their conception of intelligence, we have helped students transform a debilitating threat into an energizing challenge. In our field studies, this intervention produced large positive gains on seventh-grade exit exams, greatly boosting the reading scores of Latinos, and eliminating the gender gap on the math exam. At the college level, we found a substantial reduction in the black–white gap in college GPA, along with significant gains in the degree to which black students reported enjoyment of and psychological investment in academics.

Other researchers have conducted similarly effective interventions that improve learning and performance by affirming students' self-worth (Cohen, Garcia, Apfel, & Master, 2006) or by creating a sense of belonging among students (Walton & Cohen, 2007). Anyone familiar with Jigsaw would recognize that the reasoning underlying these interventions was prefigured by my father's work, in which the goals were to offer children a means of reducing prejudice and increasing inclusion and self-worth. These subsequent lines of research owe an enormous debt to Jigsaw. Whether we recognized or acknowledged it at a conscious level, Jigsaw's success imbued our efforts with the faith that, under the proper conditions, the achievement of the stigmatized, the excluded, and the maltreated can improve significantly. Aronson's first law about the power of the situation—*people who do crazy things aren't necessarily crazy*—applies beautifully to the classroom: People who look stupid are not necessarily stupid. They might just be in a situation that is suppressing their intelligence.

UNFINISHED BUSINESS

When, on the many occasions that I screwed up in life—failed a class, left some project unfinished, or in some way fell short of achieving important goals—my father, by way of scolding, would slip into his mother's Boston-Yiddish accent and say something like, "You futz around and you futz around, and the next thing you know everything's a mess." Often he'd be joking, speaking through his mother to let me know he had endured similar reprimands as a child, that he saw the humor in life repeating itself across generations. To futz around is to be unserious about one's goals, to waste time, to learn nothing from mistakes. It's an apt word to describe how America faces its educational problems. I read countless well-intentioned books and articles about the achievement gap, each one speculating about why it occurs and partitioning the blame among such factors as parents, the media culture, schools, economic inequality, and so on, and then offering solutions based on these analyses. Most of these discussions recognize the enormous moral and economic imperatives involved, how finding a way to effectively educate black and Latino children and keep them in school would save taxpayers billions of dollars on prisons, for example, and elevate our culture in the process. But when it comes to solutions, we tend to bicker about what matters and what works—and then we futz around with ill-considered solutions. Research suggests, for example, that No Child Left Behind has frequently exacerbated the learning problems many schools face; the higher-scores-or-else approach often backfires (see Darling-Hammond, 2007, for a review). One recent study, for example, found that making a proficiency exam mandatory for graduation significantly reduced the number of high school students who received a diploma, an effect the authors attributed to stereotype threat (Reardon, Atteberry, Arshan, & Kurlander, 2009). By attaching high stakes to the exam, significantly fewer minority students passed the same exam (and fewer girls passed the math sections) than had passed it for the previous two years, when it was simply used to gauge their progress. Another depressing trend tied to the high-stakes testing environment is the voluntary self-segregation occurring as people come to the conclusion that integration and diversity, although perhaps good for something, are not so good for achievement (e.g., Sunderman, Kim, & Orfield, 2005).

Worst of all, some hold up the failure of No Child Left Behind as a trophy for IQ fundamentalism, for the *Bell Curve* doctrine that says nothing can be done about educational inequality since we cannot make people smarter, more curious, or more academically motivated. I told you so, says Charles Murray, pointing to No Child Left Behind's failure as proof that nothing can work and that to believe we can close the achievement gap is to be out of touch, deluded by wishful thinking and educational romanticism (Murray, 2008a). This position is, of course, a non sequitur; the failure of any specific policy hardly forces the conclusion that *no* policy will work.

There's an annoying commonality to such pessimistic discussions, one that I feel acutely: No mention of Jigsaw or of cooperative education is to be found in them. And yet the Jigsaw classroom studies and much of the research that followed in its wake show consistently a significant narrowing of the minority white gap. Indeed, Robert Slavin and Eileen Oickle (1981) report a nearly complete elimination of the black–white gap in reading in a large experiment employing cooperative techniques similar to Jigsaw with black and white middle school students, an effect attributable to massive gains made by the black students. The belief that it is possible to eliminate the achievement gap flows not from romanticism, but from hard data showing the gap can be narrowed. But to believe we can succeed by continuing to use more testing, more pressure, more accountability—or any other "common sense" approach conceived in ignorance of the lessons of social psychology—is beyond romantic. It's major-league futzing around. And it is toxic to the learning process.

Things may be changing for the better. One unexpected but positive aspect of our work on stereotype threat is that we lucked into impeccable timing; we published our work right in the immediate aftermath of the publication of *The Bell Curve*, amid national discussions of affirmative action and the meaning of standardized tests and merit. The research, therefore, garnered enough attention to win us a pulpit from which to inject social-psychological ideas into the national debate on the achievement gap and affirmative action. For example, stereotype threat is cited extensively in two Supreme Court cases. Still, we have a long way to go until social psychologists are taken as seriously as economists where education is concerned. This is odd, given that beyond creating the occasional program that pays children for doing their homework, economists have been more effective at modeling the causes of the achievement gap than addressing it. Nevertheless, social psychology is getting a seat at the table and is beginning to be recognized for the powerful tool that it is, and no one has developed a more reliable tool than Jigsaw for improving educational practice. The key will be getting people to use it. I would estimate from my frequent surveys with schools that true cooperative education, á la Jigsaw, is used in 5% of American classrooms. There's much work to be done.

WHAT MURRAY MISSED

A trail of clues, including both a school for Negroes in pre-Revolutionary Philadelphia and data collected in the past few months, tells me that our traditional conception of intelligence is wrong. It is not the stable thing-in-the head that we've thought it was. Rather, like many human traits, intelligence can be thought of as an interaction between person and situation, its expression a function of the circumstances we face and the nature of our relationships. As such, it is more fragile and malleable than we tend to think. Intelligence can be distracted, suppressed, and stunted by troubled relationships and difficult circumstances. But when nurtured by positive social conditions people get smarter. This is the message of the research I've discussed in this chapter. Of the many studies that underscore this message, Jigsaw stands alone in elegantly capturing both the nature of intelligence and a key to its effective nurture. If one wants to fight the doctrine of *The Bell Curve*, or any doctrine that denies the power of the situation in shaping human accomplishment, few arguments are quite as compelling as the Jigsaw experiments and the literature on cooperation that followed in its wake (Nisbett, 2009).

Charles Murray is right about many things. He is probably right that the quality of schooling within the typical range of schools does not have much effect on student achievement. He is clearly right that policies like No Child Left Behind are wrongheaded and are doomed to failure. But he misses the point when he concludes from this pair of facts that children cannot become smarter after they enter school and that we do not know how to make them smarter. Ben Franklin's school for Negroes and Miss A's first-grade classroom proved that under extraordinary circumstances, intelligence can both manifest and grow. Yet neither Franklin, the great scientist, nor Miss A, the great teacher, left behind instructions for recreating those circumstances. It took an educational crisis and someone as gifted in both science and teaching as my father to devise a solution. In the process he produced a blueprint that any school or teacher can use to build a culture in which students get along, appreciate one another, and fulfill their intellectual promise—a system, in other words, for making extraordinary circumstances ordinary.

CODA

J. D. Salinger's *Seymour: An Introduction* was my father's favorite book during much of my childhood, something of a spiritual and creative muse in his life. It was a book that I now realize was tailor-made for him. The narrator, Buddy Glass, is a college professor and writer, reflecting on the life of Seymour, his older, smarter, brother who died young, much like my father's older (and supposedly smarter) brother who died just after I was born, when my father was an assistant professor at Harvard. In the great novella there were meditations on writing well ("remember that before you were a writer you were a reader") and living well ("all we do our whole lives is go from one piece of holy ground to the next"). Dad introduced *Seymour* to tens of thousands of students during his 40-some-year career teaching introductory social psychology, and I'm certain many of his students adopted it as their favorite novel.

In my favorite passage of the book, Buddy recalls a scene in which his father wants to know if Seymour remembers an experience he had at age 5 when Seymour was seated upon the handlebars of a shiny trick bicycle peddled by a famous vaudevillian performer named Joe Jackson. Jackson peddled the bicycle around and around in circles all over a playhouse stage. Seymour thinks for a moment and tells his father that "he wasn't sure if he'd ever got off Joe Jackson's beautiful bicycle." It's a perfect metaphor for Seymour's life and perfectly captures how I feel about my father's influence upon me, upon the work that I do—and how I became, and remain, an educational romantic. Despite everything that that ever happened to me in school, despite all the bad news in the world generally and in the world of education specifically, I have the distinct feeling of never having got down off those shoulders, going around and around our big house in Austin, dancing to the tune of "Hey, Jude," secure in the conviction that however sad the song, the day, or the world, all of it can be made better. As I reflect on the influence my father has had on the fields of psychology and education, I'm certain I'm not alone in feeling this way.

REFERENCES

Allport, G. W. (1954). *The nature of prejudice*. Reading, MA: Addison-Wesley.

Aronson, E. (2008). *The social animal*. New York: Worth Publishers. (Original work published 1972)

Aronson, E. (2002). Building empathy, compassion, and achievement in the jigsaw classroom. In J. Aronson (Ed.), *Improving academic achievement: Impact of psychological factors on education* (pp. 209–225). San Diego, CA: Academic Press.

Aronson, E., Blaney, N., Sikes, J., Stephan, G., & Snapp, M. (1975, July). The jigsaw route to learning and liking. *Psychology Today, 43*–59.

Aronson, E., Blaney, N., Sikes, J., Stephan, G., & Snapp, M. (1978). *The jigsaw classroom*. Beverly Hills, CA: Sage.

Aronson, J. (2002). *Improving academic achievement: Impact of psychological factors on education*. San Diego, CA: Academic Press.

Aronson, J., Fried, C., & Good, C. (2002). Reducing the effects of stereotype threat on African American college students by shaping theories of intelligence. *Journal of Experimental Social Psychology, 38*, 113–125.

Aronson, J., & Good, C. (2009). *Conceptions of ability, challenge seeking, and test performance in minority children*. Manuscript submitted for publication.

Aronson, J., McGlone, M. & Doyle, L. H. (2009). *Conceptions of ability influence standardized test scores*. Manuscript submitted for publication.

Aronson, J., & Steele, C. M. (2005). Stereotypes and the fragility of human competence, motivation, and self-concept. In C. Dweck & E. Elliot (Eds.), *Handbook of competence and motivation*. New York: Guilford Press.

Baumeister, R. F., Twenge, J. W., & Nuss, C. K. (2002). Effects of social exclusion on cognitive processes: Anticipated aloneness reduces intelligent thought. *Journal of Personality and Social Psychology, 83*, 817–827.

Bridgeman, D. (1981). Enhanced role-taking through cooperative interdependence: A field study. *Child Development, 52*, 1231–1238.

Ceci, S., & Williams, W. (1997). Schooling, intelligence, and income. *American Psychologist, 52*(10), 1051–1058.

Cohen, G. L., Garcia, J., Apfel, N., & Master, A. (2006). Reducing the racial achievement gap: A social-psychological intervention. *Science, 313*, 1307–1310.

Darling-Hammond, L. (2007, September 10). *Testimony before the House Education and Labor Committee on the Re-Authorization of No Child Left Behind*. Washington, DC.

Dweck, C. (1999). *Self-theories*. New York: Psychology Press.

Franklin, B. (1763). Letter to Reverend John Waring.

Gerard, H., B. (1983). School desegregation: The social science role. *American Psychologist, 38*, 869–877.

Gerard, H. B., & Miller, N. (1975). *School desegregation: A long-term study*. New York: Plenum Press.

Gladwell, M. (2007, December 17). None of the above: What I.Q. doesn't tell you about race. *The New Yorker*, 92–96.

Good, C., Aronson, J., & Inzlicht, M. (2003). Improving adolescents' standardized test performance: An intervention to reduce the effects of stereotype threat. *Journal of Applied Developmental Psychology, 24*, 645–662.

Gould, S. J. (1996). *The mismeasure of man*. New York: Norton.

Harris, J. R. (2009). *The nurture assumption: Why children turn out the way they do* (2nd ed.). New York: The Free Press. (Original work published 1998.)

Herrnstein, R. J., & Murray, C. (1994). *The bell curve: Intelligence and class structure in American life*. New York: Free Press.

Ichheiser, G. (1949). Misunderstandings in human relations: A study in false social perception [Supplement]. *American Journal of Sociology, 55*(2).

Katz, I. (1964). Review of evidence relating to effects of desegregation on the intellectual performance of Negroes. *American Psychologist, 19*, 381–399.

Lewin, K., Lippitt, R., & White, R. K. (1939). Patterns of aggressive behavior in experimentally created "social climates." *Journal of Social Psychology, 10*, 271–299.

Murray, C. (2006). Acid tests: No Child Left Behind is beyond uninformative. It is deceptive. *Wall Street Journal*, July 25.

Murray, C. (2008a, May). The age of educational romanticism. *The New Criterion, 26*(9), 35–42.

Murray, C. (2008b). *Real education*. New York: Crown Forum.

Nisbett, R. (2009). *Intelligence and how to get it: Why schools and cultures count*. New York: Norton.

Pedersen, E., Faucher, T. A., & Eaton, W. W. (1978). A new perspective on the effects of first-grade teachers on children's subsequent adult status. *Harvard Educational Review, 48*, 1–31.

Peters, W. (1986). *A class divided, then and now*. New Haven, CT: Yale University Press.

Peters, W. (Producer & Writer) & Cobb, C. (Writer). (1985). A class divided [Television series episode]. In D. Fanning (Executive producer), *Frontline*. Boston: WGBH Educational Foundation.

Reardon, S. F., Atteberry, A., Arshan, N., & Kurlander, M. (2009, April). Effects of the California high school exit exam on student persistence, achievement, and graduation. Paper presented at the American Educational Research Association, San Diego, CA.

Sherif, M., Harvey, O. J., White, J., Hood, W., & Sherif, C. W. (1961). *Intergroup conflict and cooperation: The robbers cave experiment.* Norman, OK: University Book Exchange.

Slavin, R., & Oickle, E. (1981). Effects of cooperative learning teams on student achievement and race relations: Treatment by race interactions. *Sociology of Education, 54,* 174–180.

Steele, C. M., & Aronson, E. (1995). Stereotype threat and the intellectual test performance of African Americans. *Journal of Personality and Social Psychology, 69,* 797–811.

Stephan, W. G. (1978). School desegregation: An evaluation of predictions made in *Brown v. Board of Education. Psychological Bulletin, 85,* 217–238.

Stone, J., Aronson, E., Crain, A. L., Winslow, M. P., & Fried, C. B. (1994). Inducing hypocrisy as a means of encouraging young adults to use condoms. *Personality and Social Psychology Bulletin, 20,* 116–128.

Sunderman, G., Kim, S., & Orfield, G. (2005). *NCLB meets school realities.* Thousand Oaks, CA: Corwin Press.

Thibodeau, R., & Aronson, E. (1992). Taking a closer look: Reasserting the role of the self-concept in dissonance theory. *Personality and Social Psychology Bulletin, 18,* 591–602.

Walton, G. M., & Cohen, G. L. (2007). A question of belonging: Race, social fit, and achievement. *Journal of Personality and Social Psychology, 92,* 82–96.

Zigler, E., & Butterfield, E.C. (1968). Motivational aspects of changes in IQ test performance of culturally deprived nursery school children. *Child Development, 39*(1), 1–14.

IV
Writing and Teaching

15

WRITING ABOUT PSYCHOLOGICAL SCIENCE

Carol Tavris

My comments in honor of Elliot's life work will be a departure from the usual papers in Festschrift collections because he didn't influence my choice of career, didn't teach me how to write, wasn't my earliest mentor, didn't instruct me in experimental design, and wasn't a colleague until we started working together a few years ago for our trade book, *Mistakes Were Made (But Not by Me)*. Therefore, I will be commenting from the standpoint of a professional writer about the significance of Elliot's writing about his profession.

I first met Elliot in 1970, when I was a graduate student in social psychology at the University of Michigan and an associate editor at a young magazine called *Psychology Today*. Our job was to take articles written by psychologists about their research and to translate them into English. This procedure often threw our authors into a state of dissonance: They loved having an article about their work that they could show their mothers, but they were also faintly embarrassed to have their ideas presented with full frontal nudity, as it were—with no cloak of jargon. To give you an idea of what we were up against, editing wise, I rummaged through my old *Psychology Today* jargon file. It contains a long list of the kind of academic writing we used to find in submitted manuscripts:

- A famous psychologist proposed writing an article for us on "sadists who enjoy torture" (as opposed, presumably, to sadists who don't), and assured us that his writing would be free of

"unnecessary redundancies" (as opposed, presumably, to the necessary ones).
- A behavioral psychologist explained that "the stimulus determinants of anxiety and phobic states are not necessarily confined to internal visceral of external cues. In addition self-generated symbolic stimuli, particularly self-verbalizations, can readily mediate sustained emotional arousal and avoidance behavior."
- A social psychologist wrote: "It is important to note that what has been examined in this paper is direct verbal communication about sex between mothers and daughters." "Direct verbal communication" is, presumably, talk, but is their talk about sex or about sex between mothers and daughters?
- A developmental psychologist reported: "The results indicate that an inanimate object of high cue weight, that is, one whose salient characteristics (e.g., tactual properties) have entered into a supportive relationship with an organism's ongoing behaviors, may aid in familiarizing a child to a novel situation as effectively as does a highly prominent, human social object." Translation: Security blankets help toddlers adjust to a scary new schoolroom as effectively as Mom (the "highly prominent, human social object") does.
- And a feminist gender scholar, freely abandoning the need for a subject in her sentence, wrote: "Whether abandoning the study of bodily pleasures to explore the symbolic reign of the fraudulent phallus or, distancing itself from polymorphous perversity for conventional narratives of the gender-differentiating effects of maternal attachments, the potential challenge of the infinite waywardness of infantile sexuality persisting to undermine, or at least trouble, the acquisition of sexual and gender normativity is cast aside even within many feminist versions of psychoanalysis, in both clinical and theoretical settings."

So there we were, getting articles with language like that, when we commissioned an article from this famous guy, Elliot Aronson. We thought we would get the usual kind of writing, especially once he told us his work at the time was on "interpersonal attraction." We explained to him about the unnecessary redundancy: Attraction *is* interpersonal, unless you are a narcissist whose main attraction is to yourself (which would be a case of *intra*personal attraction), or a fetishist who is sexually attracted to train sets or leg casts (a case, I suppose, of *inter-impersonal* attraction). But Elliot sent in an article that was readable and charming, and we titled it "Who Likes Whom—and Why." This change was the major editorial influence we had on Elliot, but he was a quick learner. Two years later, in 1972, the first edition of *The Social Animal* had a chapter called "Attraction: Why People Like Each Other." That's better than *Psychology Today's* title.

The problem of jargon is hardly unfamiliar to anyone in academia. Yet how did it happen that Elliot doesn't write that way, never has written that way, and gets away with not writing that way?

Decades ago, Gregory Kimble wrote an essay, unfortunately never published, called "Giving Psychology Away: The Challenge of Writing for the Public." He listed the differences between writing articles that have scholarly substance and those that have audience appeal:

Scholarly Substance	Audience Appeal
Scientific values	Humanistic values
Established fact	Newsworthiness
Credibility	Sensationalism
Intellectual value	Entertainment value
Heavy reading	Light reading
Seriousness	Humor
Research	Real life
Laboratory	Field/clinic
Behavioral regularity	Behavioral uniqueness
Normal behavior	Abnormal behavior
Impersonal data	Personal experience
Numbers, graphs, tables	Examples, anecdotes
Theory	Application
Explanation	Description
Complex causality	Simple explanation
Caution	Conclusions

When academics attempt to cross from the scholarly to the popular side, they often jettison their data as they jump. Many psychologists would submit an article to *Psychology Today* in what they thought was *Psychology Today* style, meaning that it had personal opinion, anecdotes about their cat, and no research. The result often fell smack between Kimble's two columns: Their paper lacked information, and it lacked style and appeal. Our articles—at least in those early years, when the magazine was what Elliot calls "Psychology Today Yesterday"—had the data, sometimes even reanalyzed and corrected by our methodical fact checker.

In contrast, as you look at these lists, notice how easily, seamlessly, Elliot's writing flows between them. "Scientific" versus "humanistic" values? In Elliot's world, these are not in competition. "Impersonal data, numbers and graphs" versus "personal experience and anecdotes"? Anyone who has read *The Social Animal*—or virtually anything else that Elliot has ever written, including his journal articles—knows how Elliot blurred that distinction. "The laboratory" versus "the field"? Elliot has excelled in both. "Research" versus "real life"? Visit any Jigsaw Classroom. "Seriousness" versus "humor"? Elliot has always understood that you can be funny and serious at the same time. Indeed, humor allows us to survive tragedy; and in writing and teaching, it defuses the tension produced by emotionally laden topics. "Heavy reading" versus "light reading"? Elliot takes heavy subjects—racism, aggression, conformity, war—and makes them bearable enough for readers to understand and, more important, to carry that understanding with them.

Of course, it is not the job of scientists to write for popular audiences, any more than it is the job of a novelist to conduct a great laboratory experiment. It is easy to make fun of jargon. Every occupation has its jargon, the purpose of which is to unify its members against the untrained multitudes who are not one of them; it identifies "us." Moreover, it is appropriate for scientists to avoid oversimplification and to use technical terms when there are no accurate equivalents. The appropriate use of professional language depends on finding the right balance between the complexity and usefulness of the scholarly term and the sophistication of the audience. Sometimes the term is indispensable and easy to grasp: *self-fulfilling prophecy* means just what it says. Sometimes the term is unnecessary for general audiences: In *Nobody Left to Hate,* a book for a mass audience about the psychology behind the tragic events of the murders at Columbine High School, Elliot wrote an entire chapter on attribution theory without using the word *attribution*. But in *Mistakes Were Made (But Not by Me),* a book for an audience that would want the science and theory behind our assertions, we introduced the term *cognitive dissonance* as the mechanism that would explain self-justification.

One way that Elliot bridges the two styles of writing is through the art of storytelling (a skill that pervades his teaching as well as writing, as Marti Hope Gonzales describes in her chapter for this volume). Students think a "story" means fiction, as in the child's "tell me a story." Elliot's stories emerge from life. He is the only Jewish man I know who rarely tells jokes, but who often tells stories—funny, touching, tender, wry, or sorrowful. He does not use them, as an amateur or nonscientist might, to make his argument but rather to illuminate his argument, so that the theory, the science, become memorable and alive. "What I mean by storytelling," he once said in a lecture, "is the illustration of a complex abstract idea with a vivid, powerful story, preferably a story that has some meaning for the students in the class. The story must grab their attention and keep them from going to sleep, but it needs to be much more than that. It needs to tie into the basic data of the course in such a way that it enhances the data; it makes the data understandable; it underscores the importance of the data; and it renders the data memorable."

One of my favorite examples of how Elliot does this opens the chapter on aggression in *The Social Animal*, in which he told of watching the evening news as Walter Cronkite described how American planes had dropped napalm on a Vietnamese village. Elliot's 10-year-old son asked him what napalm was:

> "Oh," I answered casually, "as I understand it, it's a chemical that both sticks and burns, so that if it gets on a person's skin, he can't remove it, and it burns him pretty badly." And I continued to watch the news. A few minutes later, I happened to glance across at my son and saw tears streaming down his face. Looking at my son, I became dismayed and upset as I began to think about what had happened to me. Had I become so brutalized that I could answer such a question so matter-of-factly—as if my son had asked me how a baseball is made or how a leaf functions? (Aronson, 2004, p. 201)

There you have it, as Elliot would say: the "vivid, powerful" story, one introducing a chapter that will answer the question he initially raised. But Elliot would be the first to add that one crucial difference always exists between an anecdote and the data: The data are sacrosanct. You don't get to smooth out the numbers to make them sound better or more persuasive. But you *are* allowed to shape a story and smooth its edges, if that better illuminates the data. You don't get to change the guts or essence of the story, but you are allowed to potchky the details. If your story doesn't clarify the research you are trying to present, it will just float there on its own; although readers (or listeners) might remember the story, they probably won't remember much about why you told it.

For example, in the list of jargony quotes at the beginning of this essay, I cheated, slightly, to enhance my story. That final example about the "fraudulent phallus," while an exact quote, was not from my *Psychology Today* folder of the early years, it was from a book written 20 years later. But for me to add that detail about the origin of the quotation would have interrupted the flow of examples, and it is an unnecessary detail. The quote is a luscious example of terrible writing, and it supports my point about how jargon muddles thinking—and how muddled thinking creates jargon.

At the annual meeting of the Association for Psychological Science in 2007, when Elliot was given the William James Award, Josh Aronson and I interviewed him the next afternoon for his award address. I asked him a question that has long been of interest to me: "Did you value good writing about psychological research because you can write well, or did you learn to write well because you value the ability to communicate psychological research?" And he said, "The chicken." Over the years many academics have asked me how to write for that amorphous beast, "the public." And the answer I would give them today is: the chicken. Not everyone can write about psychological science like Elliot Aronson, but everyone can learn to be a better writer. The first step is to take the advice that Elliot gave himself when he was starting out: Don't write in a way you wouldn't want to read. As he said to me recently, "Where is it written that a journal article cannot start the same way a popular article does: What is the problem, why is the problem important, why am I personally so passionate about it, and why should you care?" Instead, most journal articles and scholarly books start with a review of the topic going back to Aristotle. I did this myself in my first general-interest book, on anger, when I began chapter 1 with a review of the problem going back to Aristotle. My editor read it and said: "Quit the damn throat-clearing, and get on with the story." He was right. The history, by the way, is in the book, just not in the first chapter.

There is an implicit assumption at the core of much scholarly writing: namely, that you can't be comprehensive, cautious, and scientific, and *also* lucid and literate, let alone witty. Elliot has always boldly ignored that assumption. In "Writing It Up," the final chapter of *Methods of Research in Social Psychology* (Aronson, Ellsworth, Carlsmith, & Gonzales, 1990), Elliot and his coauthors observe that "a good proportion of the most memorable articles in social psychology, and in psychology in general, are beautifully written. This is no coincidence. In social psychology, the data rarely 'speak for themselves'; someone must speak for them. If the author is unwilling to take the trouble to explain why the research is interesting, it is highly unlikely that the reader will do so" (p. 329). Their chapter went on to exhort psychologists to write succinctly, to avoid jargon and all those "research has showns," and to get on with the story of the study.

Elliot is like a naïve artist, a Grandpa Moses of writing, because he never had the high school composition teachers that many professional writers and editors had, the teachers he calls the "Miss Grundys" or, in my case, the Miss Kadlicks. Those of us who had a Miss Kadlickequivalent hated them at the time for the drills they put us through, but we sure learned how to parse sentences, use language precisely, punctuate properly, avoid the wimpy passive voice, and, in the immortal words of Strunk and White (2000), "omit needless words." As Elliot and I worked on our book, he would often tease me mercilessly for my Grundyisms, though I did manage to get him down to only one "needless to say" per chapter. ("If it's needless to say," I'd say, "why say it?") Yet despite our different routes to learning to write, we agree that although rules are important, they are made to be broken in the service of grace, emphasis, and art. Sometimes it sounds better to end sentences with prepositions, sometimes you do want a few "needless" words to highlight a point, and—OK, Elliot, I agree!—sometimes a "needless to say" is worth saying.

Elliot also taught me a lesson that he and I wish had been unnecessary: the benefits of reading one's words out loud. Because of Elliot's macular degeneration, he could not see the chapters that I had drafted. Instead, he would edit and revise by listening to me read them, interrupting to flag a clumsy sentence, a failed attempt at humor, or a poorly reasoned argument. His training as a T-group leader and accomplished teacher has made him a spectacular listener. Trying to sneak a bad sentence past him reminded me of the great line that trying to pitch a fastball past Hank Aaron was like trying to pitch a sunrise past a rooster. (Or, as in an another popular version, "… like trying to pitch a lamb chop past a wolf.") Indeed, when you are reading aloud, you cannot ignore the murky sentences you failed to revise, hoping that no one would notice. If, like me, you get to read them to Elliot, you'll really learn something.

Finally, working with Elliot also brought me back full circle to my *Psychology Today* days and to one of the most enduring lessons my editors there taught me: Don't be so word proud that you can't accept editorial suggestions. Most writers will fight tenaciously for the lives of their cherished verbal creations; good writers must learn when to let them go. "Sometimes you have to kill your children," Elliot would say, as I whined about giving up some sentence I loved. "This one is a little too cute—and a little too wrong." (For his part, he would graciously yield to my editorial comments on his writing. Usually.) Academics who want to write for general audiences, or for their colleagues in a more direct and interesting style, may find it hard at first to accept editorial advice, clinging instead to their familiar technical language and that I-didn't-do-it passive voice. They should take heart in realizing that all writers, no matter how many hours we sit alone, writing, revising, and revising some more, need feedback from tough but encouraging editors.

Occasionally a student or colleague will send me a book proposal or an article and ask for my opinion on the writing, hoping—as we all hope when we send our little efforts into the world—that I will say, "Perfect! Don't change a word!" But if I like the ideas, I usually do suggest changing a word, and sometimes many words. That is the respect I owe to the writer, to the process of writing, and to my own goals of making psychological science accessible. I am sure that the recipients of my editing will be gratified to hear that I have yet to send anything to Elliot that has spurred him to say, "Perfect! Don't change a word!" He invariably says, "Perfect! But I have a few leeetle suggestions ..." His suggestions do improve my writing. Usually.

In 1940, Winston Churchill began a radio address to his country by saying, "The news from France is very bad." No Panglossian spin, no Orwellian self-delusion. Like Elliot, I feel passionate about the importance of clear language. (I feel passionately, too, but that has quite a different meaning.) Many people have praised his writing, especially *The Social Animal,* for bringing people into social psychology, but an even greater contribution is that he brings social psychology to people—to people who can use it in their everyday lives, in their work, as citizens, and even in their "interpersonal relationships." Nor does he distinguish colleague people from student people from people-in-the-street people. In Elliot's view, as in mine, everyone deserves good writing, writing that includes the data and the story. The specific way we tell that story will vary, depending on which half of Kimble's audience-divide we want to reach. But clarity, charm, narrative, and the passion to communicate need not fall only on one side. None of us can tell Elliot's stories the way he does, but everyone can learn to shed the kind of jargon that impedes understanding rather than clarifies, whether the goal is to inform, entertain, enchant, persuade, or motivate. That message is as much a part of the Aronsonian legacy in social psychology as great experimental design, socially relevant research, and inspired teaching.

REFERENCES

Aronson, E. (2008). *The social animal* (10th ed.). New York: Worth.

Aronson, E., Ellsworth, P. C., Carlsmith, J. M., & Gonzales, M. H. (1990). *Methods of research in social psychology* (2nd ed.). New York: McGraw-Hill.

Strunk, W., Jr., & White, E. B. (2000). *The elements of style* (4th ed.). Needham Heights, MA: Allyn & Bacon.

16

CHANCE ENCOUNTERS

Timothy D. Wilson

University of Virginia

One day, more than 20 years ago, I was sitting in my office preparing for class when there was a knock on the door. A psychology editor named Mary Falcon introduced herself and asked if I had a few minutes to chat. I invited her in, expecting to have the usual conversation about new offerings from her publishing house and the books I was using in my classes, and indeed we did chat about such matters. I mentioned that I was a big fan of Elliot Aronson's *The Social Animal* and had been using it in my introductory social psychology class. It was then that Mary asked me a question that seemed to come totally out of the blue: "Would you consider writing a social psychology textbook with Elliot Aronson?"

I had never given much thought to writing a textbook. For one thing, there was already a great book out there—*The Social Animal*. But I was intrigued. Although I had never met Elliot, he was one of my favorite researchers and he was obviously a fantastic writer. Who *wouldn't* consider writing a book with him?

One thing led to another. Mary arranged for me to fly to Boston to meet with Elliot, who was there to visit his daughter and graciously agreed to meet me. We had coffee at the Au Bon Pain in Harvard Square and then went for a walk along the Charles River. We hit it off, in no small part, I think, because we had similar views of the field. It probably didn't hurt that I mentioned my fondness for and fascination with cognitive dissonance theory, thereby quelling any suspicions Elliot might have had that I was one of those new-fangled, boring social–cognition types. (I may have forgotten to mention that my undergraduate honors thesis was a critical test of cognitive dissonance and self-perception theories, and that I had hypothesized that self-perception theory would win.)

So began a textbook collaboration that has lasted these many years; indeed we have just finished the seventh edition of our book. But things did not go smoothly at first. I had never written a text, and summarizing literatures clearly for an undergraduate audience did not, shall we say, come naturally to me. My initial drafts were long, detailed descriptions of research finding after research finding, and Elliot had to remind me—more than once—that students in an introductory social course did not want to read exhaustive, *Psych Bulletin*-like chapters that detailed every concept and the exceptions to it. "Tell them a story," he would say. "There is no reason a textbook can't be interesting." Adding Robin Akert as a third author on our text was a tremendous help; she made my drafts more accessible.

I learned a lot by talking with Elliot about writing and watching him compose a chapter from beginning to end. He draws the reader in with a fascinating example of social behavior, from his own personal experience, a current event, or the historical record. In one chapter, for example, he discusses a strategy that Benjamin Franklin used to win over a hostile state legislator. Rather than doing something nice for his adversary, Franklin did just the opposite, asking the legislator to do something nice for him (lend him a book). And, Franklin reports, it worked—the legislator and he became good friends. Elliot then proposes a counterintuitive lesson that we might draw from this example, namely, that people like us more after they do us a favor. He explains why, pointing out that cognitive dissonance is produced by going out of one's way to do a good deed for someone (after all, favors usually involve some effort on the part of the giver), and that this dissonance can be reduced by deciding that the recipient of the favor was well worth the effort.

But Elliot doesn't stop there. He is both an artist and scientist at heart, and at this point the scientist takes over. We can't draw definitive conclusions from an historical example, he notes, and must conduct a well-designed experiment to test the hypothesis implied by the example. He then goes on to describe a study that does just that. He has drawn the reader in with an interesting historical example that suggests a counterintuitive principle, and then shows the reader how this principle was tested experimentally. More often than not he takes readers through the experiment step by step as if they were participants, teaching them a lot about the methodological details of social-psychological research. Before students know it they are well into the chapter, curious to see what comes next.

My writing style will never be as smooth, comfortable, and inviting as Elliot's; when I read his conversational prose I always feel like I'm sitting down with him at a good meal, listening to one of his spellbinding stories. (One of the best things about our collaboration is that we have had many such meals in fine restaurants paid for by our publisher.) But I have learned a lot about writing from our collaboration and have tried to apply these lessons to all my writing projects, in addition to our textbook.

I've had the opportunity to soak up a lot more than writing tips. What is so remarkable about Elliot's career is that he excels in all facets of our discipline. He is a top-notch researcher, having conducted some of the most famous studies in social psychology. It has been an honor to collaborate with him on the chapter in the *Handbook of Social Psychology* on how to conduct an experiment, because he is one of the most successful and clever methodologists our field has produced. He is a prolific writer; I suspect he has inspired more budding social psychologists than anyone else, through *The Social Animal*, his popular books, and our textbook. He is a legendary teacher, having taught to packed lecture halls his entire career. And he has shown how to apply social psychology to solve important social problems. Many social psychologists talk the talk about wanting to explore the applied implications of their work, but few have gone out and done it as well as Elliot, such as with his influential work on the Jigsaw Classroom. If there were a Fantasy Social Psychology League, Elliot would be one of my top draft picks.

In short, it has been a privilege to be able to rub shoulders with Elliot over the years and I will always be thankful that I was in my office that day that Mary Falcon knocked on the door.

17

THE ART OF TEACHING

*Lessons From a Teacher Who Was
Never Taught How to Teach*

Marti Hope Gonzales
University of Minnesota

I began my graduate work with Elliot Aronson at the University of California at Santa Cruz in 1982. His reputation as an uncompromising taskmaster had preceded our acquaintance and I was full of more bravado than bravery, but once I could cross the threshold of his office on steady legs, I quickly fell into his orbit. I enrolled in his experimental methods seminar, served more than once as a teaching assistant and section leader in his wildly popular introductory social psychology course, and we collaborated on research. We have become lifelong friends, due in part to our commitment to teaching and learning in their myriad guises, from lectures, to seminars, to one-on-one research collaborations with colleagues and students.

As his advisee and student, I observed how skillfully he modified his teaching styles to fit those different contexts, I watched with admiration as undergraduate and graduate students responded in his classes and seminars, and I experienced firsthand what it was like to work with him in such different domains of learning. I often wondered how he did it, how he elevated the profession of teaching to an art. What did he do, why did he do it that way, and why did it work so phenomenally well? And in a more general sense, what makes for effective undergraduate instruction and for creative and fruitful work with graduate students? What "best practices" and aspects of the university teaching environment are most conducive to students' motivation, learning, and enlightened views of themselves and others?

There have been many empirical studies, of course, that have examined characteristics of the classroom environment and of the effective instructor. For example, meta-analyses have revealed that all things being equal—and they seldom are—smaller classes are preferable to larger ones in facilitating students' learning. Further, we don't have to be Elliot Aronson (who developed the Jigsaw Classroom as the prototype of a cooperative learning environment) to know that when students cooperate, they learn better and enjoy their learning experience more than when they compete with one another. And when it comes to characteristics of the best instructors, organizational skills are essential; it helps to show up at the appointed place and time with the right lecture notes and PowerPoint slides, to start and (especially) to end class on time, to hold regular office hours, to return papers when promised, and to design and to deliver a course with seamless continuity: in short, to juggle the myriad demands of instruction systematically and efficiently. In the words of domestic diva Martha Stewart, organization is a *good* thing. But it isn't artistry.

In the 1990s, a number of researchers discovered what students long before Alexander the Great (whose own teacher was Aristotle) could have told us. The best instructors are *expressive* in the classroom; they are enthusiastic about their subject and about the doggedly hard work of teaching, they use humor and make eye contact, and they move about the room. One of my more curmudgeonly colleagues remarked to me after hearing about this literature, "Great. So I'm supposed to move around the room, flapping my arms and telling jokes?" Well, that would be a start. Expressive teachers, after all, share their enthusiasm for their discipline and for the process of discovery, teaching, and learning. If we cannot muster such passion, how can we expect our students to give a damn?

Great instructors also know that the process of learning and discovery is not a purely cognitive enterprise. It's an emotional and social enterprise, as well. That is why the most gifted teachers are *caring*: They want their students to learn and to succeed; they are open, genuine, and responsive to their students' needs and perceptions; they value individual students as human beings worthy of attention and respect. When we care, students respect and trust us, and they are motivated to learn more from us.

Organization, expressiveness, and caring: Now we're getting somewhere. Still, the empirical literature leaves something to be desired. To capture the elusive quality of artistry in teaching, we need to turn to our experiences with the most gifted teachers we have known, reflecting on the ways in which they actualized their own philosophy of teaching. For me as for so many others, Elliot was that gifted teacher. Over the years he and I have spoken about teaching and mentoring, but usually in the way colleagues do: exchanging anecdotes, successes, observations, and frustrations. Like most artists, Elliot has always preferred to do it rather than to talk about how to do it. Still, in 1994, the year that he formally retired from UCSC, he delivered a lecture on teaching at a meeting of the American Psychological Association. At last, this teacher who was never taught how to teach made his tacit knowledge explicit.

At last, in the master teacher's own words, I found answers to the questions I had contemplated as I used his example to become a better undergraduate and graduate teacher myself. To begin with, according to Elliot, the most gifted and committed teachers are forever asking themselves this question: How has students' time in our courses affected their lives, the way they think, the way they feel, the way they conceive of and move through the world? If everything we work so hard to teach our students slides into oblivion the day after the final exam, or the week after, or the year after, then our efforts become an absurd exercise, not unlike the labors of Sisyphus. The most gifted and dedicated teachers expect so much more of themselves. Amen! Yet how do we achieve that lasting influence on our students? In this essay, I will consider some answers, drawing from Elliot's philosophy of the art of teaching and from my own thoughts and experiences, first as his student, and then as a professor. I'll discuss what I have learned from him about the three kinds of teaching that he loves: stand-up teaching, sit-down teaching, and mentoring.

STAND-UP TEACHING: THE ART OF THE LECTURE

I vividly remember watching Elliot bound to the stage in jeans and a sweater, and scrawl a word or two, three at most, in large chalk letters on the blackboard. He would wait just a moment for students to read the words and to wonder what lay in store, and then he'd be off and running with the day's story. And man-oh-man, is Elliot a natural storyteller. Funny, you'd think that more social psychologists would be better storytellers, given our subject matter. We might have been 40 years ago, when our questions were more about people than about processes, yet even then, few had Elliot's skills at talking about the ways in which we humans inspire, repel, enrich, amuse, frighten, hate, love, and confuse one another. Each lecture was a drama or tragedy or tragicomedy in one act, with Elliot playing all the parts. This comes as no surprise to those who understand that Elliot sees himself as a storyteller in the ancient rabbinic tradition. He worked to hold students' attention by providing them with vivid, memorable, thought-provoking examples of the day's concepts. Some of his examples were humorous, but Elliot did not rely on the telling of jokes or similar forms of flashy entertainment to get his point across (his approach to humor in writing is similar; see Carol Tavris's chapter in this volume on writing with Elliot). Far too often, we both believe, students remember our jokes, but to save their own lives they could not tell us later about the constructs, findings, or ideas the jokes were supposed to illuminate. Of course, Elliot did use humor to make his points, but the kind that flowed from an actual event, including, to his students' delight, his own foibles. For example, in making the point that not even cognitive dissonance researchers are immune to the dynamics of dissonance reduction, he would tell the story of buying a canoe in the heart of a frigid Minnesota winter, when ice on the lakes would support a pick-up truck. Why do such an apparently irrational thing? To reduce the dissonance following the family's decision to buy a house near a lake, which would be better for the children, rather than one nearer campus, which would have been more convenient for him. He now says, "To the naked eye, it might seem that the canoe was merely useless—merely taking up space in the garage all winter long. But that canoe helped me reduce the dissonance I felt over our choice." Such self-deprecating humor at the service of storytelling serves to make the material more memorable, and as important, to enable students to see their professors as "real people" not as different from themselves as they might at first assume, even without the pratfalls to which I am prone.

More often, however, Elliot's storytelling was of the more poignant variety: When talking about the academic benefits of the Jigsaw Classroom, for example, he would also describe how the method gave one young Chicano a new life of promise. When talking about the potentially deadly consequences of the psychology of commitment, he would tell the story of the physicists who worked on the Manhattan Project: They joined the project because they believed that Hitler was trying to develop such a weapon, and it was important to beat him to the punch. Still, long after those scientists learned that the United States was the only country on earth with an atomic bomb, they nonetheless forged ahead, blindly continuing down the path that led to the unprecedented devastation at Hiroshima and Nagasaki. And when teaching students about the self-fulfilling prophecy, he used a story from his own life to show them that we need not remain its prisoners: Although he once stole books for his college courses because he could not afford to buy them, he did not define himself forever after as a thief—or become one. Elliot stood behind the lectern at the front of the lecture hall and did not move about the room or gesture extravagantly; his expressiveness was in his voice, in his thoughtful choice of words, in his meaningful pauses, in these stories that would remain memorable and therefore powerful influences in his students' lives.

Artistry in stand-up teaching also requires the courage to experiment if we are to remain fresh and engaged. Unlike my own lectures, which often take the form of "Act I," "Act II," and "Stunning Conclusion" in the allotted period, Elliot's lectures unfolded as one seamless one-act performance, and he long ago abandoned the practice of encouraging students' questions along the way. In fact, he has argued that allowing students to interrupt with questions is like encouraging theater patrons to stand up and to shout comments to actors on stage in the middle of a play. After all, when a performer holds the audience in his thrall, neither the actor nor anyone in the audience wants someone hollering out, "Hey, excuse me, Prince Hamlet! I hate to interrupt here, but are you ever going to get around to killing your Uncle Claudius, or what?" Elliot regards many if not most student questions as evidence of the students' struggle for affirmation and attention in the anonymous setting of a large lecture hall rather than as a sincere expression of interest in what he is saying. When irrelevant questions arise, the carefully crafted aesthetics of a lecture can be disrupted, to no good effect.

Still, in the interest of experimenting to find ways to provide students with an opportunity to engage in a give-and-take with him, and thereby to become active participants in their own learning, Elliot decided one academic term to dismiss the class of over 300 students about 10 or 15 minutes early, so that those who were interested could hang around to ask questions and to react to the day's lecture. Unfortunately, despite this manifestation of his flexibility, the new practice was an utter failure: Few of the 300 students wanted to leave at lecture's close. After a couple of such abortive attempts, Elliot resumed the status quo, with no apparent ill effects on the students, who were perfectly happy in the role of audience members. This speaks, I believe, to the power inherent in masterful storytelling, even when experiments with pedagogical alternatives simply don't pan out.

In his stand-up teaching, Elliot gave voice to social psychologists, of course, and to other finders-of-truth, including fiction writers, philosophers, social critics, carpenters, and even his next-door neighbors. In this sense, Elliot's course was about far more than the social psychology found in textbooks or journals. Recently, we at the University of Minnesota have been revisiting the question of how best to provide students with a liberal education—an educational experience of growth and discovery that gives them a cosmopolitan vision and an understanding of the multifaceted ways in which truth, beauty, and knowledge are discovered, created, and pursued. Noble goals, no doubt. As we found ourselves stuck in the rut of identifying lists of required courses, I realized that the elements of a liberal education can be present in a single course—politics, chemistry, history, any subject—when we teach as Elliot did. In his lectures, he claimed all kinds of people as "social psychologists." Aristotle made an appearance once in a while, as did more contemporary philosophers such as Hobbes, Locke, Rousseau, and Spinoza. William Shakespeare, J. D. Salinger, Edward Albee, and Lenny Bruce had something social-psychological to say, as did Sigmund Freud and B. F. Skinner. Scientific social psychology is one route to one kind of truth, Elliot reminded students, yet there is much more to discover about ourselves and others. Literature, philosophy, and the arts offer their own paths to truth, wisdom, and enlightenment.

Artistry also demands the courage to serve as our own thoughtful and unsparing critics, and Elliot did not shy away from that activity. It was a bit of a trek from the lecture hall back to our offices, and along the way, Elliot would sometimes reflect on the day's performance. "I was *on* today!" he might observe, and would explain how he knew that his performance was spot-on. He was every bit as likely to lament a substandard (well, for him, anyway) performance, and would dissect his lecture, identifying where he went off track, again tutoring us on the whys and hows of when things go amiss. Artists in education and elsewhere, of course, continually risk nondefensive self-examination.

My experiences observing Elliot in the classroom, and my own as a professor, make me more than a little ambivalent about long-distance learning. It's one thing for students far away to watch a recording of a professor strutting her stuff. It's another matter entirely to be there with her, in the same space and time, to participate with her as she walks that tightrope between organization and spontaneity. It's like the difference between film and the theater. When we are spontaneous, or give the appearance of spontaneity as Elliot loves to do, we are telling our students in the lecture hall that what we offer is for them and for them only, right now, in this immediate moment, no matter how many times we might repeat that same riposte, remark, or aside to hundreds or thousands of students who come after them.

The ability to convey immediacy and spontaneity, whether unfolding like a meandering Miles Davis jazz riff or planfully executed as when

B. B. King plays the blues, is also an integral part of Elliot's performance artistry. For example, in one lecture about the Jigsaw Classroom, he touched all of us when he pulled out and read aloud a brittle yellow letter written to him by "Carlos," one of the first young Chicanos in Austin, Texas, to participate in that novel cooperative approach to teaching and learning. Many years later, Carlos had written to Elliot to express his profound gratitude and to let Elliot know of his achievements, including admission to Harvard Law School. In that short and powerful letter, Carlos described how Elliot had appeared to him—including his memory of Elliot's dark beard—and added, "You were very tall, *six and a half feet.*" Without missing a beat, Elliot looked up at us and said, "Well, I *was*!" We all laughed heartily before allowing him to continue. The next time I served as a teaching assistant for the same course, Elliot again pulled out the brittle, tattered letter from Carlos, and read it aloud. And damned if he didn't use the same "spontaneous" line: "Well, I *was*!" Hey, *wait* a minute! Wait a *minute* here! I felt somehow tricked or cheated, if only for a moment, before I joined in the students' laughter. It took that moment before I realized that his clever and flawlessly delivered quip was a carefully crafted aspect of performance that makes even the most well-rehearsed lecture seem immediate, intimate, and unrestrained. Never before had I better understood the pedagogical power of what I now call "orchestrated spontaneity."

SIT-DOWN TEACHING: THE ART OF THE GRADUATE SEMINAR

During my first term in the graduate program at the University of California at Santa Cruz, I took Elliot's experimental methods seminar. He assigned W. I. B. Beveridge's (1957) *The Art of Scientific Investigation,* and as I was to learn, it perfectly reflected the way Elliot thought about conducting experiments: To design and to implement the very best experiments requires both artistry and science. Beveridge, a pathology professor at the University of Cambridge, set out to take a psychological look at science and scientists, and to describe scientific research as a creative and artistic process. He wrote of hypothesis generation, systematic observation, and experimentation. He also wrote of the imagination, intuition, and creativity manifested by the most gifted and influential of the world's scientists. Wow! A research methods class with one of the most gifted experimenters in social psychology, and this guy wants us to understand artistry, as well. This is going to be some ride, I thought. And it was.

A thoughtful choice of reading assignments, of course, can make for a terrific graduate seminar, but much more than that is involved. What unfolds during discussions is even more important. One year, my students interviewed Elliot as part of their own graduate seminar and neglected to ask him about teaching. Elliot thought that was a shame. So when students got to the part about "Was there anything that we didn't ask you that you wish we had?" Elliot said that the most important thing for professors to remember when teaching graduate students—and the most difficult thing to do—is to keep our big mouths shut, and let the students do all the work. As he joked with us, "What a *racket*!"

Of course, facilitating a seminar is no racket. In fact, in many respects, it is more challenging than delivering a terrific lecture. The back-and-forth of seminar exchanges unfolds spontaneously, and it's often hard to predict what students will ask or say; for that reason, we have to be better prepared, and prepared for anything, if all participants are to capitalize on the unexpected that inevitably unfolds when there isn't a script. If professors are to use the Socratic method as skillfully as Elliot did, they encourage students to think deeply, to reach further, and to take the risk of talking more. And once students have spoken, it's essential to serve as a thoughtful, unsparing, but supportive critic, to let students know that we respect them and their work enough that we won't let them get away with anything shoddy, glib, or half-baked. Elliot was a smart, tough facilitator, indeed a sterner critic than many journal reviewers. Yet once we got over the jitters, we did indeed think more critically, reach further than we thought we could, and talk more and more intelligently with him and one another.

It was a heady and challenging experience. Under his stern yet enthusiastic direction, we students also became resources to one another, just as we would later become resources to our own students and colleagues. We learned to accept feedback from our peers with magnanimity, and to extend feedback with clarity and a commitment to helping our peers do their own work better. It was never enough to point out every real or potential flaw in reasoning, or to point to this or that possible confound in their experimental designs or demand characteristics in their procedures. Instead, we were expected to go the extra mile to help our fellow students figure out how to do their work better, to engage with them in the daunting yet fulfilling creative process of designing research.

And when Elliot did speak, his contributions often took the form of penetrating and provocative questions. A friend of mine once observed, "The best question can start us on a journey of a lifetime. The best answer can stop us dead in our tracks." I don't remember ever hearing

Elliot say those exact words, but his pedagogical strategy in graduate seminars left no doubt in my mind that he lived by them.

SIDE-BY-SIDE TEACHING: THE ART OF THE MENTOR

These same skills manifested themselves in our mentoring relationship. Notice that I didn't use the word *training*, a term that fails to reflect that crucial quality of caring. We *train* pigeons or rats; when we do it right, we *mentor* graduate students. When Elliot and I interacted, I never felt like a student who was more or less interchangeable with another. He always made me feel like Marti first, a 30-something foul-mouthed Texan in whom he saw the spirit, commitment, and intellectual acumen to do good things.

Was it all sweetness and light? Of course not. We were both too human for that, and the relationship between mentor and graduate advisee is complex. Graduate school is time of personal and professional transition, a time when students move from amateur to professional, from dependence to independence, and from self-doubt to self-assurance. Such transitions can be a source of exhilaration, and in moments despair, as mentor and advisee adjust to their changing roles, working together to ensure that along the way students become peers. Elliot could be tough on me when I had it coming, and I learned the value of being tough and critical as well as of being warm and supportive, lessons I work to apply to my own students. Like a less prickly, less intimidating version of his own mentor, Leon Festinger, Elliot did not suffer gladly fools or lazy people, and when I fell short of his hopes or expectations, I heard about it. With candor and clarity (only sometimes tinged with aggravation), he explained how and where I fell short, and what I needed to do to remedy the situation. The essential, tacit lesson he taught me was this: When we set high standards for our students, and stick to our guns, we communicate that we have confidence in them, and that we see in them potential that they might not yet see in themselves. And when we are willing to be supportively critical rather than Emily Post "polite," our words of commendation and praise mean all the more, given that our students know that they have earned them.

That is the artistry of mentoring: knowing when to be tough and demanding, and when to be supportive and flexible. Elliot set a high bar that he wanted me to clear, and when he thought that I was falling short, there were a few times when he'd give me a swift kick in the ass. But what I remember best about our mentoring relationship is that somehow he knew when he had set the bar just a bit too high, and realized I might need a boost. At those times, he was a source of support when I was either too proud to ask for it or else didn't yet recognize that I needed it. Before extending his advice, he often waited until he somehow knew that I was ready to accept it, and consequently, to benefit from it. He challenged me in the most wise and generous ways, so that I would learn to articulate my position and stick up for myself when the need arose. Were it not for his demanding yet loving mentorship, I might never have developed such essential intellectual and interpersonal skills.

And the best graduate mentors know when their formal professorial work is done. I recall a day, sometime early in my fifth year, when Elliot said with a gifted mentor's combination of nostalgia, love, and pride, "Well, kid, I think that we've taught you all there is to teach you here, so the rest is going to be up to you."

Of course, I neither learned perfectly nor embraced *all* of the lessons of my great friend and mentor. And that is as it should be. *Vive la différence*, after all. In teaching, we each combine our interpersonal style, personality, and life experience in a way that works best for us as the unique individuals we were long before we ever became professional social psychologists. Still, in my *best moments*, when I facilitate graduate seminars, teach my own large lecture courses in social psychology, mentor my own students, or talk with students or colleagues about teaching, it feels as if Elliot is perched like an angel on my shoulder and is whispering in my ear. Those are the moments when I know I'd make him proud. I wish they were more frequent.

The legendary Bette Davis once said of acting, "Without wonder and insight, acting is just a trade. With it, it becomes creation." She might just as well have been talking about the pedagogical virtuosity of Elliot Aronson, who, with wonder, insight, expressiveness, caring, and courage, has always commanded the stage. Through the daunting, demanding, and passionate work inherent in transforming teaching into art, not only has Elliot given his own life meaning and joy, but he has also shared that meaning and joy with the rest of us fortunate enough to have watched from the audience and joined him backstage.

REFERENCE

Beveridge, W. I. B. (1957). *The art of scientific investigation*. Caldwell, NJ: Blackburn Press.

V
Codas

18

ELLIOT ARONSON AND THE SPIRIT OF YOM KIPPUR: THE ADJUSTMENT TO ATROCITY

Sermon on the Occasion of Yom Kippur, Kol Nidre, 5747 (1986)

Rabbi Hillel Cohn

Congregation Emanuel
San Bernardino, California

Editors' note: *In the spring of 1986, the graduating seniors at the University of California, Santa Cruz, voted to ask Elliot Aronson to give their commencement address, which he did with pleasure. Later that summer, Elliot received a letter from a rabbi who had been in the audience. The rabbi explained that he had been so moved by Elliot's remarks that he planned to incorporate them into his sermon on Yom Kippur. With Rabbi Cohn's permission, we reprint some of that sermon because it represents to us the essence of Elliot's Judaism, his passion for the great lessons of social psychology, and the long reach of his influence.*

One of the goals we have for ourselves and for our children is that we and they be well-adjusted. That means that we want to fit in, to be in sync, to be in step with the rest of the world. People spend exorbitant amounts of time and money on psychiatrists and psychologists to attain that sense of being well-adjusted. And one of the roles of religion has traditionally been to foster such adjustment.

But most of us are pretty adept at adapting to our environments and to changes in our lives without outside help. Take the case of the person who becomes disabled at some point in his life or is disabled from birth. You and I know countless examples of the person who is blind and who adjusts to that by developing an amazing ability to "see" things and "read" with the tips of the fingers, or who sharpens the sense of smell or hearing to such a point that he can just about do all the things sighted people can do, and in some instances even do better.

With all of the value we place on adapting to change and loss, it should seem strange for me to say that if I were to add any one thing to the traditional confessional that we recite on Yom Kippur, it would be a seeking of forgiveness for the sin of adjustment.

I was not aware of the dangers of adjustment until a couple of months ago, when my wife Rita and I journeyed to Santa Cruz to witness our daughter's college graduation. I went with the expectation that I would have to sit through a boring graduation speech, but my main reasons for being there were to see my daughter get her diploma and to take a few hundred pictures. As far as the commencement address—well, it was just one of those traditions that one has to endure. But I was happily surprised. The speaker was Professor Elliot Aronson, a world-renowned social psychologist who teaches at UC Santa Cruz. Dr. Aronson is not only a beloved and inspiring college teacher and a distinguished researcher, but he is also a Jew. And he is not simply a lox-and-bagel Jew or even a Jew who spends much time in temple, but a man who embodies the spirit of Judaism in everything he does. And what he said that beautiful day in Santa Cruz is a message that is not only appropriate for a college graduation but just as important for this day of Yom Kippur.

"After some twenty-five years of doing research on how the human mind works," Professor Aronson said, "if there is one thing I know for sure, it is that as a species we are wonderful at adapting and adjusting to changes in our environment—both at doing what we need to do and at bringing our cognitions into line with what we need to do. By and large, this is a good thing. Our ancient ancestors would not have survived against the lion, the tiger, the bear, and a hostile environment if they weren't awfully good at adjusting to change." Yet, he added, there are some things we adjust to "at our own peril as a species." He told the graduates and their families and friends of an event that occurred August 20, 1936, during the Spanish Civil War: "A single plane intentionally bombed a populated area of Madrid," he said. "There were several casualties, but miraculously no one was killed. There was a huge outcry. The world was profoundly shocked by this outrage. Especially in the United States, editorials resounded throughout the land." Dr. Aronson continued, "Then, a mere nine years later, 1945, in the bombing of Hiroshima and Nagasaki, more than 100,000 people were killed and countless thousands subjected to the ravages of radiation. And at the time there was not much of an outcry. Indeed, the Gallup Poll taken shortly thereafter revealed that only 5% of Americans said we shouldn't have dropped the bomb, and an astonishing 23% said we should have used many more bombs before we allowed Japan to surrender." And the crux of Dr. Aronson's message was this: "Something very important happened to the American mind in those nine years. We had adjusted to atrocity—mindless, vengeful adjustment."

Well, some might say, that was World War II; our support of the use of nuclear weapons was justified. But Professor Aronson also mentioned the bombing of Libya a few months ago [1986], which was supposed to have reduced the presence of terrorism. Yet he pointed to a Gallup Poll in which 71% of Americans approved of the bombing but only 31% thought it would reduce terrorism. If that is the case, then what was its justification? Dr. Aronson said, "What that means is that a substantial portion of the American people thought that bombing Libyan civilians was a good idea even though it would not reduce terrorism and might even increase terrorism." The rationale was that we needed to show Colonel Khadafy who is boss. And so, because of our highly developed skill of adjusting to atrocity, we applauded as innocent civilians were killed. The fact that these innocent civilians live in a country led by a crazy colonel in no way justifies killing them.

I was deeply moved by the illustrations Professor Aronson offered, and they awakened in me a recognition for which I will be eternally grateful to him. For all the effort we make to be well-adjusted, for all of its benefits, we are all guilty of the sin of adjustment. We need not only to beat our breasts in recognition of that sin but also to activate our minds and souls to rid ourselves of it. His message to the graduates was that one of his primary goals as a teacher was to instruct his students how and when to be maladjusted, to be mindful of the world around them, to think with their hearts as well as their heads.

If you understand the role of Judaism correctly, you will understand that its role is not to enable us to be comfortable or content with atrocity. The synagogue is not a place to go for shelter and relaxation and calm. And, above all, Yom Kippur is not to be for us a day of ease, repose, and composure. The message of this day and this place and the entire system of which it is a part, Judaism, is that we need to be *maladjusted to atrocity*, to be mindful of the world around us and to think with our hearts as well as our heads.

Think with me for a few moments about how terribly skilled we have become at adjusting to brutality. We have developed an amazing capacity to turn it off. The TV's remote control has a little button that I can press to mute the sound, another button to change the channel instantly, a volume adjustment to increase or decrease the sound in a flash. And we do the same thing with our minds. We turn off the screams of the suffering, we change the channel when we get nauseated by what we see, and in so doing we think we have succeeded at making it go away. Maybe we have had to develop our skill at doing this. Maybe, because TV has such an incredible capacity to transport us all over the world, we have been so heavily inundated with atrocity day in and day out that we have become numbed to it; our capacity for pain has been dulled.

Or we can look in other directions for places to put the blame for our having become adjusted to atrocity. We can offer the excuse that those things we see and turn off, to which we adjust, are so very far away, that they afflict people so very different from us that we can't let ourselves bear the pain. We can offer as an apology that we are so helpless that one person can't make much of a difference. Some Christian fundamentalists claim that the disasters of our times are the design and work of God; the Bible predicts the Armageddon, the struggle of the forces of good and evil against each other, and that what is happening is paving the way for the last and Final Judgment. In short, atrocities are God's doing.

We are pretty proficient at coming up with excuses. You are. I am. All of us are. With whatever excuses, we adjust to the atrocities of apartheid, war, world hunger; we change the channel so that the extent of deprivation and suffering doesn't penetrate our souls. But we need to be uncomfortably maladjusted to wherever atrocity is taking place. Hunger is not just in Ethiopia. There is hunger right here in the United States. Right here in Southern California. Right here in our communities. And to confront that hunger by accusing the hungry of having brought it on themselves by not training for jobs, or depending on welfare, or hundreds of other excuses doesn't change the fact that their stomachs are empty. The Jewish tradition, going back thousands of years, insists that when it comes to providing food for another human being, there must be no asking of questions and no delay.

To be a Jew historically has been to be maladjusted to atrocity. And a fitting model of that is the prophet whose story is included in our Yom Kippur liturgy, on this, the most significant day of the year. Jonah was like all of us and like so many people in the world. He was adept at blending in with his environment, adjusting to changed conditions, fitting in with the evils of Nineveh. But then came the moment when he recognized that he was different. *"Ivri Anochi,"* Jonah says. "I am a Hebrew." And with that acknowledgement he went forth to challenge evil, to uproot atrocity. What a fitting model for us to follow! *Ivri Anochi.* I am a Hebrew. I am a Jew. That affirmation means that I am, by reason of history and tradition, a maladjusted person, maladjusted to atrocity. It means that I am able to think with my heart as well as my head—Professor Aronson's lesson of his commencement address.

On this Yom Kippur let us acknowledge that we have sinned by being adjusted to atrocity. *Avinu*—we have transgressed in the sense that it was understood by one of our teachers: "We have been mixed up and confused," we have accepted the evil as natural, the destructive as defensible. *Kishinu Oref*—we have been stubborn. "We have stubbornly, insensitively, disregarded all calamities and mishaps as coincidence." May we, all of us, attain the forgiveness for this sin of adjustment by beating our indifference out of our lives.

Thank you, Professor Aronson, for reminding us of that which we should be carrying around with us every waking minute of every day: We shall not adjust!

19

THE LAST WORD

Elliot Aronson

I loved reading these essays. My students, colleagues, and friends know me well, and were generous in their appraisal of my work and its influence on theirs. But the essays were all written in the past tense. Although that is understandable, it does feel a bit like being present at my own funeral. I felt inclined to shout, "Wait, wait! Put down those shovels! I'm still here!" As proof that I am still here, I wanted to have the last word. And, as proof that it is really me and not some imposter doing a skillful imitation, my last word will take the form of (what else?) a story.

When I was an undergraduate and started reading about some of the clever experiments in social psychology—e.g., by Asch and by Lewin and his students—I thought that experiments were done by special people. It never dawned on me that I could be one of them. Then, during my first year in graduate school at Stanford, I had a life-changing experience: Jud Mills and I designed and conducted a clever experiment. And I began to think that it was possible—not likely, but possible—that I just might be one of those special people.

After I began to teach, something else happened. I discovered that the skill of designing and conducting experiments wasn't all that special; I could train my graduate students to do it, and they picked it up easily. Moreover, I discovered that with hard work, persistence, and a smidgeon of ingenuity, my students and I could test all kinds of interesting hypotheses in the laboratory—questions about love, hate, and other workings of the human mind that had been puzzling philosophers for centuries.

It is impossible to describe the joy, the excitement, and the passion for our field that this discovery evoked in me. I can only do it by analogy. When I was a kid, I was a pretty good baseball player, but I was always afraid of screwing up and of the humiliation that would follow. So, in a tight situation, I would nervously pray that the batter would not hit the ball in my direction. ("Please, God, anywhere else, but not to me.") But then, when I was 14 years old (the age at which I reached my zenith as a ballplayer), something extraordinary happened. I remember it as if it were yesterday. I was playing second base for our neighborhood team. We were leading 6–5 in the ninth inning of a crucial game for the league championship. The opposing team had loaded the bases with no outs. And I found myself actually hoping that the batter would hit the ball in my direction. It was an epiphany: I suddenly believed that, whatever might come my way, I could handle it. At that moment, I was filled with an exquisite combination of intense concentration and serene self-confidence. The batter hit a medium slow roller past the mound; I had been playing half-way and charged the ball, scooped it up, and, in the same motion, threw it home, one step ahead of the runner; the catcher then threw it to first to complete the double play. The next batter flied out deep to center field and the game was over. But for the first time, my awareness that I could do the job well had trumped my fear of fumbling the ball.

It was a lesson I took into my professional life, because once you lose the fear of fumbling you become able to take on unexpected challenges and risks. Fumbling, however, has greater consequences in the real world than in the laboratory. For example, if my interpretation of the Aronson–Mills initiation data had been wrong, that would have been mildly embarrassing, but hardly a disaster; another scientist would offer an alternative explanation, perform an experiment to test it, and social psychology would be the better for it. In contrast, if my intervention to try to solve a problem in a highly visible public institution had been wrong, the consequences could be devastating. Accordingly, when the assistant superintendent of schools in Austin, Texas, asked me to intervene to try to reduce the interethnic hostility that was disrupting the city's newly desegregated schools, the stakes were high. To fail in an attempt to apply social-psychological wisdom in an arena that had such important implications for people's lives and for public policy would have been not only embarrassing for me, but also a black eye for the field and a further setback for desegregation. It would have been akin to fumbling a ground ball with the bases loaded and the score tied in the seventh game of the World Series.

But I have a passionate belief about the value of social psychology. I think many of its findings are important not only theoretically or intellectually, but socially. For me, nothing could have been more important than finding a way to get ethnic groups to move past their prejudices. So when that administrator pitched the possibility of using social psychology to help the Austin schools, I was quick to accept the challenge. What gave me the chutzpah to think I could come up with anything useful, especially while working under crisis conditions and the klieg lights of intense public scrutiny? For one thing, I was not alone. I was standing on the shoulders of three giants: Gordon Allport, Muzafer Sherif, and Morton Deutsch. Second, I had confidence in my skill as an experimentalist to invent the precise intervention that would work under these emotionally charged circumstances.

The major principles that have dominated my professional life have been to follow my nose (go where my curiosity leads me), follow my heart (go where my empathy leads me), and do it right. As a young professional, I loved everything I was doing: teaching, writing, and designing experiments in social psychology. At that time, in my fantasy, only one career could have been better—playing for the Boston Red Sox. Then, when I was in my early 50s, it struck me that, if my baseball dream had come true, my playing days would have been long since over; I would have been retired for well over a decade. But in social psychology, I was just coming into my prime. Someday, maybe soon, I will hit that prime. In the meantime, I stand ready to handle anything that might come my way.

ELLIOT ARONSON'S AWARDS, BOOKS, AND PUBLICATIONS

AWARDS

William James Award for Distinguished Lifetime Contributions to Scientific Psychology, Association for Psychological Science, 2007
Named one of the 100 Most Eminent Psychologists of the 20th Century, 2002
Master Lecturer, American Psychological Association, 2001
Distinguished Scientific Contribution Award, American Psychological Association, 1999
Distinguished Alumnus, Brandeis University, 1999
Distinguished Scientist-Lecturer, American Psychological Association, 1994
Distinguished Scientific Career Award, Society of Experimental Social Psychology, 1994
"Most Favorite Teacher," University of California-Santa Cruz Alumni Association, 1993
First Recipient, Award for Distinguished Research in the Social Sciences, University of California-Santa Cruz, 1992
Elected to the American Academy of Arts & Sciences, 1992
Bernhard Distinguished Visiting Professor, Williams College, 1990
Brandeis University establishes the Elliot Aronson Prize for the Best Senior Thesis in Psychology, 1990
Hovland Memorial Lecture, Yale University, November 1989
President, Western Psychological Association, 1989–1990
President, Division of Personality & Social Psychology, American Psychological Association, 1986–1987
F. Stanley Hall Lecturer on Psychology, American Psychological Association, 1986

Chair, National Academy of Science Committee on Energy Production and Consumption, 1982–1986
Guggenheim Fellowship, 1981–1982
Citation, Professor of the Year, Council for the Advancement and Support of Education, 1981
First Recipient, Donald Campbell Award for Distinguished Research in Social Psychology, American Psychological Association, 1980
American Psychological Association Distinguished Teaching Award in Psychology, 1980
First Recipient, Distinguished Teaching Award, University of California-Santa Cruz, 1979
Fellow, Center for Advanced Study in Behavioral Science, 1977–1978
Human Relations Award, Texas Teachers' Association, 1974
National Media Award, American Psychological Association, 1973
Distinguished Teaching Award, University of Texas, 1973
Fellow, Center for Advanced Study in Behavioral Science, 1970–1971
American Association for the Advancement of Science: Award for Distinguished Research in Social Psychology, 1970

BOOKS

Mistakes Were Made (But Not By Me) (with C. Tavris). New York: Harcourt, 2007.

The Social Animal. New York: W. H. Freeman/Worth. First edition, 1972; tenth edition, 2008.

Readings About the Social Animal (edited with Joshua Aronson). New York: W. H. Freeman/Worth. First edition, 1972; tenth edition, 2008.

The Adventures of Ruthie and a Little Boy Named Grandpa (with R. Aronson). iUniverse, 2006 (a children's book).

Nobody Left to Hate: Teaching Compassion After Columbine. New York: Worth/Freeman, 2000.

Cooperation in the Classroom: The Jigsaw Method (with S. Patnoe). New York: Longman, 1997.

Social Psychology: The Heart and the Mind (with T. Wilson & R. Akert). New York: Harper/Collins, 1994; Seventh edition, Prentice Hall, 2010.

Social Psychology: Volumes 1, 2, and 3 (with A. R. Pratkanis). London: Elgar Ltd., 1993.

Age of Propaganda (with A. R. Pratkanis). New York: W. H. Freeman & Co., 1992, 2001.

Methods of Research in Social Psychology (with P. C. Ellsworth, J. M. Carlsmith, & M. H. Gonzales). New York: McGraw-Hill, 1990.

Career Burnout (with A. Pines). New York: Free Press, 1988.

The Handbook of Social Psychology (3rd ed., with G. Lindzey). New York: Random House, 1985.

Energy Use: The Human Dimension (with P. C. Stern). New York: W. H. Freeman, 1984.
Burnout: From Tedium to Personal Growth (with A. Pines & D. Kafry). New York: Free Press, 1981.
The Jigsaw Classroom (with N. Blaney, C. Stephan, J. Sikes, & M. Snapp). Beverly Hills, CA: Sage, 1978.
Research Methods in Social Psychology (with J. M. Carlsmith & P. C. Ellsworth). Reading, MA: Addison-Wesley, 1976.
Social Psychology (with R. Helmreich). New York: Van Nostrand, 1973.
Voices of Modern Psychology. Reading, MA: Addison-Wesley, 1969.
Theories of Cognitive Consistency (with R. Abelson et. al.). Chicago, IL: Rand McNally, 1968.
Handbook of Social Psychology (2nd ed., with G. Lindzey). Reading, MA: Addison-Wesley, 1968–1969.

ARTICLES AND CHAPTERS

Transforming dissatisfaction with services into self-determination: A social-psychological perspective on community program effectiveness (with C. Macias). *Journal of Applied Social Psychology*, 2009, 39, 1835–1859.

The Jigsaw strategy in action: Integrating peer providers into traditional service settings (with C. Macius, P. J. Barreira, C. F. Rodican, & P. B. Gold). *Journal of Mental Health Policy Research*, 2008, 34, 494–496.

Fear, denial, and sensible action in the face of disasters. *Social Research,* 2008, 75, 1–18.

The evolution of cognitive dissonance theory: A personal appraisal. In A. Pratkanis (Ed.), *The Science of Social Influence.* New York: Psychology Press, 2007.

An autobiography. In G. Lindzey & M. Runyan (Eds.), *The History of Psychology in Autobiography* (Vol. 9, pp. 3–41). Washington, DC: APA Books, 2007.

Impact of referral source and study applicants' preference in random assignment on research enrollment, service engagement, and evaluative outcomes (with C. Macias et. al.). *American Journal of Psychiatry,* 2005, *162,* 781–787.

Reducing hostility and building compassion: Lessons from the Jigsaw Classroom. In A. Miller (Ed.), *The Social Psychology of Good and Evil* (pp. 469–487). New York: Guilford, 2004.

How the Columbine High School tragedy could have been prevented. *Journal of Individual Psychology,* 2004, 60(4), 355–360.

Drifting my own way: Following my nose and my heart. In R. Sternberg (Ed.), *Psychologists Defying the Crowd: Stories of Those Who Battled the Establishment and Won.* Washington, DC: APA Books, 2002.

Building empathy, compassion, and achievement in the Jigsaw classroom. In J. Aronson (Ed.), *Improving Academic Achievement* (pp. 209–225). San Diego: Academic Press, 2002.

Mindless propaganda, thoughtful persuasion (with A. Pratkanis). In M. H. Davis (Ed.), *Social Psychology Annual*. New York: McGraw-Hill, 2001.

Dissonance, hypocrisy, and the self-concept. In E. Harmon-Jones & J. Mills (Eds.), *Cognitive Dissonance: Progress on a Pivotal Theory in Social Psychology* (pp. 101–126). Washington, DC: American Psychological Association, 1999.

Adventures in experimental social psychology: Roots, branches, and sticky new leaves. In A. Rodrigues & R. Levine (Eds.), *Reflections on 100 Years of Experimental Social Psychology* (pp. 82–113). New York: Basic Books, 1999.

The power of self-persuasion. *American Psychologist*, 1999, *54*, 873–884.

The experimental method in social psychology (with T. Wilson & M. Brewer). In G. Lindzey, D. Gilbert, & S. Fiske (Eds.), *The Handbook of Social Psychology*. New York: Random House, 1998.

The theory of cognitive dissonance: The evolution and vicissitudes of an idea. In C. McGarty & S. A Haslam (Eds.), *The Message of Social Psychology*. London: Blackwell, 1997.

When exemplification fails: Hypocrisy and the motive for self-integrity (with J. Stone, A. Wiegand, & J. Cooper). *Journal of Personality and Social Psychology*, 1997, *72*, 54–65.

The giving away of psychology—and condoms. *APS Observer*, 1997, *10*, 17–35.

Hypocrisy, misattribution, and dissonance reduction: A demonstration of dissonance in the absence of aversive consequences (with C. Fried). *Personality and Social Psychology Bulletin*, 1995, *21*, 925–933.

On baseball and failure. *Dialogue*, Spring 1995, 4–5.

Inducing hypocrisy as a means of encouraging young adults to use condoms (with J. Stone, A. L. Crain, M .P. Winslow, & C. B. Fried). *Personality and Social Psychology Bulletin*, 1994, *20*, 116–128.

The return of the repressed: Dissonance theory makes a comeback. *Psychological Inquiry*, 1992, *3*, 303–311.

Totally provocative and perhaps partly right. *Psychological Inquiry*, 1992, *3*, 353–356.

Making research apply: High stakes public policy in a regulatory environment (with D. Archer & T. F. Pettigrew) *American Psychologist*, 1992, *47*, 1233–1236.

The jigsaw classroom: A cooperative strategy for reducing prejudice (with R. Thibodeau). In J. Lynch, C. Modgil, & S. Modgil (Eds.), *Cultural Diversity in the Schools*. London: Falmer Press, 1992.

Taking a closer look: Reasserting the role of the self-concept in dissonance theory (with R. Thibodeau). *Personality and Social Psychology Bulletin*, 1992, *18*, 591–602.

Using cognitive dissonance to encourage water conservation (with C. A. Dickerson, R. Thibodeau, & D. Miller). *Journal of Applied Social Psychology*, 1992, *22*, 841–854.

Causes of prejudice. In R. M. Baird & S. E Rosenblum (Eds.), *Bigotry, Prejudice and Hatred: Definitions, Causes and Solutions* (pp. 111–124). Buffalo, NY: Prometheus Books, 1992.

Stateways can change folkways. In R. M. Baird and S. E Rosenblum (Eds.) *Bigotry, prejudice and hatred: Definitions, Causes and Solutions. Contemporary issues*. Buffalo NY: Prometheus Books, 1992, 185-201.

How to change behavior. In R. Curtis and G. Stricker (Eds.), *How People Change: Inside and Outside Therapy*. New York: Plenum, 1991.

Subliminal sorcery (with A. R. Pratkanis). *USA Today*, 1991, *120*, 64–66.

Leon Festinger and the art of audacity. *Psychological Science*, 1991, *4*, 213–217.

Overcoming denial and increasing the intention to use condoms through the induction of hypocrisy (with C. Fried & J. Stone). *American Journal of Public Health*, 1991, *81*, 1636–1638.

Applying social psychology to prejudice reduction and energy conservation. *Personality and Social Psychology Bulletin*, 1990, *16*, 118–132.

The social psychology of energy conservation (with M. H. Gonzales). In J. Edwards (Ed.), *Social Influence Processes and Prevention* (pp. 48–59). New York: Plenum Press, 1990.

Analysis, synthesis and the treasuring of the old. *Personality and Social Psychology Bulletin*, 1989, *15*, 508–512.

Desegregation, jigsaw and the Mexican-American experience (with A. Gonzalez). In P. Katz & D. Taylor (Eds.), *Eliminating Racism* (pp. 301–314). New York: Plenum, 1988.

Using social cognition and persuasion to promote energy conservation: A quasi-experiment (with M. H. Gonzales & M. Costanzo). *Journal of Applied Social Psychology*, 1988, *18*, 1049–1066.

Answering behavioral questions about energy efficiency in buildings (with P. Stern et al.). *Energy*, 1987, *12*, 339–353.

Energy conservation behavior: The difficult path from information to action (with M. Costanzo et al.). *American Psychologist*, 1986, *41*, 521–528.

The effectiveness of incentives for residential energy conservation (with P. Stern et al.). *Evaluation Review*, 1986, 10, 147-176.

The social-psychological foundations of successful energy conservation programmes (with S. Coltrane & D. Archer). *Energy Policy*, 1986, *14*, 133–148.

Teaching students what they think they already know about prejudice and desegregation. In V. P. Makosky (Ed.), *The G. Stanley Hall Lecture Series*, Volume 7. Washington, DC: American Psychological Association Press, 1986.

Experimentation in social psychology (with M. Brewer & J. M. Carlsmith). In G. Lindzey & E. Aronson (Eds.), *The Handbook of Social Psychology* (3rd ed., pp. 99–142) New York: Random House, 1985.

Social behavior and mental attitudes. In D. Nelkin (Ed.), *The Human Mind: The Brain and Beyond*. New York: The American Broadcasting Company Press, 1985.

Social-psychological aspects of energy conservation (with S. Yates). In D. Hafemeister, H. Kelly, & B. Levi (Eds.), *Energy Sources: Conservation and Renewables*. New York: American Institute of Physics Press, 1985.

What ever happened to dissonance theory? *Contemporary Social Psychology*, 1985, *11*, 132–136.

Improving utility conservation programs: Outcomes, interventions, and evaluations (with L. Condelli et al.). *Energy*, 1984, *9*, 485–494.

Energy conservation research of California's utilities: A meta-evaluation (with L. White et al.). *Evaluation Review*, 1984, *8*, 167–186.

Characteristics of effective feedback. In R. S. Cathcart & L. Samovar (Eds.), *Small Group Communication*. Dubuque: W. C. Brown, 1984.

Modifying the environment of the desegregated classroom. In A. J. Stewart (Ed.), *Motivation and Society* (pp. 319–336). San Francisco, CA: Jossey-Bass, 1984,.

Residential energy conservation: A social-psychological perspective. In B. Morrison & W. Kempton (Eds.), *Families and Energy* (pp. 11–24). East Lansing: Michigan State University Press, 1984.

Forderung von Schulleistung, Selbstwert und prosozialem Verhalten: Die Jigsaw-Methode. In G. L. Huber, S. Rotering-Steinberg, & D. Wahl (Eds.), *Kooperatives Lernen* (pp. 48–59). Weinheim und Basel: Beltz Verlag, 1984.

Cooperation in the classroom: The impact of the jigsaw method on inter-ethnic relations, classroom performance and self-esteem (with S. Yates). In H. Blumberg & P. Hare (Eds.), *Small Groups*. London: John Wiley & Sons, 1983.

The social psychology of aggression (with L. White). In M. Draaganov (Ed.), *Sociopsychological Problems in Personality*. Sofia, Bulgaria: Science and Art Press, 1983.

Behavioral and Social Aspects of Energy Conservation (with P.C. Stern). Washington, DC: National Academy of Sciences, 1983.

Combatting burnout (with A. Pines). *Children and Youth Services Review*, 1983, *5*, 263–275.

Antecedents, correlates and consequences of sexual jealousy (with A. Pines). *Journal of Personality*, 1983, *51*, 108–136.

A social-psychological perspective on energy conservation in residential buildings (with S. Yates). *American Psychologist*, 1983, *38*, 435–444.

Polyfidelity: An alternative lifestyle without sexual jealousy? (with A. Pines). *Journal of Alternative Lifestyles*, 1982, *4*, 373–392.

The relative effectiveness of models and prompts on energy conservation: A field experiment in a shower room (with M. O'Leary). *Journal of Environmental Systems*, 1982, 219–224.

Energy conservation as a social science problem. In J. Harris & J. M. Hollander (Eds.), *Improving Energy Efficiency in Buildings*. Berkeley: University of California Press, 1982.

Cooperation, prosocial behavior, and academic performance: Experiments in the desegregated classroom (with N. Osherow). In L. Bickman (Ed.), *Applied Social Psychology Annual* (Vol. 1, pp. 163–196), 1980.

Persuasion via self-justification: Large commitments for small rewards. In L. Festinger (Ed.), *Four Decades of Social Psychology*. New York: Oxford University Press, 1980.

Training teachers to implement jigsaw learning: A manual for teachers (with E. Goode). In S. Sharan, P. Hare, C. Webb, & R. Hertz-Lazarowitz (Eds.), *Cooperation in Education* (pp. 47–81). Provo, UT: Brigham Young University Press, 1980.

Jigsaw groups and the desegregated classroom: In pursuit of common goals (with D. Bridgeman). *Personality and Social Psychology Bulletin*, 1979, 5, 438–446.

Attributions to success and failure in cooperative, competitive and interdependent interaction (with N. Presser, C. Stephan, & J. Kennedy). *European Journal of Social Psychology*, 1978, 8, 269–274.

Attributions for success and failure after cooperation, competition, or team competition (with C. Stephan & M. A. Burnham). *European Journal of Social Psychology*, 1979, 9, 109–114.

Interdependent interactions and prosocial behavior (with D. Bridgeman & R. Geffner). *Journal of Research and Development in Education*, 1978, *12*(1), 16–27.

The effects of cooperative classroom structure on student behavior and attitudes (with D. Bridgeman & R. Geffner). In D. Bar Tal & L. Saxe (Eds.), *Social Psychology of Education*. Washington, DC: Hemisphere, 1978.

The theory of cognitive dissonance: A current perspective. In L. Berkowitz (Ed.), *Cognitive Theories in Social Psychology* (pp. 215–220). New York: Academic Press, 1978.

The interpersonal consequences of self-disclosure and internal attributions for success (with W. G. Stephan & G. W. Lucker). *Personality and Social Psychology Bulletin*, 1977, *2*(3), 252–255.

Interdependence in the classroom: A field study (with N. T. Blaney, C. Stephan, R. Rosenfield, & J. Sikes). *Journal of Educational Psychology*, 1977, 69, 121–128.

Therapy for a competitive society. In P. B. Zimbardo & F. Ruch, *Psychology and Life* (9th ed., pp. 12A–12D). Glenview, IL: Scott, Foresman and Co., 1977.

Research in social psychology as a leap of faith. Invited address, 1976 Meetings of Society of Experimental Social Psychologists, Los Angeles. *Personality and Social Psychology Bulletin*, 1977, 3, 190–195.

Attribution of luck or skill as a function of cooperating or competing with a friend or acquaintance. *Sociometry*, 1977, 40, 107–111.

Performance in the interdependent classroom: A field study (with W. Lucker, D. Rosenfield, & J. Sikes). *American Educational Research Journal*, 1976, *13*(2), 115–123.

Current developments in small group theory. In M. Cernea (Ed.), *Perspectives in American Sociology*. Bucharest: Encyclopedia Romana, 1976.

The effect of cooperation on interpersonal attraction. A report to the special conference on International Social Psychology, Budapest, Hungary. *Bulletin of the Hungarian Academy of Sciences*, 1976, *31*(3), 322–327.

Busing and racial tension: The jigsaw route to learning and liking (with N. Blaney, J. Sikes, C. Stephan, & M. Snapp). *Psychology Today*, February 1975, 8, 43–50.

Affective reactions to appraisal from others (with D. Mettee). In T. L. Huston (Ed.), Foundations of Interpersonal Attraction (pp. 236–283). New York and London: Academic Press, 1974.

A two-factor theory of dissonance reduction: The effect of feeling stupid or feeling "awful" on opinion change (with T. Chase, R. Helmreich, & R. Ruhnke). *International Journal of Communication Research*, 1974, *3*, 340–352.

Attribution of fault to a rape victim as a function of respectability of the victim (with C. Jones). *Journal of Personality and Social Psychology*, 1973, *26*, 415–419.

The rationalizing animal. *Psychology Today*, May 1973, *6*, 46–52.

The reciprocation of attraction from similar and dissimilar others: A study in person perception and evaluation (with E. E. Jones, & L. Bell). In C. G. McClintock (Ed.), *Experimental Social Psychology* (pp. 142–179). New York: Holt, Rinehart & Winston, 1972.

Does a woman's attractiveness influence men's nonsexual reactions? (with V. Aronson). *Medical Aspects of Human Sexuality*, 1971, *5*, 12–27.

The cooperative subject: Myth or reality? (with H. Sigall & T. Van Hoose). *Journal of Experimental Social Psychology*, 1970, *6*, 1–10.

Who likes whom—and why. *Psychology Today*, 1970, *4*(3), 48–50, 74.

To err is humanizing—sometimes: Effects of self-esteem, competence, and a pratfall on interpersonal attraction (with R. Helmreich & J. LeFan). *Journal of Personality and Social Psychology*, 1970, *16*, 259–264.

Experimentation in social psychology (with J. M. Carlsmith). In G. Lindzey & E. Aronson (Eds.), *Handbook of Social Psychology* (2nd ed., Vol. II, pp. 1–79). Reading, MA: Addison-Wesley, 1969.

Liking for an evaluator as a function of her physical attractiveness and nature of the evaluations (with H. Sigall). *Journal of Experimental Social Psychology*, 1969, *5*, 93–100.

The influence of the character of the criminal and his victim on the decisions of simulated jurors (with D. Landy). *Journal of Experimental Social Psychology*, 1969, *5*, 141–152.

Beyond Parkinson's law: III. The effect of protractive and contractive distractions on the wasting of time on subsequent tasks (with D. Landy & K. McCue). *Journal of Applied Psychology*, 1969, *53*, 236–239.

Opinion change in the advocate as a function of the persuasability of his audience: A clarification of the meaning of dissonance (with E. Nel & R. Helmreich). *Journal of Personality and Social Psychology*, 1969, *12*, 117–124.

The theory of cognitive dissonance: A current perspective. In L. Berkowitz (Ed.), *Advances in Experimental Social Psychology* (Vol. 4, pp. 1–34). New York: Academic Press, 1969.

Normative adaptation, cognitive dissonance, and conflict denial. For RIAS, Berlin, 1969.

A theoretical restatement of dissonance theory in the light of recent experiments. *Proceedings of the XIX International Congress of Psychology*, London, July 1969.

Some antecedents of interpersonal attraction. In W. J. Arnold & D. Levine (Eds.), *Nebraska Symposium on Motivation 1969* (pp. 143-173). Lincoln: University of Nebraska Press, 1969. (Won AAAS Socio-Psychological Prize for 1970.)

My enemy's enemy is my friend (with V. Cope). *Journal of Personality and Social Psychology*, 1968, 8, 8–12.

Dissonance theory: Progress and problems. In. R. P. Abelson, E. Aronson, W. J. McGuire, T. M. Newcomb, M. J. Rosenberg, and P. H. Tannenbaum (Eds.), *Theories of Cognitive Consistency: A Sourcebook* (pp. 5–27). Chicago: Rand McNally, 1968.

Dissonance theory and the formation of values. In C. D. Speilberger, R. Fox, & B. Masterson (Eds.), *Contributions to General Psychology* (pp. 366–369). New York: Ronald Press, 1968.

Dishonest behavior as a function of differential levels of induced self-esteem (with D. R. Mettee). *Journal of Personality and Social Psychology*, 1968, 9, 121–127.

Liking for an evaluator as a function of his discernment (with D. Landy). *Journal of Personality and Social Psychology*, 1968, 9, 133–141.

The effect of expectancy of task duration on the experience of fatigue (with B. Walster). *Journal of Experimental Social Psychology*, 1967, 3, 41–46.

Opinion change and the gain-loss model of interpersonal attraction (with H. Sigall). *Journal of Experimental Social Psychology*, 1967, 3, 178–188.

Further steps beyond Parkinson's law: A replication and extension of the excess time effect (with D. Landy). *Journal of Experimental Social Psychology*, 1967, 3, 274–285.

Beyond Parkinson's law: The effect of excess time on subsequent performance (with E. Gerard). *Journal of Personality and Social Psychology*, 1966, 3, 336–339.

Threat and obedience. *Trans-action*, March–April 1966.

Similarity versus liking as determinants of interpersonal attractiveness (with P. Worchel). *Psychonomic Science*, 1966, 5, 157–158.

Avoidance of inter-subject communication. *Psychological Reports*, 1966, 19, 238.

Try a little dissonance. *New York Times Magazine*, Part I, September 11, 1966.

Problem: To find evidence of discomfort as a function of "dissonant" success. In *Methodological Problems of Social Psychology*, Proceedings of the XVIII International Congress of Psychology, 34th Symposium, Moscow, August 1966.

The psychology of insufficient justification: An analysis of some conflicting data. In S. Feldman (Ed.), *Cognitive Consistency* (pp. 109–133). New York: Academic Press, 1966.

Self evaluation versus direct anxiety reduction as determinants of the fear affiliation relationship (with J.M. Darley). *Journal of Experimental Social Psychology*, Supplement I, 1966, 66–79.

Choosing to suffer as a consequence of expecting to suffer: An unexpected finding (with E. Walster & Z. Brown). *Journal of Experimental Social Psychology*, 1966, *2*, 400–406.

On increasing the persuasiveness of a low prestige communicator (with E. Walster & D. Abrahams). *Journal of Experimental Social Psychology*, 1966, *2*, 325–342.

The importance of physical attractiveness in dating behavior (with E. Walster, V. Aronson, D. Abrams, & L. Rottman). *Journal of Personality and Social Psychology*, 1966, *4*, 508–516.

Opinion change as a function of the communicator's attractiveness and desire to influence (with J. Mills). *Journal of Personality and Social Psychology*, 1965, *1*, 173–177.

Gain and loss of esteem as determinants of interpersonal attractiveness (with D. Linder). *Journal of Experimental Social Psychology*, 1965, *1*, 156–171.

Some hedonic consequences of the confirmation and disconfirmation of expectancies (with J. M. Carlsmith). *Journal of Abnormal and Social Psychology*, 1963, *66*, 151–156.

The effects of expectancy on volunteering for an unpleasant experience (with J. M. Carlsmith and J. M. Darley). *Journal of Abnormal and Social Psychology*, 1963, *66*, 220–224.

Effect of the severity of threat on the devaluation of forbidden behavior (with J. M. Carlsmith). *Journal of Abnormal and Social Psychology*, 1963, *66*, 584–588.

Communicator credibility and communication discrepancy as determinants of opinion change (with J. Turner & J. M. Carlsmith), *Journal of Abnormal Social Psychology*, 1963, *67*, 31–36.

Effort, attractiveness, and the anticipation of reward. *Journal of Abnormal and Social Psychology*, 1963, *67*, 522–525.

Modification of the rat's saline intake gradient by experience with specific concentrations (with J. Theios & J. de Rivera). *Psychological Reports*, 1962, *10*, 487–490.

Performance expectancy as a determinant of actual performance (with J. M. Carlsmith). *Journal of Abnormal and Social Psychology*, 1962, *65*, 178–182.

The effect of relevant and irrelevant aspects of communicator credibility on opinion change (with B. W. Golden). *Journal of Personality*, 1962, *30*, 135–146.

The effect of effort on the attractiveness of rewarded and unrewarded stimuli. *Journal of Abnormal and Social Psychology*, 1961, *63*, 375–380.

Arousal and reduction of dissonance in social contexts (with L. Festinger). In D. Cartwright and Z. Zander (Eds.), *Group Dynamics* (3rd ed., pp. 125–136). New York: Harper & Row, 1960/1968,.

The effect of severity of initiation on liking for a group (with J. Mills). *Journal of Abnormal and Social Psychology*, 1959, *59*, 177–181.

Selectivity in exposure to information (with J. Mills & H. Robinson). *Journal of Abnormal and Social Psychology*, 1959, *59*, 250–253.

Personality rigidity as measured by aniseikonic lenses and by perceptual tests of metabolic efficiency (with M. Wertheimer). *Journal of General Psychology*, 1958, *58*, 41–49.

The need for achievement as measured by graphic expression. In. J. W. Atkinson (Ed.), *Motives in Fantasy, Action and Society* (pp. 249–265). New York: Van Nostrand, 1958.

Some attempts to measure tolerance for dissonance (with L. Festinger). Wright Development Center, Technical Report 58-492, December 1958. ASTIA Document No. 207-337.

AUTHOR INDEX

A

Abel, T., 260, 262
Abelson, R. P., 33, 36
Abrahams, D., 207
Allen, J. J. B., 121, 122
Allport, F. H., 21
Allport, G. W., 21, 25, 42, 273, 274, 293
American Psychological Association, 263
Amodio, D. M., 120, 121
Anderson, N., 58
Apfel, N., 304
Araragi, C., 25
Archer, D., 26, 256, 261, 262
Aron, A. P., 84
Aronson, E., 24, 25, 26, 31, 33, 34, 36, 41, 43, 51, 52, 56, 67, 68, 71, 75, 79, 80, 81, 82, 84, 85, 87, 88, 90, 91, 92, 96, 98, 99, 101, 103, 109, 110, 111, 112, 114, 124, 125, 134, 135, 137, 142, 144, 146, 147, 148, 150, 152, 154, 159, 160, 161, 162, 163, 164, 176, 178, 179, 191, 204, 205, 206, 207, 215, 221, 224, 234, 238, 242, 253, 255, 256, 260, 261, 262, 270, 272, 273, 275, 279, 285, 294, 299, 302, 317, 318
Aronson, J., 190, 290, 293, 297, 303
Aronson, V., 207
Arrow, K., 49
Arshan, N., 305

Asch, S., 86
Atteberry, A., 305
Audrain, P. C., 100
Ax, A. F., 85

B

Bailey, D. A., 225, 229
Banaji, M. R., 273
Barch, D. M., 120
Bargh, J. A., 146
Baron, R. M., 115
Barron, K. E., 188
Bartels, J. M., 76
Batson, C. D., 124
Baumeister, R. F., 36, 69, 72, 73, 74, 75, 76, 83, 92, 99, 101, 102, 176, 303
Bayer, U., 117
Beauvois, J. L., 111
Becker, C. B., 178
Beckmann, J., 117, 119
Behrens, W. W., 254
Bellotti, A. C., 254
Bem, D., 33
Bem, D. J., 218
Benthin, A., 144
Berent, M. K., 179
Berkowitz, L., 115
Berscheid, E., 205, 206, 207
Beveridge, W. I. B., 331
Birbaumer, N., 122
Black, J. S., 257, 261, 262
Blaney, N., 43, 294

Blanton, H., 190
Bloom, P., 134
Boden, J. M., 74
Boninger, D. S., 179
Bonoma, T. V., 72
Botvinick, M. M., 120
Bowdle, B. F., 103
Brainerd, C. J., 241
Braver, T. S., 120
Brehm, J., 148, 149, 187, 190
Brehm, J. W., 52, 83, 111, 113, 117, 118, 119, 120, 124, 138, 144, 145, 177
Brenner, L., 57
Brewer, M., 24, 204
Brickman, P., 139
Bridgeman, D., 294
Brinol, P., 143
Brock, T., 139, 141
Brock, T. C., 179, 183
Brothen, T., 207
Bryk, A. S., 89
Buckley, J. P., 212, 221, 223, 227, 233, 235
Butterfield, E. C., 303
Byrne, D., 206

C

Cacioppo, J. T., 182, 183
Campbell, D., 60
Campbell, D. T., 87, 101, 102
Campbell, J. D., 74
Cantril, H., 21
Carlsmith, J. M., 24, 31, 32, 33, 34, 41, 68, 80, 82, 84, 85, 86, 87, 90, 91, 95, 96, 98, 99, 101, 109, 110, 134, 135, 137, 142, 144, 154, 159, 160, 161, 162, 178, 191, 204, 207, 270, 272, 318
Carter, C. S., 120, 121
Catanese, K. R., 76
Cavender, J., 122
Ceci, S., 291
Cesafsky, L., 252
Chappells, H., 252
Chartrand, T. L., 146
Chojnacki, D. E., 217, 239
Cialdini, R. A., 221, 228
Cialdini, R. B., 36, 97

Ciao, A. C., 178
Ciarocco, N. J., 76
Cicchini, M. D., 217, 239
Cobb, C., 302
Coffman, K. A. J., 217
Cohen, A. R., 52, 83, 111, 120, 177, 179
Cohen, D., 103
Cohen, G. L., 150, 304
Cohen, J. D., 120, 121
Coles, M. G. H., 120
Collins, B. E., 111, 161
Collins, M. E., 23
Collins, N. L., 208
Coltrane, S., 256, 262
Comaroff, J. L., 257
Cooper, J., 72, 109, 110, 111, 112, 124, 125, 145, 146, 147, 150, 161, 163, 164, 165, 167, 169, 171, 177, 190
Copeland, L., 47
Cordova, D. I., 35
Costanzo, M., 25, 56, 154, 205, 256, 261
Costanzo, M. A., 26
Cottrell, N. B., 141
Covert, A., 120
Crain, A. L., 25, 110, 111, 112, 150, 163, 164, 205, 299
Crogan, M., 25
Crompton, T., 260
Curtin, J. J., 120

D

Dailey, E. M., 217
Darley, J., 86
Darley, J. M., 162, 253, 258
Darling-Hammond, L., 305
Dashiell, J. F., 21
Davidson, R. J., 121
Davis, D., 213, 218, 221, 223, 225, 226, 229, 233, 234, 235, 237, 239, 240, 241, 242
Davis, K. E., 161
Davis, R. M., 145
Deci, E. L., 34
Demaree, K. G., 143
Denizeau, M., 190
Deutsch, M., 23, 25, 42
Devine, P. G., 113, 120, 179, 188
DeWall, C. N., 76

Dickerson, C., 163
Dickerson, C. A., 25, 56, 103, 110, 152, 256
Dietz, T., 253, 258, 259, 260, 261, 262
Dipboye, R. L., 138, 141
Disston, L. G., 57
Dixon, J., 281
Donchin, E., 120
Doob, A. N., 84
Dovidio, J. F., 272
Downhill, J. E., 121
Doyle, L. H., 303
Drake, M., 36
Driver, E. D., 218
Drizin, S. A., 217, 221, 222, 223, 224, 230, 231, 233, 235, 236, 238, 239, 240, 242
Durrheim, K., 281
Dutton, D. G., 84
Dweck, C., 303

E

Eagly, A. H., 179, 188
Eaton, W. W., 290
Ebbesen, E. B., 33
Edelman, S. K., 139, 141
Edwards, D. C., 139, 141
Egan, L. C., 134
Eggleston, T. J., 144
Eisenstadt, D., 177, 178, 182, 183, 185, 186, 190, 192, 195
Ekman, P., 100
Eliot, C. W., 278
Elkin, R. A., 113, 119, 183, 194, 195
Elliot, A. J., 113, 188
Ellsworth, E., 24
Ellsworth, P., 109, 318
Ellsworth, P. C., 41, 85, 86, 87, 91, 95, 96, 99, 100, 101, 102, 191, 204
Elworth, J. T., 257, 261, 262
Ely, R. J., 208
Eppler, R., 25
Epstein, G. F., 139
Etgen, M. P., 141
Everett, P. B., 260

F

Fabrigar, L. R., 179, 189

Fanning, J. J., 189
Faucher, T. A., 290
Fazio, R. H., 109, 110, 145, 146, 163, 177
Fearn, M., 123, 145
Fernandez, N. C., 152
Festinger, L., 31, 32, 50, 82, 84, 85, 96, 98, 109, 110, 114, 115, 135, 144, 160, 177, 178, 195, 270
Field, P., 69
Findley, K. A., 238
Fisher, J. D., 281
Fisher, R., 49
Fiske, D. W., 101, 102
Flor, H., 122
Floyd, J., 207
Fointiat, V., 148, 152
Follette, W. C., 221, 223, 225, 229, 234, 241
Fong, G. T., 36, 122
Ford, L. H., Jr., 139
Forster, M. J., 254
Franklin, B., 288
Freedman, J. L., 84, 87, 101, 102
French, T., 241
Fried, C., 110, 163, 303
Fried, C. B., 25, 110, 111, 112, 150, 152, 163, 164, 205, 299
Friedman, R. D., 241
Frijda, N. H., 124
Fulero, S. M., 212, 239, 240
Funder, D., 83, 92, 99, 101, 102
Funder, D. C., 36

G

Garcia, J., 304
Gardner, G. T., 253, 256, 257, 258, 259, 261
Garrett, B., 219, 238
Gawronski, B., 182
Geller, E. S., 260
Gerard, H. B., 115, 117, 292
Gerber, W.-D., 122
Gerdjikov, T., 121, 122, 123
Gerhing, W. J., 120
Gibbons, F. X., 144
Gibson, J. J., 115
Gilligan, J., 253, 259
Gilovich, T., 44, 47, 48
Gingras, I., 34

Gladwell, M., 300
Glass, D. C., 144
Glick, P., 272
Goethals, G. R., 111
Goffman, E., 69
Gollwitzer, P. M., 117, 118, 123
Gonzales, M. H., 24, 25, 41, 56, 85, 86, 87, 91, 95, 99, 101, 109, 154, 191, 204, 205, 256, 318
Gonzalez, A., 25
Gonzalez, R., 91, 100, 102
Good, C., 303
Gosling, P., 190
Goss, B., 120
Gossard, M., 252
Gotz, J., 190
Gotz-Marchand, B., 190
Gould, S. J., 285
Graziano, W. G., 207
Greenberg, J., 75, 113, 119, 145, 148, 149, 187, 190
Greene, D., 34, 44, 86
Greenwald, A. G., 195, 273
Gringart, E., 178
Grisso, T., 221, 222, 223, 224, 230, 231, 233, 235, 236, 238, 239, 240, 242
Grosbras, J.-M., 152
Guagnano, G., 261
Guagnano, G. A., 260, 262
Gudjonsson, G. H., 218, 221, 222, 223, 224, 230, 231, 233, 235, 236, 238, 239, 240, 242

H

Hardin, G., 254
Hardyck, J. A., 195
Harmon-Jones, C., 117, 118, 121, 122, 123, 145
Harmon-Jones, E., 111, 113, 114, 115, 117, 118, 119, 120, 121, 122, 123, 124, 145, 177
Harris, J. R., 290
Hartley, S., 120
Harvey, O. J., 24, 25, 293
Hass, R. G., 181, 192
Haynes, G. A., 144
Heerey, E. A., 103
Heine, S. J., 170

Helmes, E., 178
Helmreich, R., 111, 161, 176, 178, 179
Henderlong, J., 34, 35
Henkel, L. A., 217
Henley, M. D., 111
Henriques, J. B., 121
Herrnstein, R. J., 286
Hertz-Lazarowitz, R., 25
Hill, D. H., 253
Hill, R., 100
Hirsch, A., 238
Hirst, E., 253
Hodell, M., 34
Hogg, M. A., 166, 167, 169, 171
Holland, R. W., 145
Holmes, J. G., 208
Homans, G. C., 49, 206
Hood, W., 293
Hood, W. R., 25
Hoshino-Brown, E., 170
House, P., 44, 86
Hovland, C., 160
Hovland, C. I., 188
Hoyt, M. K., 111
Huber, G. L., 25
Huesmann, L. R., 139
Hunter, J. E., 140
Hurd, L. E., 254
Hutton, D. G., 74

I

Ichheiser, G., 301
Inbau, F. E., 221, 223, 227, 233, 235
Inzlicht, M., 303
Irle, M., 117, 190
Iyengar, S. S., 35

J

Janis, I., 160
Janis, I. L., 69, 177
Jayne, B. C., 212, 221, 223, 227, 233, 235
Johnson, B. T., 179, 188
Johnson, P., 123, 145
Joncas, A. J., 33
Jones, E. E., 23, 44, 69, 72, 115, 117, 161
Jones, S. C., 138
Joule, R. V., 111

K

Kagan, J., 101, 102
Kahneman, D., 54
Kalof, L., 260, 262
Kamiya, J., 122
Kardush, M., 195
Kassin, S. M., 218, 221, 222, 223, 224, 226, 230, 231, 232, 233, 235, 236, 238, 239, 240, 242
Katz, I., 181, 192, 303
Katz, M., 53
Katzev, R., 260
Keavney, M., 36
Kelley, H. H., 160
Kelly, M., 179
Keltner, D., 100, 103
Kemmelmeier, M., 241
Kempton, W., 253, 258
Kiechel, K. L., 218
Kim, S., 305
King, B. T., 177
Kitayama, S., 170
Klineberg, O., 21
Klockars, A. J., 139
Knaack, D., 225, 229
Koestner, R., 34
Kopelman, S., 258
Kotchoubey, B., 122
Kramer, B. M., 274
Kropp, P., 122
Krosnick, J. A., 179
Krueger, J. I., 74
Krug, M. K., 120
Kübler, A., 122
Kuhl, J., 117, 119
Kunda, Z., 147
Kurlander, M., 305

L

Lackenbauer, S., 170
Lamm, L. W., 47
Landauer, T. K., 33, 84
Lassiter, G. D., 233, 242
Latané, B., 86
Lawrence, D. H., 114
Leary, M. R., 74, 75
Lee, C., 276
Lehman, D. R., 170

Leo, R., 213, 221, 223, 225, 229
Leo, R. A., 215, 217, 218, 219, 221, 222, 223, 224, 225, 226, 229, 230, 231, 232, 233, 234, 235, 236, 237, 238, 239, 240, 241, 242
Lepper, M., 45
Lepper, M. R., 33, 34, 35, 36, 41, 45, 58, 63, 113, 119, 177, 178, 179, 182, 183, 185, 186, 190, 192, 194, 195
Lewin, K., 21, 22, 293
Li, W., 152
Liberman, V., 58
Lindberg, M. J., 242
Linder, D., 206
Linder, D. E., 72, 161
Lindzey, G., 81
Lippitt, R., 293
Liu, T. J., 164
Locke, K. D., 100
Lord, C. G., 45
Lowin, A., 139
Lutzenhiser, L., 252
Lykken, D. T., 226
Lynch, M., 145, 164

M

MacDonald, A. W., III, 121
Maoz, I., 53
Maracek, J., 139, 141, 142
Markus, H., 147, 170
Marti, C. N., 178
Martinie, M. A., 148
Master, A., 35, 304
Master, S. L., 121
Matsumoto, D., 100
McArthur, L. Z., 115
McGlone, M., 303
McGuire, W. J., 36, 83, 88
McKenna, S. J., 47
McNall, K., 218
Meadows, D. H., 254
Meertens, R. M., 145
Meissner, C., 233
Mesquita, B., 101
Messick, D. M., 258
Mettee, D., 139, 141, 142
Mettee, D. R., 67, 68, 71, 75
Meyer, D. E., 120

Michel, S., 152
Milgram, S., 24, 31, 86
Miller, D., 25, 56, 103, 110, 152, 163, 256
Miller, N., 292
Mills, J., 24, 31, 84, 85, 90, 96, 109, 122, 160, 177, 206, 270
Misak, J. E., 145
Mnookin, L., 49
Mnookin, R. H., 49
Moezzi, M., 252
Monarch, N. D., 103
Monin, B., 167, 169, 171
Moran, D., 252
Moran, G., 139
Mullen, B., 140
Munsterberg, H., 218
Murray, C., 285, 286, 300, 305, 300
Murray, S. L., 208

N

Nadler, A., 281
Nail, P. R., 145
National Research Council, 251, 253, 257, 258, 261
Nel, E., 111, 176, 178, 179
Nelson, D. E., 113, 119, 145
Newcomb, T. M., 36
Nisbett, R., 291, 307
Nisbett, R. E., 34, 44, 87, 98, 101, 103
Noll, D., 120
Norton, M. I., 167, 169, 171
Norwick, R. J., 223
Nosek, B. A., 273
Nuss, C. K., 303

O

Oakes, P. J., 166
Oberle, D., 190
O'Donohue, W. T., 221, 233
Oemig, C., 103
Ofshe, R. J., 215, 217, 237
Oickle, E., 305
Oka, I. N., 254
O'Leary, M., 255, 260
Olson, J. M., 144
Orfield, G., 276, 305
Oskamp, S., 258
Ostrom, E., 258

Ostrom, T. M., 179

P

Patnoe, S., 25, 43, 152, 275
Pedersen, E., 290
Peters, W., 302
Peterson, A. A., 144
Peterson, H., 124
Pettigrew, T., 256, 261
Pettigrew, T. F., 26, 272, 274, 280
Petty, R. E., 143, 182, 183
Pimentel, D., 254
Pines, A., 25
Pizzagalli, D. A., 121
Poehlman, T. A., 273
Pool, G. J., 144
Pratkanis, A. R., 215, 221, 224, 242, 279
Presnell, K., 178
Prislin, R., 144
Pronin, E., 47, 48
Pyszczynski, T., 75

R

Rabbie, J. M., 111, 120
Randers, J., 254
Ratcliff, J. J., 242
Rauch, S. M., 185, 186
Raudenbush, S. W., 89
Reardon, S. F., 305
Redlich, A., 218
Redlich, A. D., 221, 222, 223, 224, 230, 231, 233, 235, 236, 238, 239, 240, 242
Regan, D. T., 86
Reicher, S. D., 166
Reid, J. E., 221, 223, 227, 233, 235
Reyna, V. F., 241
Riecken, H. W., 84
Rivers, J. A., 182, 185, 186
Robinson, R. G., 121
Roediger, R., 104
Rogers, H. L., 179
Rosen, E. F., 141
Rosenberg, M. J., 36
Rosenthal, R., 140
Ross, L., 36, 41, 44, 45, 46, 47, 48, 49, 52, 53, 57, 58, 63

Ross, L. D., 86
Rottman, L., 207
Rudman, L. A., 272
Ryan, R. M., 34

S

Sandvold, K. D., 138, 139
Santos, L. R., 134
Sarup, G., 179
Schachter, S., 31, 84, 85
Schacter, D. L., 241
Schlenker, B. R., 72, 176
Schmidt, F. L., 140
Schooler, J. W., 120
Schuck, J. R., 139, 141
Schwartz, D., 87
Schwartz, S. H., 260
Schwarz, N., 101, 103
Scott, M. S., 238
Sechrest, L., 87
Senese, L., 230
Sharan, S., 25
Shaw, H., 178
Sheeran, P., 117
Sherif, C. F., 24, 25
Sherif, C. W., 179, 293
Sherif, M., 24, 25, 42, 188, 293
Sherman, D. K., 150
Sherwood, R. J., 121
Sholes, O. D., 254
Shrauger, J. S., 138
Sigall, H., 122
Sigelman, J., 121
Sigelman, J. D., 123, 145
Sikes, J., 43, 294
Simon, L., 113, 119, 145, 148, 149, 187, 190
Singer, J. E., 31
Siniatchkin, M., 122
Slavin, R., 305
Smart, L., 74
Smith, L. M., 178
Snapp, M., 43, 294
Snyder, M., 144
Solomon, S., 75
Somat, A., 152
Sommers, S., 93
Son Hing, L. S., 152
Soryal, A. S., 189

Sparling, S., 86
Speelman, C., 178
Spencer, S., 164
Spencer, S. J., 36, 122, 145, 170
Spoor, S., 178
Stambush, M., 182
Stambush, M. A., 185, 186, 187, 188, 194
Starzyk, K. B., 189
Steele, C., 164
Steele, C. M., 109, 145, 153, 176, 190, 290, 302
Steinberg, R., 25
Stenger, V. A., 121
Stephan, C., 43
Stephan, G., 294
Stephan, W. G., 273, 292
Stern, P. C., 25, 252, 253, 255, 256, 257, 258, 259, 260, 261, 262
Stice, E., 178
Stone, J., 25, 110, 111, 112, 115, 116, 124, 125, 140, 144, 145, 146, 147, 148, 150, 152, 163, 164, 165, 205, 299
Strack, F., 182
Strehl, U., 122
Stroop, J. R., 121
Strunk, W., Jr., 319
Stucke, T. S., 76
Sunderman, G., 305
Swann, W. B., Jr., 138, 140, 141, 208

T

Tajfel, H., 166
Takaku, S., 152
Tanke, E. D., 144
Tannenbaum, P. H., 36
Tauer, J. M., 188
Tavris, C., 99, 234, 238
Taylor, S., 139
Taylor, S. E., 121, 123
Tedeschi, J. T., 72
Thibodeau, R., 24, 25, 56, 103, 110, 144, 146, 147, 148, 152, 163, 256, 299
Thøgerson, J., 260
Tice, D. M., 72, 73, 74, 75, 76, 176
Tiedens, L. Z., 101
Tittler, B. I., 179
Tom, S., Jr., 84

Tredoux, C., 281
Tropp, L. R., 272, 274, 280
Turner, J. C., 166
Turner, M. E., 279
Tversky, A., 49, 54
Twenge, J. M., 76
Twenge, J. W., 303

U

Uhlmann, E., 273
Ury, W., 49

V

Vallone, R. P., 45
Vance, K. M., 188
Vandenbergh, M. P., 253, 259
van Veen, V., 120, 121
Van Vugt, M., 145
Vaughn, K., 124
Vohs, K. D., 36, 74, 83, 92, 99, 101, 102
Vrij, A., 224, 233, 236

W

Walker, I., 25
Walster, E. H., 206, 207
Walton, G. M., 304
Ward, A., 41, 46, 49, 52, 53, 57, 58, 63
Ward, A. H., 36
Ward, W. D., 138, 139
Warden, R., 234
Ware, L. J., 242
Waterman, A. S., 139
Weaver, T., 226
Webb, E. J., 87
Weber, J. M., 258
Wells, C. L., 183
Wells, T., 236
Wetherell, M. S., 166
Whitcher-Alagna, S., 281

White, D. J., 24, 25
White, E. B., 319
White, J., 293
White, L. T., 217, 239
White, R. K., 293
Whiting, J. W. M., 90
Whitman, R. J., 254
Wicklund, R. A., 52, 138
Wiegand, A. W., 124, 125, 150, 164
Wilbanks, T. J., 253, 258
Wilhite, H., 252
Willerman, B., 207
Williams, M., 86
Williams, W., 291
Wilson, R., 49
Wilson, T., 24
Wilson, T. D., 87, 98, 101
Winett, R. A., 260
Winslow, M. P., 25, 110, 111, 112, 150, 163, 164, 205, 299
Woolverton, M., 35
Worchel, S., 110
Wrightsman, L. S., 218

Y

Yee, C. M., 121
Young, R. C., 103
Yow, W. Q., 35

Z

Zajonc, R. B., 139
Zanna, A. S., 170
Zanna, M. P., 33, 36, 111, 122, 152, 170
Zigler, E., 303
Zimbardo, P. G., 177, 218
Zuwerink, J. R., 179

SUBJECT INDEX

A

ABASS, *see* Assembly of Behavioral and Social Sciences
ACC, *see* Anterior circulate cortex
ACEEE, *see* American Council for an Energy-Efficient Economy
Achievement, 36
Acknowledgment condition, 57
Action-based model (cognitive dissonance), 115
Action-orientation manipulation, 118
Action versus state orientation questionnaire, 119
Advocacy condition, 191
African National Congress (ANC), 52
Age of Educational Romanticism, The, 285
Age of Propaganda, 220–221
Aggression, 36
Altruism, 36, 80, 99
American Council for an Energy-Efficient Economy (ACEEE), 249
American Psychological Association (APA), 7, 17
ANC, *see* African National Congress
Anterior circulate cortex (ACC), 120
Anxiety, terror management theory, 75
APA, *see* American Psychological Association
Arab–Israel wars, 281
As-if feelings, 1

Assembly of Behavioral and Social Sciences (ABASS), 251
Assimilation bias, 45
Atrocity, adjustment to, *see* Yom Kippur
Attitude(s)
 –behavior relationships, 261
 change, alternative to, 189
 confounding of, 53
 -discrepant behavior, 176
 formation, value–belief–norm theory of, 260
 important, 178
 questionnaires, 47, 83
Attribution, behavioral consequences of, 58
Audience transfer procedure, 72
Authority sanctioned contact, 274
Aversive consequences model, 111
Awards, books, and publications, 347–357
 awards, 347–348
 books, 348–349
 publications, 349–357

B

BECC conferences, *see* Behavior, Energy, and Climate Change conferences
Behavior, Energy, and Climate Change (BECC) conferences, 263
Bell Curve, The, 285
Belongingness, 74
Benjamin Franklin's Philadelphia, 301

Subject Index

Bias(es)
  assimilation, 45
  confirmation, 58, 234
  disciplinary, 261
  experimenter, 139, 142
  false consensus, 44, 46
  guilt, 224
  information-processing, 234
  interpretation of evidence, 240
  media, 45
  motivational, 48
  publication, 97
  self-confirming, 234
  self-report, 101
  student, 48
Black–white race relations, 273
Bonneville Power Administration, 253
Brainwave activity, 122
Brown v. Board of Education, 273, 292

C

California v. Page, 215
Caucusing procedures, 56
Chance encounters, 321–323
  chapter composition, 322
  cognitive dissonance theory, 321
  counterintuitive principle, 322
  Franklin's strategy, 322
  summarizing literatures, 322
  textbook collaboration, 322
  textbook writing, 321
  writing style, 323
CHDGC, *see* Committee on the Human Dimensions of Global Change
Christian philanthropy, experiment in, 288
Citizen Tania, 277
Cognitive consistency models, 206
Cognitive dissonance, 159–174, *see also* Decisions, actions, and neuroscience
  Boy Scouts, 166
  charitable donation, 165
  collectivist culture, 171
  controversies, 172
  counterattitudinal advocacy, 169
  counterattitudinal speech, 162
  dissonance-inducing choice, 170
  early days, 160–165
  disagreement, 161–162
  hypocrisy, 163–165
  true cognitive dissonance, 162–163
  experimental psychology, 160
  finding derived from, 159
  group identity, 166–171
    social self and culture, 170–171
    though experiment, 166–167
    vicarious dissonance, 167–170
    vicarious dissonance in East and West, 170–171
  hypocrisy paradigm, 163
  indirect dissonance-reduction technique, 165
  individualistic culture, 170
  in-group condition, 168
  linguistic subcultures, 167
  microcultures, 171
  new look model, 163
  out-groups, 166, 168
  personal dissonance, 169
  procondom speech, 164
  Rotary Club, 166
  self-affirmation, 164
  self-esteem, group membership and, 166
  theoretical disagreements, 161
  universality, 170
  vicarious affect, 169
  vicarious dissonance
    empathic transmission of, 171
    testing, 167
  Yale Communication and Attitude Change Program, 160
Columbine High School, 316
Committee on the Human Dimensions of Global Change (CHDGC), 258
Confirmation bias, 58, 234
Conflict, 39–66
  acknowledgment condition, 57
  assimilation bias, 45
  attitude questionnaire, 47
  bias, 47
  caucusing procedures, 56
  confirmation bias, 58
  confounding of attitudes, 53
  divergent perceptions of actors and observers, 44

dual-track strategy for victory, 46
exhortation and hope, 63–64
false consensus effect, 43–44, 46
forced compliance experiment, 51
free-riders, 42
functional magnetic resonance
  imaging, 46
hostile media effect, 45, 47
interethnic conflict, 41
intergroup hostility, 42
intuitive scientist, 41
Israeli–Palestinian stalemate, 50
loss aversion, 54
media bias, 45
motivational bias, 48
naïve realism, 45–48
overcoming reactive devaluation and
  other barriers, 55–60
  managing attributions, 56–58
  negotiation expectations, 58–60
presidential debates, 45
psychological barriers to dispute
  resolution, 49–55
  cognitive dissonance and
    rationalization, 50–52
  pursuit of fairness, justice, and
    equity, 49–50
  reactive devaluation, loss
    aversion, and reluctance to
    trade concessions, 52–55
reactive devaluation, 49, 52, 54, 56
real-world lessons, 60–63
  conversion from militant to
    peacemaker, 62–63
  futility of trying to convince
    people, 61–62
  relationships and trust, 61
  shared view of mutually bearable
    future, 61
  spoilers and internal politics, 61
real-world negotiations, 58
rejectionists, 51
school integration, 41
subjective experience of reality, 46
third-party mediator, 57
Conformity, 80
Consistency, *see* Rejection, consistency,
  and interpersonal processes
Convergent validity, 102

Counterattitudinal advocacy, 146, 176,
  187

D

Deadline technique, 228
Decisions, action, and neuroscience,
  109–131
  action-based model of dissonance,
    115–117, 124
    action orientation and spreading
      of alternatives, 117–119
    increasing strength of action
      tendencies and discrepancy
      reduction, 124–125
    neural activity associated with
      discrepancy reduction,
      120–124
    neural activity underlying
      dissonance arousal, 119–120
  action-orientation manipulation, 118
  action versus state orientation
    questionnaire, 119
  aversive consequences model, 111
  brainwave activity, 122
  cognitive discrepancy, 115
  confederate statements, 113
  counterattitudinal statements, 111
  difficult-decision paradigm, 122
  discrepancy reduction, 115
  dissonance manipulations, 109
  dissonance reduction, 116
  emotional responses, 124
  hypocrisy experiments, 110
  inconsistency and dissonance
    outcomes, 110–115
    cognitive inconsistency vs.
      self-concept inconsistency,
      114–115
    hypocrisy experiments, 110–112
    inconsistency as motivating force,
      112–114
  inconsistency model, 113
  induced compliance paradigm, 112,
    116
  mind-set condition, neutral, 118
  neurofeedback, 122
  personality questionnaires, 118
  postdecision dissonance paradigm,
    119

370 • Subject Index

postdecision mind-sets, 118
self-concept violation, 114
self-consistency model, concerns, 115
self-image threat, 109
spreading of alternatives, 118
standard dissonance paradigm, 112
Department of Energy (DOE), 250
Desegregation, 13
baseball, 279
Brown decision and, 273, 292
court-ordered, 51
difficulties, 277
retreat from, 276
setback, 344
Difficult-decision paradigm, 122
Disciplinary biases, 261
Discriminant validity, 102
Dissonance, *see also* Cognitive dissonance
action-based model, 115, 124
arousal, 148
-inducing choice, 170
manipulations, 109
reduction, 33, 116, 148
attitude importance in, 180–194
generalization of, 181
indirect technique, 165
theory, self-consistency version of, 176
unresolved, 195
vicarious, 167–170
empathic transmission of, 171
potential to cause, 170
predictions, 169
testing, 167
DOE, *see* Department of Energy
Dual-track strategy for victory, 46

E

Earth Day, 254
Educational romanticism, 283, 286, 295, 305
EEG activity, *see* Electroencephalographic activity
Effort-justification principle, 270
Ego involving attitudes, 188

Electroencephalographic (EEG) activity, 121
Emergent attitude object, 260
Encounter-group leader, 8
Energy Efficiency in Buildings: Behavioral Issues, 253
Energy policy, 249–268
attitude–behavior relationships, 261
barriers to behavioral change, 252
Behavior, Energy, and Climate Change conferences, 263
Bonneville Power Administration, 253
cap-and-trade regime, 264
Committee on the Behavioral and Social Aspects of Energy, 250–253
Committee on the Human Dimensions of Global Change, 258
debates, 264
disciplinary biases, 261
Earth Day, 254
efficiency and curtailment behaviors, 258
emergent attitude object, 260
energy crisis, 253
energy tax, 264
environmental problems, 261
environmental sustainability, 254
global environmental change, attitudes about, 260
Google Scholar, 263
high-impact consumer behaviors, 261
human–environment interactions, 261
induced hypocrisy, 256
past 25 years, 262–264
physical–technical–economic model, 252
polygraph, spy detection using, 257
price elasticity of demand, 253
problem-driven versus psychology-driven perspectives, 254–257
problem-oriented approach to policy, 257–262
resource-depleting behavior, 255
social-psychological model, 255
value–belief–norm theory of attitude formation, 260

zero-cost behaviors, 260
Environmental sustainability, 254
Evaluation index, 186
Experimental psychology, 160
Experimental realism, 204, 272
Experimenter bias, 139, 124
Expert witnesses, 239

F

False confession, *see* Lies (crime)
False consensus effect, 43–44, 46
False feedback, 70
Fear of fumbling, 344
Feedback
    bogus, 68
    brainwave activity, 122
    false, 70
    inconsistent, 142
    negative, 122, 140
    peer, 332
    perceptual, 36
    performance, 141
    personality, 70, 71
    positive, 138
    public versus private, 72
    social sensitivity trials, 137
    task, 143
fMRI, *see* Functional magnetic resonance imaging
Forbidden activity, 31–38
    behavioral measures of social phenomena, 36
    bowling game, 33
    children's obedience, 32
    dissonance reduction, 33
    high-impact experimentation, 31
    insufficient justification, 31, 34
    intrinsic motivations for learning, 35
    obedience studies, 32
    oversufficient justification, 34
    perceptual feedback, 36
    slice of life dramas, 31
Forced compliance experiment, 51
Fourth degree, 226
Functional magnetic resonance imaging (fMRI), 1, 46, 99

G

Gain–loss theory, 207
Gender norms, adherence to, 99
Generalization effect, 193
Global environmental change, attitudes about, 260
Google Scholar, 263
Guilt
    bias, 224
    likelihood of, 191
    presumption of, 212, 240

H

Handbook of Social Psychology, 24, 81, 323
Helpful contact, 281
High-impact experiment, 31, 79–106
    adherence to gender norms, 99
    attitude questionnaires, 83
    belief that subjects are people, 88–90
    bureaucratic demands, 93
    confederate, 86
    convergent validity, 102
    demand for process measures, 99
    device control conditions, 98
    discriminant validity, 102
    events and behaviors, 86–87
    fake polygraph machine, 85
    fun, 91–92
    functional magnetic resonance imaging, 99
    future, 103
    independent and dependent variables, 86–87
    institutional review board, 93
    IQ test, 89, 91
    judgment-type experiments, 92
    manipulation checks, 100
    measures of inner processes, 99
    Measure This Experiment Is About, The, 86
    methodology, 92
    Modern Racism Scale, 100
    phenomenon-oriented research, 80
    pilot testing, 90–91, 98
    polygraphs, 99
    Puritanism, 91
    questionnaires, 97, 102

rarity of studies, 92–102
    demand for multiple studies in single article, 96–98
    emphasis on measuring "process," 98–102
    institutional review board, 93–96
    real situations, 84–86
    self-report bias, 101
    studies, 97
    systematic replication, 102
    verbal manipulations, 102
Hostile media effect, 45, 47
Hostile mediator effect, 56
Hydraulic model, 190
Hypocrisy
    energy policy, 256
    experiments, 110–112
    paradigm, 150, 163

I

Identity-analytic model, 176
Importance–change relation, 182
Importance groups, questionnaires, 188
Improving Energy Demand Analysis, 253
Inconsistency model, 113
Indirect dissonance-reduction technique, 165
Induced-compliance paradigm, 112, 116, 180, 191
Institutional review board (IRB), 93
Insufficient justification demonstrations, 31
Intelligence(s), *see also* Jigsaw method
    changed conception of, 304
    children's, 302
    circumstance and, 300
    differences in theories, 303
    distracted, 306
    evidence on improving, 286
    fragility of, 301–304
    group differences in, 299
    growing of, 303
    incorrect conception of, 306
    intervention, 300
    multiple, 286
    nature of, 291
    nurturance of, 285
    production, research on, 294

suppression of, 304
test scores, African American, 21
Intergroup contact, 269–283
    Arab–Israel wars, 281
    authority sanctioned contact, 274
    Benjamin Franklin, 278
    black–white race relations, 273
    Brown v. Board of Education of Topeka, Kansas, 273
    cases, 276–280
        bank robberies, 277–278
        baseball, 279–280
        book loan, 278–279
        proof, 280
        prototypical equal-status contact, 276–277
    Citizen Tania, 277
    contact hypothesis, 280
    cooperation, 275
    desegregation, 273
    effort-justification principle, 270
    equal status, 274
    experimental realism, 272
    helpful contact, 280–282
    Hull–Spence behavior theory, 270
    Jackie Robinson, 279
    Jigsaw Classroom, 275, 276
    Major League Baseball, 280
    military draft, 269
    Patty Hearst, 277
    recipe, 273–276
    shared goals, 275
    stereotypes, intergroup relations, 272
    Stockholm syndrome, 278
    Symbionese Liberation Army, 277
Interpersonal attraction, 206
Interpersonal processes, *see* Rejection, consistency, and interpersonal processes
Intuitive scientist, 41
Invisible jails, 301
IQ
    fundamentalism, 300, 305
    student gains in, 289
    test, 89, 91, 303
IRB, *see* Institutional review board
Israeli–Palestinian stalemate, 50

J

Jigsaw Classroom, 40
Jigsaw method, 285–310
    achievement gap, 299–301
    African American stereotypes, 302
    Bell Curve doctrine, 286, 290
    Benjamin Franklin's Philadelphia, 301
    Brown v. Board of Education, 292
    Christian philanthropy, experiment in, 288
    college GPA, black–white gap in, 304
    common goals, 293
    control group, 295–297
    cultural blueprint, 307
    desegregation, 292
    educational romanticism, 283, 286
    experiment, 289–290
    extreme romanticism, 286
    galling chains of slavery, 301
    Hares, 296
    higher-scores-or-else approach, 305
    intelligence
        changed conception of, 304
        children's, 302
        circumstance and, 300
        differences in theories, 303
        distracted, 306
        evidence on improving, 286
        fragility of, 301–304
        group differences in, 299
        growing of, 303
        incorrect conception of, 306
        intervention, 300
        nature of, 291
        nurturance of, 285
        production, research on, 294
        suppression of, 304
    interracial dynamics (Franklin's), 301
    invisible jails, 301
    IQ fundamentalism, 305
    IQ gains, 289
    Jigsaw, 293–294
    Jim Crow South, 301
    Milgram experiment, 291
    minority white gap, 305
    miseducation, 297
    mock prison, 291
    multiple intelligences, 286
    No Child Left Behind, 305, 307
    optimism, 293
    power of situation, 304
    prejudice, 301–304
    proficiency exam, 305
    Pygmalion effect, 286
    quality of schooling, 307
    reasoning, IQ-like test of, 303
    Robbers Cave experiment, 293
    romantic delusion, 286
    SAT scores, 301
    school culture, 306–307
    scientist and school, 287–289
    self-actualization, 287
    self-esteem, minority students, 294
    social exclusion, 301–304
    social psychologist and school, 290–293
    Stanford Prison Experiment, 291
    stereotype threat, 295, 301–304
    student letter, 298–299
    Supreme Court cases, 306
    Tortoises, 296
    unfinished business, 304–306
Jim Crow South, 301
Judgment-type experiments, 92

K

Katz–Hass scale, 185, 186

L

Landscaping, 224
Law enforcement, *see* Lies (crime)
Law of infidelity, 4, 207
Lewinian tradition, 21–29
    African American intelligence test scores, 21
    first-generation Lewinians, 22–23
    founder of social psychology, 21
    National Training Laboratories, 22
    second-generation Lewinians, 23–26
    self-esteem, minority kids, 13
    sensitivity training, 22
    T-groups, 22
    Zeigarnik effect, 26
Lies (crime), 211–247
    behavior analysis interview, 235

biased information-processing, 234
biggest lie, 212
California v. Page, 215
coercive interrogation, 226
confession evidence, 240
confirmation bias, 234
context, 218–219
contradictory information, 213
coperpetrator, 238
criminal interrogation, 212
damning damned lie, 235
deadline technique, 228
detective confidence, 224
detective self-deception, 234
DNA evidence, 237
effects, 219–238
    Borg maneuver, 225–226
    crime story construction, 229
    false confession, 226–227
    impaired judgment, 221–233
    initial interrogation failure, 231–232
    interrogation, 220–221
    Miranda warnings, 222–224
    preinterrogation interview, 224–225
    pretext for interrogation, 227–228
    set-up question, 225
    sympathetic detective, 228–229
    taking the confession, 232–233
    wrongful conviction, 233–238
exonerating evidence, 241
expert witnesses, 239
failures of memory, 241
false confessions, 212
    internalized, 226
    police-induced, 219
    preconceptions, 240
fourth degree, 226
future, 238–243
going easy, 236
good cop–bad cop, 228
guilt bias, 224
interrogation training, 234
investigating guilt, 227
judges, 240
landscaping, 224
leading comments, 236
minimization, 230, 231
Miranda v. Arizona, 221

Miranda warnings, 222
murder case, 214–218
narrative, 232
polygraph
    interrogation following, 215, 218
    misrepresented results, 226
preinterrogation interview, 228
pre-persuasion, 224
presumption of guilt, 240
pretrial motion to suppress confession, 239
proven-false confessors, 217
real truth, 230
reciprocity principle, 227
self-aggrandizement, 234
self-confirming biases, 234
self-deception, 234
self-justifying motivations, 238
stepping stone approach, 230
taped confession, 2126
tentativeness, 236
theme development, 230
tunnel vision, 234, 241
voice stress analysis, 226
vulnerability to interrogative influence, 218
Life-changing experience, 343
Limits to Growth, The, 254
Linguistic subcultures, 167
Litigation
    Brown v. Board of Education, 273, 292
    California v. Page, 215
    Miranda v. Arizona, 221
Loss aversion, 54

M

Media bias, 45
Mentoring, 333–334
Methods of Research in Social Psychology, 24, 109
Milgram experiment, 80, 291
Mind-set condition, neutral, 118
Minnesota tradition, 204
Miranda v. Arizona, 221
Miranda warnings, 222
Mismeasure of Man, The, 285
Mistakes Were Made, 40
Model(s)

Subject Index • 375

action-based (cognitive dissonance), 115
aversive consequences, 111
cognitive consistency, 206
hydraulic, 190
identity-analytic, 176
inconsistency, 113
new look, 163
physical–technical–economic, 252
self-consistency, concerns, 115
self-resource, 145
self-standards, 145, 146
social-psychological, 255
translational research, 12
Modern Racism Scale, 100
Motivational bias, 48
Multiple intelligences, 286

N

Naïve realism, 45–48
Narrative History of Experimental Social Psychology: The Lewinian Tradition, A, 152
National Research Council (NRC), 251
National Science Foundation (NSF), 73
National Training Laboratories (NTL), 22
Nature of Prejudice, The, 273
Nazi Germany, 80, 291
Neurofeedback, 122
Neuroscience, *see* Decisions, actions, and neuroscience
New look model, 163
Nobody Left to Hate, 40
No Child Left Behind, 305, 307
NRC, *see* National Research Council
NSF, *see* National Science Foundation
NTL, *see* National Training Laboratories

O

Obedience, 36
  to authority, 80
  behavioral measures of, 36
  studies, 32
Observations on the Increase of Mankind, 288
Orchestrated spontaneity, 331

Out-groups, 166

P

Paradigm
  counterattitudinal advocacy paradigm, 146, 178
  difficult-decision paradigm, 122
  hypocrisy, 111, 150, 163
  induced compliance paradigm, 112, 116, 180, 191
  performance expectancy paradigm, 134, 138, 145
  postdecision dissonance paradigm, 119
  prejudice-relevant issue paradigm, 185
Peer feedback, 332
Perceptual feedback, 36
Performance expectancy paradigm, 134, 138, 145
Personal dissonance, 169
Personality
  feedback, 70, 71
  questionnaires, 118
  test, 68
Phenomenon-oriented research, 80
Physical–technical–economic model (PTEM), 252
Pilot testing, 90–91, 98
Police interrogation, *see* Lies (crime)
Polygraph(s)
  fake, 85
  inner processes measured using, 99
  interrogation following, 215, 218
  misrepresented results, 226
  spy detection using, 257
Postdecision dissonance paradigm, 119
Power of situation, 304
Preinterrogation interview, 228
Prejudice-relevant issue paradigm, 185
Pre-persuasion, 224
Presentation of Self in Everyday Life, The, 69
Price elasticity of demand, 253
Pro- and Anti-Black Beliefs Questionnaire, 181
Prosocial behavior, 76
Psychological science, writing about, 313–320

audience appeal, 315
award address, 318
Columbine High School, 316
editorial suggestions, 319
Grandpa Moses, 318
heavy vs. light reading, 316
jargon, 313, 315, 317
needless words, 319
Psychology Today Yesterday, 315
redundancies, 314
scholarly substance, 315
storytelling, 316
styles of writing, 316
T-group leader, 319
Psychological sensitivity, test of, 141
Psychology Today Yesterday, 315
PTEM, *see* Physical–technical–economic model
Public self, 69
Puritanism, 91
Pygmalion effect, 286

Q

quasselstrippe, 63
Questionnaire(s)
  action versus state orientation, 119
  attitude, 47, 83
  college participants, 188
  emotional responses, 124
  importance groups, 188
  multiple studies, 97
  personality, 118
  postdecision mind-sets, 118
  Pro- and Anti-Black Beliefs, 181
  responses, 102

R

Racial symbolism, 183
Rational economic theorists, 1
Reactive devaluation, 49, 52, 54
Regret, 99
Rejection, consistency, and interpersonal processes, 67–77
  anxiety, 75
  audience transfer procedure, 72
  belongingness, 74
  bogus feedback, 68
  counterattitudinal essays, 72
  inner processes, 75
  interpersonal functions, 75
  no-choice manipulation, 72
  null results, 69
  personality feedback, 70, 71
  personality test, 68
  prosocial behavior, 76
  public–private manipulation, 72
  public self, 69
  public versus private feedback, 72
  self-defeating behavior, 76
  self-esteem, 67
    false feedback affecting, 70
    manipulation, 68, 69
    measured, 69
    reconceptualization of, 74–75
    self-presentation versus, 74
  self-presentation, 71
  sociometer theory, 74
  supreme human motivation, 75
  terror management theory, 75
  theory development, 68
Relationship science, 203–210
  cognitive consistency models, 206
  experimental realism, 204
  gain–loss theory, 207
  influence, 208–209
  interpersonal attraction, 206
  interpersonal phenomena, 205
  interpersonal theories, 208
  Jigsaw Classroom, 205
  law of infidelity, 207
  Minnesota tradition, 204
  preparation, 205–208
  self-verification theory, 208
  study validation, 205
Research Methods in Social Psychology, 24
Robbers Cave experiment, 293
Romanticism, *see* Jigsaw method

S

SAT scores, 301
Self-actualization, 12, 287
Self-affirmation, 164
Self-aggrandizement, 234
Self-concept inconsistency, 114–115
Self-confidence, 344
Self-consistency model, concerns, 115

Self-consistency motive, 133–158
    audacity, tenacity, and scientific
        progress, 152–154
    counterattitudinal advocacy
        paradigm, 146
    dissonance, 134–144
    dissonance arousal, 148
    dissonance reduction strategies, 148
    experimental priming conditions, 147
    experimenter bias, 139, 142
    external validity, 153
    hypocrisy paradigm, 150
    inconsistent feedback, 142
    Jigsaw Classroom, 133
    performance expectancy paradigm,
        134, 138, 145
    performance feedback, 141
    personal standards for morality, 144
    photo-judging task, 139
    positive feedback, 138
    positive self-views following
        hypocrisy, 149–152
    prediction, 151
    preexisting inconsistency, 150
    process, 144–149
    psychological sensitivity, test of, 141
    self-affirmation theory, 149
    self-esteem
        cognitions underlying, 146
        high, 144, 147
        low, 142, 147
    self-inconsistent behavior, 149
    self-rating scale, 136
    self-resource model, 145
    self-standards model, 145, 146
    social sensitivity, 136, 141
    task feedback, 143
    track record of replication, 139
    trivialization, 148
Self-esteem, 67
    cognitions underlying, 146
    dissonance manipulation and, 114
    false feedback affecting, 70
    group membership and, 166
    high, 144, 147
    low, 142, 147, 207
    manipulation, 68, 69
    measured, 69
    minority students, 13, 294
    reconceptualization of, 74–75

    self-presentation versus, 74
Self-image threat, 109
Self-persuasion, 175–199
    advocacy condition, 191
    attitude-discrepant behavior, 176
    attitude expression, 189
    attitude importance in dissonance
        reduction, 180–194
        caring and values, 188–190
        generalization, 190–194
        personal cost, 182–186
        personal relevance and
            trivialization mode, 186–188
        prejudice studies, 180–182
    counterattitudinal advocacy, 176,
        177–179
    counterattitudinal position, 188
    dissonance-reduction strategy, 189
    "don't remind me effect", 194
    ego involving attitudes, 188
    essay-writing behavior, 193
    evaluation index, 186
    generalization of dissonance
        reduction, 181
    generalization effect, 193
    high dissonance conditions, 188
    humanitarianism, 192
    hydraulic model, 190
    identity-analytic model, 176
    implications, 194–196
    importance–change relation, 182
    importance groups, 188
    important attitudes, 178
    induced-compliance paradigm, 180,
        191
    Katz–Hass scale, 185, 186
    low-relevance advocates, 188
    mental attitude-discrepant behavior,
        183
    no-advocacy condition, 192
    personal relevance, 183
    pillars of importance, 175
    postadvocacy changes in racial
        beliefs, 191
    prejudice-relevant issue paradigm,
        185
    Pro- and Anti-Black Beliefs
        Questionnaire, 181
    racial symbolism, 183
    Rodney King beating, 180

self, attitude importance, and cognitive dissonance, 176–177
self-betrayal, 176
self-consistency version of dissonance theory, 176
self-persuasion, 178
semi-compliers, 181
symbolic importance, 183
trial simulation, 191
trivialization, 187, 189
unresolved dissonance, 195
values-relevant attitudes, 188
Self-resource model, 145
Self-standards model, 145, 146
Semi-compliers, 181
Sensitivity training, 22
SLA, *see* Symbionese Liberation Army
Slice of life dramas, 31
Social Animal, The, 40, 109, 203, 249, 285, 321
Social life, self-consistency motive in, *see* Self-consistency motive
Social psychology
    career, 133
    course, 25, 31, 249, 271, 291, 325
    data, 318
    dubious policy, 97
    epiphany, 79
    experiments, 12, 343, 272
    father of, 40
    founder of, 7, 21
    future of, 153
    hard-won insights, 60
    Lewinians, 81
    major force in, 160
    Minnesota tradition, 204
    objective, 75
    popularizing of, 16
    premier textbook, 17
    real-world problems, 22
    recognition, 306
    reshaping of, 21
    school achievement, 297
    self in, 166, 176, 207
    social influence, 221
    theory development, 68
    value of, 9, 345
    Willie Mays of, 39
Social Psychology Network (SPN), 16
Social sensitivity, 136, 141
Sociometer theory, 74
SPN, *see* Social Psychology Network
Spoilers, 61
Spreading of alternatives, 118
Stanford Prison Experiment, 291
Stereotype(s)
    African American, 302
    children's, 13
    dispelled, 41, 274
    intergroup relations, 272
    threat, 295, 301–304
Stockholm syndrome, 278
Symbionese Liberation Army (SLA), 277
Sympathetic detective, 228

T

Teaching, art of, 325–334
    caring teachers, 326
    classroom expression, 326
    commendation, 333
    cooperative learning environment, 326
    empirical literature, 327
    experiment design, 331
    graduate seminar, 331–333
    humor, 328
    interpersonal styles, 334
    lecture, 327–331
    long-distance learning, 330
    mentoring, 333–334
    orchestrated spontaneity, 331
    peer feedback, 332
    reading assignment choice, 332
    side-by-side teaching, 333–334
    sit-down teaching, 331–333
    stand-up teaching, 327–331
    storytelling, 328
    student participation, 329
Terror management theory, 75
T-group(s), 8
    leader, 16, 319
    workshop, 22
Theories of Cognitive Consistency, 35
Tikkun olam, 9
Translational research, model for, 12
Trivialization, 189
    counterattitudinal advocacy, 187
    low-relevance advocates and, 188

low self-esteem and, 148
Tunnel vision, 234, 241

U

Unresolved dissonance, 195
Uprooting of atrocity, 341

V

Value–belief–norm theory (attitude formation), 260
Values-relevant attitudes, 188
Verbal manipulations, 102
Vicarious affect, 169
Vicarious dissonance, 167–170
    empathic transmission of, 171
    potential to cause, 170
    predictions, 169
    testing, 167
Voice stress analysis, 226

W

When Prophecy Fails, 84
Writing, 313–320
    audience appeal, 315
    award address, 318
    Columbine High School, 316
    editorial suggestions, 319
    Grandpa Moses, 318
    heavy vs. light reading, 316
    jargon, 313, 315, 317
    needless words, 319
    Psychology Today Yesterday, 315
    redundancies, 314
    scholarly substance, 315
    storytelling, 316
    styles of writing, 316
    T-group leader, 319
Wrongful conviction, *see* Lies (crime)

Y

Yale Communication and Attitude Change Program, 160
Yom Kippur, 337–341
    adapting to environment, 338
    bombing of Libya, 339
    dangers of adjustment, 338
    hostile environment, 338
    liturgy, 340
    recognition of sin, 339
    role of religion, 337
    uprooting of atrocity, 341

Z

Zero-cost behaviors, 260